Presidents versus Senators

Presidents versus Senators

*Conflicts and Rivalries
That Shaped America*

F. Martin Harmon

McFarland & Company, Inc., Publishers
Jefferson, North Carolina

LIBRARY OF CONGRESS CATALOGUING-IN-PUBLICATION DATA

Names: Harmon, F. Martin, 1951– author.
Title: Presidents versus senators : conflicts and rivalries that shaped America / F. Martin Harmon.
Description: Jefferson, North Carolina : McFarland & Company, Inc., Publishers, 2021 | Includes bibliographical references and index.
Identifiers: LCCN 2021035150 | ISBN 9781476683140 (paperback : acid free paper) ∞
ISBN 9781476643410 (ebook)
Subjects: LCSH: United States. Congress. Senate—History. | Executive-legislative relations—United States. | Presidents—United States—History. | Legislators—United States—History. | United States—Politics and government. | BISAC: HISTORY / United States / General | POLITICAL SCIENCE / American Government / General
Classification: LCC E183 .H324 2021 | DDC 328.73/07456—dc23
LC record available at https://lccn.loc.gov/2021035150

BRITISH LIBRARY CATALOGUING DATA ARE AVAILABLE

ISBN (print) 978-1-4766-8314-0
ISBN (ebook) 978-1-4766-4341-0

© 2021 F. Martin Harmon. All rights reserved

No part of this book may be reproduced or transmitted in any form or by any means, electronic or mechanical, including photocopying or recording, or by any information storage and retrieval system, without permission in writing from the publisher.

Front cover image: Known for his confrontational style of politics, Lyndon Johnson could even resort to the same tactics with allies, as was the case after becoming president when he met with old friend and mentor Georgia Senator Richard Russell to let him know in no uncertain terms that he intended to pass meaningful civil rights legislation over the objections and obstruction of Russell's Southern Bloc in the Senate (courtesy LBJ Presidential Library, W98-30)

Printed in the United States of America

McFarland & Company, Inc., Publishers
Box 611, Jefferson, North Carolina 28640
www.mcfarlandpub.com

To the memory of George Norris, a truly great senator from Nebraska between 1913 and 1943, who always put country ahead of party, as well as more recent bipartisan Senate greats like Lyndon Johnson of Texas, Mike Mansfield of Montana, Everett Dirksen of Illinois, Howard Baker of Tennessee, Ted Kennedy of Massachusetts, and John McCain of Arizona. Would that their spirit of bipartisan understanding could bring a rebirth for America.

Table of Contents

Preface: Great Political Rivalries and Conflicts — 1
Introduction: Landmark Political Confrontations — 3
Prologue: All-Time Greats and Taking on the White House — 5

Section One. Battle Over the Bank: Andrew Jackson vs. Henry Clay

1. Setting the Stage with Campaign Strategy — 10
2. Chronological Review of a Political Gamble — 20
3. The Ensuing Expansion of Presidential Power — 33

Section Two. The Bleeding Kansas Fight: James Buchanan vs. Stephen Douglas

4. Breakdown of the Jacksonian Democrats — 42
5. Lack of Leadership Amidst Drift to Disunion — 54
6. Lincoln, Civil War and Republican Rule — 67

Section Three. The Reconstruction Conflict: Andrew Johnson vs. Charles Sumner

7. Political Opposites on a Collision Course — 78
8. The Rage Over Southern Reconstruction — 86
9. "Glorious Failure" or What Might Have Been — 112

Section Four. Crusade for the League: Woodrow Wilson vs. Henry Cabot Lodge

10. Political Enemies on a Collision Course — 120
11. The Ammunition of Lasting Animosity — 132
12. One-and-Done and Back to Normal — 147

Table of Contents

Section Five. Surviving the Red Menace: Harry Truman vs. Joseph McCarthy

13. The Cold War Launch of a Red Hot Demagogue — 158
14. Turning the Other Cheek in a No-Win War — 170
15. From Fearmongering to Covert Action — 187

Section Six. Civil Rights or Segregation: Lyndon Johnson vs. Richard Russell

16. Anatomy of an Impending Political Breakup — 198
17. The End of Debate; the Start of Equality — 212
18. Personal Legacy Waylaid by Foreign Escalation — 228

Section Seven. The Canal Giveaway: Jimmy Carter vs. Paul Laxalt

19. From "Perpetuity" to "Inviting Disaster" — 238
20. Reversing Course into a Proxy War — 245
21. The Diminishing Returns of Global Leadership — 256

Epilogue: If Keeping Score, Closer Than Anticipated — 264
Chapter Notes — 265
Bibliography — 281
Index — 285

Preface: Great Political Rivalries and Conflicts

As a former sportswriter at two daily newspapers for seven years and a sports communications professional at three different state universities for more than 22, I am well versed in the integral role rivalries play in the American athletic landscape. No matter the level of competition, rivalries inspire a greater intensity for any athletic contest. And under the canopy of major pro and/or college sports, it doesn't require die-hard fandom to recognize our most renowned, athletic rivalries—traditional confrontations like Packers–Bears, Yankees–Red Sox, Cowboys–Redskins, Giants–Dodgers, Celtics–Lakers, Michigan–Ohio State, Auburn–Alabama, or North Carolina–Duke. The mere mention of those rivalries prompts images of big games past that live on through constant reminders and annual hype.

By contrast, all-time political rivalries are not so much remembered by the individuals involved as by the issues. Usually these have been started by an influential senator of the opposition party taking on the White House—someone with the public persona and political clout to directly challenge the president. It has made for some of America's most intense political conflicts, with presidents emerging victorious most of the time, but not always.

The rivalries and issues to be covered here commence with the rise of congressional influence and populist impact following the War of 1812, sometimes referred to as "America's Second Revolution," and illustrated by the partisan divide over such things as a National Bank. They are continued through the battle over slavery and its expansion; emancipation and the aftermath of racially motivated, sectional civil war; the international transition brought on by U.S. involvement in World War I; the repeated threats and suspicion of communist infiltration of our federal government after World War II; the final move towards actual racial civil rights in America;

and the controversial give-away of one of our most celebrated accomplishments and prized possessions, the Panama Canal.

Sources for such legendary battles abound. From biographies of the great and would-be great men who waged these protracted political showdowns, to detailed examinations of each historic episode, and from period overviews of some of our most famously defined American eras and specific institutional histories, to related books that either set the stage or confirm the results.

Among the biographies used were a series on Andrew Jackson, Henry Clay, and Daniel Webster by Robert Remini, undoubtedly one of the foremost historians of the "Jacksonian Era" (1820s and '30s); three on Abraham Lincoln, including one by two-time Pulitzer Prize winner David Donald Herbert titled—simply—*Lincoln*; as well as recognized bios of presidents Andrew Johnson, Woodrow Wilson, and Harry Truman, and a Pulitzer winner titled with just another last name—*Truman*—by yet another two-time Pulitzer recipient, David McCullough. Add to those accepted biographies on the administrations of presidents Jimmy Carter and Lyndon Johnson, and the careers of senators Charles Sumner, Joseph McCarthy, and Richard Russell, and you get the idea of how much attention was paid to the vast array of biographical works available from the nearly 150-year span of American history covered in this book.

Additionally, targeted histories like *The Rise and Fall of the American Whig Party* by Michael Holt; *Almost President: Men Who Lost the Race but Changed the Nation* by Scott Farris; *Reconstruction: America's Unfinished Revolution* by Eric Foner; *Paris 1919: Six Months That Changed the World* by Margaret MacMillan; *The Wise Men: Six Friends and the World They Made* by Walter Isaacson and Evan Thomas; and most recently *Heirs of the Founders: Henry Clay, John Calhoun, and Daniel Webster, the Second Generation of American Giants* by H.W. Brands are all examples of the wide ranging support sources used to fill in blanks of each of the major political battles examined here.

Each confrontation has been examined in three parts, with the first involved in setting the stage for the battle; the second a chronological breakdown of the events that occurred during each battle; and the third a summation of the results of those famous Washington wars—winners and losers and what it meant for the country in the aftermath.

Introduction: Landmark Political Confrontations

The battle over a National Bank of the United States in the country's post-colonial, still formative years; the escalating battle over slavery and its expansion into the Western territories during the 1850s; the battle over Reconstruction and the rights of African American freedmen in the post–Civil War South; the battle over the League of Nations and whether or not the United States should continue foreign entanglements following World War I; the battle over the supposed threat of communist infiltration into our government during the Cold War; the battle over civil rights and voting rights as a result of the Civil Rights Movement of the 1960s; and the controversial decision and battle over returning the Panama Canal to the nation of Panama. Those are the great president versus senator battles this book is about, or, more specifically, the great personal and political rivalries that turned those issues into transformative Washington wars.

If that sounds like a series of domestic war stories, it's because they were—high stakes political confrontations usually won by the White House, but not always. Each exacted a toll on the nation's psyche that would never be forgotten. Some were titanic clashes between some of the biggest names in American history, while others relegated their participants to historical also-rans by virtue of what resulted and was revealed for posterity.

Some affected legacies in unexpected ways and some so lowered the bar that their mere mention remains a derisive footnote for an entire era. Others were doomed to failure because of competing ideologies or aversion to compromise. And some became the epitome of partisan intransigence, that bane of our democratic existence to the present day.

Return with us now to these famous battles on Pennsylvania Avenue, when Senate legends and sitting presidents duked it out between the Capitol Dome and the Oval Office with partisan divides seething below the surface of every congressional debate or presidential veto. Watch for the moments when cooler heads might have prevailed and spared the nation needless turmoil. Consider the combatants for each of these conflicts, their personalities, their supporters, and their agendas, and connect the dots with what were usually larger, ideological wars. They exemplified American politics at its most combative, a take-no-prisoners approach that too often takes way too long to resolve or justify. In each instance, too bad it had to be that way ... and still does.

Prologue:
All-Time Greats and Taking on the White House

In 1955, a young Massachusetts senator, John Fitzgerald Kennedy, authored a book that would win a Pulitzer Prize, *Profiles in Courage*. It featured the inspiring stories of previous United States senators who, despite intense political pressure from constituents, powerful colleagues, or even their party as a whole, exemplified courage in the choices they made and the votes they cast during some of the nation's most dramatic moments. A year later, while seeking to further elevate the history of Congress' "Upper House," Senate Majority Leader Lyndon Johnson asked JFK to head a five-man committee charged with selecting what in essence was a Senate Hall of Fame, a task that resulted in the naming of five all-time greats on May 1, 1957—the original, so-called "Famous Five."

After initially struggling over the attributes that should define senatorial greatness, Kennedy's committee settled on statesmanship transcending party or state lines, and national leadership on legislation. Sixty-five candidates were recommended for consideration by a prestigious scholars' committee for the five all-time slots, an obviously daunting task that resulted in the "Great Triumvirate" of the early 1800s—Kentucky's Henry Clay, South Carolina's John C. Calhoun, and Massachusetts' Daniel Webster—all having their greatness confirmed along with progressive icon Robert La Follette of Wisconsin and staunch conservative Robert Taft of Ohio, two influential Senate fixtures of the early and mid–1900s, respectively.

Surprisingly left off of the Senate committee's top quintet—to the consternation of the 160 nominating scholars who voted for him unanimously—was Nebraska Republican George Norris, perhaps the most independent, nationally focused senator ever. His legacy between the world wars as "Father of the TVA"; as the primary advocate for the Rural Electrification Act; and as the first outspoken opponent of the Electoral College in presidential politics remains unmistakable, proving that progressive ideas and bipartisan accomplishment do not necessarily rate with congressional colleagues (or rivals) the way they do with more objective observers. Indeed, nearly a half century later in 2004, when this so-called Senate HOF was updated with the addition of two more all-time greats, Norris, maybe the last truly progressive Republican, was again left out in favor of Michigan's Arthur Vandenberg and New York's Robert Wagner, one a Republican and the other a Democrat (respectively) from roughly the same chronological era as Norris.

In September of 2018, in an article titled "The Senate's Incomplete Hall of Fame," the History News Network termed the omission of Norris a "historical wrong" that should be righted, while also recommending the addition of more recent Senate greats, John McCain of Arizona and Ted Kennedy of Massachusetts (again, a Republican and a Democrat). Like

Despite being a unanimous choice of 160 nominating scholars charged with helping select the top U.S. senators of all-time in 1956, Nebraska's George Norris was not among the five inaugural honorees and has continued to be mysteriously omitted even after four have since been added to what amounts to a Senate Hall of Fame (Library of Congress Prints and Photographs Division—Reproduction Number LC-DIG-hec-37934).

Norris, both were well known for working across the proverbial aisle with the opposition party to get things done.

After all, two senators from America's previously ignored founding generation, Roger Sherman and Oliver Ellsworth (ironically, both from Connecticut), were added in 2006 and portraits of what has now been termed the "Famous Nine" are displayed in lasting recognition in the Senate Reception Room at the Capitol. So why not at least three more for what would truly be the "Deserving Dozen"?

Initially, these and other giants of our Upper Chamber were to be the focus of this book, but gradually the rivalries and battles waged by certain senators against sitting presidents warranted more attention and precedence. Once termed a "Millionaires Club" and later the world's "Most Exclusive Club," senators actually were the winners in several of these wars, but certainly not all.

Indeed, except for the legendary Clay, it's surprising (but no less revealing) that none of the other Senate combatants examined in this book came close to the Kennedy committee's final honorees. Not Stephen Douglas, Charles Sumner, Henry Cabot Lodge, Joseph McCarthy, Richard Russell, or Paul Laxalt, all among the most influential (or infamous) senators of their individual eras, but also-rans when Hall of Fame status was being conferred. Unlike Norris and Taft, none were worthy of Kennedy's award-winning *Profiles* either.

And in no way is this an attempt to elevate them "senatorially," either. Instead, this book's purpose is to simply reveal in detail these career-defining confrontations as congressional titans took on the "Bully Pulpit" and often overreaching power of the presidency. These were Washington wars pure and simple, and as with most conflicts, to the victors went the spoils, politically shaping U.S. history over some of our most contentious landmark issues.

Prologue sourcing: John F. Kennedy, *Profiles in Courage*, New York: Harper & Row, 1955; "The Famous Five," senate.gov (March 12, 1959); Andrew Glass, "Senate Creates Members 'Hall of Fame,'" politico.com (March 11, 2017); Gene A. Budig and Don Walton, *George Norris, Going Home*, Lincoln: University of Nebraska Press, 2013; Ronald Feinman, "The Senate's Incomplete Hall of Fame," (September 9, 2018); "United States Senate Reception Room," en.wikipedia.org.

SECTION ONE

Battle Over the Bank
Andrew Jackson vs. Henry Clay

1

Setting the Stage with Campaign Strategy

Orphaned by the age of 14; unbeaten as an American military hero in wars against the Seminoles, Spanish, Creeks, and British; and our first truly populist president, Andrew Jackson felt vindicated when he was elected to the White House over John Quincy Adams in 1828, having been denied the presidency four years earlier by Adams' and Henry Clay's so-called "Corrupt Bargain." Despite receiving the most popular votes of four major candidates in the 1824 election, Jackson ultimately lost when no candidate received a majority in the Electoral College, thus casting the top three into a runoff election in the House of Representatives. That's when Speaker of the House Clay, the frustrated fourth place finisher, threw his extensive congressional support to Adams, the runner-up and eventual winner, reportedly in exchange for the supposed next-in-line position of secretary of state. It would prove the opening salvo in a political rivalry that some historians actually termed hatred that has echoed in American history ever since, a Washington war pitting trans–Appalachia stars from Tennessee (Jackson) and neighboring Kentucky (Clay) in a multi-decades confrontation epitomized by their brazen battle over the Second National Bank of the United States as a prelude to President Jackson's second term.[1]

Why Clay would back Adams over Jackson, a New England mainstay over a fellow Westerner, was the question most people could not fathom in 1824 unless the nefarious quid-pro-quo was actually in play, but there are reasons other than political deal-making that historians in the know have pointed to as a basis for the Kentuckian's obvious lack of regional loyalty. Foremost among those was Clay's apparent disdain for the very idea of a "military chieftain," as he termed it, being installed as the head of state. To a judge of the time he wrote, "As a friend of liberty, and to the permanence of our institutions, I cannot consent, in this early stage of their existence, by contributing to the elevation of a military chieftain to give the strongest guarantee that this republic will march in the fatal road which has conducted every other republic to ruin." And as fate would have it with much of the high-profile correspondence of that era, Clay's letter found its way into the *Washington National Intelligencer*. "From that moment [forward] Jackson conceived a hatred for Clay he would carry to the end of his life," H.W. Brands confirmed as recently as 2019 in *Heirs of the Founders*.[2]

Also, there was the sudden rise of a regional rival and proverbial political outsider. As any nationally ambitious politician understands, serious consideration for high office usually requires unmitigated support from one's home community and region, the kind of support the veteran Clay suddenly saw eroded by this military marvel—this "Hero"—the kind of Western support he did not wish to share.[3]

Eight years and two presidential terms later, by the time of Jackson's re-election bid in 1832, Clay was still a congressional force to be reckoned with; by then returned to the Senate, where he had served twice before, and well on his way to becoming one of three legendary senators of that era, a renowned trio that included Daniel Webster of Massachusetts and John C. Calhoun of South Carolina.[4] All three would oppose Jackson at some point in his presidency, but it was towards Clay that he would always muster the most animosity, referring to him as "Judas of the West" and "a profligate demagogue." Undoubtedly, those sentiments were mutual. Clay, in fact, would sarcastically label Jackson "Caesar" or "King Andrew," while leading Upper Chamber efforts to censure the rather autocratic president when impeachment proceedings proved too much to ask.[5]

Having risen to national prominence and mass popularity by sheer audacity and the notoriety of his military exploits, Jackson and his advisers were the first to take advantage of a growing electorate, where the abolishment of property qualifications had opened voting rights to virtually all adult White males. The Jacksonian managers were the first political organizers to fully mobilize the common man, especially in the new Western states where the frontier had only recently been conquered.[6] After all, "Andy" Jackson was a man's man who had survived several duels and other notorious confrontations, and was known to his soldiers as "Old Hickory" because of his toughness. Although his leadership style could be brash and irreverent, it was offset by a natural charisma that had always elevated Jackson in the company of other men, even before his military achievements. Jon Meacham noted as much in his Pulitzer-winning *American Lion*, when he mentioned Jackson's "sense of adventure" and "infectious fearlessness" that contributed to an undeniable "raw ability to lead" and (in turn) "be followed."[7] Later, when Jackson was an incoming U.S. senator himself in 1823, Robert Remini wrote of his early days in Washington as "nothing less than brilliant. No sooner did he take his seat in the Senate than he set off a dazzling display of Jacksonian charisma and presence. The figure he cut! The commanding style he revealed! He came like a thunderclap and left observers overwhelmed."[8]

Equally charismatic, if not as intimidatingly so, the same biographer recognized similar attributes in Clay, one of the most renowned legislators of his or any other American era. Unlike Jackson, the product of a very large family, with eight siblings and seven half siblings (once his mother remarried following his father's death), Clay also displayed early leadership capabilities. But instead of illustrating those at the head of a militia, his powers of persuasion and ability to lead became rapidly apparent once he attained elected office at just 26 years of age.[9] On that topic, Neil MacNeil and Richard A. Baker wrote in their history of the U.S. Senate: "Henry Clay was elegant in debate, haughty and imperious at times, gracious and chivalric at others, he commanded a fiery eloquence that won him national popularity. As an orator, he could be witty and clever, dignified and high-toned, bold and impetuous—whatever posture seemed appropriate—and he was especially genial and winning."[10] Offering equal praise of Clay, Remini confirmed: "Over the years he had developed the extraordinary skill of drawing people to him. This magnetic quality to his personality attracted followers and admirers, both male and female. His amiability, his love of conversation, his ready smile, his delightful manners, his devastating wit, his remarkable intellect, and his profound understanding of the issues facing the nation all combined to produce a dynamic and charismatic personality that most Washingtonians found irresistible."[11]

Such adulation by a group in Congress known as the "War Hawks" (advocates for further national expansion) propelled Clay at 34 to become the second youngest House Speaker ever and the youngest before 1939. There followed 11 years of House leadership and four more as secretary of state before three separate stretches in the Senate, including an 11-year run from 1831 until 1842 during which most of his run-ins with Jackson would occur.[12]

These would lead to weeks (even months) of bitter political struggle. For starters, Western farmers were interested in cheap land; New England industrialists were demanding protective tariffs; Southern planters wanted those tariffs kept low; and internal improvements were on the minds of most as the country moved west. Both Clay and Jackson had to remain attuned to those trends, and the economic and social ramifications they inspired as they developed competing party programs. And by the 1830s, it was indeed competing parties. Jackson's mass following bore the Democratic Republican mantle of the agrarian/states' rights philosophy first espoused by two of our founders and former presidents, Thomas Jefferson and

1. Setting the Stage with Campaign Strategy 13

America's first national hero since George Washington, General Andrew Jackson was a dashing, charismatic, and very willful character on the national stage by the time he reached the White House in 1828. After being denied the presidency in 1824, when the election had to be decided by the House of Representatives, his immense popularity offered him the chance to expand presidential power (Library of Congress Prints and Photographs Division—Reproduction Number LC-DIG-det-4a26552).

Perhaps the most renowned legislator in American history, Henry Clay was a wily, gifted, and audacious participant on the national stage for more than four decades, beginning with his elevation to Speaker of the House at age 34 and three separate stints as a dominant voice in the United States Senate. Ambitious to a fault, however, he would become one of only two three-time U.S. presidential losers (Library of Congress Prints and Photographs Division—Reproduction Number LC-USZ62-71603).

James Madison, while Clay's so-called "American System" would become the basis of a new party, the Whigs, an offshoot of the earlier Federalists of the first secretary of the treasury, Alexander Hamilton, and his belief in a powerful central (aka federal) government.[13]

Clay's new twist on a more assertive federal government was all about financing internal improvements, including those involving more than one state, in order to spark more rapid development of the nation as a whole. Meanwhile, the Jacksonians would shorten and keep only the name Democrats, a designation that has been in place ever since, while Clay's Whigs, who wouldn't be officially called that until two years later (1834), stuck with National Republicans for the time being. That moniker would also be shortened and recalled 22 years later, when the new/current Republicans replaced the short-lived Whigs in 1856.[14]

In keeping with his "every-man" approach to democracy, Jackson sought to weed out over-governance by and for the country's elite. To his way of thinking, it was the same principle that had inspired America's Revolutionary generation to break away from British monarchy and he capitalized on angry voters bent on venting their discontent. No sooner had he avenged his presidential loss of 1824 than he began to target what he considered federal over-reach, especially anything he regarded as in direct competition with his own, executive agenda. Such a malignant force, at least in Jackson's mind, was the Second Bank of the United States. According to one presidential scholar: "When Andrew Jackson didn't like something, there were few half measures. He built his military career by attacking his enemies with little restraint [and] his political enemies were no different. In 1829, he made clear his hatred of the National Bank."[15]

As the centerpiece of the United States' original federal economic system, Jackson felt the National Bank "exerted too much control over the nation's economy." He viewed it as a political adversary that made loans to influence elections and re-elections, and paid retainers to favored lawmakers. And with the Bank's 20-year charter set to expire during what would be his second term, Jackson made known he had no intention of it seeing it renewed.[16]

Seizing upon such avowed opposition, Clay, the unanimous National Republican nominee, slyly sought to make the Bank a campaign issue in 1832. Although there were many other issues on which they disagreed, including Jackson's forced removal of Native American tribes, pushing them west to what was then "Indian Territory" in present day Oklahoma, as well as the President's opposition to federal funding of interstate or "national roads," an example of the kind of internal improvements he felt should be funded solely by the states, Clay saw in the Second Bank an issue where the destruction of a trusted financial institution might lead to the electoral repudiation of a popular incumbent. While Jackson had thoroughly avenged his controversial 1824 loss to Adams in 1828, his foremost Western rival, Clay, was angling for a way to mount a more formidable challenge in 1832.[17]

Despite the fact Jackson had recently ignored a Supreme Court ruling, which upheld existing treaty rights and the sovereignty of the most progressive of Southern tribes, the Cherokees, who along with the Creeks, Choctaws, and Seminoles were nonetheless compelled to leave their homelands and move west on their infamous "Trail of Tears," Clay chose the National Bank issue over all others for the coming campaign.[18] And despite the fact Jackson had previously vetoed federal funding for the "Maysville Road," which would have linked Clay's hometown, Lexington, to the Ohio River, the Kentucky senator chose to make that direct affront to him and his constituency secondary to the Bank in his plan of attack on the incumbent.[19] Not only as a sitting president had Jackson openly defied the Supreme Court, he also had the pleasure of curtailing a popular pet project of his personal rival and presidential opponent. Nevertheless, Clay's campaign focus would remain on the Bank.[20]

The Second National Bank had come into existence in 1816, a full five years after expiration of the First. As already noted, the brainchild of Alexander Hamilton, the original version had been signed into law in 1791 by then President George Washington. Federal Reserve historian Andrew Hill called it a "grand experiment" designed to assist the post–Revolutionary War economy. Hamilton's concept of a central bank was to help re-establish commerce and industry, repay war debts, and restore value to the currency by lowering inflation. All this was to be accomplished by the Bank issuing banknotes (paper money); to provide a safe place for public funds and commercial transactions; and to act as the government's designated fiscal agent in the collection of tax revenue and payment of debts. Its design was based on the Bank of England.[21]

Not all of America's "Founding Fathers" agreed with the concept, however, including Hamilton's chief rival, then Secretary of State Jefferson, who felt the federal government was creating a financial monopoly that would undermine smaller, state banks and cater to merchants and financiers at the expense of its agrarian based citizens and economies. Basically, it was the same argument Jackson would use 40 years later (with Jeffersonian-Jacksonian ideology usually referenced as a key part of Democratic Party heritage).[22]

When the First Bank's charter expired 20 years later in 1811, then Vice President George Clinton, a Jeffersonian disciple, broke a tie vote in the Senate by which it was not renewed. Five years later, however, it was brought back (as the Second Bank) as a result of financial issues left over

1. Setting the Stage with Campaign Strategy

from the War of 1812. It was re-chartered, surprisingly, with another Jeffersonian, President Madison, still in charge. Many historians have even interpreted that as Madison abandoning the principles of his mentor, but regardless of the reason for "Little Jemmy's" change of heart in the White House (as Madison was called due to his five foot, four-inch stature), the Bank was back in business by 1817.[23]

Over the next decade and a half, the Second Bank would gain in power and influence, especially under the leadership of Nicholas Biddle, its third and final president. In 1822, then President James Monroe, the third consecutive Virginia-born president (following Jefferson and Madison), heeded the advocacy of Biddle—one of the Bank's most active proponents as a wealthy three-term Pennsylvania congressman—by naming him to head the expanding institution, which was located in his hometown, Philadelphia. It would prove a great or toxic match, depending on one's status or station in life, for Biddle was, in the words of business historian Steve

The Second Bank of the United States, as it appeared in the early 1800s in Philadelphia, Pennsylvania. After the First National Bank was dissolved in 1811, America's involvement in the War of 1812 led to a desire for a rebirth of the federal repository and lending institution, leading to its creation by 1816 (Library of Congress Prints and Photographs Division—Reproduction Number LC-USZ62-56349).

Fraser, "an unapologetic patrician ... politically tactless enough to advertise his disdain for the popular will." Nevertheless, what's not debatable is that the Bank prospered under his leadership, serving as a useful market source for government bonds and commercial operations throughout the young country.[24]

Although not certifiably a monopoly, it exerted a large amount of control over foreign and domestic exchange, and if an asset in many ways, it could also be viewed as a liability, especially by not being subject to any kind of government constraint. That's what would become irritatingly obvious to President Jackson when the Bank doled out favors to influential people, including up-and-coming opposition voices like New York State Senator William Seward, newspaper editors like the *New York Courier and Enquirer's* James Watson Webb, and even powerful opposition senators like Webster and Clay, both of whom borrowed from it extensively. Already suspicious of all banks and banking in general, it was easy for Jackson to reach the conclusion that Biddle's Bank was, in his words, "a hydra of corruption—dangerous to our liberties by its corrupting influence everywhere"—"a monster," no less, that should not be re-chartered.[25]

With such intense opinions made manifest, imagine the Jackson administration's surprise when Biddle opted not to wait to seek the Bank's re-charter (not due until 1836), but to instead inject such a request into national politics four years early. Prodded by Clay, who obviously sought to back Jackson into a corner and a fight he felt had the potential to render him a one-term president, Biddle tossed a political grenade, the Bank re-charter legislation, onto the campaign landscape a full four years early in the winter of 1832.[26]

Needing a unifying issue to rally around versus the Jackson incumbency, Clay and his supporters enthusiastically endorsed the early re-charter idea, basically daring the President to veto a major (and by then accepted) component of the U.S. financial system during an election year. They were anticipating an equally major backlash at the ballot box. What they got instead was a divisive, wedge issue that enabled Jackson to inflate his presidential prerogatives and force systematic changes whether the country was ready for them or not. It was presidential autocracy on steroids, an all-powerful approach not seen before and utilized by only a few presidents since. It was first standardized during the reign ... err, administration of Andrew Jackson.[27]

As confirmed by two separate but related entries in *The American Senate, An Insider's History*: "Jackson expanded the president's power and prestige beyond anything seen before. He saw no reason to defer to Congress—especially the Senate—and his defiance of the Senate changed the very nature of the presidency, of the Senate, and of the relationship between them." "Such a polarizing figure, fiercely intent on subordinating the Senate to his purposes, he also summoned [or disparaged] into existence an identifiable class of visible and eloquent Senate leaders"[28]—chief among them, Henry Clay.

2

Chronological Review of a Political Gamble

When Henry Clay urged Nicholas Biddle to inject the re-charter of the Second Bank of the United States into the presidential campaign of 1832, it seemed a gamble worth taking. Faced with trying to take down the immensely popular Andrew Jackson, the anointed "Hero of New Orleans" following his landmark generalship in the War of 1812, was going to be an onerous, uphill climb, even for a political pro like Clay. But it was an issue with a chance to succeed based on the increasingly influential stature of Biddle's 15-year-old Bank.[1]

Knowledge of Jackson's well-established contempt for the Bank and its expanding footprint on the national landscape were at the heart of Clay's prodding and Biddle's early re-charter request. Putting Jackson on the spot for his acknowledged plan to stop the Bank's re-charter whenever it came up was in essence a political plot designed to trap the autocratically prone President, something that should he follow through on might prove manifestly offensive to a majority of American businessmen and breadwinners—White males, who in those days were the only voters. As a by then mostly accepted and relied-upon part of the fledgling U.S. financial system, the Clay-Biddle assumption was that forcing Jackson's hand on the early re-charter with his re-election looming would compel him to either back down on his veto intention or face electoral judgment on what would surely seem unnecessary overreach. In other words, if the American financial system wasn't broken and in need of fixing, why go there?[2]

Clay had Biddle convinced that to wait on his re-charter request until after the election, without the threat of Jackson facing electoral backlash, was to court veto and disaster. On the other hand, to go ahead and have the re-charter bill submitted and passed in Congress might ensure reluctance by the President to act on his previously stated opposition to the Bank. As a matter of survival, Biddle was an easy convert.[3]

2. Chronological Review of a Political Gamble

Obviously, this ploy held potential advantages for the Clay campaign, and especially so should Jackson go ahead with his pre-determined Bank intentions. According to Robert Remini, a principal biographer of both, "He [Clay] was certain he could defeat Jackson on the issue if the President dared veto a re-charter bill." To his way of thinking, that would constitute "a blatant act of political self-interest" and as stated in *The American Senate*, Clay was always "willing to take high political risks to achieve his purposes."[4]

Meanwhile, Biddle anticipated the President wouldn't dare veto re-charter in an election year for fear of reducing what he hoped would be his huge re-election turnout and majority. Also, Biddle could not afford to offend Clay, whose support seemed necessary for the continued life of his Bank.[5] And as late as December 1831, Jackson was

Perhaps contemplating the uncertain status of his Second Bank of the U.S., a young and very pensive Nicholas Biddle was at the center of the National Bank controversy as its president. His 1832 request for re-charter four years early became the main issue in the presidential campaign that year, fueling the already intense rivalry of Senator Henry Clay and President Andrew Jackson (Library of Congress Prints and Photographs Division—Reproduction Number HABS PA,9-ANDA,134).

still sending mixed signals about his intentions on the Bank based on his third annual message to Congress. Clay even said, "The President is playing a deep game to avoid at this session [of Congress] the responsibility of any decision on the Bank question." Any retreat from his earlier veto indications, however, were quickly put to rest when Biddle responded to Clay's call for action by following through on his petition to Congress in January 1832, an act Jackson proclaimed was instituted with "treachery and malice" and one he vowed to stop.[6]

Almost immediately, Jackson's advisers assured him his worst intuitions were correct and that Biddle's early re-charter request was indeed a political ploy to intrude on the immediate electoral process on behalf of Henry Clay. Attorney General Roger B. Taney told the President what it meant in plain English: "Your next election is at hand—if you re-charter, all's well and good—if not, beware your power."[7]

Equally compelling evidence of Senator Clay's subterfuge came in the way the Bank re-charter was to be combined with the protective tariff question and the distribution of public lands, other major issues that, at least in Clay's politically astute way of thinking, had the power "to blow the old man out of the White House." Returning to Washington via the then state legislature-appointed Senate, in fact, following over 10 years as Speaker of the House, was proof of Clay's desire (and expectation) to dominate the legislative process from a different congressional platform. He was looking to secure campaign momentum from any presidential missteps on the tariff, public lands, or Bank issues, and especially so if a Jackson veto happened to be issued on the last one.[8]

Sure enough, on January 20, 1832, the bill for the Bank's re-charter came up for debate on the Senate floor.[9] It was brought there not by Clay, who it had been agreed would concentrate on the tariff issue, but by his National Republican (and soon to be Whig) colleagues, George Dallas of Pennsylvania, the Bank's home state, and the iconic Webster. For optic reasons, it had been agreed this arrangement would work better, with Clay shepherding the tariff, which meant much to Webster's New England, while "Godlike Dan," who would also be immortalized as "Black Dan" in the 1936 *Saturday Evening Post* short story "The Devil and Daniel Webster," argued for the Bank. This would relieve Clay, the party nominee, from direct initiation of the issue and wishfully, at least some political suspicion.[10]

Opposing Webster and speaking for the Jackson administration would be Thomas Hart Benton of Missouri. Nearly as eloquent as the oratorically renowned Webster, Benton based his attack on the Bank on what he labeled illegal bank drafts issued by different branches of the institution in various cities throughout the country. His attack preceded a surprise maneuver by Webster and Dallas, as they requested a committee of five Senators, including Thomas Ewing of Ohio, Robert Hayne of South Carolina, and Josiah Johnston of Louisiana, all of whom were pro–Bank, to be set up to examine the re-charter issue, something the Jacksonians in the Senate were unable to block. As a result (and before any more charges could be levied by Benton or any other Democrats), that select committee was formed and returned a recommendation for re-charter by March 13.[11]

Although recommended with new restrictions, including limiting the National Bank's right to hold real estate and establish branches; the prohibition of bank drafts; the reinforcement of Congress' power to forbid issuance of certain small bank notes; and a requirement of presidential authorization for any new member of the Bank's board of directors—all minor compromises designed to speed passage—the Jacksonians still sought delay. At least one third of the Democrats in Congress favored its passage, so congressional opposition was mostly sectional from the South and West, Jackson strongholds. Nevertheless, the forces of Webster and Clay managed to push it through by votes of 28–20 in the Senate and 107–85 in the House. Only four Northern senators voted nay, reinforcing the final tallies along sectional rather than party lines.[12]

Clay, Webster, and their backers were jubilant. Clay even said: "The congressional session has indeed been one of glorious triumph for the country and our cause." Biddle, too, expressed delight, congratulating "our friends most cordially upon this satisfactory result" before adding that he still expected the President to veto the bill. As to that possibility, Clay remarked, "Should Jackson veto it, I will veto him."[13]

One of America's greatest orators, Senator Daniel Webster of Massachusetts argued the case for re-chartering the Second Bank of the United States. Making the case for his National Republican colleague and presidential nominee Henry Clay, the words and performance of Godlike Dan were deemed major drawing cards when the Senate opened debate on January 20, 1832 (Library of Congress Prints and Photographs Division—Reproduction Number LC-US762-8231).

In other words, the trap had been laid and "Prince Hal," as Clay was sometimes called, was eager for the sitting president, whom he truly detested, to fall into it. Perhaps his best (or only) hope of unseating the popular incumbent, it at least provided a possible path to the White House and fulfillment of his lifelong ambition—a burning ambition that had already been denied once and would ultimately be again (and again). It was a gamble for both him and Biddle, but a gamble they both felt worth taking as the election of 1832 and the Bank's future hung in the balance. Fully in the crosshairs of an unforgiving political enemy, they braced themselves for his next move.[14]

24   Section One—Battle Over the Bank

At the same time, "Washington readied for political war." So stated Brands again in *American Lion*.[15] "Old Hickory knew what he meant to do," accorded earlier Jacksonian historian Glyndon VanDeusen. "The Bank is trying to kill me, but I will kill it," he reportedly told Martin Van Buren, the New York Democrat who had become his most trusted Cabinet confidant as secretary of state, soon-to-be second vice president, and eventual White House successor. Relying on a trio of political advisers—newspaper magnate Amos Kendall, Attorney General Taney, and Secretary of the Navy Levi Woodbury—Jackson carefully prepared his response, a ringing veto that would characterize the National Bank as a "monster" with far-reaching tentacles and political friends that influenced and infected American democracy. His veto message, also in VanDeusen's words, "pilloried" the Bank as "a dangerous centralization of power at the expense of the states" and "its proposed capital [assets] of $35 million was declared to be far in excess of what was necessary."[16]

GENERAL JACKSON SLAYING THE MANY HEADED MONSTER.

Using evocative imagery to make a point, President Andrew Jackson described the National Bank in 1832 as a "monster" with far-reaching tentacles aimed at killing him if he didn't kill it first, prompting this political cartoon. In it, he was portrayed attempting to slay the multi-headed monster he considered an elitist threat to the nation (Library of Congress Prints and Photographs Division—Reproduction Number LC-USz62-1575).

Taking the rhetoric to another level, Jackson also declared the Bank unconstitutional despite an earlier Supreme Court ruling (*McCullough vs. Maryland*) that had deemed it otherwise. To the contrary, Jackson argued that each public official was bound to the Constitution only as he understood it, not as actually interpreted by the Supreme Court, a "highly questionable thesis" to be sure, as again, rightly interpreted by VanDeusen in his 1959 book, *The Jacksonian Era*.[17]

One thing for sure, "to differ with Old Hickory or his policies guaranteed retaliation" and because of his popularity with the electorate, most Democratic politicians found it safer to toe the presidential line. To disagree would be to exit the party, as Jackson assumed tighter and tighter control of the Dems ... and the government as a whole.[18] That according to Remini in his biography of Clay, while adding in a later entry: "Not only did the President 'vilify' the Bank, but he repeatedly asserted presidential authority and privilege" over it. As an agent of the executive branch, at least to his way of thinking, the re-charter would renew (or confirm) powers for the institution that were "unnecessary and dangerous to the nation." He ended his veto with a "flourish" and a glimpse of what he planned to do. To paraphrase, it read:

> It is regrettable that the rich and powerful too often bend the acts of government to their selfish purposes so that when laws are enacted that make the rich richer and the potent more powerful, the humble members of society have a right to complain of the injustice of their government. The true strength of the government consists in leaving individuals and states as much as possible to themselves—in making [government] felt, not in its power, but in its beneficence; not in its control, but its protection; not in binding the states more closely to the center, but in leaving each to move unobstructed in its proper orbit.[19]

Not at all surprised by the veto, but totally appalled by the President's tone and content, Biddle compared it to "the fury of a chained panther biting the bars of its cage." Clay also called it "a manifesto of anarchy," but neither imagined the propaganda benefits Jackson's words would have in the upcoming campaign.[20]

With his veto, Jackson basically began to accuse the nation's rich of stealing from the poor with the Second Bank of the United States as the instrument of their theft. Soon thereafter, Webster rose in the Senate to denounce the President for "seeking to inflame the poor against the rich" and Clay's reputation as a political fighter quickly came to the forefront when he gave voice to his own contempt for Jackson's "verbiage." He called it "a perversion of the veto power established by the founders and only to be used in extraordinary circumstances" and not as President Jackson had already done four times in three years. Clay also accused the President of "invading the legislative process by seeking to impose his own will upon Congress, an act hardly reconcilable with the genius of representative government, if not downright revolutionary." Candidate Clay then warned of potential economic and social consequences to be incurred from President Jackson's action, hinting at possible "catastrophe," which drew rousing cheers and applause from Bank partisans in the Senate gallery.[21]

A short time later, Benton rose again to confront both Clay and Webster on behalf of the administration. He chided them for speech lacking in courtesy, "indecorous and disrespectful to the President of the United States," and he feigned shock at things that had been said in response to the chief executive's exercise of veto power as defined in the Constitution.

Upon hearing that, Clay literally jumped to his feet in response, chastising his big rival from Missouri as a "ruffian and street brawler," and unqualified to offer anyone "etiquette" lessons. Resurrecting circumstances surrounding a confrontation and duel between Benton and the President when they were not on such friendly terms years before, he also sought to embarrass his Border State colleague with knowledge and exposure of that 1813 incident (even though Clay, too, had previously dueled), when he said, "At least I never had any personal rencontre [meeting] with the President; I never complained of the President beating a brother of mine after he was prostrated and lying apparently lifeless."

"False, false, false," Benton screamed in retaliation, and in his biography of Clay, Remini recounted how everyone in the chamber "steeled" themselves in anticipation of the fight that now seemed inevitable between the two Senate

Opposing Daniel Webster and Henry Clay on the Senate floor over re-chartering the Second Bank of the United States, Senator Thomas Hart Benton was a powerful voice for the Jackson administration and its intention to contain the National Bank. Ironically, the big man from Missouri had once dueled with the President during their younger, frontier days before becoming a stalwart Jacksonian Democrat (Library of Congress Prints and Photographs Division—Reproduction Number LC-US762-1112).

2. Chronological Review of a Political Gamble   27

leaders. But with the Chair frantically gaveling and calling for order, cooler heads prevailed, and decorum was eventually restored. The two storied combatants apologized to the Senate, though not to each other, and "on [that] low note, debate over Jackson's misuse of power ended."[22]

What followed was the failure of the Clay-Webster forces to override the veto by a close 22–19 margin. What remained was for the American people to have final say on the issue's ultimate winner and loser in the upcoming presidential election, and towards that result the campaign battle intensified throughout the spring and early summer of 1832.[23]

The remaining fight over the Bank would take place amidst other political grievances and confrontations during one of the Senate's most bellicose eras. Making these matters worse for the aging President was a severe bout of influenza early in the year, an improper fitting of his artificial teeth, and removal of a festering bullet that was lodged in his left arm 19 years earlier following one of several previous duels he had survived.[24] Added to these acute, physical challenges, Jackson also suffered through some difficult confirmation proceedings for his nominees to several Cabinet and diplomatic posts, an unusual presidential nuisance in the days before organized partisan opposition became commonplace.[25]

Amazingly (at least to modern Americans used to a vice president being chosen as part of his party's ticket and in total homage to his or her presidential running mate), Jackson's original and separately elected VP was the previously mentioned John C. Calhoun, who had criticized then General Jackson's controversial invasion of Florida in pursuit of Seminoles in 1818 while secretary of war, and who, as a future South Carolina senator, would openly clash with Jackson over the idea of a state's right to reject (or nullify) and not enforce any federal law it disagreed with. Needless to say, Calhoun would prove nearly as much a Jackson foe as Clay and was delighted as vice president in 1832 to cast a tie-breaking Senate vote rejecting Jackson's nomination of New York's Martin Van Buren for minister to Great Britain. "By the eternal, I'll smash them," Jackson was reportedly heard to say upon learning of Calhoun's vote to defeat Van Buren, something he considered a personal affront and ironically something that would hasten his choice of Van Buren as Calhoun's VP replacement and his own presidential successor in 1836. Indeed, Remini termed the diplomatic rejection the best thing that could have happened to Van Buren and his political career, as it only served to solidify the little New Yorker's place as a Jackson favorite.[26]

At the same time, Clay's highly anticipated call to arms soon came from the Senate floor, when he said, "We are in the midst of a revolution, hitherto bloodless, but rapidly tending towards a total change of the pure republican character of the government, and to the concentration of all power in the hands of one man." He also argued that Jackson was "destroying" the America the Founding Fathers had created by turning the (federal) government into "an elective monarchy—the worst of all forms of government."[27]

Political satirists of the day were quick to draw attention to Henry Clay's gamble to hamstring President Jackson by injecting the National Bank issue into their 1832 campaign. This cartoon was typical, showing Clay aggressively attempting to shut his rival's mouth by forcibly sewing it up (Library of Congress Prints and Photographs Division—Reproduction Number LC-USZ62-92612).

It was at this point that the wily Kentuckian called on Congress to "apply an instantaneous remedy" for the good of the American people. Otherwise, in his words, "fatal collapse ... abject slavery ... scorn and contempt [would] be heaped upon mankind," a warning he issued to applause and cheers so continuous that the Senate galleries had to be cleared. According to Meacham in *American Lion*, this was Clay "striking at what Jackson cherished most: his power and his honor ... and in response, Jackson 'took joy in the fight.'"[28]

To his Cabinet, the President had already shared his belief that "the people wanted—and expected—the Bank to die," and to accomplish this financial makeover, he made known his plans to remove all federal deposits from the Second Bank of the United States and re-deposit them in a series of state banks throughout the country.[29] Accepting the challenge, Jackson was equally ready for the Bank to become the defining campaign issue. As Michael Holt stated in the early pages of his *American Whig Party*, he would use it to "bludgeon" Clay.[30]

According to Francis Preston Blair, a pro–Jackson editor of the time who had been brought east by the administration to head the *Washington Globe*, "The sublimity of [a] moral spectacle" had been "presented to the American people in the person of Andrew Jackson" and as a result, the President had thrown down the gauntlet, challenging the "moneyed aristocracy," an "insidious enemy and creeping poison," and a "germ of American nobility."[31] Comments like those would be part of what Holt termed "a masterpiece of political propaganda aimed directly at voters." Jackson denounced the Bank as unconstitutional and an excess of national authority; as "a monstrous concentration of private power that threatened popular liberty"; and as an aristocratic privilege that inherently "favored the rich at the expense of the poor." Such proclamations were aimed at enhancing the President's reputation as the champion of republicanism, and the enemy of the corrupt and entrenched political establishment found in Congress.[32]

Despite such idealistic pronouncements, however, "the veto's reasoning remained weak." So, admitted VanDeusen in the *Jacksonian Era*, adding:

> [The] argument that a national bank in the 1830s needed no more capital than the one that had existed 30 years before betrayed reluctance to face realistically the problems of a rapidly developing economy that was characteristic of the Jacksonians. The veto repeatedly stated that the Bank was a monopoly, which was true only if monopoly were defined in such a way as to divest the word of its real meaning. It ignored the Bank's enormous services to the national economy. Neither then, nor later did the President offer an effective substitute.[33]

Along with Webster and his other backers, Clay hoped to take full advantage of the anticipated concern this financial void might create, or at least hoped the American people would be smart enough to recognize the unnecessary disruption an end to the Bank could cause. As with so many political debates, feasibility and believability were critical components of the argument to alter the developing nation's financial system without economic chaos.[34]

Clay warned of economic consequences and social ones as well. "It would bring catastrophe," his biographer, Remini, repeated, amplifying the Kentuckian's dire warnings from the summer of 1832. Included would be a lengthy, high-profile layover for him at society-conscious White Sulphur Springs (still known as "America's Resort") in present day West Virginia, while en route to his "old Kentucky home"—Ashland. Once back in the "Blue Grass," Clay confidently awaited the voters' verdict, secure in his belief that he had engendered an issue with the power to upset the incumbent, whose autocratic tendencies had finally and sufficiently been exposed.[35]

Over the next three months (from the end of July through October), Clay remained heartened by the reception he received wherever he went. "I believe the redemption of our country from an arbitrary administration is at hand," he stated on more than one occasion, while also predicting President Jackson would not receive over 100 electoral votes. In the meantime, only the defeat of his party's candidate in the Kentucky governor's race by a Jacksonian gave him pause to reconsider his own chances in November.[36] Although it seemed a bad sign, Clay indulged in what Remini termed "his old propensity for self-delusion" and "kept asserting his own victory was assured." To his way of thinking, the governor's race was merely a bi-product of Jackson's popularity in the Upper South and not indicative of the popular will in the rest of the country.[37]

Biddle further buoyed Clay's "unrealistic interpretations" of recent events with comments like "You are destined to be the instrument of the nation's deliverance," while polling reports from New York, Pennsylvania, Louisiana, Ohio, Missouri and New England all remained positive.[38] In addition, the four-year-old Anti-Masonic Party (1828), the nation's first third party, had emerged in Upstate New York primarily as an alternative to Jackson's Democrats with former Attorney General William Wirt of Maryland as its reluctant nominee, and Clay assumed this new voting bloc would most likely take votes away from the man who had recently vetoed the already proven National Bank and much needed internal improvements like the Maysville Road.[39]

But even with other domestic and foreign policy issues crowding his calendar during the summer months and early fall of 1832, Jackson also remained resolute in keeping the Bank issue front and center on the minds of voters as election day approached. The issue, in fact, was rarely absent from his thoughts. Many pundits and politicians wrote to him at his Tennessee home outside of Nashville, the Hermitage, currying favor by lauding his Bank veto, praising its message as Remini recorded, "a document worthy of the purest days of our republic" and one that would "bring us nearer the original principles and spirit of our founders." Not since Jefferson, many enunciated, had the nation's chief executive stood so solidly for "the people."[40]

Unlike Clay and his National Republicans, however, Jackson's Democrats were counting on much more than the Bank issue to make the difference. In an age of advancing professionalism, they already understood the importance of political organization to any election cycle and they had been working for years to build majorities for the President in virtually every section of the country. Local committees called "Hickory Clubs" were established and active, generating support for the Dems' national ticket at spontaneous rallies, especially in the West, where patriotic pride and Jacksonian spirit were considered one and the same. In addition, barbecues involving whole communities became an important Jacksonian technique and opportunity for political propaganda, with the President himself even appearing at a few in cities where his calendar and travels allowed it. And partisan newspapers like the previously mentioned *Globe*, were relied on to trumpet the Dems' party line message in perhaps the nation's first partisan media campaign. Earlier portraits of General Jackson in his military attire or later ones as a gentleman farmer with his famous cane began to appear everywhere during the campaign's final months, with the Jacksonian blitz consuming town halls throughout the country.[41]

It all became too much for Clay and his congressional allies to overcome, as most so-called "common men" applauded Jackson's characterization of the Bank "as a symbol of special privilege and manipulation." Presidential historians also confirmed the Democratic press's promotion of Clay as an irredeemable "gambler" capable of immoral behavior, a reputation that dogged the Kentucky legend whenever compared to the heroic, military image of the President. So, despite the Anti-Masonic addition to the race, Jackson still dominated voting in the West and South and even improved his anticipated support in New England. The final popular vote tally was 687,502 for Jackson (55 percent), 530,189 for Clay (37 percent), and 100,715 (eight percent) for Wirt. The Electoral College count was even more one-sided with Jackson claiming 16 states to Clay's six—a final judgment that left little doubt the political gamble that caused the battle over the Bank had failed dramatically.[42]

Nevertheless, while still preaching the virtues of his American System amidst yet another losing presidential campaign over a decade later, Clay would again look for political traction from the idea of a restored National

Bank. In 1844 he would actually use it as a diversionary tactic, seeking to distract from the major issue that was by then Texas annexation and westward expansion (Clay being on the wrong side of history for that one as well), but once again it failed to move the public opinion needle in any significant way and certainly not enough to aid his never-ending quest for the White House. Finally admitting defeat and the fact his career goal was beyond reach, the aging Kentuckian said at the time, "My duty now is that of resignation and submission, cherishing the hope that some others more fortunate than myself may yet arise to accomplish that which I have not been allowed to effect."[43]

3

The Ensuing Expansion of Presidential Power

Most historians now agree: Jackson's veto of the Second Bank of the United States ushered in the climactic final chapter of the 1832 presidential campaign.[1] Despite optimistic reports almost daily from friends and supporters around the country, and his own delusional expectations that destiny had chosen him to deliver the nation from a finally-exposed autocratic despot, Clay's unrealistic interpretations of the campaign were obviously impaired by his failure to realize the Bank issue was being spun to Jackson's benefit more than his own.[2]

A normally astute and shrewd politician, Clay's gamble on the Bank issue was nonetheless one in a series of political long shots he employed for personal advancement throughout his career, while seeming to always lag behind his immediate rivals organizationally.[3] Other examples included his misguided 1824 strategy whereby not having a majority Electoral College winner among the four presidential contenders would give the final decision to the House of Representatives where he was speaker. He anticipated that would ensure his chances of victory if only he could make the top three—a gamble proven wrong when he missed the cut by finishing fourth. Also, his gamble in the 1844 presidential election that opposition to Texas annexation, its expansion of slavery, and what figured to be a resulting war with Mexico would earn him more Northern votes than what it would ever cost him in the South and West—an error in judgment confirmed by his narrow loss to the nation's first "dark horse" candidate, James K. Polk.[4] Although Clay would always recognize the value of well-placed campaign propaganda, Jackson's Democrats proved infinitely more adept at it in 1832.[5] The only states Clay carried were Delaware, Connecticut, Rhode Island, Massachusetts, and his own—Kentucky.[6]

The most obvious, first result of the election (and lack of a backlash to Jackson's Bank veto) was the demise of the National Republicans as a national party. The electoral outcome seemed to confirm that National

Republicans were "out-of-touch advocates of the Northeastern elite" and a party "unfit to make converts." Also illustrated by period historian Michael Holt's extensive research, "Competing on even terms with the Jacksonians [Democrats] would mean abandoning the National Republican Party" for a more enticing partisan model—what would become the Whig Party— which, ironically, would also come and go from the American political scene by the 1850s.[7]

Another immediate result of the 1832 Clay-Jackson political conflict was the re-elected president's re-configuring of American finances. Only months after his battle over the Bank was electorally resolved, Jackson ordered all federal deposits in the National Bank to be withdrawn and deposited in state banks. When Treasury Department officials refused to comply with his wishes, he simply replaced them with those he could trust to conform, including Attorney General Taney, who suddenly went from heading the Justice Department to serving as acting secretary of the treasury. And despite the Senate's refusal to confirm Taney at Treasury on a permanent basis, he was there long enough to carry out Jackson's wishes. As a result, by October 1, 1833, all surplus federal funds were no longer in the Second Bank of the United States, having been deposited instead in smaller "Pet Banks," effectively sounding the death knell of the Philly-based, Biddle-led National Bank, which would re-charter as the United States Bank of Pennsylvania in 1836 before going bankrupt and gone entirely by 1841.[8]

Although his authority to remove the deposits at the time was questioned, even by his own Cabinet, Jackson had no doubt he had the right to do it and was determined to make sure the issue did not outlast his administration. In response to the President's devastating action, Biddle attempted to survive by recalling all of the Bank's outstanding loans, thus starving the U.S. economy of cash flow and attempting to prove to the country it indeed needed a National Bank. Jackson's abrupt actions and stubborn resolve following the veto, as well as Biddle's understandable response, would lead to investment limbo throughout the country and set in motion what ultimately became the "Panic of 1837," a national recession that lasted well into the 1840s. Focusing on the administration's seemingly high-handed removal of the deposits and the resulting contraction of credit, businessmen throughout the country flooded Washington with petitions asking for relief and prompting Jackson to angrily remark, "Come not to me! Go to the monster! Go see Nicholas Biddle. It is folly, sir, to talk to Andrew Jackson. The government will not bow to the monster."[9]

Meanwhile, the President's detractors in the Senate were equally appalled at the economic hardship he had so flagrantly instigated and led by Clay they moved to censure him for "the exercise of power over the

3. The Ensuing Expansion of Presidential Power 35

Treasury not granted by the Constitution and dangerous to the liberties of the [American] people." Clay even felt it was a revolution of sorts, "tending," as Brands wrote in *Heirs to the Founders*, "towards a total change of the pure republican character of the government to concentration of all power in the hands of one man." Clay basically accused Jackson of seizing the nation's financial assets and "scattering them to the winds."[10] While under Whig control the censure would be upheld, specifically because of Jackson's failure to turn over documents related to his Bank actions, but once Democrats were back in control of the Senate before Jackson's second term ended, they wasted no time having that official rebuke expunged from the congressional record.[11]

All the while, Jackson blamed Biddle for implementation of the financial distress and held Clay responsible for continuing to put ideas in the Bank executive's head. The President also took obvious delight in what Brands framed as Clay's "personal impotence" on the banking question. Most Americans did not understand the arguments, pro and con, but generally took Jackson's side (as had the majority during the election), believing the President was waging a battle for them against the financial aristocracy.[12] At the same time, despite the nation's economic anxiety and ongoing political debate, Jackson felt empowered enough to issue an executive order known as the "Specie Circular." It required that all land purchased from the federal government be paid for in gold or silver (specie) instead of paper money, furthering the financial depression Biddle's loan recall had initiated and leaving the worst of the resulting economic woes to the next administration—Van Buren's.[13]

Among those heavily involved in land speculation, both before and after the Specie Circular, was none other than Daniel Webster, and to the Massachusetts senator and others in Congress this was yet another example of Jackson unjustly increasing the powers of the executive branch. It was one more result of the failure of the Bank battle to derail an incumbent bent on expanding presidential power to never before seen constitutional limits. Along with the Specie Circular, Webster and Clay also decried a "spoils system" of unchecked patronage that Jackson was employing to excess, affirming the argument that the President alone, as Remini confirmed in his book *Daniel Webster* (yet another of his massive biographical texts), was the sole "representative of the whole American people."[14] Pressure for repeal of the Specie Circular mounted under Van Buren and it would eventually be rescinded, but there can be no denying the American chief executive's influence over national finances and patronage was irrevocably increased during Jackson's leadership.[15]

In addition, Jackson's victory over the Bank and Clay had been preceded by his veto of federal funding for the Maysville Road from Lexington,

As the designated successor to President Andrew Jackson, Martin Van Buren inherited his hard money policies, including the 1836 Specie Circular, which contributed to the Panic of 1837, the subject of this political cartoon of the time. Notice the devil hovering over the well adorned new White House resident (Library of Congress Prints and Photographs Division—Reproduction Number LC-USZ62-26455).

Kentucky, Clay's hometown, to the Ohio River, one of the internal improvements nearest and dearest to Clay's heart and his beloved American System. Along with the National Bank, which unlike Jackson Clay had fully embraced after the War of 1812 and resulting national debt, the Kentuckian advocated federal dollars for internal, multi-state improvements, believing those to be in the best interests of the entire nation. Jackson, on the other hand, was decidedly of the opinion that funding for internal improvements should be the sole responsibility of the individual states (example: the Erie Canal, built solely by the state of New York between 1817 and 1825). Obviously, his re-election and the administrations of his Jacksonian Era successors—Van Buren (1837), the Democratic defector and accidental president John Tyler (1841, having ascended as vice president when William Henry Harrison died in office), and Polk, America's great Western expansionist (1845)—would set back the concept of federally funded internal improvements for decades.[16]

Another legislative pillar of the formula for Clay's American System was the tariff—what amounted to taxes (or duties) levied on imports from other countries that in that age made up the largest share of U.S. revenue. Before the election in 1832, according to presidential historian William DeGregorio, a new, more "moderate" tariff was enacted, but one only slightly "less exacting" than the so-called "Tariff of Abominations" of 1828, so-named by its Southern detractors in Congress because of the debilitating effect it would supposedly have on their section's economy.[17] Unlike their Northern counterparts, where manufacturing and industry were beginning to proliferate, the Southern state economies remained agrarian based, so that while high duties on incoming imports were obviously beneficial to Northern manufacturers striving to compete with European makers of the same products, they were not so in the South, where the price of all goods went up without the accompanying product protections being reaped by the North. As a result, many Southern legislators continued to feel the tariff was "unconstitutional, unequal, and oppressive" (even the modified 1832 version), making their constituents what Glyndon VanDeusen called the "serfs of the system." Needless to say, they looked for a way to rescind it.[18]

With Jackson securely back in the White House and wielding presidential power in extraordinarily new and more assertive ways, this sectional disagreement over the tariff exploded shortly after the election in early 1833, when Calhoun-led South Carolina, in an act of Southern brinksmanship (as occurred often before the Civil War), drafted its "Ordinance of Nullification" that ruled collecting the tariff null and void in the "Palmetto State." It was an act of states' rights defiance that Jackson would not tolerate, leading to passage of his Force Bill the following month, which gave him the authority, as president, to use the U.S. military to enforce the tariff in states where its collection might be obstructed and to overpower and jail anyone, if necessary, involved in obvious obstruction of this or any other federal law. Defiantly Jacksonian in its aggressive, out-front approach, its passage quelled the budding Southern resistance of the moment, but it was a precursor of the looming sectional conflict that would not go away until civil war and the emancipation of Southern slavery in the 1860s.[19]

At the same time, despite his crushing defeat in the presidential race the year before, Henry Clay remained integral to actually solving the "Nullification Crisis" in 1833, as debate and animosity between the sections continued to escalate. Just as with the "Missouri Compromise" of the 1820s, when Missouri could not be admitted as a slave state until Maine was also added as a balancing, non-slave, free state, Clay led the way to yet another tariff, the lesser known "Compromise Tariff." To do so, he had to secretly consult with the increasingly radicalized Calhoun to concoct a gradual, decade-long lessening of import duties to pre–1820 levels that a reluctant South and disgruntled North could both accept—at least for the time being (through 1842).[20] While never able to fulfill his lifelong ambitions for the White House, his service to the nation would continue as the "Great Compromiser," repeatedly staving off what always seemed America's inevitable march to civil war. His last introduction of such legislation would happen in 1850, what became known as the "Compromise of 1850," but it would be for a younger and equally appeasement-conscious senator, Stephen A. Douglas, to push that one across the finish line by breaking the initially large omnibus bill into more acceptable parts for the 72-year-old and ready-to-retire Clay, probably America's greatest legislator and most battle-scarred politician of all time (and the first deceased American to be honored by having his body lie in state at the Capitol, 1852). Nine years after his death when Abraham Lincoln became president, he remembered Clay's influence over 40-plus years of federal government service and how he had always been his "beau ideal as a statesman." Even more revealing, Lincoln called Clay "*the* man in a crisis."[21] Along with Democratic firebrand William Jennings Bryan—whose populist message and thunderous oratory made him a political star in the late 19th and early 20th century—Clay remains one of America's only two three-time, major party presidential losers.[22]

Politically the Jacksonian Democrats obviously benefited from the Bank confrontation, as they were able to characterize their opponents as "lackeys of a 'mammoth corporation.'" In other words, according to VanDeusen, "friends of the wealthy and powerful" and "exploiters of the masses." Vice President Van Buren would also write, "The opposition labor[s] hard to shake off the Bank, but we are determined to hold them to it," and for the foreseeable future that's exactly what they did, returning to the issue again and again throughout Jackson's second term and again during his VP's successful succeeding campaign in 1836.[23] Van Buren, in fact, would be the last vice president to ascend to the White House on the coattails of his preceding presidential running mate until George H.W.

Bush succeeded Ronald Reagan in 1989. Paraphrasing historian Kenneth C. Davis in that regard, he wrote: "Like his long ago predecessor Martin Van Buren, Bush would be a one-term president—and one who was measured against [the] presidential giant [who preceded him]."[24]

That sort of "giant" status among American presidents has rarely been unanimous, however, and the major expansion of presidential power that occurred under Andrew Jackson has always had its share of detractors. One such historian, Brian McClanahan, even labeled the Jackson administration "the first imperial presidency" for the way it "arrogated enormous power not authorized by the Constitution." In other words, executive overreach—examples of which McClanahan pointed to in Jackson's handling of both the Bank and Nullification controversies. As to the first of those, he called Jackson's Bank veto mostly a "personal vendetta" against Clay and his administration's removal of federal deposits patently unlawful in light of the fact Congress was not notified first. On Jackson's aggressive approach to Nullification via the Force Bill, McClanahan took the side of Calhoun, the primary author of South Carolina's ordinance, arguing that his presidential power play was not only aimed at an individual state's authority, "but also at the expense of the entire federal system and Constitution itself," permitting the executive branch to eventually "consume" powers of the other federal branches as well as the states.[25]

Also, Jackson's expansion of presidential authority clearly coincided with the push for equality and economic opportunity by the middle and lower classes of the White population throughout the country.[26] This was especially true in the Deep South and early West, where his Indian Removal Act of 1830 proved a major operation with no precedents that callously pushed Native Americans westward, opening their homelands to Caucasian settlement and increased Democratic voter rolls.[27] No longer would such ironies as a "Virginia Dynasty," where four of our first five presidents all hailed from the same state, be conceivable, or the financial influence of one or two regions of the country, such as New England and the Middle Atlantic, hold sway over national decision-making.[28] Instead, Jacksonian-style democracy had effectively ushered in populist appeal and massed partisan support.

After feeling burned by insider politics in his first national run in 1824, the general that was Jackson made sure to marshal his forces the second and third times around, and he did so, in part, by exemplifying and enhancing presidential control while in the White House. Among the ways he did so was by the presidential veto, blocking more congressional bills (12) than all his predecessors combined; by doubling the size of the federal government and rewarding his supporters with government jobs (what we now term patronage) in our original spoils system; and by asserting the supremacy of the federal government over state governments more than any of his predecessors.[29] Although other presidents, most notably Theodore Roosevelt at the turn of the 20th century and his fifth cousin, Franklin Roosevelt, in the 1930s, could rightly be credited with greatly extending the powers of the presidency, Jackson clearly set the early standard for presidential empowerment or overreach, depending on one's point of view. Either way, he's been called the "founder of the modern presidency" as a result.[30]

SECTIONTWO

The Bleeding Kansas Fight
James Buchanan vs. Stephen Douglas

4

Breakdown of the Jacksonian Democrats

Not every Washington war has originated as a purely partisan squabble. Occasionally, intra-party conflicts have also influenced national policies, reshaping politics and constituencies for decades and maybe none more so than the battle that beset the Democratic Party before the Civil War. "Popular sovereignty," a concept so democratic in its premise that it seemed to sneak up on the nation when it narrowly became law with passage of the Kansas-Nebraska Act of 1854, brought about this breakdown through a clash of executive overreach and legislative leadership that led to party dysfunction, division, and ultimately disunion.[1]

At the same time, rarely, if ever, in American political history has a phenom so dramatically risen in the hearts and minds of his countrymen, or at least his party, when it came to Senator Stephen A. Douglas—the "Little Giant" of Illinois at only five feet, four inches tall—in the decade leading up to the war. And just as rarely, if ever, has a sitting U.S. president so abused and abdicated presidential leadership as Pennsylvania's only chief executive, James Buchanan, during the years overlapping Douglas' prominence between 1856 and 1860.[2]

Both were Jacksonian Democrats when the party of Jackson was still supreme and worthy of national leadership at a time of real need in America, as the country continued to careen towards sectional animosity and division. Douglas was a certified political wunderkind by the time he rescued Henry Clay's Compromise of 1850 from the scrapheap of sectional discord in his mid-30s, securing its passage through the separate passage of its individual parts with legislative slight of hand that endeared him for the moment to wishful peacemakers nationwide. Buchanan, still America's only bachelor president (as a rumored though never proven homosexual) and its oldest up that time at age 65, had held about every governmental pay grade by the time his party turned to him and put him in the White House almost by default, including state assemblyman, congressman, senator, secretary of state, and ambassador to both Russia and Great Britain.³

Ironically, both Buchanan and Douglas would become focused on rendering American debate over slavery in the mid–1800s as mute as possible, but they would veer to completely divergent paths in trying to make that wish reality. Although both were Northerners, Buchanan, as president, would display Southern empathy and preferences, apparently cultivated during his earlier Washington years of socializing and boarding with legislators from the Southern states, while Douglas would attempt to toe middle ground in the slavery debate designed to keep his future at the forefront of Democratic politics.

With consideration of slavery's expansion into new territories at the forefront of national discussion, this irony would be exacerbated despite both seeking ways to lessen (or even diffuse) the slavery debate. Both hoped the nation's attention could be refocused on transcontinental or even hemispheric development without the brewing sectional divide. For Douglas it was a logical and constitutional solution that he championed as a cure-all for the North's abolitionist motivation and the South's mounting sense of disrespect and potential isolation. Buchanan, on the other hand, sought a quick resolution to the territorial slavery issue in order that his presidency could move on to other, more acclaim-worthy accomplishments. And from his lofty new White House platform, he saw no reason that a man of his vast experience should not expect his party and his nation to follow his lead.⁴

Each of their respective outlooks on the North-South conflict had been shaped by Clay's two earlier compromises, his initial Compromise of 1820, which allowed Missouri's entrance to the Union as a slave-condoning state only because of Maine's simultaneous entry as a new slave-prohibiting state. This maintained what was deemed the all-important balance of free and slave states in the U.S. Senate. In addition, what came to be known as the "Missouri Compromise" also established an imaginary, horizontal line of 36 degrees 30 minutes north latitude along Missouri's southern border and extending westward through the unorganized remainder of the 1803 Louisiana Purchase; in theory all the way to the Pacific Ocean should that vast, adjacent area ever belong to the U.S. instead of Mexico.⁵ As a permanent solution to the slavery question, most Northerners had never accepted the Missouri Compromise and they were urging Congress to reject it and prohibit any further extension of the nation's "original sin" into the Western territories.⁶

Nonetheless, for three decades this Missouri Compromise line of demarcation survived the increasing controversy of what to do about slavery and its potential expansion into the West as an accepted part of "Manifest Destiny," the long-running American impulse to extend the nation's borders in that direction regardless of roadblocks. This became especially so before, during, and after the U.S. war with Mexico from the mid– to late 1840s. It began with the annexation of the Republic of Texas (1845), formerly the northeasternmost Mexican state, and was followed by the war and Treaty of Guadalupe Hidalgo (February 1848) by which Mexico relinquished the future states of New Mexico, Arizona, California, Nevada, and Utah to the U.S., as well as parts of Oklahoma, Colorado, and Wyoming.[7]

Many Northerners of the time considered this so-called "Mexican Cession" nothing more than a "land-grab" (many Mexicans still do). Suddenly, as of February 1848, the United States had over 500,000 additional square miles to fill at a cost of $15 million. It was the second largest American land acquisition up to that time—second only to the previously mentioned 1803 Louisiana Purchase (from France)—and would remain so until Alaska (from Russia) proved slightly larger less than two decades later in 1867.[8] Along with the Oregon Territory, annexed away from British claims by a previous 1846 treaty establishing the 49th parallel as the U.S. border with Canada, America truly stretched from "sea to shining sea" and such things as the Santa Fe Trail, California Gold Rush, Mormon Migration, and Oregon Trail all figured prominently in White America's populating of the westernmost parts of the country.[9]

Two years after the Mexican Cession and with Oregon already a territory, the nation reached another landmark moment made necessary by the surge of people into its other, would-be Western territories. Settlers were pouring into these newly accessible lands from both North and South, while "politically, slavery infected the nation like a virus" as "slave-owning Southerners supported territorial expansion as a strategy for their survival." So stated Fergus Bordewich in *America's Great Debate: Henry Clay, Stephen A. Douglas, and the Compromise that Preserved the Union*, his excellent retelling of the Compromise of 1850.[10]

Foremost among the issues in need of compromise at that time was California's readiness for statehood. Since General Stephen W. Kearney, John Sutter, John C. Frémont, and Kit Carson had all had a hand in the tearing away of Mexican influence on the West Coast, and the discovery of gold at Sutter's Mill in January 1848 had ensured a surge in population growth—the soon-to-be "Golden State" had become prime real estate in a relatively short amount of time with its entry into the Union inevitable. As early as September 1849, delegates were meeting to decide the territory's immediate future, including one of their earliest priorities—making sure slavery did not gain a foothold in California. In other words, admittance as a free state despite pressure "back East" to open California to slave-owners. President Zachary Taylor, a general and hero of the Mexican War (and president as a result), was a leading proponent for admitting California as a free state before his untimely death in July 1850 put a far more amenable personality into the White House. Vice President Millard Fillmore, in fact, was a Northerner who leaned South (much as Buchanan would, too) and in contrast to Taylor's view, California's statehood without slavery wasn't the only part of the compromise being put forward by Clay that he endorsed. Fillmore understood that while admitting California with its economic boost as a free state was what the majority of its settlers desired, such a move could spark disunion without something to satisfy Southern interests in return. Thus did New Mexico and Utah gain acceptance as new territories with no restrictions on slavery; thus did Texas receive $10 million to pay off debts incurred while an independent republic following its disputed severance of ties with Mexico in 1836 and before entering the Union as a slave state in 1845; and thus (and most accommodating of all) did a new Fugitive Slave Act become enacted to provide tougher federal oversight in assisting slave owners with their recovery of runaway slaves escaping north. Along with California, Northerners, in return, could take solace in the ending of the slave trade in the District of Columbia, what had been a lingering embarrassment in the nation's capital, but distaste for the tougher fugitive slave law would increasingly inflame sensibilities above the "Mason-Dixon Line."[11]

Ultimately (as previously indicated) it would take addressing Clay's compromise as individual parts by Douglas to win passage in Congress of all that was in the original omnibus bill, the acceptance of which has traditionally been credited with "staving off the [eventual] fracturing of the nation [via the Civil War] for a few years." Bordewich also confirmed "the nation rejoiced, most of it anyway," and in that moment, President Fillmore asserted: "We have been rescued from the wide agitation that surrounded us." A more recent interpretation put it this way: "Most of the country enjoyed the fruits of the compromise and strived to persuade itself that it would endure. Most people earnestly desired to believe the slavery question settled forever."[12]

Still, the controversy of the new territories and their future with or without slavery would not go away. While California was a long way from the gathering storm in the East, the land just west and/or north of the newer tier of states that included Missouri (1821), Arkansas (1836), Texas (1845), Iowa (1846), Wisconsin (1848), and also Indian Territory (originally set aside for the so-called "Five Civilized Tribes" pushed west by President Andrew Jackson in the 1830s that would eventually become Oklahoma in 1907) remained ripe for settlement and yet to be spoken for in the ongoing slavery debate.[13]

Unlike previous territorial bills for the still expanding country, the Compromise of 1850 (as already implied) did not specify free or slave holding status for the new territories of New Mexico and Utah despite the fact no slaves had been allowed there previously under Mexican rule. In addition, the drier climate of the West and Southwest was obviously not conducive to agrarian, slave-based labor. Instead, Congress agreed it would let the residents of those territories, old and new, decide for themselves via elections and make that decision part of their constitution when they applied for statehood. This became an idea known as popular sovereignty (or derisively as "squatters' sovereignty") first espoused by Lewis Cass of Michigan, the Democratic nominee for president in 1848, and later co-opted by Douglas. Cass had warned against federal interference in the territorial slavery question, stating at the time: "If the relation of master and servant may be regulated or annihilated [by the federal government], so may the relation of husband and wife or parent and child, and of any other conditions which our institutions and the habits of society recognize."[14]

Although already aspiring to the presidency, when Douglas adopted the popular sovereignty concept it was "less a product of political calculation than a reflex conditioned by an intimate relationship that he enjoyed with voters," according to Martin H. Quitt in his 2012 Douglas biography. But when he spoke of democracy and political sovereignty, they were "exclusionary." Douglas never intended to empower people of anything but European descent and his indifference to the bondage of African Americans would eventually become "notorious," again according to Quitt.[15]

Nevertheless, by the time he put the concept forward as the basis for organizing another of the new territories, he was at the height of his prestige and legislative power. West of Iowa and Missouri were vast stretches of unorganized land, the northern remnants of the Louisiana Purchase. The settlers already there were frustrated. Initial territorial status had been rejected by Congress in March 1853 and by December of that same year, Senator Augustus Dodge of Iowa had introduced another bill calling for a new territory to be named Nebraska, a word taken from the Oto Native American language meaning "flat water" for the placid Platte River that flows the length of what is now that state (and already a guiding landmark for settlers moving west along the Oregon Trail).[16]

As chairman of the Committee on Territories in the Senate, Douglas was integral to the new bill's passage the second time around, but he was also advised of a lingering problem early on when Missouri Senator David Atchison, an in-state rival of venerated, Manifest Destiny architect Thomas Hart Benton, let him know that as long as the Missouri Compromise line remained on the books, the Southern members of Congress would never support additional territories north of parallel 36°30.' Obviously, anyone possessing slaves would not be eligible to move there unless the demarcation line was rescinded. As political leaders of the only slave

Because he stood only five feet, four inches tall, Illinois Senator Stephen A. Douglas was known as the Little Giant in the decade before the Civil War after a meteoric rise through the Democratic Party that culminated in his guidance of the Compromise of 1850 through Congress; his advocacy for the concept of popular sovereignty as chairman of the powerful Senate Committee on Territories; and his passage of the controversial Kansas-Nebraska Act in 1854 (Library of Congress Prints and Photographs Division—Reproduction Number LC-BH82-2460A).

state west of the Mississippi River and north of the Missouri Compromise line, the Benton and Atchison factions were on opposite sides of the issue, creating pressure for Chairman Douglas.[17] At the same time, then President Franklin Pierce, the current leader of the Democratic Party of which Atchison, Benton, and Douglas were all part, hoped to avoid language that risked making repeal of the 30-plus-year-old compromise line an issue, while Douglas, knowing Atchison was right, understood that Southern support would be strictly contingent on repeal. To not go along, he convinced Pierce, would be to risk the administration's Senate support on other issues. So, with the President's backing, Douglas astutely offered a substitute bill that would create two territories instead of one, thus splitting the Dodge legislation into a southern territory and a northern territory, the Kansas-Nebraska Bill of January 23, 1854.[18]

Douglas' revised bill was based on the popular sovereignty premise "that all questions pertaining to slavery in the territories and in the new states to be formed are to be left to the decision of the people residing therein through their appropriate representatives," as defined in Nicole Etcheson's book *Bleeding Kansas: Contested Liberty in the Civil War Era*. And although faced with some criticism for dividing the original territory into two territories and what skeptics surmised to be the increasing chances that one would be open to slavery, both of the existing neighboring states, free state Iowa and slave state Missouri, endorsed the division, which would prove of minor consequence compared to elimination of the Missouri Compromise line. Regardless, Douglas continued to preach that popular sovereignty was all about local self-government and remained the most basic of democratic principles.[19]

In the North, however, Douglas' democratic approach to the remaining territories was not well received, both during and after four-month long debate and final passage of Kansas-Nebraska. President Pierce did not sign the act into law until May 30, 1854, and the *New York Times* was typical of Northern reaction, when it called the Kansas-Nebraska Act's repeal of the Missouri Compromise line "a gross violation of a sacred pledge" before predicting its passage would turn the new area "into a dreary region of despotism inhabited by masters and slaves."[20] Southerners, on the other hand, found the act easy to accept. It opened them and their property to territory formerly closed. Georgia Senator Robert Toombs argued that repeal of the Missouri Compromise line was proper because it had already been violated by Northern refusal to apply it to the Mexican Cession, and other Southerners renewed the argument of their patron spokesman from a generation before, John C. Calhoun, who had maintained that Congress had no right to interfere with slavery in the territories as slaves were "common property" in all states. For them, Douglas' formula merely confirmed Calhoun's doctrine.[21]

Final voting on the Act further illuminated the differing sectional (if not partisan) views. In the House of Representatives, Northern Democrats, presumably Douglas' most connected colleagues, were split evenly, 44 in support and 44 opposed, while Southern Dems overwhelmingly supported his bill with only two exceptions. At the same time, no Northern Whigs supported it, while their Southern counterparts were split with two-thirds in favor, 14–7.[22]

The Senate exhibited even more sectional division with 15 Northern Democrats for it and only five opposed, while all but one Southern Dem, Texas' legend Sam Houston, voted in support. As for the Senate Whigs, no Northern members of that party supported it, while 11 of 13 Southern Whigs voted yea. Obviously, popular sovereignty provided the South more chance of bringing slavery into the territories and a better chance of retaining power in a divided Senate. As Etcheson succinctly concluded: "While less certain a guarantee to protect property in slaves, a chance was nevertheless preferable [for the South] to the Missouri Compromise's exclusion."[23]

Douglas, meanwhile, was suspected of ulterior motives in his passionate advocacy. While he championed popular sovereignty as his bill's "contribution to freedom," and defended it by pre-empting opposition amendments with some of his own, he was accused of possible conflict of interest motives, such as remuneration from his home state hopes that a

4. Breakdown of the Jacksonian Democrats 49

transcontinental railroad would begin in Chicago and proceed across Illinois before continuing west through at least one of the new territories, as well as potential political gain. In that regard, an unsigned editorial in the *New York Daily Times* said Douglas would "sacrifice any public principle, however valuable, and plunge the country into foreign war or internal dissention, however fatal they might prove, if he could thereby advance himself a single step towards the presidential chair."[24]

If political profit was what Illinois' up-and-coming senator was all about, however, the Kansas-Nebraska Act did not seem to offer much in the way of national laurels. Missouri's Benton, speaking rather immoderately off the record to another congressional colleague, surmised as much when he supposedly stated: "Douglas, Sir, is politically dead, Sir. If he fails to carry his bill the South will kick him in the rear, Sir; and if he does carry it, the North will beat his brains out, Sir."[25]

But while sectional loyalty seemed uppermost in the Kansas-Nebraska Act vote, the other political issue at play was party loyalty—or the perceived lack of any. The Democrats held the majority in both Houses, while the gradually disappearing Whigs still managed 33 percent in the Senate and 30 percent in the House, and a third party of the time known as "Free Soilers" enjoyed a grand total of six seats, two in the Senate and four in the House of Representatives. Any political party sectionally split over slavery seemed certain to lose congressional seats in the 1856 election, not to mention the problems that could present for any presidential candidate. There were those, like Senator Houston and by then Congressman Benton, who felt that because the Missouri Compromise had been adopted as a settlement for divisive questions of the era, it should never be disturbed. And indeed, once it was, contentious rejoinders were issued on the Senate floor by the likes of New York's William Seward, a leading abolitionist and Northern presidential hopeful, who famously said: "Come on then gentlemen of the slave states. Since there is no escaping your challenge, I accept it on behalf of the cause of freedom. We will engage in competition for the virgin soil of Kansas, and God give the victory to the side which is stronger in numbers as it is in right."[26]

Those would prove fighting words and Kansas, the more southerly of the two new territories, would become the battlefield. While Nebraska Territory—the original name given the entire area before Douglas' split was introduced for passage purposes—would escape the controversy and conflict of its southern neighbor, Kansas would be subjected to probably the most dysfunctional and contested entry of any state (or territory) into the Union. After all, did any of our other 50 states ever suffer a more disturbing moniker than "Bleeding Kansas"?[27]

Essentially in repealing both the Missouri Compromise and Northwest

Ordinance of 1787 (whereby the federal government was first established as sovereign over territorial expansion rather than existing states), Douglas knew the Kansas-Nebraska Act would "raise a hell of a storm," but even he underestimated the sectional, political, and confrontational blowback it would provoke. On August 1, 1854, a large party of New England emigrants sponsored by the Massachusetts Emigrant Aid Company arrived in Kansas and began establishing the new town of Lawrence, which was named for their largest benefactor, New England merchant and philanthropist Amos Lawrence. It was located just 30 miles inside the territory's eastern border and with the expressed goal of setting up homesteads and initiating the process by which a free state would eventually be voted into existence.[28]

In neighboring slave-state Missouri, meanwhile, the arrival of the free-state settlers did not go unnoticed and given their close proximity, vast numbers of Missourians began to infiltrate Eastern Kansas as well, establishing their own settlements—towns such as Lecompton and Leavenworth. It would be the start of what Etcheson labeled "the race for Kansas," the challenge Senator Seward had foreseen and accepted after passage of the Kansas-Nebraska bill. Majority rule was now uppermost on the minds of both abolitionists and slave-owners, as they recruited settlers (or squatters as they were also known) to make their way west to what would become the center of the country and become a voting resident of Kansas as soon as possible.[29]

Unfortunately, in addition to a race for settlers, Kansas also became an arms race ... and a corrupt race. "Border Ruffians," so-named backcountry residents of Missouri who wanted neighboring Kansas to also be open to slavery, made their presence felt by burning, looting, and in a few instances even taking lives in free-stater enclaves like Lawrence. In return, free state emigrants learned to give as good as they got, inflicting retribution on pro-slavery settlers, including violent acts like the radical abolitionist John Brown's brutal massacre of six pro-slave settlers along Pottawatomie Creek on the night of May 24, 1856. It was, as Etcheson again described, "revenge heaped upon revenge," with the ultimate goal of both sides being to drive enough of the other away to ensure the territory's upcoming decision at the polls would produce a majority in their favor. In other words, popular sovereignty gone mad.

Adding to this mess of territorial democracy would be some corrupt elections and voter fraud aimed at elevating one side and one philosophy on slavery over the other; a series of failed governors appointed by the President; and competing legislatures in Lecompton (pro-slavery) and Topeka (anti-slavery), with each holding constitutional conventions and supposed territory-wide elections, the results of which were then submitted to

Congress for approval in order to gain Kansas statehood—their way. One of those votes (Lecompton), however, was subject to a boycott by the other side, rendering it entirely suspect from the start with only one third of eligible voters taking part. As a result, one thing was certain—the majority of the people of Kansas were not in favor of the Lecompton constitution.[30]

Ironically, one very important person who did favor the Lecompton document was President Franklin Pierce. The New Hampshire–born Pierce was still in the White House when Douglas introduced popular sovereignty as a means of circumventing the intensifying debate over slavery in the territories, and his unequivocal support of the Kansas-Nebraska Act inflamed New England abolitionists, whom he actually blamed for much of the agitation and violence occurring in Kansas. Along with favoring the pro-slavery, Lecompton version of Kansas' constitutional efforts, Pierce also denounced the Topeka, free state constitution. Thus was the Pierce administration's stance on Kansas ripe for criticism and second guessing (especially in the North) by the time the Democratic Convention of 1856 rolled around, creating a desire by many Democrats to replace their incumbent, who was not even favored in his own home state (actually, it would be 50 years after Pierce's death before New Hampshire would honor him with a statue).[31]

To take Pierce's place, the most likely candidate seemed Douglas based on his lofty senatorial standing and national notoriety, but there was another who had been out of the country for three years and missed the long and acrimonious Kansas-Nebraska debate, keeping James Buchanan free of the sectional taint that plagued both Pierce and Douglas. "Old Buck," in fact, suddenly seemed immensely qualified and electable following his many years in Congress; as secretary of state; and most recently in the diplomatic corps. Gradually, the remaining Pierce supporters disappeared amidst the mounting criticism of his administration and shifted their allegiance to Douglas. On the convention's 18th ballot, however, with Illinois' Dems steadfast in their desire to retain him as their senator, the relatively young Douglas (age 43) forsook his presidential ambitions, at least for the time being, by suddenly withdrawing his name to unify the party behind the 65-year-old Buchanan. John Breckinridge, a popular young congressman from slave state Kentucky, was then quickly added as Buchanan's vice-presidential running mate.[32]

Douglas, meanwhile, would enter perhaps the most famous Senate race in American history versus a little known former congressman, Abraham Lincoln, seven years removed from his Illinois congressional seat. As one historian phrased it, "Douglas had let the genie out of the bottle" with his Kansas-Nebraska Act and Lincoln would represent the anti-slavery frenzy its passage unleashed. Their series of debates throughout Illinois would become famous for the compelling focus they brought to the slavery

The only bachelor president in American history and the oldest president when he took office in 1856 at the age of 65, James Buchanan of Pennsylvania had a vast array of congressional and diplomatic experience when he ascended to the White House, but also the misfortune of preceding Abraham Lincoln, the president generally regarded as America's greatest chief executive (Library of Congress Prints and Photographs Division—Reproduction Number LC-USZ62-96357).

issue nationwide, and although Douglas would be re-elected by the state legislature and retain his Senate seat, the exposure Lincoln received and the name recognition he gained through such things as his now famous "house divided" speech ("A house divided against itself cannot stand…"), regarding slavery and union, would propel him to the presidential nomination and election four years later as the first Republican president.[33]

At the same time, Buchanan would go on to win the presidency in 1856 in a three-way race, defeating the first Republican presidential nominee, John C. Frémont, the celebrated California explorer and former military governor mentioned earlier, who by then was known as "The Pathfinder," and former President Fillmore, the last Whig chief executive who ran as a candidate of the nativist anti–Catholic, anti-immigrant American Party (also as the "Know-Nothings"). Previously, while minister to England, Buchanan had been the primary author of the Ostend Manifesto, an American diplomatic report justifying U.S. interest in the nearby island nation of Cuba. It proposed a $100 million purchase of Cuba from Spain "on the grounds it was a natural geographic appendage of the United States" and its "location commanding the mouth of the Mississippi" River. If, after offering Spain "a fair price," the sale of the island was refused, that same manifesto also justified the use of force by the U.S. to "wrest" it from Spain. Such an acquisition had long been the dream of Southern statesmen hoping to extend their dominion to Cuba and, perhaps, other Latin American areas where an agrarian, slave-based economy like theirs could flourish. Indeed, the fact Buchanan would renew this unfulfilled proposal three years later while still in the White House serves to illustrate the Southern aspirations that made this Pennsylvania native such an enigma as leader of the Democratic Party and nation right before the Civil War.[34]

5

Lack of Leadership Amidst Drift to Disunion

Before James Buchanan was even inaugurated as president, he had inserted himself into the federal system in a way most newly elected chief executives have shied away from. For instance, with the country in the midst of the worst economic depression in history when Franklin D. Roosevelt was elected for the first time in 1932, he withdrew from the spotlight as president-elect, even when his defeated opponent, Herbert Hoover, reached out to him for joint consultation while finishing out his term. At the time, FDR was criticized for what he privately termed "staying away from the kitchen until he was made the head cook," especially given the nation's desperate state. Instead of inserting himself into a joint decision making process when he was not yet the chief decision maker, Roosevelt maintained his distance until Hoover's time was up, knowing full well that he needed total control to implement any new course of action, even if that meant putting off much needed change for several months. Whatever might have been possible sooner if FDR had conferred and coordinated with Hoover we will never know, but it is clear that he wanted to enter the White House as the hero with unchallenged authority to make things happen, and to accept the outgoing president's personal entreaties to jointly address the nation's financial woes would have rendered that highly unlikely, if not impossible.[1]

Similarly, Buchanan had the dream of quickly righting the Democratic ship of state and succeeding in everything his outgoing, one-term predecessor, Franklin Pierce, had left messy and unresolved, including a reasonable solution for slavery and a way of ending the Kansas controversy. Having been out of the country for most of the previous three years as a highly respected American diplomat, both goals seemed attainable if he could only insert himself into the process rapidly, even before Inauguration Day.[2]

Actually "from Buchanan's perspective," the demands of the presidency

5. Lack of Leadership Amidst Drift to Disunion 55

required "a man of calm and firm temperament, a commanding leader," as Jean Baker took from his own 1852 writings when she authored a biography of him as part of the American Presidents Series. In concurrence with how Buchanan probably arrived at this personal point of view, another presidential historian labeled him: "The last of the Democratic heirs to Andrew Jackson," the first president he served under as minister to Russia (1832–1833) before also serving under Jacksonian protégé, James K Polk, as secretary of state (1845–1849). From the moment he achieved the White House, Buchanan was convinced he, too, possessed the Jacksonian trait of knowing what would best serve the country at that crucial moment in time and making it happen. It was this uncompromising self-assurance, in fact, that would prompt him to follow the opposite pre-inauguration course to that chosen by FDR, instead inserting himself into the administrative process before his term actually began.[3]

One way he did that was by showing up in Washington over a month before his inauguration to interview and select his Cabinet on-site. But it was another preliminary and very questionable insertion of himself and presidential influence into the judicial system that attracted condemnation at the time and rumors of corruption ever since. This historic innuendo was made possible by a case out of St. Louis making its way through the federal courts that would become a landmark in American judicial annals. It involved a slave, Dred Scott, who had been taken by his master from pro-slavery Missouri into Illinois and later Wisconsin Territory before being returned to Missouri. Because both Illinois and Wisconsin Territory did not permit slaves, Scott sued for his freedom, which was first rejected by the Missouri Supreme Court and then famously upheld, 7–2, by the U.S. Supreme Court of Chief Justice Roger B. Taney on March 6, 1857, two days after Buchanan was inaugurated.[4]

To many observers, it did not seem mere coincidence that two days before Taney's announcement, Buchanan had stated in his inaugural address that the slavery question "belongs to the Supreme Court of the United States, before whom it is now pending and will, it is understood, be speedily and finally settled." Speculation that Buchanan knew the Court's decision before it was announced began immediately and, in fact, was supported by pretty damning evidence, including correspondence the President-elect had with Associate Justice John Catron, who apparently confirmed the Southern majority on the Court would probably rule against Scott. In so doing, Catron had also indicated that slaves were protected property under the Constitution, which could be instantly interpreted to mean the government had no right to bar slavery in any territory before statehood.[5]

In *The Worst President: The Story of James Buchanan*, Garry Boulard wrote: "Bumptiously inserting himself into preliminary deliberation of the Court, Buchanan had not only corresponded with Catron on the matter, but also with Associate Justice Robert Grier," an old Pennsylvania friend of his whom he may have influenced to side with his Southern colleagues. And if those suspicions weren't bad enough, the President had also been seen kibitzing privately with the Chief Justice "in front of thousands" at the inaugural ceremonies.[6]

Regardless "of what the President knew and when he knew it" (a phrase now common in America's political lexicon), Buchanan hoped to seize on the opportunity presented by the Dred Scott case to put an end to the slavery issue forever. Based on the Supreme Court's decision and with the new president in agreement, no African American could be a citizen and, as a result, Dred Scott should have not been able to sue for his freedom. Also, with repeal of the Missouri Compromise line, slaves interpreted as private property by the due process clause of the Fifth Amendment could not be prohibited before statehood even during the more ambiguous territorial period, opening the door to slave owners being able to move into the new, and as yet "unconstitutionalized" territories, and bring their slaves/property with them just as any other property owner could. Basically, Buchanan believed slavery had always been rooted in the U.S. Constitution and therefore could not be legislated out. The Dred Scott decision did nothing but reinforce that belief.[7]

Interestingly, it also reinforced Southern confidence in Buchanan, whose "pronounced pro–Southernism," as Baker termed it, and belief that the North still needed to permit its Southern neighbors to manage their own affairs had paid dividends. Indeed, Buchanan would not have been elected if not for the South. While failing to carry all but three Northern states, Illinois, Indiana and his own, Pennsylvania, Buchanan was victorious in all but one slave holding state, including all six states of the Deep South, all four in the Upper South, and three of the four soon-to-be Border States. California also went for Buchanan, while Maryland was the only state for Fillmore and Frémont captured the eleven other Northern states.[8]

Even in victory, however, Buchanan was subdued as he faced the prospect of a nation that had given him just 45.3 percent of its total vote and an Electoral College tally that was 80 votes less than his Democratic predecessor four years earlier. In addition, the brewing toxicity surrounding Northern anti-slavery feeling was becoming increasingly evident and the Republican Party had made huge inroads by adopting that cause and becoming "the party of the North," basically relegating the Democrats' immediate future to the South. "For Buchanan, the Republican Party was anathema," according to Baker. It was made up of "extremists who threatened the South with their anti-slavery propaganda." So, despite his

5. Lack of Leadership Amidst Drift to Disunion   57

ascension to the White House after years of seeing younger men reach the presidency ahead of him, Buchanan was relieved, but he was not happy.[9]

At the same time, the construction of his Cabinet, four Southerners and three Northern Democrats, revealed a chief executive uninterested in peacemaking and intent on having his own way. Armed with the Kansas-Nebraska Act and the Dred Scott decision, he planned to make short shrift of the territorial dilemma he had inherited so that he could move on to other, more gratifying issues like expansion and foreign affairs, both of which he felt well qualified to tackle. Even during the financial Panic of 1857 and what became a crisis in the desert, when Mormon leader Brigham Young briefly challenged federal authority in Utah, Buchanan never wavered in his primary focus—a speedy resolution of the presidential headache that was Kansas.[10]

Douglas, meanwhile, having had the slavery controversy again rear its ugly head, necessitating another round of legislation (as it had in 1820 and 1850), approached the Buchanan presidency confident in his popular sovereignty remedy, the resulting Kansas-Nebraska Act, and his defense of both during the debates with Lincoln. Richard Baker and Neil MacNeil, combining on their 2013 history of the American Senate, summarized his supreme confidence in that moment when they wrote of and quoted him thusly: "With great skill, Senator Douglas managed that legislation to final approval, and he dismissed the Senate's extended debate as meaningless. 'I had

This vintage poster advertised a series of statewide campaign debates between Stephen A. Douglas and Abraham Lincoln that made the 1856 Illinois senatorial race one of the most remembered in American political history. Douglas would retain the Senate seat, but it was the start of the little-known Lincoln making a national name for himself and his elevation to the presidency in 1860 (Library of Congress Prints and Photographs Division—Reproduction Number LC-USZC2-5233).

the authority and power of a dictator throughout the whole controversy,' he bragged later. 'The speeches were nothing. It was the marshaling and directing of men, guarding from attacks, and with ceaseless vigilance preventing surprise.'"[11]

Even in his hard-won victory over Lincoln and return to the Senate, however, he had also misjudged the power of the anti-slavery message. "For Douglas, Lincoln's proposition that the United States could not endure half slave and half free was belied by American history since 1776," according to Martin Quitt in his biography of the other, lesser known giant from Illinois. "He genuinely believed that territories should have the right to decide the question of slavery for themselves and that federal intervention deprived territorial inhabitants of their right to self-government." That's also why his revision of Dodge's original territorial bill had been a masterstroke for overcoming the issue of sectional Senate balance, a necessity in that era for the admission of new states. Through it all, Douglas remained the dominant figure in the Democratic Party before the 1856 election, but anti-slavery concerns had necessitated him giving way to the unblemished Buchanan when it came time to face the national electorate. He had survived the vote in his home state, where his seniority, chairmanship, and notoriety were still seen as valuable, but the shine had come off his appeal nationwide and given the sectional signs of the time, that would be something he could never recover.[12]

Because the Dred Scott decision seemed to contradict the need for his Kansas-Nebraska legislation, Douglas suddenly had to navigate his popular sovereignty concept past not only an increasingly anti-slavery North, but also a South embracing the 7–2 Supreme Court ruling, which had reduced the issue to simple property rights. Even as he resumed his Senate seat, he was not in great shape politically and he knew it.[13]

Also feeling the political heat but determined there had to be a quick way out was the new president. Buchanan had been counting down the days during his first year in office to the time when an important vote would be held in Kansas. That's when settlers there were to decide for themselves if they would allow slavery within their borders, the first step towards statehood. And finally, that day arrived, December 21, 1857, with a statewide vote on the result of what had been a very contested constitutional convention held in Lecompton two months earlier and a similar convention that had taken place in Topeka the year before. That meant the results were in; two sets of results, in fact. The first, the Topeka constitution, which would have banned slavery, had been condemned by the Pierce administration and tabled by the Senate following passage in the House. As with Topeka, the pro-slavery Lecompton vote had been tainted by a boycott (each by the other side), but that was not going to stop Buchanan from endorsing it, regardless of the fact that like its predecessor, it had already been proven a sham in terms of democratic process. Understandably, the sitting territorial governor at the time, who was also an old Buchanan ally, began to doubt the entire statehood process and resigned.[14]

Nevertheless, as Baker emphasized, Buchanan continued to insist he did not wish to interfere "with the decision of the people of Kansas, either for or against slavery," even though he clearly hoped the Lecompton constitution could be accepted by Congress and the nation could move on with Kansas set to become another slave state, offsetting eventual free state Nebraska (1867). What Buchanan failed to realize was control of Congress was teetering over Kansas and while he naively sought to maintain a coalition of free-soil and pro-slavery Democrats with the Dred Scott decision as his constitutional insurance, sectional division over slavery was already trumping partisan allegiance. The President's willing acceptance of the governor's resignation and his perseverance in sticking with Lecompton drew the attention of Northern Democrats and the outrage of Northern Republicans, but it simply reinforced his pro–Southern reputation and conviction to make Kansas a slave state—at least that's the shared opinion of biographers, presidential historians, and mid–1800s political observers alike. Jean Baker, in fact, concluded that more than any other of his presidential decisions, including those in late 1860 like his conciliatory treatment of Southern secessionist aggression at the start of the Civil War, his management of Kansas demonstrated not just his commitment to the South and determination to have things his way, but his fusion of the two as a "hardheaded resolve to use executive power for Southern interests." The last Jacksonian president was, after all, "as stubborn for the South as Andrew Jackson was for the Union."[15]

Into this political hornet's nest that Buchanan had created over Lecompton strode Douglas. With his own political viability in question, especially among Northern Democrats, the President's course had put the party in a very precarious position heading into the 1858 midterms and beyond. Once again, the outspoken senator from Illinois reminded the nation that had it not been for his withdrawal as a candidate in 1856, Buchanan would probably not be president. Famously he declared, "By God Sir, I made James Buchanan, and by God, Sir, I will unmake him."[16]

Although successful in his bid to hold off Lincoln and retain his Senate seat, Douglas faced a steadily increasing public backlash over his legislation, even in his own state. In addition, with the President determined to force a quick acceptance of the deeply flawed, pro-slavery Lecompton constitution, Douglas' idea of popular sovereignty had been corrupted, leaving him in a tenuous place politically in Illinois if he did not oppose Buchanan's intentions. To remain relevant among Northern Democrats, his core constituency, it became increasingly obvious he would need to marshal congressional forces in rejecting Lecompton on the grounds most people in Kansas had been denied a chance to vote on it.[17]

Nonetheless, the prospect of an "obvious break between the two most powerful Democrats in the country would not only be bad for the party, but ruinous for an administration that [needed] every vote it could get in Congress in the wake of anticipated Republican gains in the coming midterms." So wrote Garry Boulard in his 2015 biography of Buchanan, *The Worst President*, before elaborating on the standoff, face-to-face meeting the two top Dems had in December 1857. Indeed, Douglas' visit and attempt to find common ground would open with the President remarking how he was tired of hearing about Kansas (and) once a constitution had passed, it should be over and done with. Douglas, on the other hand, considered that

STEPHEN FINDING "HIS MOTHER."

In a political cartoon from the 1850s, the Goddess Columbia, the female personification of both the "New World" and the United States in its earliest days, is shown whipping Senator Stephen Douglas of Illinois for his role in passing of the controversial Kansas-Nebraska Act of 1854, while the original Uncle Sam, who also came to symbolize America as her male counterpart after the War of 1812, urges on the punishment (Library of Congress Prints and Photographs Division—Reproduction Number LC-USZ62-14832).

5. Lack of Leadership Amidst Drift to Disunion 61

"a shockingly ignorant" take on events, and urged, instead, that Buchanan "save himself and his presidency by disowning Lecompton" and by starting the ratification process over anew. Douglas also emphasized he had no choice but to openly oppose the Lecompton constitution, even though that would mean opposing the President.[18]

Obviously angered by this "Democratic impertinence," Buchanan reportedly replied, "Mr. Douglas, I desire you to remember that no Democrat ever yet differed with an administration of his own choice without being crushed," to which Douglas supposedly (and just as famously) replied, "Mr. President, Andrew Jackson is dead." If true, and biographers for both men agree such a reply took place, Douglas' retort, one Jacksonian to another, would have certainly commenced the rare intra-party war that took place from that moment onward through the presidential election of 1860, nearly three full years later.[19]

Douglas biographer William Gardner elaborated further on the Democratic conflict when he wrote: "The Buchanan administration and Southern extremists [in his own party] openly declared war on Douglas for his cool indifference to their own special interests," including "his carelessness whether slavery was voted up or down in the territories and his [apparent] hostility to their plans for planting it in Kansas." To retain any hope of a presidential audition in the future, Douglas had to know he would face an uphill climb. His majority party was headed for a major split that would obviously work to the benefit of the new anti-slavery Republicans. To hold onto his Senate seat, it had been necessary to stay true to his Illinois constituents, now he would need a plan to re-conquer Southern Dems, who would obviously align with the President. As a keen political strategist, he concluded the treacherous course of all-out Washington war would be necessary to force Buchanan and his Cabinet to, as Gardner put it, "sue for peace."[20]

It would never happen. Despite the bold front he would take with the South and despite his willingness "to go to them" and campaign in their midst in secessionist-leaning places like New Orleans and Baltimore, he would never be able to recover from what Southerners by then considered his "abhorrent doctrine"—that despite what the Supreme Court had said, it was still up to the people of the territories to decide about slavery within their borders. When addressing Southern audiences from then on, he would attempt to take the sting out of his philosophy by showing that it was entirely harmless—that despite the Court's constitutional ruling, the people still had "the practical power to exclude slavery" if their attitude towards it was unfriendly. And according to Gardner, "If slavery would be profitable, their attitude would be friendly, and it would take root and flourish under the protection of law." But "if by any reason of soil or climate it was unprofitable, their attitude would be unfriendly and not the law nor the

Constitution could successfully foster it." In other words, while trying to coax the South back to his way of thinking, it was an argument at that time that he could not win.[21]

As for Buchanan, his biographers have confirmed he too went to work to try and maintain control of a party in rebellion. Baker described how throughout the spring of 1858, using tactics often assumed to be the creation of 20th century chief executives, the President sent Cabinet members to lobby congressmen, while "dangling" government contracts before wavering representatives, as well as patronage jobs and commissions. So much so, in fact, that two years later a House committee would investigate whether Buchanan by money, patronage, or other improper means sought to influence Congress. During that same spring, the *Washington Union*, a pro-administration newspaper of that era, "turned itself into" what Baker termed "an advertisement for the merits of the Lecompton constitution." At the same time, Buchanan argued that free state residents who had voted for the Topeka constitution had actually been in open rebellion, much like the Mormons in Utah, defying legitimate authority as "mercenaries" for abolitionists. His stubborn advocacy of the Lecompton constitution despite its "forgery by a minority," as Boulard labeled it, even refuted his earlier commitment to majority rule, and was done with a complete lack of appreciation for how his Kansas actions were negatively affecting the national narrative and boosting the opposition of the still infant Republican party.[22]

He was actually still urging Congress to accept Lecompton even after a second vote in Kansas had rejected the document. In Massachusetts, the *Springfield Daily Republican* called his continued efforts in that regard "a disgrace" and his home state *Philadelphia North American* labeled his "embrace" of the fraudulent constitution "so evidently the work of a mind determinedly defending the wrong as to destroy all credit that the President had before possessed." Adding to this disdainful Northern media chorus, the *Ohio Repository* wrote: "Mr. Buchanan, with the most astounding duplicity and inconsistency [has] violated [his] pledges to the people of Kansas and joined the ranks of their enemies."[23]

To try and bridge the national turmoil, a compromise was attempted by Indiana Congressman William English, who conceived an amendment to try and make the Lecompton constitution more palatable, whereby if Kansas residents would accept the President's preferred course and vote to approve Lecompton, the state would be allowed to enter the Union early without going through the normal territorial waiting period and required population of at least 93,000, upon which representation in the House of Representatives was then based. This timing concession, however, was considered nothing more than a bribe by the majority of Kansas' voters, who would summarily reject it when given the chance.[24]

5. Lack of Leadership Amidst Drift to Disunion

Alas, it would not be the last time a U.S. president's stubborn resolve to his way or no way would doom a unique leadership opportunity for country over self and damage his legacy. Thus pitted against a solid bloc of Republicans and breakaway Northern Democrats, Buchanan "dug in," still determined to push the Lecompton constitution through a deeply divided Congress.[25] In Kansas, meanwhile, settlers re-armed themselves against the prospect of renewed violence should the President's will come true and Congress bow to his wishes. "Every man is getting his rifle in good order [and] God help the few pro-slavery men and women in the territory for there will be no mercy shown if 'Old Buck' forces that upon them," one of his former territorial governors wrote to an Ohio legislator at the time, as national debate on the issue intensified.[26]

On March 22, 1858, Douglas, in his capacity as chairman of the Committee on Territories, rose in the Senate to give voice to his official opposition to the admission of Kansas as a U.S. territory under the Lecompton constitution. His address that day was a direct assault on the preferred policy of President Buchanan, but also a deliberate attempt to defend his recent legislative efforts and to bridge, if possible, the gaping divide threatening to consume his Democratic Party. Even for an accomplished speaker and politician like Douglas, it was a nearly impossible task. Permanently preserved in print by the Library of Congress, excerpted highlights from his memorable address that day follow.

On the issue of popular sovereignty:

> In as much as the time-honored and venerated policy of the Senate and the other House of Congress saw no remedy but to return to the true principles of the Constitution—to those great principles of self-government and popular sovereignty was to leave the people of the territories and the states free to decide the slavery question, as well as all others, for themselves. The object was to localize, not to revolutionize the controversy in regard to slavery, to make it a question for each state and territory to decide for itself, without any other state, any other territory, the federal government, or any outside power interfering to influence or control the result.

On the question of Lecompton:

> Have the people of Kansas been left perfectly free to form and regulate their domestic institutions in their own way, subject only to the Constitution? If not, you have no right to impose it upon them. I come back to the question ought we to receive Kanas into the Union with the Lecompton constitution? Is there satisfactory evidence that is the act and deed of the people [?] ... that it embodies their will? Is the evidence satisfactory that the people of that territory have been left perfectly free to form and regulate domestic institutions in their own way? I think not! But for the slavery clause, could this Lecompton constitution even receive a single vote in either House of Congress? Were it not for the slavery

clause, would there be any objection to sending it back to the people for a fair vote? I say to my Southern friends they must act on the right of the people to decide for themselves.

On Lecompton being a party test:

I am told this Lecompton constitution is a party test, a party measure that no man is a Democrat who does not sanction it, who does not vote to bring Kansas into the Union with the government established under this constitution. Sir, who made that a party test? Who has interpolated this Lecompton constitution into our party platform? Oh; we are told it is an administration measure, [but] is it the right of this administration to declare what are party measures and what are not? That has been attempted [before] and failed.

As to Congress being in charge of the admission of new territories and not the President:

The Constitution of the United States says that new states may be admitted into the Union by the Congress—not by the President, his Cabinet, or administration. This constitution shall be submitted directly to the Congress, not to the President—the President [has] nothing to do with it.

On the right of a president to dictate to senators:

I do not recognize the right of the President or his Cabinet, no matter what my respect may be for them, to tell me my duty in the Senate chamber. The President has no more right to prescribe tests to senators than senators have to the President. If the will of my state is one way and the will of the President is the other, am I to be told that I must obey the executive and betray my state or else be branded as a traitor to the party and hunted down by all the newspapers that share the patronage of the administration. What despotism on earth would be equal to this if you establish that the executive has a right to command the votes, consciences, [and] the judgment of senators and representatives instead of their constituents? The President says in effect: Do as you please on all questions but one—that one is Lecompton [and] he intends to brand every Democrat in the United States a traitor who is opposed to the Lecompton constitution. For my part, Mr. President, I stand by the time-honored principles illustrated by Jefferson and Jackson, those principles of state sovereignty and strict construction on which the Democratic Party has ever stood. I will stand by the Constitution and neither the frowns of power nor the influence of patronage will change my action or drive me from my principles. I would prefer private life to abject servile submission to executive will.[27]

It had to be one of the most ringing rebukes of a sitting president ever delivered by a member of his own party, but it failed to dissuade the Senate and its Democratic majority, two-thirds of whom represented slave-holding states, and by a comfortable margin the Upper House backed the President in approving Lecompton. The Lower House, however, with its composition based on population was a different story, mostly because Northern Democrats—guided by Douglas—viewed Lecompton as fraudulent and

5. Lack of Leadership Amidst Drift to Disunion

voted against it. The congressional split should have provided Buchanan the perfect, face-saving opportunity to send the pro-slavery document back to Kansas for a re-write, but instead all his administration could offer was a renewed push for acceptance based on inclusion of the English amendment. Ultimately the document did get through both houses, but as already noted, Kansans had the final say and overwhelmingly rejected what Baker termed "the bribe" by 9,500 votes of the 13,100-total cast in what was—at least that time—a fair election.[28]

"So long stifled by the Buchanan administration" and their aggressive pro-slavery neighbors, as Baker also affirmed, new Kansas delegates to a new convention returned a new constitution, the anti-slavery Wyandotte constitution (named after yet another new Kansas border town), which despite being bitterly opposed by Southern legislators, was eventually ratified by Congress. As a result, Kansas finally got to enter the Union as a free state in January 1861—just four months before the first guns of the Civil War were fired.[29]

Despite obviously being on the wrong side of the issue from the start, Buchanan would seek to save face by taking credit for "resolving the Kansas conflict" in his annual message to Congress at the end of 1858, while blaming "reactionary abolitionist sentiment" for all the violence and controversy that had transpired. Needless to say, it was a hollow message. While claiming that with the crisis of the economy, the Mormons, and Kansas over, the nation could finally address foreign policy and other issues he hoped to pursue, the central issue of slavery continued to linger for all Americans—North and South—and Buchanan's inability to deal with or offer anything of substance for the coming national storm would render him a one-term president. Even more telling would be one biographer's label as the worst president ever and another's judgment of his Kansas policy as one of the "greatest blunders" in American history.[30]

Meanwhile, facing the same divided country would prove just as problematic for Douglas. Although not aligned with the sentiment of one section over another, as Buchanan was with the South, Douglas was a national leader trapped in the middle of the transformational conflict that would soon envelope the country. Despite making every effort to straddle and bridge the gargantuan gap between the sections, Douglas could only defend his earlier efforts on behalf of what he considered constitutional doctrine—never backtracking, even with his political ambitions under siege.[31] And yet, with the sectional divide driving a wedge through his party, past prestige and credentials would still earn him its official presidential nomination in 1860 after 160 days of intense electioneering in more than 150 towns and 23 of the 33 states. Casting aside any false pretense of his ongoing White House ambitions, in fact, Douglas staged what biographer Martin Quitt termed "the first overtly political campaign" by an American presidential candidate.³² Unlike 1856, he was on the ballot and Buchanan was not, but after Buchanan and the war they had waged, the Democrats would have had trouble electing anybody, especially given the fact Douglas would not be the only Dem—or even Illinois candidate—in the presidential field.³³

6

Lincoln, Civil War and Republican Rule

The presidential election of 1860 was a watershed moment for America made all the more likely by a dysfunctional Democratic Party, four major candidates instead of the usual two, and the rise of a Republican Party that would rule the political landscape for most of the next five decades. With the divisive election of President Abraham Lincoln confirming for Southerners what had been forecast for years—that the North's true intention was to subdue the Southern way of life and end slavery—the last vestiges of Unionist sentiment in "Dixie" were overruled, leading to the secession of eleven Southern states and the nation's greatest disaster—the Civil War. Afterwards, following the unprecedented carnage caused by four years of brutal conflict, "Waving the Bloody Shirt" became the modus operandi for Republicans whenever they wished to remind voters of past failures of the Democratic Party, upon whose tenure they repeatedly placed blame for disunion and the war.[1]

The Buchanan-Douglas feud over Kansas had staggered the Democrats. Douglas, in fact, "had reached the brink of the abyss," as biographer William Gardner put it, desiring, if possible, to "conciliate the South without alienating the North." At the same time, Republicans had looked on as "pleased spectators." Advising the son of a friend at the time, the Illinois senator evidenced his frustration when he said, "Never go into politics. If you do, no matter how sincere and earnest you may be, you will be misinterpreted, vilified, traduced, and finally sacrificed to some local interest or unreasoning passion."[2]

Douglas, after all, was a pragmatist, who like Henry Clay was famous for seeking compromise. He openly despaired at what secession and war between the sections could mean for American democracy, but his selection in 1860 as the Democratic presidential nominee had as much to do with bringing on the colossal conflict as the Lincoln nomination on the Republican side—the event normally attributed as the last straw leading to

THE GREAT MATCH AT BALTIMORE,
BETWEEN THE "ILLINOIS BANTAM", AND THE "OLD COCK" OF THE WHITE HOUSE.

Portrayed as a staged "cock fight," something that was common in early rural America, Senator Stephen A. Douglas of Illinois emerges victorious in this political cartoon from the mid 1800s over a prostrate President James Buchanan. Illustrating the intra-party conflict that emerged between these two leading figures of the Democratic Party, the cartoon makes reference to Baltimore, site of the 1860 Democratic National Convention where Douglas was named the official party nominee to replace the outgoing Buchanan, while Vice President John Breckinridge, candidate of the breakaway Southern Democrats, is also seen entering the ring (Library of Congress Prints and Photographs Division—Reproduction Number LC-USZ62-10365).

war—or at least that's the verdict assessed by Scott Farris in *Almost President: The Men Who Lost the Race but Changed the Nation*. Farris also cited the Southern "Fire-Eaters," radical secessionists like Alabama's William Lowndes Yancey, South Carolina's Robert Rhett, Texas' Louis Wigfall, and Mississippi's William Barksdale, as being those who conspired to bring about a split in the Democratic Party at the 1860 national convention in Charleston, South Carolina, a hotbed of Southern secessionist sentiment. Indeed, once it was determined that Douglas would be the party's official nominee, eight Southern state delegations walked out, forcing the convention to adjourn for lack of a two-thirds majority and to reconvene in Baltimore, Maryland, six weeks later.[3]

In the interim, Douglas offered to withdraw his name if a compromise

6. Lincoln, Civil War and Republican Rule   69

candidate could be agreed upon, but his Northern supporters would not allow it and refused to even let his offer be made public. "Unless he is nominated, our party is gone for all time to come," one leading Northern Democrat was heard to say and "Douglas or nobody" seemed to be the prevailing sentiment when the Democrats tried to regroup in Baltimore still minus the Southern delegations, who had resolved to meet on their own in another part of town and to hold a "rump convention." They would nominate John Breckinridge, Buchanan's outgoing vice president as the Dems' Southern nominee in the newly formed National Democratic Party, and, as if the presidential field wasn't large enough, it got even more crowded when Tennessee Senator John Bell, an aging, former anti–Jackson Whig, was nominated by the Constitutional Union Party, a coalition of Southern conservatives.[4]

By entering the race, both Breckinridge and Bell hoped the election could be thrown into the House of Representatives via a deadlocked Electoral College, leaving no clear majority winner, as had happened two previous times (1800 and 1824). That way a Southern compromise candidate might emerge. In his anger over the Democratic breakup, however, Douglas indicated he would rather "throw the election to Lincoln" than see either of his other opponents elected by the House.[5] And that's what he did by staying in the four-way race, even when it was clear Democratic and Southern voters would be split, allowing Lincoln and the Republicans to be first time winners of the White House with only 40 percent of the vote. Douglas came in second with 29 percent, Breckinridge third at 18 percent, and Bell fourth with 13 percent.[6]

Despite his campaigning throughout the country (the only candidate who did) and warning of the inevitability of secession should Lincoln win, Douglas' fate and that of the country were all but sealed by the crowded field, as Lincoln took all 18 Northern states as well as California. It would be the start of a Republican dominated North for a long time to come. Thus the practice of "waving the bloody shirt" would come into political play in the decades immediately after the Civil War—even for Ulysses S. Grant, who as the Union's greatest general would be the most obvious two-term "waver" from 1869 through 1877. After Grant, Rutherford B. Hayes waved it again during his extremely contested election versus Democrat Samuel Tilden in 1876 and James Garfield, another Union general, would wave it yet again in 1880 and win despite being matched against an even more famous Union war hero, Gettysburg frontline commander Winfield Scott Hancock.[7]

Except for the two non-consecutive terms of Democrat Grover Cleveland, in fact, the Republican Party would control the White House from Lincoln in 1860 through William Howard Taft in 1913, and

Section Two—The Bleeding Kansas Fight

"UNCLE SAM" MAKING NEW ARRANGEMENTS.

With outgoing President James Buchanan shown packing his bags in the White House (far right) after only four years, this political cartoon shows U.S. symbol Uncle Sam (early version) welcoming Abraham Lincoln, the President-elect from Illinois who was known as the "Rail Splitter," while former Tennessee Senator John Bell, Vice President John Breckinridge of Kentucky, and Illinois Senator Stephen Douglas are advised they are too late in their hope of ascending to the executive mansion (Library of Congress Prints and Photographs Division—Reproduction Number LC-USZ62-12424).

thanks to its influence in the "dynamically growing, industrializing, immigrant-attracting North, the party that dominated the nation's manufacturing districts—which is to say the Republican Party" (as H.W. Brands said in *American Colossus: The Triumph of Capitalism, 1865–1900*)—would enjoy a decided advantage in national elections throughout the second half of the 19th century. But American elections do have consequences and no election ever had more consequence than the one in 1860. Presidential historian Kenneth Davis acknowledged as much when he called it, "without question the most momentous in American history," while according to Walter Stahr, who authored a biography of William Seward, Lincoln's secretary of state: "The Republicans generally saw themselves as the party of clean government" and a necessary answer to the "corruptible" Buchanan years.[8]

Actually, the last two years of the Buchanan administration were also about the President's unfulfilled ambitions and/or overreach when it came to foreign policy. As established by the Ostend Manifesto he co-authored before becoming president, Buchanan always hoped to purchase and annex Cuba as the nation's 16th slave state and those desires only intensified once he was in the White House. He argued that his so-called "Pearl of the Antilles" remained essential to American security, less than 100 miles off the coast of Florida and within easy reach of both Mobile Bay and the mouth of the Mississippi River. He also issued a dramatic proposal involving Mexico, asking Congress for authority to establish military outposts across the Arizona border in Mexican territory, and also permission to raise a military force to police that area. Legislators who remembered only too well the political discord that accompanied the Mexican War a decade earlier absorbed both requests with understandable disbelief, but such were the kind of ideas Buchanan hatched—foreign policy suggestions that led biographer Jean Baker to label him "one of the most aggressive and hawkish of our chief executives," but also one Congress routinely "avoided or opposed."[9]

Suspected corruption by his administration was also the subject of a congressional investigation once the Republicans gained control of the House of Representatives in 1858. John Covode, a Pennsylvania Republican, headed the probe of his home state president. Known as "Honest John," Covode was convinced Buchanan had benefited from illicit campaign funds in 1856 and was fairly certain the President had tried to bribe individual members of Congress during the Lecompton debate. When created, the Covode Commission drew praise from the *New York Times*, which reported "a general conviction throughout the country that the administration of Mr. Buchanan has been profligate and corrupt beyond all precedent." Once testimony began, there were accusations by Democratic insiders and Buchanan appointees, but the findings were inconclusive and served only to illustrate the great disparity of opinion when it came to the President by those who disliked him and his loyalists, who felt he had done nothing wrong. Afterwards, Buchanan ridiculed his accusers, when he said, "I defy all investigations. Nothing but the basest perjury can sully my good name."[10]

Just one week before Lincoln's election, Buchanan encountered probably the most disturbing moment of his presidency. According to biographer Garry Boulard, that was the moment he received a message from Winfield Scott, the commanding general of the United States Army, advising him of "imminent danger of disruption of the Union by the secession of one or more of the Southern states." In the same communiqué, Scott indicated that federal forts along the Mississippi and Atlantic coast "were at risk of invasion" and recommended garrisoning those immediately in order to deter any thought of surprise attacks, while also predicting, "The danger of secession may be made to pass away without one conflict of arms, one execution, or one arrest for treason." Famous last words—no message could have been more annoying to Buchanan, who felt that by even hinting at such alarm, Scott had only made matters worse.[11]

In *Lincoln: A Life of Purpose and Power*, Richard Carwardine, a British biographer of America's most revered president, used the word "hapless" to describe Lincoln's predecessor in the White House, particularly in the four months between the 1860 election and Inauguration Day. With the states of the Deep South following South Carolina's lead and seceding in near unison, Buchanan was being derided nationally for his "feeble argument that it was beyond his power to stop." Despite disunion and the seceding states seizing federal arsenals and forts within their boundaries, Buchanan could only urge caution and conciliation, and a call for a convention at which compromise proposals could be submitted by Congress, including a hopeful scheme by Senator John Crittenden of Kentucky, a would-be political heir to his in-state predecessor Henry Clay, that attracted the most attention. It called for a series of constitutional amendments that would remove slavery from the reach of the federal government for all time, with the Missouri Compromise line restored and a guarantee of slavery's permanence south of that line, literally binding future generations to its provisions. Of course, the key to the Crittenden proposal was getting enough Republicans to support it, the majority of whom were opposed to slavery, but also deeply concerned about the financial chaos disunion promised.[12]

Lincoln, however, was not open to any such compromise. Like FDR's previously discussed decision not to work with Hoover before taking office in 1932, the President-elect in 1860 let it be known that he wanted no part of compromise on the question of extending slavery before taking the oath. He was not about to relinquish the platform he and his new party had run on, and won on, before assuming the reins of power (and his heroic moment), even in the face of the Southern states breaking away and the awful, overwhelming sense of responsibility that by then filled his every waking hour.[13]

Basically, the U.S. government had no policy to deal with the crisis. Buchanan vacillated between believing secession unconstitutional while at the same time concluding he was powerless to do anything about it. In the first three months following his election victory, Lincoln made no public statements or formal addresses. When he did speak, he offered what biographer David Herbert Donald called "bland observations" designed to reassure the citizens of the North who had voted him into office, feeling there was no way Southerners would actually dissolve the Union despite their threats, the same kind they had issued so many times before—before the Missouri Compromise of 1820; during the Nullification Crisis of 1832;

6. Lincoln, Civil War and Republican Rule   73

throughout debate over the Compromise of 1850; and while deciding the ongoing fate of the territories acquired by the Mexican Cession of 1848— all of which had extracted some sort of Northern concessions. Buchanan sincerely believed that was all Southerners really wanted: that once again it was "the trick by which the South breaks down every Northern man." But should he agree to it, he also felt, would render him "as powerless as a block of buckeye wood."[14]

Regardless, the chances of Lincoln and the Deep South ever achieving compromise were slim and mostly none. Once again according to Donald, whose 1995 biography of Lincoln followed two earlier Pulitzer Prizes, "The President-elect's commitment to maintaining the Union was absolute." Although pressed to accept concessions that might give a measure of support to Southern Unionists, he was immovable on one thing: stopping the extension of slavery into the new territories, the thing that had gained him so much national exposure during his 1856 Senate race with Douglas. On that point alone he told Republican congressmen: "Stand firm. The tug has to come and better now than at any time hereafter."[15]

On March 4, 1861, James Buchanan and Abraham Lincoln began the ride down Pennsylvania Avenue to the Capitol together. Their inauguration journey followed the President-elect literally being snuck into Washington in order to foil a rumored assassination plot uncovered by the Pinkerton National Detective Agency during Lincoln's victorious, 12-day train trip from his home in Springfield, Illinois, to the District of Columbia on a circuitous route that took him through as many Northern cities as possible. Knowing that to complete the last leg of the trip, travelling through slave state Maryland and particularly Confederate-sympathizing Baltimore, Lincoln would be required to change not only trains but stations, a secret train and sleeping car were arranged to transport the President-elect from Philadelphia to Washington under the cover of darkness, a ploy that would be exposed and derided by the *New York Times* and *New York Tribune* upon his arrival. Nine days later, as soon as Lincoln had finished his inaugural address, which included his famous appeal to "the better angels of our nature," he was faced with the dilemma of re-supplying the federal garrison at Fort Sumter in Charleston Harbor, the place where the Confederate forces of General P.G.T. Beauregard would initiate the Civil War with their historic bombardment 39 days later.[16]

At least one author of more recent vintage has suggested Lincoln was not all that taken aback by the South's headlong rush to secession and, in fact, was actually "all in" on a Republican plot to initiate the confrontation all along in the hope the new party would gain complete control and power of the central government. Talk about re-writing history; Robert Broadwater set out to at least threaten "Honest Abe's" saintly reputation in his *Did*

Lincoln and the Republican Party Create the Civil War?: An Argument, written in 2008. In the book's Introduction Broadwater wrote:

> The true cause of the war is one as old as civilization itself: the power to rule. The Republican Party, a relative newcomer to national politics, had, by a twist of fate, secured the election of Abraham Lincoln to the presidency in only its second presidential election. The Democratic Party had become split, divided into three factions [with] each nominating its own candidate. Lincoln won with a decided minority of the popular vote and his presidency promised to be of limited power and influence. It became apparent to the Republicans from the beginning that even with the presidency they could exert no great influence over national politics unless the hold of the Democrats was broken [and] the most expeditious manner to accomplish that was to eliminate the solid Democratic [voting] bloc that was the South. The sectional crisis that erupted with the election of Lincoln could have been avoided through mediation and diplomacy, but the [Lincoln] administration opted against such a course. Vowing to save the Union, the Republicans [instead] did everything in their power to dissolve the confederation [Union of states] and split the nation.

Totally revisionist in theory to say the least, Broadwater's controversial premise seems even more ironic when one considers how Stephen Douglas, Lincoln's most formidable opponent, was actively striving to preserve the Union to the bitter end of his 1860 presidential campaign, even when Lincoln's victory had become inevitable. Douglas' biographers agree he was working on keeping the country together more than ever, specifically because of the new, soon-to-be resident of the White House—an assumption that makes a lot of sense if Broadwater's argument is to be believed. "During the entire last month of his presidential campaign, when Douglas recognized the probability of Lincoln's victory, he focused on the need to preserve the Union by explaining why the South should remain wedded to the established constitutional order. [And] immediately after the election, he continued to articulate the same message"—at least that's how one of his biographers put it while emphasizing economic arguments and Lincoln's repeated promise to leave Southern slavery alone. Another Douglas biographer confirmed: "He was sincerely alarmed for the safety of the Union in case of Lincoln's election, which he believed probable. [And] he urged upon the South the duty of submitting to the result, whatever it might be."[17]

Easily the most recognized Democratic spokesman, with Buchanan having faded from relevancy by the time of the 1860 presidential election, Douglas was also instrumental in the previously mentioned Crittenden compromise, the last gasp of those trying to again compromise their way out of disunion. Reflectively, he would also revise his previous career-long political approach by claiming to regret having had to vote for compromise so often, an example of his tendency to reconstruct the past to accommodate more immediate goals. Of necessity, he would end his political days vigorously supporting Lincoln before dying of typhoid fever at the even-then young age of 48, while on a grueling speaking tour on behalf of (you guessed it) saving the Union, less than two months after the fall of Fort Sumter.[18]

Buchanan, by contrast, would simply retire to his Wheatland estate in Lancaster, Pennsylvania, and live out the remaining seven years of his life in relative anonymity, seeking only to defend his administration by authoring *Mr. Buchanan's Administration on the Eve of Rebellion*, a memoir of his one-term presidency with more positive spin than what most pundits remembered from that four-year drift to disunion that he had not only failed to resolve, but accelerated. To the end of his life at age 77, he would seek to justify and draw similarities between his policies and those of his successor, especially once Lincoln was lionized in death by an assassin's bullet that made him a national saint.[19]

Yet, although Lincoln has nearly always been regarded as our greatest president, such levels of adulation have not left him immune to detractors—one of whom, Brion McClanahan, in his *Nine Presidents Who Screwed Up America*, even had the temerity to include Lincoln as one of those nine. In so doing, he admitted that in "presiding over the most traumatic and defining moment in American history," a war between states, there may have been need for a "careless disregard [of] executive restraint" and the "wholesale transformation from federal republic to consolidated nation," but Lincoln, "more than any other president before him," including the often executively autocratic Andrew Jackson, "created the blueprint for the modern presidency."[20]

To support this argument, McClanahan expressed Lincoln's own understanding of the national situation he assumed leadership of in 1861 as a state of "anarchy," while at the same time classifying the Union of that nation as "perpetual" and "indissoluble." These two rarely used words, which mean "never ending" and "unable to be destroyed," obviously meant a lot to Abraham Lincoln because in upholding their meaning in regard to the nation, he was forced to play what McClanahan cited as "a dangerous balancing act with the Constitution and his oath of office." Examples would be his initial call for 75,000 troops to put down the Southern "rebellion," since the secession of individual states by state governments was an illegal act without law on which to base the so-called Confederate States of America. And his unilateral suspension of habeas corpus by arresting secessionist-leaning office holders in Maryland in April 1861 that was ruled unconstitutional by the Taney Supreme Court. That was a ruling he would ignore two more times during the Civil War by sanctioning the detainment of perceived foes through his war powers and finally his January 1863

Emancipation Proclamation, which has always been hailed as a seminal act in American history for freeing the slaves, but also questioned by legal scholars for its invalidating of state laws and property rights via presidential decree.[21]

In other words, the conflict between Senator Douglas and President Buchanan and the overall breakdown of the Democratic Party between 1856 and 1860 undoubtedly resulted in political control by the Republican Party for the foreseeable future; actually escalated the sectional divide over slavery that had long threatened the nation's unity; and eventually paved the way for the election of a little known former congressman to be president, who rightly (as has always been taught) or wrongly (as constitutional law might indicate), expanded presidential power to never before seen levels. Ultimately this personal, intra-party, Washington war helped precipitate the Civil War, the worst catastrophe in American history and one that planted the seeds of so many things that still confront and divide us.

Section Three

The Reconstruction Conflict
Andrew Johnson vs. Charles Sumner

7

Political Opposites on a Collision Course

Boston-bred, Harvard-educated, and European-experienced, with an impressive array of mentors and friends that included Supreme Court Justice Joseph Story and esteemed poet Henry Wadsworth Longfellow, Charles Sumner was a polished lawyer, teacher, and United States senator ahead of his time in the 1850s. Indeed, how many American politicians have been elected to their first office—a major, statewide office—by an unlikely coalition of two separate parties joining forces to oust the state's prevailing "money power"? Such was the case in Massachusetts in 1851 when Sumner's short-lived Free-Soil Party coalesced in a controversial alliance with the state's traditionally second place Democrats to capture the Senate seat long held by the iconic Daniel Webster and his Whigs.

By all accounts, it was a radical changing of the guard in the "Bay State" that took 26 ballots to consummate in the Massachusetts House of Representatives, but that's not why Sumner was ahead of his time. Instead, that status would be earned by the leading role he played in the nation's first African American civil rights movement—both the anti-slavery agitation he brought and personified in the U.S. Senate before and during the Civil War, and the Radical Republicanism he would eventually subscribe to and lead during the nation's "Reconstruction" after the war. Barry M. Goldenberg confirmed as much in his 2011 book *The Unknown Architects of Civil Rights*, when he wrote: "Sumner lived his life as a means to fight for Black equality, his source of passion as a U.S. senator." Also quoting the leading Sumner biographer, David Herbert Donald, who actually authored two books on the Massachusetts senator, Goldenberg agreed that he was "'a man inflexibly committed to a set of basic ideas as moral principles.' Those principles that defined Sumner were grounded in equality, social justice, and civil rights."[1]

But if Sumner was a senator ahead of his time in 1851, Andrew Johnson would prove a president terribly behind the times upon his sudden elevation from vice president to the White House following the shocking assassination of Abraham Lincoln just six days after the end of the Civil War in 1865. Unlike Sumner, Johnson, who had aspired to higher office for decades, was a battle-tested career politician by the time he became the nation's chief executive, having risen steadily through Tennessee's Democratic Party. In a period history he authored in 1988, in fact, Eric Foner argued that in terms of sheer political experience, few men could have appeared more qualified for the presidency than Andrew Johnson did by the 1860s.[2]

And yet, Johnson had been fatherless, unschooled, and apprenticed at an early age, when he and his brother escaped dire financial straits in Raleigh, North Carolina, crossing the Appalachian Mountains in order to start anew as tailors (their acquired profession) in the still young "Volunteer State." There Johnson would settle in the lovely East Tennessee village of Greeneville, within sight of the Great Smoky Mountains, where he established a successful tailor's shop, acquired a self-taught education, raised a thriving family, and jumped into local and state politics, winning early and often as a disciple of Andrew Jackson.[3] In 1843, representing Tennessee's 1st Congressional District, he reached the U.S. House, where he thrived before becoming governor in 1854, senator in 1858, military governor in 1862 after Tennessee seceded and was partially re-conquered by Union forces early in the war, and vice president as a Unionist "War Democrat" on Lincoln's revised re-election ticket of 1864 (replacing Lincoln's highly regarded first term VP, Maine's Hannibal Hamlin).[4]

Johnson's move to the Republicans as military governor and vice president was a matter of political necessity, as well as a reflection of the strict constitutional beliefs that kept him in his Senate seat in Washington when all other Southern senators were abandoning theirs in early 1861, returning to their respective seceded states before the war's inevitable start. He truly believed secession illegal and caused by a treasonous "slaveocracy" in the South, the wealthy, plantation-owning minority who were determined to take the rest of the White population to war with them in order to protect their influence and property. As a result, he subscribed to the belief the Southern states had never actually left the Union and were in a state of rebellion only because the vast majority of people in the South had been duped into believing their way of life was threatened. Eventually Johnson had to accept political reality and his lack of a home state constituency, as well as Lincoln's Emancipation Proclamation ending slavery in January of 1863. What he would never surrender, however, were his roots and belief in White supremacy. "Everyone must admit that the White race is superior to the Black," Johnson was recently credited with saying by a current, national media outlet.[5]

At the same time, an ironic bit of commonality in their connected saga was the fact both Sumner and Johnson had been elevated to hero status in the North by the time the Civil War began. Sumner would ascend the Mount Olympus of anti-slavery and abolitionist sentiment following a speech he gave in May 1854 during debate over the Kansas-Nebraska Act. It became known as his "Crime Against Kansas" speech and in it he attacked "the one idea that Kansas, at all hazards, must be made a slave state." Castigating repeal of the Missouri Compromise line as a pro-slavery conspiracy and "swindle" by Stephen Douglas, the Pierce administration, and their legion of Southern adherents in Congress, who, he said, "shamelessly acquiesced around the concept of popular sovereignty as a means of expanding slavery into the territories," he also personally chastised other members of the South's Senate delegation, including James Mason of Virginia, "where human beings are bred as cattle," and South Carolina's Andrew Butler, whom he branded the "Don Quixote of slavery" with "a mistress [slavery], who though lovely to him is polluted in the sight of the world." Unbeknownst to Sumner, the aging Butler had a younger, more radicalized second cousin representing South Carolina in the House at the same time, who took it upon himself to defend family honor and that of the South by attacking Massachusetts' anti-slavery spokesman in broad daylight as he sat at his desk in the Senate chamber. Congressman Preston Brooks, in fact,

As the first American president whose ascent to the White House was due to an assassination, Andrew Johnson was thrust into national leadership at the most troubling of times—the bitter end of the Civil War with its ongoing sectional hostility, and the death of the man (Abraham Lincoln) who had seemingly willed the country back together. Despite a long political career, Johnson would prove ill-equipped to deal with the enormous challenges still facing the nation (Library of Congress Prints and Photographs Division—Reproduction Number LC-USZ62-13017).

7. Political Opposites on a Collision Course   81

would use a walking cane to repeatedly strike Sumner about the head and shoulders, rendering him bleeding and unconscious before the few other senators in attendance that day could restrain the assailant and get the victim medical attention.

This impressive 1878 statue of Massachusetts Senator Charles Sumner still stands in Boston's Public Garden. A Boston native and graduate of Harvard College, Sumner was regarded as one of the most important members of Congress for more than two decades. Ahead of his time in terms of civil rights, he was also the victim of the worst assault ever inflicted in the Halls of Congress by an opposition congressman, but recovered from his injuries to lead the Republican Senate during Reconstruction (Library of Congress Prints and Photographs Division—Reproduction Number LC-DIG-def-4111405).

Although expelled from the House and convicted of assault, Brooks would never be incarcerated and was fined only $300. On the other hand, Sumner faced a three-year rehabilitation from his injuries and resulting infection, a period in which he was absent from the Senate though retaining his seat, and a time during which he would become a heroic symbol for the North's growing anti-slavery fervor. Not surprisingly, he would be re-elected to the Senate in 1859 despite never fully recovering from what has come to be diagnosed as post-traumatic stress disorder, obviously the neurological result of Brooks' attack.[6]

Following Lincoln's election in the fall of 1860, Johnson would also attain Northern hero status, when his urgent pleas in support of the Union and decision to remain at his post in the U.S. Senate, regardless of Southern secession, made him the target of abuse in his home state and throughout the South to the point of having his likeness burned in effigy and being threatened by mob violence in Virginia while en route to his home in East Tennessee. That visit, in fact, had to be cut short to allow him to slip out of Tennessee by another, more circuitous route through neutral Kentucky to avoid becoming a political hostage. Needless to say, he was treated to a hero's welcome upon his return to Washington, becoming a much sought after Unionist spokesperson as the nation continued its plunge to war over the next several months.[7]

Both were good speakers, with Johnson an effective backwoods debater and Sumner an eloquent orator, especially whenever the slavery issue was addressed. Otherwise, while Johnson was already a very experienced politician by the time he rose to the U.S. House at age 35, Sumner needed coercion to get over his political reluctance at age 40 before being swept along by his Free Soil colleagues to their coalition nomination with the Democrats and the opportunity to end Webster's two decades of Whig influence in the Senate.[8] Like Johnson, Sumner would eventually change parties for political expediency, finding a more appropriate and lasting home in what he considered the new, "fusion" party (aka the Republicans) before that party's first presidential nomination in 1856.[9]

Although Sumner would find a useful role in the pre-war and wartime Republican ranks, Johnson's days of party influence were numbered once he reached the post-war White House and crossed paths (and purposes) with Sumner and the other, so-called "Radical Republicans." It was there that the new President's plans for Reconstruction and those of congressional leadership diverged, setting up one of the most intense Washington wars ever—a confrontation that would lead to the first presidential impeachment in the House of Representatives and the first of our four presidential acquittals by the Senate, with this one closer to conviction (a single vote) than the other three. What's interesting in hindsight is that no one in leadership at the federal level saw such drama coming, even in the anger that followed the Lincoln assassination. Once the overwhelming shock of that tragedy had subsided, Congress prepared to embrace Johnson as someone it could work with; maybe even more so than would have been possible with the re-elected Lincoln, who was expected to take total ownership of what he was calling his "restoration" policy had he not been assassinated. After all, Lincoln's intentions were well known by that time in terms of the more moderate olive branch he planned to extend to the defeated South. Perhaps "Honest Abe's" more lenient Reconstruction would have been accepted verbatim—it would seem he had earned that right by his leadership through the country's worst-ever, four-year nightmare—and it is doubtful anyone in the House or Senate would have been brazen enough to challenge his designs on national reconciliation.[10]

Instead, his successor was generally regarded by congressional leaders as more amenable to their own desires to treat the traitorous Southerners a lot more stringently than what Lincoln had prescribed; thereby forcing them to show the proper contrition in order to re-enter the Union as reconstituted states. This was an understandable conclusion on their part given Johnson's early and total rejection of secession; his oversight of his re-conquered home state as Tennessee's military governor during the war; his acceptance of emancipation before becoming Lincoln's running mate; and, most of all, comments he made on April 15, 1865, during his first meeting as president with congressional Republicans. According to his principal biographer, Hans Trefousse, his message that day opened with: "I am very much obliged to you gentlemen and I can only say you can judge my policy by the past. I hold to this: robbery is a crime; rape is a crime; treason is a crime; and crime must be punished. The law provides for it; the courts are open [to it]. Treason must be made infamous and traitors punished." After applause for those words from his congressional visitors, they departed, apparently satisfied and confident in his viewpoints. Their confidence was even more assured a few days later when he agreed with bombastic Radical Senator Ben Wade of Ohio that even hanging might become necessary for "a number of the rebel leaders" to drive home the essential requirement of Southern submission to the Reconstruction process.[11]

According to co-Senate historians Richard Baker and Neil MacNeil, the "Radicals believed they now had one of their own as president" and along with other, conservative Republicans, they had been reassured by President Johnson's initial pronouncements. At the same time, Trefousse emphasized how the President "was taking particular care not to commit himself to any specific program," while going out of his way to reassure the general public, including "holding over" Lincoln's entire cabinet.[12] His response to the Radicals was obviously contrived and those same Senate historians confirmed, "In less than a month, Johnson began to slip from their grasp." After initially speaking about "harsh, punitive measures towards the Confederates," Johnson's actual Reconstruction approach softened to resemble that of his deceased predecessor. In *The Complete Book of U.S. Presidents*, William DeGregorio summed it up this way:

> Taking the position that, technically, the rebel states had never left the Union because constitutionally it is in dissoluble, Johnson set out to restore their legal status swiftly, without recrimination, and with the least possible disruption in the lives of his fellow Southerners. His plan was to appoint a local provisional governor, who was to call a state constitutional convention, which, in turn, would draft a new constitution repudiating secession, slavery, and Confederate war debts. Full rights of citizenship were to be restored to Southerners on swearing a simple oath of allegiance to the federal government. Once these objectives were accomplished, the people of the Southern states were to be free to govern themselves and send men of their own choosing to Congress. As for the emancipated slaves, it was Johnson's hope that the South would recognize the value of giving the vote to literate, responsible Blacks.[13]

No sooner had Johnson started implementing this Reconstruction policy, however, than what would become irrevocable disagreements between the President and Congress began to surface. Writing about the impending conflict, Seward biographer Walter Stahr noted: "Radicals were in no hurry to welcome the Southern states back." Previously, when Louisiana, already under federal control, had attempted to form a state government before the war's end and sent representatives to Washington, the Radicals had prevented them from taking seats. The Radicals argued that unless Southern Blacks were given the vote, Southern states could not have "republican governments" as required by the Constitution, even though many of their own Northern states also prohibited or limited Black suffrage. They also wanted not just a temporary Freedmen's Bureau, which had been initiated by Lincoln to ensure provisions to the newly freed slaves, but a permanent independent federal agency charged with helping and protecting the Southern Blacks.[14] Such demands by the Radical Republicans even before Johnson instigated Reconstruction—his way—undoubtedly made clear their expectations to the new president, but he chose to ignore their input anyway. DeGregorio, again, simplified the brewing divide when he wrote: "The South had no intention of sharing political power with former slaves; Radical Republicans, led by Charles Sumner in the Senate and Thaddeus Stevens in the House, were determined to punish the South and prevent a resurgence of Southern Democratic power"[15]; and Johnson had finally revealed his commitment to re-admitting his fellow Southerners "under his own authority" in the quickest, most accommodating manner possible.[16] It was a recipe for political mayhem—or, at the very least, a

7. Political Opposites on a Collision Course

Washington war that would pit one of the most stubborn, outmoded presidents against a senator having to reinvent himself, but still very much ahead of the game.

Perhaps their individual biographers said it best when each took time to summarize their subjects. In the case of Johnson, Trefousse ended his Epilogue with the admission our 17th president's "refusal to adjust his racial views" rendered him "a child of his time, who [unfortunately] had failed to grow with it," while Donald's second Preface made manifest "what was unique about Sumner [was] the way he implemented his principles—[for] between the age of Thomas Jefferson and that of Woodrow Wilson, [he] was the one American who had equal claim for distinction in the world of intellect and the world of politics."[17] How's that for critical judgment of one and high praise for the other?

8

The Rage Over Southern Reconstruction

If the Civil War was indeed America's most pivotal historic event as usually portrayed, then surely the Southern Reconstruction that followed the war had to be among its most defining. Amid the residue left over from four years of sectional strife, President Andrew Johnson inserted himself confidently into the breach. And why not? After all, he was a Southerner who had rejected secession, loyally served the Union, and was suddenly positioned to take ownership of reconstituting the country in what he considered the quickest, least offensive, most historically accurate, and constitutionally appropriate manner possible. As president after the assassinated Abraham Lincoln, he would make every effort to put the country back together as his great predecessor would have wanted, but as it turned out, with his own South-condoning twist.[1]

While assuming leadership and attempting to reassure the nation during the earliest weeks of his administration, Johnson held off on policy, saying just enough to keep the Republican Congress on board, but not enough to raise red flags among its more assertive Radical leadership. The new President hoped the Radicals would accept the need for the most painless reunification process possible without inserting themselves into the mix any more than necessary. To his way of thinking, it should be a process his fellow Southerners could also accept, with slavery gone, fealty to the nation renewed, and states' rights restored, the Confederate States could return to their rightful place in the federal government as before—without further restrictions or needless retribution.[2]

All very neat and tidy as possible was how Johnson envisioned Reconstruction—something along the lines of what his deceased predecessor had hoped for before he was murdered, but with one important difference. That difference would be Johnson's abiding racism, which has since caused political pundits to claim, "he abandoned Lincoln's agenda," as was published in late 2019 in the magazine *The Week*. As re-quoted there, Johnson rather infamously once said, "America is a country for White men and will remain so as long as I am president." What more could the Radical Republicans have possibly needed to hear before having serious doubts about the man who had assumed "The Great Emancipator's" place at the head of Reconstruction?[3]

Apparently gone was the leader who had said "treason must be made odious" and "traitors must be punished and impoverished" as Johnson had done as vice president in 1864—the same man who had once offered himself as a would-be "Moses" to lead African Americans to a promised land of freedom once the war was over and Lincoln's emancipation policy and Reconstruction took over in the defeated South, including confiscation of large Southern estates and their division among "small freeholders."[4] Instead, according to Trefousse, Johnson whiffed as president on the opportunity to inaugurate a policy that would have "protected minimum rights of the freedmen," when he ignored the "admonitions" of advisers by deciding to leave voting restrictions up to the states, where, in his estimation, they had always resided; by appointing provisional governors and laying down his own terms for reunion; by beginning to reunify Southern states as they met his previously specified requirements, both constitutionally and by their citizens taking a loyalty oath; and most of all, when he vetoed a bill that would have strengthened the Freedmen's Bureau started by President Lincoln in March 1865.[5] Originally established to ease the transition of the emancipated slaves to post-war, emancipation reality in the South, its start was a rocky one as the defeated states began enacting their own, earliest "Black Codes," restricting the movement of the former slaves and conditions of labor. In other words, ways to approximate the servitude African Americans in the South had supposedly just been freed from.[6] Johnson vetoed the new Freedmen's Bureau Bill, which would have expanded the agency's functions, and one other civil rights measure designed to counteract Black Codes on February 19, 1866, with a strongly worded message to the Senate. The President objected to the legislation because it would substitute military jurisdiction in the South for civilian law, something he doubted the need or rationale for with the country in the midst of restoring peace.[7]

As a Democrat at heart and a Southerner, he had no qualms whatsoever when it came to reversing his tough, earlier stance once he became president and actually dictating policy. That's when he shifted back to his lifelong conviction that the federal government had no business usurping the rights of individual states. Johnson also came to believe that states' rights offered the best and easiest way to reconstruct his still divided country regardless of what that might portend for the South's suddenly free mass of unschooled Negroes, who would be left to fend for themselves in a very different world.[8]

Proclaiming this "a country for White men as long as I am president," then President Andrew Johnson's efforts to restore the defeated South to the Union after the Civil War with few if any safeguards for the newly freed slaves was the subject of numerous political cartoons like this one, as Reconstruction became a very contentious political period in post-war America (Library of Congress Prints and Photographs Division—Reproduction Number LC-USZ62-121735).

8. The Rage Over Southern Reconstruction

Some historians have maintained that Johnson tried to "counteract" the image of being totally indifferent to the freedmen's plight by suggesting to his newly appointed governors that they at least extend voting rights to their "most literate and propertied Blacks," certainly a minuscule number of all the African Americans in the South in the 1860s. What he never wavered from, however, were his twin beliefs that the federal government did not have the authority to impose total Black enfranchisement on individual states and that the newly freed Negroes should not be made an impediment "to the speedy completion of Reconstruction."[9] If anything, he hoped to use Reconstruction as a means of assisting what he considered the "yeomanry" of the South, the majority poor White population whose ranks he had risen from and the people he hoped would lead the way in establishing new state governments no longer beholden to the plantation-owning gentry, who he held responsible for secession and war. The poor Whites were the ones he wished to elevate—not the African Americans of whom he once said: "The subjugation of the states to Negro domination would be worse that military despotism," and "they possess less capacity for government than any other race of people." Ultimately, such deeply felt racial prejudices would explain his stubborn Reconstruction resolve every bit as much as the constitutional principles he professed.[10]

Meanwhile, Charles Sumner was among the Radical Republicans who were initially duped by the President. Along with others during early meetings at the White House, Sumner heard the President assert his inclination to punish "traitors." He also heard him say on more than one occasion, "There is no difference between us," when their discussions turned to equality before the law in regard to skin color. Like his Radical colleagues, he had taken those kinds of comments as presidential nods in support of civil rights in the reconstructed South, even though the President felt such breakthroughs could be achieved without the presence of occupying federal troops. Also, Eric Foner indicated in his book *Reconstruction* that Sumner was easily the most persistent of the Radicals, the one who "waited upon" Johnson almost daily during the first month of his administration, reiterating constantly the theme around which his whole political career would be built—"justice [for] the colored race."[11]

Sumner remained optimistic that even though the Lincoln assassination had been a stunning setback. Perhaps this new president, who he admittedly barely knew despite having served together in the Senate for five years and more recently with Johnson briefly overseeing the Senate as vice president, might prove more amenable to Radical aims than his revered predecessor. Unfortunately, soon enough that would become a baseless hope.[12]

According to Donald, it did not occur to Sumner at the time "that he had all along allowed his hopes to deceive him as to Johnson's [true] policy," but by May 29, 1865, Johnson's appointment of William Holden as provisional governor of North Carolina and his call for the election of a (state) constitutional convention "to be chosen by loyal White voters" spoke volumes about his actual objectives. At first, Sumner could not believe the President had decided to exclude Negroes from the polls, given all he had previously said or at least signaled, but as Johnson's repeated proclamations calling one Southern state after another to reorganize on the basis of their same old White supremacy, he was forced to accept the "change" as renunciation of the good faith he and other Senate Republicans had placed in him. Of this change, Donald would write:

> More perceptive observers had all along been aware that there were real differences in the Reconstruction policies of the President and the Senator. British Minister Sir Frederick Bruce had alerted his government as early as May 5 to the probability of a quarrel between the two men. When Johnson recognized the [Governor Francis] Pierpont government in Virginia and failed to use his [home state] influence to secure impartial suffrage in Tennessee, a number of [other] Radical Republicans began to feel that he had betrayed them, and it took Sumner and [Ohio's Ben] Wade to convince the rest at a caucus held at the National Hotel on May 12 that "the President [really] was in favor of Negro suffrage." Despite such assurances, the *Springfield Republican* announced nine days before Johnson issued his North Carolina proclamation that Sumner's theory of Reconstruction was not the theory of the administration.[13]

Sumner could not help but feel betrayed. He attributed Johnson's about-face to political pressure. In truth, the President was being influenced in three directions at once—by Sumner and his fellow Radicals; by Seward and more moderate Republicans hoping to lead a new Union Party; and by prominent Democrats, who hoped the President might rejoin their ranks—but on their terms. As a result, Sumner was forced to revert to his familiar role as crusader for African American rights by seeking to delay the Reconstruction process of the President, or at least prevent the readmission of Southern states until Congress reassembled in December while at the same time mobilizing public opinion against Johnson's program.[14]

Meanwhile, the Southern provisional governors put in place by Johnson had begun to initiate his Reconstruction desires by calling state conventions to officially abolish slavery within their borders; to nullify or repeal their previous secession ordinances; and to repudiate all Confederate debts. What the President refrained from doing, for some reason, was apply extra pressure to get those things done as quickly as possible. In not doing so, perhaps he felt restricted by his strong state sovereignty beliefs, but regardless of the reason, his reluctance to do so would prove disastrous to his hopes of installing new blood in the positions of Southern leadership, as voters in those states turned to the same conservatives who had been consumed in the South's "Lost Cause"—the same ones primarily responsible for the already mentioned Black Codes that all but renewed slavery. As a result, Sumner and the other Radicals had even more reason to be alarmed.[15]

Their fears would only intensify over the next several months, as Johnson became obstinate and unwilling to compromise. Although hard to understand given his extensive political experience, the President often chose the more difficult political path of my-way or no-way during his long career when it came to compromise, and Trefousse makes clear he definitely did so once again when it came to Reconstruction. The reason, his biographer maintained, was either his hope of returning soon to his previous lifelong affiliation with the Democratic Party or his hope of rallying enough conservatives to assemble a new party with him at its head. Either way, it rapidly became apparent that he could not embrace the brand of Republicanism the Radicals of that party were preaching and although the course he chose would be "strewn with political pitfalls," he was not about to reverse course, exhibiting the same, uncompromising demeanor that led Trefousse to title one of his chapters "Pugnacious President."[16]

When it came to Johnson's shortsighted political point of view, the newly freed African Americans were to remain "outside the bounds of citizenship"—maybe forever, but certainly for the foreseeable future, according to Eric Foner in *Reconstruction: America's Unfinished Revolution*. He also wrote of Johnson's tongue-in-cheek suggestion that absent presidential directives, the individual Southern states might take the initiative to give Blacks the vote, a very "disingenuous" assertion, to be sure, especially given the fact no Southern state since the founding had ever contemplated extending such political rights to Negroes ... and absolutely no American alive could have conceived the possibility of any former state of the Confederacy willingly doing so in 1866. As Foner deduced, using a not-so politically correct dialect of the time: "For the freedmen, it already seemed clear that they had been hurt by 'Mr. Lincoln gettin' kilt.'"[17]

Such sentiments were further magnified when President Johnson not only did not severely punish Rebel leaders as he initially hypothesized, but reinforced his suddenly emerging image as the South's Reconstruction champion by pardoning more than 7,000 Confederates, who had first been excluded from the nation's general amnesty because of a $20,000 wealth clause. Instead, this largely landed Southern gentry had their property restored by Johnson minus, of course, their slaves. No mass arrests followed the Confederate collapse and only Henry Wirtz, the commandant of the South's most notorious prison camp, Andersonville (in Southwest Georgia), and Tennessee guerrilla fighter Champ Ferguson were the only two Confederates hung for war crimes. Otherwise, Confederate President Jefferson Davis of Mississippi would be freed after just two years of prison time and his vice president, Georgia's Alexander Stephens, would return to Congress and even serve as governor of his home state before dying in 1883. Why Johnson so quickly abandoned the idea of depriving the prewar Southern elite that he had always disdained, allowing them to regain much of their economic and political ascendancy, has been an oft debated question. One obviously hostile congressman of the time referenced this presidential change of heart when he commented: "The President is no poor White trash now. They [wealthy planters] have taken him on their platform at last and he is wonderfully elevated and elated by their flattery and shared White supremacy." If Johnson was to have any chance at a second term, he knew he would need the Southern elite and their remaining influence in the post-war South. And so, Southern leaders began predicting a coming breach between the Southern-born president, who had suddenly become their protector, and the Radical Republicans in Congress. For that break, they would not have to wait long.[18]

After presiding over the Massachusetts Republican State Convention, where he began openly challenging "presuppositions" of the President's Reconstruction program, Sumner rallied New England businessmen and bond holders by warning them "not a single ex–Rebel will vote to pay interest on the national debt," while also rallying his past anti-slavery partners to the threat of Johnson's adherence to a pro–Southern process that would speed reunification but deliberately impede African American opportunity and development. He also did what he could to educate as many legislators as he could to the inherent danger in the President's course. Donald reported his message to each as the same: "Johnson had broken his promises" and "the Rebels are springing into old life." Furthermore, he argued, "The President's policy was illegal and flagrantly unconstitutional because it set up a discrimination of color." It was, he added, "against common sense, common humanity, and openly against God."[19]

Nevertheless, the response to Sumner's entreaties was initially discouraging, as most Republicans, weary of his war of words in addition to four years of actual warfare, worked to simply bring their state parties in line with the President's policy in hopes of just moving on. Even the handful of Radical congressmen most disturbed by the President's fast-tracking and back-tracking on Reconstruction, including normally aggressive anti-slavery co-conspirator Thaddeus Stevens of Pennsylvania, felt powerless to do anything about it. At the time, Stevens reportedly posed questions like "Is there no way to arrest the insane course of this President?" "Is it possible to devise a plan to stop this government in its ruinous course?" To which another Radical leader in the Senate, the irascible Wade, reputedly answered: "The colored people of the South will be compelled to hew out their own way to liberty by the power of their own right arm ... if by insurrection they could slay one half of their oppressors, the other half would hold them in respect and no doubt finally treat them with justice."[20]

Although discouraged by this lack of opposition and consensus, Sumner nonetheless determined to make one more face-to-face appeal to Johnson. On Saturday, December 2, 1865, two days before Congress was to reconvene, Sumner returned to Washington early and went to the White House to see the President. "Ostensibly," according to Donald, he was prepared to beg Johnson to change course, "but believing him irreclaimable" and his "rupture" with the Radicals inevitable, he wanted to make sure that it was the President making the break and not something he could later claim was the other way around. Johnson, from his perspective, was also anticipating a clash and hoped to provoke Sumner "into firing the first shot." Donald reported their meeting lasted for two and a half hours. "Both were on guard and both were vulnerable." After earlier approving of Johnson's apparent direction on Reconstruction, Sumner was in no position to claim the President had usurped power by acting without waiting on Congress or by not calling it back into special session. At the same time, Johnson's position was equally awkward. After repeatedly declaring his support for Negro suffrage, he was ultimately permitting each Southern state to decide for itself, knowing full well they would all fall back on White supremacy they had always known. As host, Johnson coyly went on the defensive, forcing Sumner to eventually erupt into an angry accusation that the President "had thrown away the fruits of the victories of the Union Army," to which Johnson called his bluff by asking him to be more specific. Following is their supposed dialogue in that moment:

> **SUMNER:** The poor freedmen in Georgia and Alabama are frequently insulted by the Rebels.
> **JOHNSON:** Mr. Sumner, do murders ever occur in Massachusetts?
> **SUMNER:** Unhappily yes, Mr. President, sometimes.
> **JOHNSON:** Would you consent that Massachusetts should be excluded from the Union on this account?
> **SUMNER:** No, Mr. President, surely not.

From this type of inane cross-examination, irreconcilable differences between the two emerged. Johnson considered Sumner's manner "arrogant and dictatorial," and realizing he represented the entire Radical group, the President knew he could expect "open war." On the other hand, Sumner left believing Johnson "ignorant, pig-headed, and perverse." He also decided that Congress must do whatever it could to alter the President's course—one he was obviously determined to take regardless of concerns on Capitol Hill and one without compromise.[21]

In partnership with Stevens in the House, Sumner immediately went to work. Donald stated he "seized" the Senate floor as the new session began two days later and introduced "a barrage of resolutions, bills, and constitutional amendments" that would come to make up the bulk of the Reconstruction program preferred by Congress instead of the one introduced months earlier by the President. At the same time, Stevens introduced a motion in the House calling for the creation of a Joint Committee to which all measures on Reconstruction must be automatically referred. The different techniques they employed would characterize their distinct roles in the coming battle with the White House. While Stevens, who was in his 70s, would be the behind-the-scenes organizational man, the much younger Sumner would assume his customary, out-front role as spokesperson for the Radical approach—a very different Reconstruction agenda than what the President had previously unveiled—one that called for sweeping change in the defeated South.[22]

With Congress in charge of approving each state's constitution, Donald described how the Radical approach would wipe away the regimes already set up by the President and ensure "all persons" regardless of race or color "would be equal before the law" with "no denial of rights, civil or political, in the courtroom or at the ballot box." And to further ensure this goal, each provisional governor would be required to register all male citizens of his state, requiring them to take an oath repudiating secession, upholding the national debt, and most telling of all, pledging them

The Radical Republican leader of the anti-slavery and pro-civil rights movement in the U.S. House of Representatives before, during, and after the Civil War, Thaddeus Stevens of Pennsylvania was the primary partner of Charles Sumner in setting the congressional Reconstruction agenda after the war. He also led the House during the impeachment of President Andrew Johnson (Library of Congress Prints and Photographs Division—Reproduction Number LC-USZ62-63640).

to always "discontinue and resist any laws making distinction on race or color." Once a majority of males in each Southern state had adhered to this oath, then and only then would a state be eligible to hold a constitutional convention, but with no former officer or even soldier of the former Confederacy allowed to serve as a delegate to those conventions. Also, the new state constitutions would be expected to "disavow secession, prohibit slavery, permanently disqualify high-ranking Confederate officers or officials from holding government office, and pledge henceforth that there would be 'no distinction among inhabitants founded on race, former condition, or color.'" When each state's male majority ratified these constitutions, they would be eligible to apply for readmission and representation in Congress. Under Sumner's plan, Negro males would be included but most ex–Confederates would not; terms he had to know were bound to be summarily rejected by Whites in every Southern state, especially given that Johnson's original plan had been far more generous.[23]

In anticipation of that happening, Sumner's plans, if rejected, would leave a state as a provisional government with Negro rights protected by an occupying military force. Donald surmised these occupations were what the Senator actually preferred in order to provide federal protection for the newly freed African Americans until they had been given a chance "to grow in independence; in knowledge; and in political wisdom." Not surprisingly, Sumner's new Reconstruction program was met with derision in the Senate, even by many Republicans, who labeled it "absurd" and too "visionary." Johnson's initial messages, on the other hand, were greeted warmly as the session opened. It was the President's already operational plan that set the tone in early debates and not the Senator's resolutions. For instance, when Sumner denounced the President's report of peaceful conditions throughout the South as a "whitewashing" of the mischief and mayhem bound to occur in Dixie if his Reconstruction was allowed to proceed unchanged, his reasoning was rebuked by many of his Senate colleagues. It was certainly not the first time, however, that the senator from Massachusetts had assumed what his primary biographer described as an "uncomfortable and lonely role," and one that was the subject of heated protests. While Stevens' committee approach in the House proved more acceptable and a Joint Committee of 15 on Reconstruction was established, Sumner, as a result of his verbal onslaught, would not be included.[24]

Increasingly under political pressure (even in his home state) from Johnson's quicker plan for Southern reunification and from overwhelming resistance to political interference in the South, Sumner nonetheless introduced a stopgap amendment that would have made congressional representation in the House based on the number of voters rather than total population. Conspiratorially, its passage would have actually made African

American voters advantageous to Southern interests in Congress, but at the same time it made Massachusetts interests question their own senator's logic and what exactly he was trying to do. In the meantime, Stevens' Joint Committee had also found time to introduce a constitutional amendment, the Fourteenth, that would continue representative apportionment on the basis of total population, but one that also declared "whenever the elective franchise shall be denied or abridged in any state on account of race or color, all persons of such race or color shall be excluded from the basis of representation," accomplishing what Sumner had set out to do with his amendment without the attendant cost to his or any other Northern state. Having painted himself into a political corner versus his instate rivals, Sumner had no choice but to come out in opposition to that one even though it was entirely similar to his own.[25] At the time, he would claim he had chosen "the high road of morality" while his colleagues "had fallen into the slough of compromise with slavery."[26]

Again, according to Donald, that was the ironic and unfamiliar political place the nation's foremost advocate of African American civil rights found himself in when, in June of 1866, "Congress approved the Fourteenth Amendment granting citizenship to all those born in the United States" while also "prohibiting states from depriving 'any person of life, liberty, or property without due process of law' or from denying any person 'equal protection of the laws.'" Also known as the "Reconstruction Amendment," it did not address Black voting rights, a disappointment to Stevens as well as Sumner, but almost all the other Radical Republicans in Congress voted for it along with their more moderate partisan colleagues.[27]

Although far from the voting rights protection preferred for the new freedmen by Sumner and Stevens, it was something—a start for civil rights in a reconstituted country. Johnson, however, remained opposed to anything that amended the U.S. Constitution until all new Southern senators and representatives had been selected and seated, and until that happened, he chose to use the influence of the presidency to stop ratification. According to Trefousse, the President believed the Fourteenth Amendment to be in direct opposition by Congress to his expressed (and already commenced) Reconstruction program and he was not about to yield, either to compromise or the will of his congressional opponents. As a result, Reconstruction became a far more contentious proposition. "To Johnson," Trefousse would confirm, "as long as Congress was 'in the hands of the Radicals,' bringing the Southern states back in and returning all the states to their proper relationship would be impossible."[28]

His biographer also revealed that once the amendment received the necessary two-thirds vote in Congress at about the same time the Joint Commission issued a report containing the President's assertion that

8. The Rage Over Southern Reconstruction

the Southern states were ready for re-entry and representation, Johnson rebuked the legislation and the process on the basis that no one in his administration had even been forwarded a copy of the resolution before it was voted on. Nevertheless, as stipulated by federal law, he instructed Secretary of State Seward to officially transmit the amendment to the states for their consideration. Following Seward's transmission, however, he described that step as "merely ministerial," while continuing his tirade that "the people" had not been consulted and there being "no precedent for such a course."[29]

Made to look irrelevant by the congressional action, Johnson vetoed another version of the Freedmen's bill. Suddenly weakened by the amendment and his reaction to it, however, that veto was overridden with even moderates voting against him. On that point, Trefousse concluded: "By the summer of 1866, it had become evident that Johnson's effort to restore the Southern states by executive fiat without any significant conditions or safeguards [for African Americans] was in deep trouble."[30]

Because of his political quarrels with Republicans during the first half of 1866, the President's interest in a new political party intensified. Along with Seward, Congressman Henry Raymond of New York, a co-founder of the *New York Times*, and Secretary of the Navy Gideon Welles (like Johnson a former Democrat), the President initiated calls for a National Union Convention in an attempt to bring together all those who had approved of the administration's Reconstruction policy. Johnson even asked his Cabinet to back the convention en masse, a presumptive request that resulted in three Cabinet members, all Republicans, resigning. Other than Seward and Welles, the only Cabinet members remaining after Johnson's politically motivated request were Secretary of the Treasury Hugh McCullough and Secretary of War Edwin Stanton, who openly sided with the Radical Republicans even though he refused to resign. Stanton's decision to remain at that time and Johnson's decision to allow him to stay would foreshadow confrontation—the kind that has reverberated in American political history.[31]

During this presidentially induced Cabinet shakeup, meanwhile, Sumner's own political irony played out about as well as possible for him, as the Reconstruction Amendment that had passed Congress even without his support survived yet another Johnson veto. He rationalized his position by claiming the amendment did not go far enough in its civil rights protections for Southern Blacks and would thus leave them still vulnerable to Southern Whites and their Black Codes. This however, according to Donald, was regarded by most of his congressional colleagues as totally inconsistent with his lifelong advocacy of African American civil rights "to the point of indecency." Before its passage, Stevens even "begged" that if the amendment his Joint Committee had fashioned "was to be slain, that it not be by the votes of friends," with everyone in both chambers knowing that comment was directed at his longtime anti-slavery partner more than anyone else. And Sumner was acutely aware of the frustration his surprising stance had caused among Republican colleagues, many of whom supposed his obstinacy on the issue had to do with a full-blown hatred of the President. Equally ironic, however, in the ongoing Reconstruction saga would be what Johnson did next that actually got Sumner off the hook, relieving the ostracism the Massachusetts Senator was suddenly experiencing within his own party.[32]

That summer, through the combination of centrist politicians like Seward, Edgar Cowan of Pennsylvania, James Doolittle of Wisconsin, and influential political gurus like Thurlow Weed, a Republican from New York, and Montgomery Blair, a Democrat from Maryland, the President's coveted political convention did come off in mid–August in Philadelphia, with delegates attending from across the country and across party lines. With the expressed goal being the formation of a new Union Party, many Republicans in Congress reacted angrily to this bipartisan effort at party reconstruction. At the same time, race riots erupted in Memphis and New Orleans, resulting in the deaths of at least 98 people and the President blaming the Radicals and their new amendment for inciting the violence. Obviously, the riots in the South also contradicted Johnson's earlier claims of calm in the Southern states, so Congress and its new amendment offered convenient scapegoats. Shortly thereafter, the first presidential impeachment rumblings were heard in the House of Representatives. Despite the racial turmoil and ongoing Washington squabbles, however, Johnson's hoped-for bipartisan convention did come off in Philly and did feature such gestures at unity as Massachusetts and South Carolina delegations entering the hall arm-in-arm, with everything aimed at providing the President a public relations coup. In its wake, participant reports proclaimed it "the most important proceeding since 1787," the year of the U.S. constitutional convention, and an emerging resolution was even billed as "a second Declaration of Independence." Continuing the PR campaign, Johnson next embarked on a series of presidential speeches designed to make his case to the Northern people for Reconstruction his way. Included were the cities of Baltimore, Philadelphia, New York City, Albany, Buffalo, Cleveland, Toledo, Detroit, Chicago, Springfield, St. Louis, Indianapolis, Louisville, Cincinnati, Columbus, and Pittsburgh in what was called the "Swing Around the Circle" between August 27 and September 15, 1886. It was an unprecedented presidential speaking tour for that era, but also one that would destroy any conceivable possibility for peace between the Johnson administration and the Radical Republicans.[33]

Speaking in the same, direct, confrontational manner he had always

8. The Rage Over Southern Reconstruction   99

used during his decades on the Tennessee stump, Johnson castigated his opponents in Congress and repeatedly responded irrationally to hecklers in his crowds. During one stop in St. Louis about halfway through the tour, Trefousse acknowledged he even became "blasphemous," and somewhat incoherently so, when he stated:

> I know I have been abused and traduced. I have been slandered. I have been maligned. I have been called Judas Iscariot. There was a Judas, and he was one of 12 apostles. Oh yes, the 12 apostles had a Christ. The 12 apostles had a Christ and he never would have a Judas unless he had 12 apostles. If I have played Judas, who has been my Christ? Was it Thad Stevens? Was it Charles Sumner? These are the men that stop and compare themselves to the Savior—and everybody that differs with them—and to try and stay and arrest their diabolical and nefarious policy, is to be denounced as a Judas.

Quoting what the *Chicago Tribune* had to say afterwards, his biographer confirmed this harangue as "the crowning disgrace of a disreputable series." And once his tour concluded, the *New York Independent* pretty well summed up how the Northern media as a whole felt about it by reporting: "For the first time in the history of our country, the people have been witness to the mortifying spectacle of a president going from town to town denouncing his opponents, bandying epithets with men in the crowd, praising himself and his policies. Such a humiliating exhibition has never been seen."

Casting himself as the only thing standing between Whites and "Negro domination," according to the previously referenced magazine *The Week* in 2019, Johnson's speeches provided ammunition for his opponents. Having already labeled Sumner and Stevens traitors, he may have actually been relying on Northern racism to sway moderates to his side in the Reconstruction argument, but the fact Republicans carried most elections for the House of Representatives that fall by overwhelming majorities portended major problems ahead for Tennessee's third president (after Jackson and Polk).[34]

Following those midterms, Seward advised Johnson to strike a more conciliatory and compromising tone. The secretary of state even drafted an annual message for the President that would have had him accepting the Fourteenth Amendment after all, if only Congress would admit the Southern representatives still pending from Johnson's original Reconstruction plan. The President, however, rejected Seward's attempted overtures, stubbornly persisting in his my-way or no-way attitude towards the Reconstruction process. With three Border States having already voted against ratification and the former states of the Confederacy all but certain to follow suit, it was Johnson's political calculation that compromise would be unnecessary since the amendment would not secure the necessary votes of three-fourths of all the states to become law unless Congress resorted to harsher measures to coerce the South. In other words, long-term military rule. He was basically gambling that neither the House nor the Senate would ever go that far and if they did, he believed that could also work to his advantage in time for the 1868 presidential election.[35]

This would prove an ill-conceived calculation on his part because he had unwittingly relieved Senator Sumner's ostracized position within his own party and reunified the Radicals with his speaking tour. Johnson hoped for a coalition of Northern Democrats, moderate Republicans, and the White Southerners he hoped to merge into his new Union Party once all the states regained statehood and the opportunity to vote, especially after his Philadelphia convention had been orchestrated from the White House. Only the most well-to-do Southern "traitors" were ultimately targeted by Johnson for retribution (example: Confederate President Jefferson Davis, who was imprisoned at Fortress Monroe on the Virginia coast), including estates worth more than $20,000 as he sought to reposition and repatriate less fortunate Southern Whites in his sphere of influence.[36]

Despite his original opposition to the Fourteenth Amendment, Sumner had found time to propose a number of supplementary bills to strengthen the milestone legislation; enough so, in fact, that he would eventually vote for it after all. Following its passage, he almost immediately renewed his efforts to win even more precise legislation for African Americans, a nearly decades long campaign that he would carry through to the Fifteenth Amendment in 1870, which more specifically addressed minority voting rights, and the even more landmark Civil Rights Act of 1875, which guaranteed equal access to public accommodations. Even though he died in 1874, a year before its passage, that 1875 bill would become Sumner's lasting legacy, according to Barry Goldenberg, the last meaningful civil rights legislation until the 1960s. In defining his renewed effort on behalf of African Americans, Sumner once orated:

> Show me a creature with lifted countenance looking to heaven, made in the image of God, and I will show you a man who, of whatever country or race, whether browned by equatorial sun or blanched by northern cold, is with you a child of the heavenly father, and equal with you in all the rights of human nature. You cannot deny these rights without peril to the republic ... by the same title that we claim liberty do we claim equality also. One cannot be denied without the other. What is equality without liberty? What is liberty without equality? One is the compliment of the other. The two are necessary to begin and complete the circle of American citizenship. They are inseparable organs through which the people have their national life.[37]

This excerpt from an 1871 Senate debate on what Sumner termed the "equality of man" helped explain the new chapter of his career that he entered

8. *The Rage Over Southern Reconstruction*   101

As perhaps the leading anti-slavery agitator in the U.S. Senate before the Civil War, Charles Sumner was regularly portrayed as a patron of Black civil rights in both the North and South, as exemplified by this political cartoon of the time with the Massachusetts senator shown favoring a needy Negro child over an equally needy White child (Library of Congress Prints and Photographs Division—Reproduction Number LC-USZ62-12771).

into in 1866. By the second half of the 1860s, he had regained his political balance and purpose following the Lincoln assassination. The new president had proven a disappointment and their paths had diverged sharply; enough, in fact, to shed light on what his new resolve needed to be.[38]

Following Sumner's speech, the President immediately sought to divide and conquer given the Senator's remarks. Before Sumner's renewed attack had time to spread, Johnson hoped to nip it in the bud by inviting other leading Republicans to the White House, hoping to profit from their initial hesitancy over what Sumner and Stevens (in the House) were suddenly preaching. Johnson, by then, was resigned to full-scale war with the two leading Radicals, so manipulating a truce with the majority party's other leaders seemed a good idea to the embattled chief executive.[39]

Gradually during the fall of 1866, Sumner's political fortunes began to change for the better, in large part because of Johnson's intrusion into the Republican ranks, seeking possible inroads to displace his most aggressive opponents. Largely through his own blunders, including being baited into rash accusations and name calling at political events, the President had painted himself into a corner without benefit of an existing political organization to call his own, much less one to which he could look for loyalty. About the only group he could increasingly turn to were Southern Democrats and they were still waiting on congressional approval of their new state constitutions just to re-enter the Halls of Congress. Only Tennessee, his home state, which had the head start of being under Union control since 1862, was the only Confederate state to re-enter by 1866. As for the others, Alabama, South Carolina, Florida, Louisiana, Arkansas, and North Carolina would be denied return until 1868, and the last three, Texas, Virginia, and Georgia, until 1870.[40]

Given the President's own self-destructive tendencies and increasing political isolation, Republican candidates largely swept to victory in the 1866 mid-term elections with the vast majority of those being of the Radical persuasion, a further boon to Sumner and Stevens in the Reconstruction debate. That's when Congress stole a page from the Johnson playbook, becoming increasingly more inflexible. With more senators and representatives feeling the return of the Southern states could not be completed as long as Johnson opted not to work with the congressional majority, they began to look for ways to ensure their influence over the process. One of those ways was the 1867 Tenure of Office Act by which all authorized administration officials approved via the Senate were henceforth required to remain in their office until the Upper Chamber had also approved any successor. According to Eric Foner in his history of Reconstruction, this was "intended primarily to protect lower level patronage functionaries [and] also barred the removal, without Senate approval, of

8. The Rage Over Southern Reconstruction

Cabinet members during the term of the president who appointed them. It remained uncertain, however, whether this [new law] applied to Secretary of War Edwin Stanton, who [as previously noted] had been named to his post by Lincoln and had retained it even when most of the other Lincoln-appointed, Republican-leaning Cabinet members had resigned in protest earlier in the Johnson administration."[41]

And within a day of that legislation, Congress had also passed its own Reconstruction Act of 1867. In its final form, again according to Foner, the former states of the Confederacy, minus already readmitted Tennessee, were divided into "five military districts under commanders empowered to employ the U.S. Army to protect life and property. And without immediately replacing the Johnson governors, it laid out the steps by which new state governments could be created and recognized by Congress." The steps included the writing of new constitutions to include universal manhood suffrage; the approval of each constitution by a majority of the state's eligible voters; and ratification of the recently passed Fourteenth Amendment. Ratification of this other Reconstruction amendment would also qualify returning states for representation in Congress as before the Civil War. The military commanders in each district would then be authorized to register voters and hold elections.[42]

What Foner termed the congressional "evolution" away from Johnson's Reconstruction policy to the policy endorsed by Sumner and Stevens that followed passage of the Fourteenth Amendment was rapid and the result of not only the President's obstinacy when it came to states' rights and Black suffrage, but also the obvious obstinacy of the White South. Military rule was deemed necessary but temporary as long as the new civil rights and new political orders became established. Just as obviously, however, what could not be legislated into submission would be the deeply held beliefs, prejudices, resentments, and animosity of a mandatorily reconstructed Southern White population. No two-thirds vote of the then all–Northern Congress was going to change that and therein lay the essence of the Reconstruction dilemma.[43]

Perhaps Johnson's original plan had merit when considered from the standpoint of a chief executive trying to put the country back together after one of the most massive internal bloodlettings in recorded history and the assassination of the one man with the understanding and proven leadership qualities to (perhaps) pull off a less contentious Reconstruction process. Even the revered Lincoln's presence, however, might have not been enough to rein in the politics that ensued. What is certain is that Johnson's plan was dead almost on arrival when Congress was not included from the outset; when large Southern race riots with lots of fatalities began occurring; and especially when the South's reluctance to accept the new freedmen and their suddenly equal rights after generations of slavery became increasingly manifest ... the "better angels of our nature" that Lincoln talked about in his first inaugural address be damned.[44]

"The landmark advances in the wake of Lincoln's assassination would largely come about in spite of [Andrew] Johnson, not because of him." So wrote Pulitzer Prize–winning historian Jon Meacham in one of his latest offerings, *The Soul of America*. "The presidency which under Lincoln had been a tool of transformation had become under Johnson, a refuge from modernity."[45] Into this breach and opportunity lost by our 17th president, Sumner inserted himself to try and achieve the African American suffrage he had always dreamed about along with their freedom. He believed the question of Black voting rights had to be resolved or "every state and village between Washington and the Rio Grande River [border with Mexico] would be agitated by it."[46]

Donald acknowledged: "Washington was a lot pleasanter place for Sumner in the winter of 1866–67 than it had been in years." With the President leaning towards Democrats as his last resort for support, the Republicans in their congressional caucuses were becoming more and more sympathetic to the plight of Southern freedmen and once again receptive to the senior senator from Massachusetts and his more radical way of thinking. Although he had nothing to do with the Tenure of Office Act, Sumner enthusiastically endorsed its attempt to rein-in the President by limiting his power to remove subordinates. He liked it so much, in fact, he wanted its restrictions made stronger to include the power of appointing and removing Cabinet members, a power he said should "more properly reside with the Senate as the more fixed branch of government rather than individual presidents who came and went more frequently." Sumner also believed "the Senate was less likely to become depraved and base than the President."[47]

Also, according to Donald, Sumner had privately "made up his mind" that Johnson must not only be contained, "but removed." With enough executive power, still, to frustrate Radical Republican efforts to reconstitute the South with its racist social fabric, especially in the way he could be expected to exercise his presidential veto—something Johnson would do 29 times, 15 of which Congress would override (still a record). Even with a dependable Republican majority to provide overrides, however, his repeated vetoes had the power to needlessly encourage obstinacy and non-compliance in the South. And worst of all, as president he possessed the power to virtually negate congressional Reconstruction policies through non-enforcement whenever he so desired. All the while, Sumner said, "If we go forward and supersede the sham governments set up in the Rebel states, we [will still] encounter the appointing power of the President, who

8. The Rage Over Southern Reconstruction

would put in office only men who sympathize with him. It is this consideration which makes ardent representatives say he must be removed."[48]

With another Stevens' led committee in the House already investigating the President, the Lower House was in a position to bring charges. That would cast Sumner and his fellow senators as jurors in an impeachment court, but for the time being he refrained from urging what he termed "the full remedy" of presidential removal. But by early 1867, with Southern states still taking Johnson's lead by refusing to ratify the Fourteenth Amendment, Sumner's constraint was vindicated as more and more Republicans began to express hostility to any measure or presidential pronouncement that openly recognized the White race as superior to the Black. In the months since passage of the Fourteenth, they had begun to understand how astute Democratic lawyers could (and would) "exploit every concession made to Northern racism," as Donald explained it, and use that as a precedent for Southern actions and prejudice. A prime example of that occurred in the final days of the previous congressional session, when Tennessee had been readmitted to the Union without the required Negro suffrage component by exploiting what Donald termed "an awkward fact" in the amendment that "seemed to give states the right to exclude citizens from the polls" if that state also agreed to reduced representation in Congress. Almost alone, Sumner had voted against that loophole ever since Tennessee's early re-entry, and his consistent stance on the subject started reaping benefits when reluctant senators began to follow his lead, voting nearly verbatim as he did. Donald confirmed "by mid–January he could boast that the Senate had adopted his views" and in one of his letters his biographer found the quote: "It cannot be said now that the Republican Party is not fully committed to Negro suffrage."[49]

Being able to write that must have been a very gratifying moment for a lawmaker who had devoted his political career to equality for America's Black population. While Presidents Lincoln and Lyndon Johnson a century apart have always been credited with getting African American civil rights started and finally complete, there's no doubt that Charles Sumner was one of the most important catalysts between the two on an issue that has unfortunately always defined American history. And as Goldenberg related in his book on early architects of civil rights, "to justify past racism would be to wash away the efforts of men like Stevens and Sumner, who were responsible for the first major legislation that advanced Black equality."[50]

Thus, by the 40th Congress of 1867–68, what could be considered "the unmaking" of a president had begun. By then, Sumner had denounced Johnson as "the defender of slavery, the arch enemy of country, and the betrayer of liberty," strong accusations that Donald indicated set in motion the Senator's expressed remedy—"removal from office" of the nation's chief executive. As talk of impeachment began to filter through both congressional chambers, especially whenever a caucusing of Radical Republicans occurred, Sumner tried to remain above the fray publicly, while keeping abreast of anti–Johnson feeling in the House and undoubtedly "egging" it on despite the fact that chamber's Judiciary Committee had yet to establish the presidential high crimes and misdemeanors required by the Constitution. In August of 1867, however, that abruptly changed when the President finally saw fit to suspend his secretary of war. Actually, no one in the Johnson administration was surprised when the suspension was announced, as many had been advocating for a replacement atop the War Department ever since those three earlier Cabinet resignations occurred. After all, Secretary Stanton shared a likeminded affection for Radical Republican ideology with those earlier Cabinet defections and an obvious difference of opinion when it came to the Johnson's plan for Reconstruction. Obviously reluctant to remove the Lincoln appointee who had played a major role in the Union's military turnaround and mostly winning final years of the war, the President was either still indebted to Stanton for his support while military governor of Tennessee; was hesitant to remove someone so connected and important to Grant, still the commanding general of the Army; or because of his fear that Congress would never confirm a replacement given its current state of conflict with the administration. Perhaps that last reason, as acknowledged by Johnson biographer Hans Trefousse, had the most validity when borne out by America's first impeachment proceeding over the next nine months.[51]

"Relations between Johnson and Stanton had been worsening steadily," Trefousse confirmed, and despite the undoubtedly targeted Tenure of Office Act hanging over any personnel moves the President hoped to make, he was prepared to go out on that limb anyway while Congress was adjourned and remove Sumner by the summer of 1867. With his stubborn streak ultimately consuming any better judgment he might have entertained in open defiance of Congress and its Tenure Act, Johnson finally sent a curt letter to Lincoln's trusted man at the War Department, asking him to vacate his office, with Grant to be put in charge of his duties for the immediate future. Grant, who did not wish to take on the added role and responsibilities or see his benefactor and colleague so summarily dismissed, reminded the President that the Tenure Act prohibited such a decision. Undeterred a week later, however, following charges and counter charges in the press, Johnson officially suspended Stanton as secretary of war, with all his duties indeed transferred to General Grant.[52]

Along with Stanton, Johnson also set about getting rid of the Radical-preferred military district commanders in the South, including General Phil Sheridan in the Louisiana-Texas district, but Grant rejected

8. The Rage Over Southern Reconstruction

this removal of one of his most trusted Civil War subordinates. Also, the President's choice to replace Sheridan was Winfield Scott Hancock, a Democrat and future presidential nominee, who naturally aroused suspicion in the Republican ranks as a perceived threat to congressional Reconstruction. Trefousse reported "Johnson was furious" and fearing Grant was also siding with the Radicals, he even sought to replace him with another Union hero, William Tecumseh Sherman, who, not surprisingly, refused the post in deference to Grant, his wartime commander and colleague.[53]

Not to be quelled, however, Johnson continued his aggressive and defiant tactics heading into the 1868 elections by issuing a proclamation requiring the Army to "sustain law and order as expounded in the civil courts" of the South and by ordaining "a general amnesty for all but the most prominent Confederates." It was a calculated presidential provocation based on the fact Johnson felt Democratic gains in elections that fall in state after state would sustain him, and initially that seemed a wise bet as November's elections did indeed favor Democrats even before the Democratic South had been restored. To the President's way of thinking, it had become all about "rescuing the South from 'Negro rule,'" according to Trefousse, and he flagrantly incorporated a constituent's wish for the "restoration to the White men of the South the Constitution as it was" in his annual message to Congress.[54]

Meanwhile, complaints Republicans in Congress were receiving from Southern Unionists made manifest the effect the President's opposition to the Reconstruction Amendment was having among rank and file Southerners, and that, along with his obvious disregard for the Tenure of Office Act, prompted many of them to ultimately accept the impeachment mode of their Radical brethren as the only realistic solution.[55] There's no doubt, in fact, that Southern intransigence encouraged by the President and Johnson's stubborn resolve to challenge the very Tenure Act that had been put in place to curb his autocratic tendencies "played right into Radical hands," as both Donald and Foner attested. Sumner and company had their issue, repressive as it was of executive privilege, and their one fear was that Stanton would eventually accept the President's wishes and resign. So, to prevent that happening, the Senate rushed through a resolution denying Johnson's right to oust the War secretary, whose selection under Lincoln and retention by the sitting president had nullified his ability to remove him from office of his own volition. It was a controversial bill when it passed over Johnson's veto and it was still controversial a year later, especially once it was established that Stanton would abide by the Senate Radicals' wishes and remain at his post in the War Department, relinquishing nothing to Grant or the President's demands.[56]

"Stick" is the term Donald indicated Senate Radicals used to implore

Stanton to remain on the job no matter what, and stick is exactly what he did, barricading himself in his office for approximately two months, beginning February 21, 1868. Three days later, the Stevens-led House of Representatives voted to impeach Johnson by a vote of 126–47 for high crimes and misdemeanors related mostly to his breach of the Tenure of Office Act.[57]

Ardently, Sumner began to push for the start of a Senate trial, what would become the first of a sitting U.S. president. He argued that all other public business should be suspended, and a prompt conclusion and verdict rendered once a jury of all the senators had been sworn in and the evidence presented. Throughout the legal proceedings in the Senate chamber with Chief Justice Salmon P. Chase presiding, Sumner sat close to Stevens and the other House managers. He would argue that the Senate trial was not really a courtroom trial at all, but "a political proceeding before a political body with a political purpose." Also, since the trial was, in his view, a political proceeding, he urged all evidence, no matter how minute or based on hearsay be allowed, but when it came to permitting Cabinet members to testify on the President's behalf as to his intent in removing Secretary Stanton, that was another matter altogether. As his biographer noted, consistency for him was "no hobglobin" in that moment as intent as he was on "ridding the country of Johnson."[58]

When William Evarts, one of the President's attorneys, defended his client's right to interpret the Constitution for himself "just as President Andrew Jackson had done in a previous day," and "just like Senator Sumner in 1852, when he had defied court and Congress by calling the new Fugitive Slave law unconstitutional"—that same senator did not blink. Instead, according to Donald, he "impatiently brushed aside all technicalities and legal quibbles" when a few Republicans were troubled by the fact Johnson had not actually removed Stanton, who still occupied his office; when discussion centered on the intolerability of keeping someone in the Cabinet against the president's wishes; and when the validity of the Tenure Act even applying to Stanton was questioned due to the fact he had been appointed by Lincoln and had never received a formal commission from Johnson. To Sumner, all this legalese was irrelevant. Disgustedly, he voiced regret that the House had brought articles on "such narrow ground," since, he felt, there were other transgressions by the President that also warranted impeachment.[59]

Desiring impeachment to save Reconstruction in the South regardless of any specific crime the President may have committed, Sumner was, in fact, infuriated when Johnson was acquitted by a single, surprising vote—that of Republican Edmund Ross of Kansas, one of the senators John F. Kennedy would feature in his book, *Profiles in Courage* for exactly that reason. Although representing one of the most anti–Johnson, pro-civil rights states in in the country, his unexpected vote to acquit on the first article of impeachment on May 16, 1866, along with fellow Republicans William Fessenden of Maine, John B. Henderson of Missouri, Peter Van Winkle of West Virginia, Lyman Trumbull of Illinois, Josiah Fowler of Tennessee, and James W. Grimes of Iowa, "saved a president," according to JFK. By the time Ross was called on to cast his vote, 24 "guilties" had been pronounced, with 10 more certain and one practically certain, rendering the newly elected Kansas senator's vote decisive to the final tally. In describing that moment, Kennedy dramatically wrote: "Every voice was still; every eye was upon the [young, 39-year-old] freshman senator. The hopes and fears, the hatred and bitterness of past decades were entered upon [that] one man. Then came the answer in a voice that could not be misunderstood—full, final, definite, unhesitating, and unmistakable, 'Not guilty.'" Presidential historian William DeGregorio credited the resulting acquittal as "owing to the courage of seven senators who risked their political careers to bolt party ranks."[60]

Those seven previously mentioned Republicans plus 12 Democrats made the final margin 35–19—oh so close to the required two-thirds necessary for conviction and removal. Ten days later, Johnson would be acquitted again of two more articles of impeachment by the same count. Sumner would never forgive the seven "recusant Republicans" and would go to his grave believing Ross had been bribed.[61] Johnson, meanwhile, got word of his acquittal that same day and was so delighted with the verdict that he had the White House thrown open to well-wishers. While Democrats publicly hailed the trial's result, privately they would have preferred a more lasting condemnation of the Radicals for having foisted it upon the country.[62]

Ten days later, the Republicans nominated the immensely popular but initially reluctant Grant for president. The Democrats would nominate former New York Governor Horatio Seymour, who would win just eight of the 34 eligible states, including two of the initial eight Southern states to ratify the Fourteenth Amendment, the result of so many Southern Whites being disenfranchised by the ongoing Reconstruction process while the many former slaves in those states, with their first chance at the polls, voted overwhelmingly for Grant.[63]

Having narrowly survived impeachment, Johnson would never realize his hope of founding and leading a new Union Party, and would finish a distant memory at the Democratic National Convention, where he somehow got 65 votes on the first ballot—less than a third of what was needed for nomination—before dropping out. Thus denied re-nomination by both major parties, he would finish out his final nine months in office as the lamest of lame duck presidents, except during his last annual message to

"FAREWELL, A LONG FAREWELL, TO ALL MY GREATNESS!"

Shown crying his eyes out in this political cartoon during his final, inglorious days as an impeached president, Andrew Johnson would go down in history as one of our worst chief executives largely because of the stubborn, uncompromising approach he took to Reconstruction and his racist Southern roots, both of which became evident during his four years in the White House (Library of Congress Prints and Photographs Division—Reproduction Number LC-USZ61-2017).

Congress in December of 1868, when he "minced" no words, according to Trefousse, in assailing the "military dependencies" that Congress had put in place in the South and the "attempt to place the White population under the domination of persons of color." A White supremacist to the bitter end, Johnson would not attend the inauguration of his successor, Grant, but would retire a hero in his home state, where his Reconstruction efforts on behalf of the defeated South had not gone unnoticed and where he would end up regarded as a patriot after all.[64]

At the same time, Sumner would go on to serve in the Senate for eight more years and continue to battle for Black suffrage in a prejudiced country and still hostile political environment. Seven years after the Reconstruction Act of 1867, he would attempt to pass another civil rights bill—the kind that would finally get done almost a century later (1964), during the previously mentioned administration of Lyndon Johnson. Aimed at granting full

8. The Rage Over Southern Reconstruction

Pictured here later in life, Charles Sumner of Massachusetts was the foremost advocate of African American equality and civil rights before, during, and after the Civil War. His efforts on behalf of the first American civil rights legislation in the 1860s and 1870s earned him folk hero status among Blacks, North and South, as the architect of modern legislation that resulted during America's Civil Rights Movement a century later (Library of Congress Prints and Photographs Division—Reproduction Number LC-US762-66840).

citizenship and social equality to African Americans—almost unthinkable in those days in both North and South—Goldenberg indicated that amendment was struck down twice in committee in 1872 and again in 1874. But barely a month later after Sumner's death on March 11, 1874, the bill that had only survived due to his tireless advocacy was passed in a watered-down version that, among other things, did not include his visionary goal of school desegregation.

Nevertheless, when it was finally signed into law on March 1, 1875, it would be another milestone in the long struggle of African American civil rights due primarily to the senator honored in death just a year earlier like Henry Clay—by lying in state in the U.S. Capitol Rotunda. At Sumner's burial in the Boston area's prestigious Mount Auburn Cemetery, his pallbearers included lifelong friend Longfellow, Supreme Court Justice Oliver Wendell Holmes, renowned New England essayist Ralph Waldo Emerson, and the great American poet John Greenleaf Whittier, a star-studded sendoff for the man to whom "more than any" (including Lincoln), according to another friend and biographer, Moorfield Story, "the colored race owed its emancipation and such measure of equal rights as it could enjoy" in the aftermath of Reconstruction.[65]

9

"Glorious Failure" or What Might Have Been

Just as Charles Sumner can now be regarded as a visionary senator ahead of his time and perhaps the rightful father of African American civil rights, so too the Reconstruction period from which he departed in 1874 would have proven a real disappointment to him had he lived any longer. Eric Foner subtitled the period "America's Unfinished Revolution," but it might just as easily have been the era of what might have been or, as Philip Dray referenced in his Preface to *Capitol Men*, a "glorious failure." With America on the verge of achieving at least a semblance of racial equality as Sumner dreamed, it was all gone in less than a decade, as the same old White supremacy and racism exhibited by the administration of Andrew Johnson, Sumner's political opposite and eternal rival, would resurface almost immediately, ending whatever chance Radical Republican hopes of equality had in the South. After all, if it had been up to Sumner, Lincoln would have emancipated America's Southern slaves much earlier than September 22, 1862, as from the war's beginning the outspoken Massachusetts senator was urging exactly that as a "military necessity."[1]

Indeed, the deceased Sumner may have turned over in his grave in late 1876, only two and a half years after his passing and just over a year since his Civil Rights Act of 1875 had passed, when Republican Rutherford B. Hayes followed Grant to the White House only because of another controversial political bargain being struck after another U.S. presidential election was thrown into the House of Representatives. Unlike what had become known as the Corrupt Bargain in 1824, when none of four presidential candidates, including our previously reviewed rivals Andrew Jackson and Henry Clay, received an Electoral College majority, this one came about when votes from four states, South Carolina, Louisiana, Florida, and Oregon, were contested and an electoral majority unable to be decided as a result. The real controversy would occur, however, when a combined and supposedly equally divided Electoral Commission of 10 congressmen and five Supreme Court justices (seven Democrats, seven Republicans, and allegedly one Independent) established by Congress to decide things turned out not so bipartisan as portrayed. The one supposedly Independent member, Justice Joseph Bradley, was later exposed as a Republican after maliciously proclaiming his "nonpartisanship." Thus did what Foner term the "maddeningly ambiguous" Constitution become the underlying reason for one of the most disputed elections in American history. Hayes would go into the history books as the winner by one electoral vote, 185–184, after the Commission tally was 8–7 along strict party lines. The narrow popular vote winner, however, had been Democrat Samuel Tilden, the former governor of New York, with a 51 percent majority, setting the stage for what could have become the worst possible constitutional crisis had not Tilden "restrained his supporters" and Hayes "mollified them," using Foner's words, with a compromise ending Reconstruction's military occupation of the South, something Southerners and most Democrats actually preferred over winning the White House. It would be the second of five American presidential elections in which the popular vote winner would not become president—ironically, all Democrats.[2]

To the country at large it was obvious—the Republicans had cut a deal with the Democrats. But for African Americans living in the South this deal meant the end of the Reconstruction on which they had based all their hopes. Gone overnight was the military safeguard put in place by Sumner, Stevens, and the other Radical Republicans to federally protect African American rights over Johnson's strenuous objections and vetoes. The South would become less and less Republican with the evaporation of Black votes through White intimidation and voter suppression. As presidential historian Kenneth Davis re-quoted Republican chronicler Lewis Gould: "After a generation of trying to build a freer and more open society for all its citizens, the United States lapsed back into the customs and prejudices of old." And over the next quarter century, as a result of this abandonment by the "Party of Lincoln," the "Solid South" would become more Democratic and segregated.[3]

Though given enormous credit by the comments of Foner and other historians for his "tireless advocacy" and the civil rights bill passed after his death, Sumner's last contribution to Black equality was also criticized for what it did not include. Along with the previously mentioned lack of school desegregation, it also lacked enforcement mandates and has usually been considered an anomaly in the history of race relations after the Supreme Court ruled it unconstitutional in 1883 ... and because so few Southern Blacks of the time were willing to use it when discriminated against, rendered it a "dead-letter law" in the Court's opinion.[4]

On the other hand, current diversity experts referenced by historian

Barry Goldenberg, such as Penn State University Professor Kirt Wilson, have maintained the 1875 act had "extreme importance" as a symbolic presence within the African American community, especially through all the decades of "Jim Crow" segregation in the South leading to LBJ's previously mentioned landmark civil rights legislation in the 1960s. As a result, regardless of any deficiencies of the age in which it was enacted, Goldenberg emphasized it should always be recognized as a "milestone" in the evolution of America's civil rights history. He properly eulogized Sumner when he concluded:

> Charles Sumner was not a prototypical politician concerned only with his political career. Nor was he a man who succumbed to the prejudiced restraints of his era. Instead, Sumner was a visionary; he was a man who wholeheartedly believed that until the nation offered complete equal rights to Blacks in every possible arena, the country would continue to be an inhumane society that slandered its own claim of universal equality. Political shortcomings aside, he should be remembered for his vision; his unique accomplishments; and a life dedicated to civil rights in an unprecedented era.[5]

Unfortunately, as established, Sumner's grand vision would only be enforced and maintained for a short amount of time, and the man who managed to do it even that long was another of Goldenberg's "unknown architects," the before mentioned, two-term president, Ulysses Grant. While always better recognized for his commanding generalship during the Civil War and especially the single-minded, win-at-all-cost mentality so necessary to bringing the nation's greatest conflict to a final resolution, Grant's presidency has generally been best remembered for some noteworthy scandals, particularly the so-called "Whisky Ring," whereby distillers and federal officials were diverting liquor taxes into their own pockets, and Credit Mobilier, the name of a railroad construction company founded upon a scheme to defraud the U.S. Treasury during the linking of the East and West Coasts by rail. In addition, his oversight of the financial Panic of 1873 has always been questioned. All three served to tarnish his presidential legacy and compromise his overall standing among U.S. chief executives, but none of those ever reduced his fame, leaving him one of the most revered and popular Americans ever.

Having played such a leading role in the war and its resolution, Grant came to office believing African Americans' right to vote would be essential to successful Reconstruction and that Black political support would be equally essential to keeping the Republican Party in power. For both of those reasons, Goldenberg contended that Grant's influence on Negro suffrage provided lasting benefit in the nation's rehabilitation and struggle for civil rights despite almost immediate indications of voter discrimination in the South.[6]

9. "Glorious Failure" or What Might Have Been 115

Despite having been part of the Johnson administration, "the new president felt an overwhelming responsibility to protect the results of the costly war" that he as much as anyone had propagated. Also, according to Goldenberg, he understood that reuniting the country with the emancipated slaves was a "very fragile proposition" and felt duty bound by the war, an attitude that not only made but kept him a veritable symbol for African Americans anxious about their civil rights. As to his dedication to the Negro race, he once stated: "I hope sincerely that the colored people of the nation may receive protection, which the laws have given them. They shall have all my efforts to secure such protection and they should prove by their acts their advancement, prosperity, and obedience to the laws worthy of all privileges the government has bestowed [and] by their future conduct prove themselves deserving of all they now claim."[7]

Grant also called "the sacred heart" of Reconstruction "protecting the Negro in his new freedom," and to do that he continued to align himself with the Republican Party to ensure that Union victory in the war would translate into establishing and protecting the rights of Southern Blacks. Again according to Goldenberg, he "fought" to ensure military protection for African Americans in the South by enforcing the Reconstruction Acts and "pushed" for ratification of the Fifteenth Amendment, which guaranteed continuation of the five Southern military districts in order to contain lynchings and other forms of assault on the South's new Black citizenry. To his way of thinking, ratification was a necessary component of each Southern state's reunification process and when the Fifteenth Amendment

Although often cast as a scandal-marred president following his glorious military career as overall commander of the winning Union armies in the Civil War, Ulysses Grant does deserve credit for the role he played in African American civil rights during his eight years in the White House. Under Grant's determined oversight, Black citizenship was allowed to gain a foothold in the South (Library of Congress Prints and Photographs Division—Reproduction Number LC-USZ62-79351).

was finally sufficiently ratified and added to the U.S. Constitution on February 3, 1870, he called its prevention of a citizen's "race, color, or previous solitude" from affecting his right to vote anywhere in the United States, "the most important event since the nation came to life." Without question, his personal popularity played a major role in its passage, helping to ensure 28 of 37 states voted for ratification.[8]

With what Goldenberg termed a "methodical approach" throughout his first term, Grant was responsible for the "relative stability" of this "unprecedented time in American history." While striving to maintain "sectional peace," he had to do so without enacting policies that would put the Republican Party in political jeopardy. Nonetheless, under his watch, the Enforcement Acts of 1870 and 1871 and the Ku Klux Klan Act of 1871 granted the federal government "unprecedented power to protect Black Americans."[9]

Standing in stark contrast to the administration of Johnson, Grant's embrace of Black America ushered in a time of change, at least temporarily, and nothing exemplified that change more than the presence of African American officeholders populating courthouses and statehouses throughout the South and even the national capitol. Philip Dray's book *Capitol Men* memorializes this unique group of Black officeholders, who filled local positions like county tax assessor and sheriff, all the way up to two Black Southern senators, Mississippi's Hiram Revels and Blanche Bruce (when state legislatures still decided U.S. senators), as well as seven Southern Black congressmen between 1870 and 1877. Dray even related how South Carolina, the birthplace of Southern secession, would hold its convention to write a new, post-war state constitution with 77 of its 124 total delegates being Black, and how it would become one of three Deep South states, along with Mississippi and Louisiana, to send mostly African Americans to Congress during the Reconstruction years.[10]

Along with the Freedmen's Bureau, which had been set up to assist the newly freed slaves with their transition to emancipation, another private organization begun in the North during the war, the Union League, also came to the aid of the freedmen in their conversion to citizenship, helping them with land and labor issues. Aligned with the Republican Party, it was a springboard for identifying capable Southern Blacks for government service, mostly charismatic men who largely came from the African American clergy ... ministers like South Carolina's Richard "Daddy" Cain, who would serve one term in the State Senate and two in the U.S. House between 1868 and 1879. Despite real strides in universal education for Southern Whites as well as Blacks during Reconstruction, including the first public schools in the South and the first historically Black colleges, as well as "the forging of Black political know-how and leadership," according to Dray, the brief,

9. "Glorious Failure" or What Might Have Been   117

approximately eight-year run of African American officeholders would end when federal intervention in local politics became too much for Northern voters to stomach or stay involved with once national attention became diverted by things like the Panic of 1873.[11]

Meanwhile, in addition to the triumph of Radical Republicanism in the Reconstruction process of the mid- to late 1860s, the popular, eight-year presidency of Grant with his pro–African American support system, and the brief surge of Black officeholders in the South during his administration, there were a number of other Southern developments resulting from the aftermath of the Sumner-Johnson, congressional-presidential political warfare. Among those with lasting significance was the very necessary economic offshoot of slavery—sharecropping—as a new labor arrangement was needed to accommodate both post-war Southern landowners and the newly emancipated slaves in their sudden need for personal income and a means of family sustenance. Another was growing Southern White resistance to what had been deemed Negro rule, which could be any situation that reminded Whites of the suddenly equal standing of African Americans in their midst. Also, the influx of Northern businessmen, speculators, and opportunists in the South, the so-named "Carpetbaggers," who were initially welcomed because of the much-needed, post-war financial capital they contributed, before becoming demonized for their unexpected influence in local politics and economies. There were the previously mentioned Black Codes, colluded restrictions by Southern Whites designed to keep African Americans economically dependent and later to curtail political or judicial participation, as well as secret societies like the Ku Klux Klan and others that introduced organized terror to the Southern landscape in an effort to intimidate Black citizenship through group violence under the cover of darkness and disguise. And ultimately, out of the tragedy of Reconstruction lasting such a short time, there was the emergence of the so-called "Lost Cause" mentality, the South's mythical attachment to the defeated Confederacy and its heroes despite its connection to slavery. Memorialized and past down from generation to generation of White Southerners, it relentlessly re-enforced institutional segregation of the races as the accepted (and preferred) Southern way of life for decades.[12]

According to H.W. Brands in *American Colossus*, following the presidential election (and bargain) of 1876, the former White ruling classes of the South almost immediately regained political power in a takeover and backlash proudly referred to as "Redemption." The White North basically stood aside to better consolidate the country and restart economic prosperity in the coming age of industrialization and technological advancement. That would be priority numero uno for both the Republicans and Democrats in the last quarter of the 19th century. Of that same time, Jon

Meacham would acknowledge: "The post 1877 period was bleak" for Southern Blacks. He would also quote a former slave, who said, "The whole South—every state in the South—had got into the hands of the very men who held us as slaves" and that's how it would remain until another Washington war to be covered later in this book—one involving another President Johnson, but that one on the side of civil rights.[13]

SECTION FOUR

Crusade for the League
Woodrow Wilson vs. Henry Cabot Lodge

10

Political Enemies on a Collision Course

Like the Southern football rivalry between the University of Georgia and Georgia Tech that has always hyped its annual games as "Clean, Old Fashioned Hate," perhaps no political rivalry in American history could be characterized so aptly as the one that developed between President Woodrow Wilson and Massachusetts Senator Henry Cabot Lodge during the decade before 1920. From the landmark, four-nominee presidential campaign of 1912 that famously split the Republican Party and gave Wilson the victory, through World War I and the resulting Treaty of Versailles, theirs was a rivalry that got personal and left a lasting stain on U.S. international affairs and American foreign policy.[1]

Lodge, the great grandson of George Cabot—one of the wealthiest New England merchants and shippers of the 19th century—grew up a member of one of Boston's most prominent families and in a home where our previously reviewed Charles Sumner was a frequent guest. Along with Sumner, in fact, Lodge would become one in a series of high-profile senators from the "Bay State" that started with Daniel Webster and would later include such recent political luminaries as Ted Kennedy, John Kerry, and Elizabeth Warren. Certainly a well-known group, it also included the first popularly elected African American senator, Edward Brooke, in the midst of the Civil Rights Movement of the 1960s—a fact that would have obviously made Senator Sumner very proud.[2]

Born in 1850, Lodge was old enough to remember the Sumner visits, the Civil War, and the assassination of Abraham Lincoln in 1865, and he would eventually aspire to become a reform-minded entrant into local politics over the objections of his entrepreneurial family, winning election to the Massachusetts House of Representatives at age 39 after graduating from Harvard and beginning his professional life as a history instructor at his alma mater. While in that role, he also established a long history of his own as an author, writing and editing numerous historical narratives and biographies, including one of the best on his own great-grandfather, *The Life and Letters of George Cabot*.[3] By the 1880s, while serving as chairman of the Republican State Central Committee and as chief architect for the state's party platform, his ever-expanding coterie of cultural and political friends would encourage his political aspirations. One of those would be lifelong friend and confidant Theodore Roosevelt. Already a New York assemblyman although eight years Lodge's junior, the hyperenergetic "TR," as he would come to be known throughout his meteoric rise to the U.S. presidency at age 43 (still the youngest ever), had actually been a student at Harvard while Lodge was an instructor, but they would not cement their long political relationship until working together at the 1884 Republican Convention in Chicago. There, with Lodge also running for the U.S. House, they were reluctantly forced to support the party's nominee, James G. Blaine, the secretary of state for both the assassinated James Garfield (1881) and his vice presidential successor Chester Arthur (1882), but also a very polarizing figure during earlier years as the leader of one faction of the Republican Party while both Speaker of the House and a senator from Maine. Blaine would lose to New York reform Governor Grover Cleveland, the first Democratic president since before the Civil War, and Lodge would also lose in his initial bid for Congress.[4]

The election year of 1884 would prove one of reassessment for Republicans, as young

One of a long line of influential Massachusetts senators, Henry Cabot Lodge was a leading voice of the Republican Party for four decades. As the closest political friend of President Theodore Roosevelt, he was also the best-known political enemy of President Woodrow Wilson and is best remembered for his leadership of the Senate opposition to the League of Nations that Wilson conceived at the end of World War I (Library of Congress Prints and Photographs Division—Reproduction Number LC-USZ62-72073).

party stalwarts like Lodge and Roosevelt sought to distance themselves from the political arena—TR in the wilds of North Dakota to try cattle ranching (while he also struggled to recover from the sudden, unrelated deaths of his wife and mother on the same day), and Lodge by returning to his editorial endeavors, including a book on the *Works of Alexander Hamilton* and as president of the *Boston Daily Advertiser* "in order," in his own words, "to make it a strong Republican newspaper."[5] Both would return to politics in 1886, with Roosevelt the loser this time in the New York City mayoral race as the Republican nominee and decided underdog in a three-man race, while Lodge would also get another party nod and win in his second try for the U.S. House from Massachusetts' heavily industrialized 6th District north of Boston.[6]

Theirs would be a political friendship forged by identical views on most issues and one able to stand the test of time by constant communication, discussion, and reinforcement. When TR first moved to Washington as an appointee of Republican President Benjamin Harrison on the federal Civil Service Commission for six years (1889–1895), he would begin his life in the nation's capital by lodging at Congressman Lodge's home. Very often, in fact, according to Roosevelt biographer H.W. Brands, Lodge was the only person outside TR's immediate family circle "to whom he could entrust his feelings," while Pulitzer Prize winning historian Doris Kearns Goodwin went a step further in her book *The Bully Pulpit*, when she pointed out that Lodge was TR's "closet friend for more than a quarter century." And Lodge biographer John Garraty obviously concurred, when he wrote: "The friendship of these two men was fascinating; it grew out of their early political adventures yet soon came to transcend politics completely."[7]

All of that to say…. Henry Cabot Lodge and Theodore Roosevelt shared the same political opinion and attitude on just about anything or anyone they encountered in their nearly 30 years of partnership in the Republican Party, including how they both felt about Democrat Woodrow Wilson, the 28th president of the United States and the great antagonist they would criticize, challenge, and ultimately confront in the very public sphere of foreign policy before, during, and after the First World War. While Wilson would come to be regarded as one of our more successful presidents by most historians, to the two of them he was anathema and the wrongheaded villain at the head of American government at a most inopportune time.[8] But who was this Democratic sorcerer, who suddenly rose from the ivy-covered walls of academia to national political prominence, and how did he come to inspire such political vitriol from the two Republicans most confounded by his presence and persona on the national stage?[9]

While Lodge was the product of an elite Northeastern entrepreneurial family and Roosevelt the scion of an old New York City family of Dutch heritage and community commitment, Wilson was the son of a preacher man, a Southern based Presbyterian minister, to be specific, who was born in Staunton, Virginia, and spent most of his formative years growing up in Augusta, Georgia, and Columbia, South Carolina. From there, he spent one year at Davidson College in North Carolina before transferring to Princeton University, the previous College of New Jersey from its founding in 1746 and the fourth oldest college or university in the nation, with the same kind of upper-crust, "Ivy League" education as what Lodge and Roosevelt had both enjoyed at Harvard, the nation's oldest institution of higher learning (1636). In other words, while the lineages and childhoods of these future political antagonists were very different, their educational backgrounds were similar.[10]

One other marked difference was the sectional legacies from whence they came, with Wilson harboring the innate racial prejudices and attitudes of a Southern boy who was nine years old when the Civil War ended and who would return south after graduating from Princeton to study law and enlist in a law firm in the heart of the segregated "New South," Downtown Atlanta, Georgia (1886). Although TR, whose mother hailed from Roswell, Georgia, heard family tales of heroic uncles serving in the Confederate Navy, his young allegiance was always to the Union, just as Lodge would grow up to the sound of Civil War fife and drum and never forget lessons about the North being right and the South wrong.[11]

While impossible to totally grasp the political esprit de corps that existed between Lodge and Roosevelt, it is instructive to see what the former had to say about the latter even when TR bolted the Republican Party in the election of 1912. Even then, although ever the party loyalist, Lodge would cheerily comment: "Theodore remains one of the most loveable as well as cleverest and most daring men I have ever known. The more I see of him, as the fellow says in the play, 'the more I love him.'" Nonetheless, that election would come the closest to disrupting their friendship while also setting the stage for Lodge's eventual Washington war with Wilson.[12]

In 1892, Lodge was elected to the U.S. Senate after three terms in the House. It was the start of a senatorial run that would last 32 years, ended only by his death in office in 1920. During the earliest years of that same span, TR would go from the Washington-based Civil Service Commission to a series of government positions that put him on a rapid trajectory towards the presidency, including his start as a news-making president of the New York City Board of Police Commissioners in 1895; his 1897 return to Washington as assistant secretary of the Navy; his recruitment and leadership of an all-volunteer cavalry regiment in the 1898 Spanish-American War (remembered famously as "Roosevelt's Rough Riders"); his heroic fame from that venture, which catapulted him to the governorship of New

York in 1899; and reluctantly, his party-mandated acceptance of the vice presidency under President William McKinley in 1901. He would only have the VP role for six months as a result of McKinley becoming the third of four American presidents to be assassinated when he was shot in Buffalo, New York, which suddenly elevated TR to the White House. Throughout that succession of jobs, Senator Lodge was always consulted and often aided each stop along Roosevelt's way, especially in his assistant secretary appointment, his special military deployment, and even in convincing his acceptance of the VP role after "ulteriorly" promoting someone else first.[13]

Meanwhile, Wilson's ascension to the top of Democratic politics was much more surprising and much less scripted. Despite the study of law on his own after dropping out of the University of Virginia Law School for health reasons, leading to his being admitted to the bar in 1882 and joining the previously mentioned Atlanta law firm, Wilson gave up being an attorney (a job he only wanted in hopes it might lead to a political career) and instead pursued what had become his more desired career as an educator. After he became the only future U.S. president to earn a PhD at Johns Hopkins University in Baltimore, Maryland (in political science), he authored a five volume *History of the American People* as well as a controversial treatise on *Congressional Government* before starting his teaching career in 1885 at Bryn Mawr College in Pennsylvania, a liberal arts school for women. He moved to Wesleyan University, an all-male school in Connecticut, to teach history in 1888. From there it was an easy choice to return to Princeton when the opportunity arrived to teach jurisprudence and political economy in 1890, a role he continued until becoming the 13th university president at age 46 in 1902. As such, he would transform Princeton from a venerable Ivy League college to a nationally recognized model of higher education by doing away with the big, impersonal lecture hall method of instruction in favor of smaller group settings; by redesigning the curriculum and reorganizing academic departments; and by attempting to abolish social cliques on campus, something that would, unfortunately, eventually prove his undoing at his alma mater. More importantly, it was during his eight-year tenure as university president that he actively embraced progressive politics.[14]

As a result, he was well positioned when New Jersey's Democratic Party hierarchy went looking for a gubernatorial candidate in 1911. New Jersey was in the midst of a run of five consecutive Republican governors when the state's most powerful Democratic boss, James Smith, Jr., decided a new kind of statewide candidate was needed to break the Republican string. In his *Wilson* biography, Scott Berg, a Princeton grad himself, uses Smith's terminology to reference his most famous fellow alum as "that Presbyterian priest" before also conceding that at a time when greedy business interests and corrupt political machines were under attack, "nobody" seemed more appropriate to articulate against such "special privilege than [Princeton's] politically untarnished moralist." Smith and his cronies also believed Wilson's political inexperience would leave him beholden to them and their guidance, basically allowing them to run state government if he won. Ironically, at the same time Wilson was involved in the previously alluded to conflict at Princeton with his Board of Trustees, which made it all the more convenient, attractive, and not particularly difficult for him to decide to resign and enter the political arena he had always wanted to try. The timing could not have been better.[15]

Making it known from the start that any effort to draft him for the governor's race would need to be unanimous, Wilson passed every test with the New Jersey Democratic Committee, while unbeknownst to him, he was also being sized up by influential *Louisville Courier Journal* Owner/Editor Henry Watterson and several other leading Democrats for a possible future presidential run. As amazing as that sounds, especially with the reminder Wilson had never held elected office, it was nonetheless true for a national Democratic Party just as desperate for a presidential winner, having had none since Cleveland's second, nonconsecutive win in 1892, as it was the frustrated "Garden State" Dems. So, at the urging of Watterson and *North American Review* Editor George Harvey, the suddenly in-demand academic, progressive, reform-minded Woodrow Wilson became the 1910 New Jersey Democratic gubernatorial nominee—with the potential, strange as it seemed, of a U.S. presidential run only two years later (1912).[16]

The son of a Presbyterian minister, Woodrow Wilson was raised in the South during the Civil War and rose to prominence as a transformational educator at New Jersey's Princeton University. As the only U.S. president to obtain a PhD, he was also the first Democrat to earn consecutive terms since Andrew Jackson (Library of Congress Prints and Photographs Division—Reproduction Number LC-USZ62-13028).

With the support of the statewide Democratic machine, but much more the backing of the growing progressive movement (especially after he declared his independence from the surprised state party bosses), Wilson posted a relatively easy win over his Republican opponent en route to the governor's mansion. And just over a year later, he scored the Democratic nomination for president, a shockingly quick political ascent made easier by the backing of William Jennings Bryan, a three-time presidential loser but still a beloved party icon and orator. John Milton Cooper, another Wilson biographer, actually listed that as one of a trio of things the relative political newcomer did to earn the nomination. In total those were: "First made himself known throughout the country; second convinced Bryan Democrats that he was one of them; and finally, burnished his credentials as a progressive."[17]

An unexpected opponent would be Roosevelt. Back from African safari and a royal tour of Europe, the two of which absorbed his first 15 months away from the White House, TR had grown increasingly concerned and increasingly vocal about the lack of a progressive agenda being carried on by his hand-picked successor, William Howard Taft, another longtime friend who never really wanted the job of president but a Supreme Court judgeship instead. Taft, especially, would have rather not followed his charismatic and hugely popular predecessor. Nevertheless, he did so, accepting TR's anointment as heir apparent and expectations to continue his progressive lean in 1909. But influenced by the Republican "Old Guard" in Congress, who had seen their power diminish during the Roosevelt years, Taft refused to be cowed by his forerunner's increasingly public critiques of his administration and vowed to fight for his re-nomination rather than be pushed into one-term irrelevance by, in his own words, his "dangerous, egotistical, and demagogic" former friend.[18]

The 1912 Republican Convention, where this clash of wills would play out, was in Chicago and according to the two-part historical narrative of that event provided by James Chace:

> There would be a total of 1,078 delegates at the convention, with 540 needed to win the nomination. Roosevelt entered having won 278 delegates, Taft 48, and [Senator Robert] La Follette [of Wisconsin, another progressive] 36. The rest of the delegates would be chosen by district conventions, caucuses, state conventions, or some combination of those that nonetheless did not permit voters to directly elect delegates. At the end of the primary season, 254 seats were contested with the disputes to be adjudicated by the Republican National Committee before the convention opened. Since the Civil War, the Republican Party had become a party of conservatism, but the primaries indicated that the great mass of voters had clearly moved into the progressive column. [Yet] of the 254 contested seats, the National Committee awarded 235 to Taft and [only] 19 to Roosevelt. There [was] no question TR was entitled to more delegates. Roosevelt's own estimate was that he should have 80 or 90 more [and if he] had just won 70 of the contested seats, he would have had enough to obtain the nomination.[19]

10. Political Enemies on a Collision Course

Two days after the convention began and the Republican National Committee's ruling on the contested delegates was endorsed by the credentials committee, every effort to rectify the obvious controversy was summarily rejected by the aforementioned Old Guard Republicans. As a result, the Roosevelt progressives walked out en masse and staged their own rump convention nearby, nominating TR under the banner of the new Progressive or "Bull Moose" Party. The Republican split was official, and Governor Wilson suddenly found himself not only the Democratic nominee, but the prohibitive favorite in a presidential race that would feature both Taft and Roosevelt. Also added to this four-way mix would be Eugene Debs, a political activist and trade unionist nominated by the Socialist Party of America, who one writer termed "the country's most appealing radical politician" in an era of working class revolutionary change in other parts of the world (namely Russia), and Debs would win six percent of the popular vote, the largest share ever for a socialist candidate in America.[20]

At the same time, professing a brand of progressivism known as "New Freedom," Wilson would capture 42 percent of the popular vote to easily best Roosevelt's runner-up 27 percent, most of which was driven by his competing and equally progressive "New Nationalism." The more conservative incumbent, Taft, got only 23 percent. Nonetheless, Taft's total proved more than enough to deny Roosevelt a third, non-consecutive term. The vote for Taft would also be the worst ever for a presidential incumbent running for a second term, a clear sign of just how impactful TR's entry had been and how damaging

Among the most popular Americans ever and still the youngest U.S. president, Theodore Roosevelt would fail in his bid for a third (nonconsecutive) term and famously split the Republican Party by running as a third-party candidate. Pictured here in his later years, he would remain a constant critic of Woodrow Wilson, the progressive Democrat he lost to in 1912 (Library of Congress Prints and Photographs Division—Reproduction Number LC-DIG-ggbain-21824).

it was to the Republican Party. On the other hand, Wilson's seemingly out-of-nowhere victory and his eventual re-election four years later (1916) would make him the first Democrat to win consecutive presidential terms since the party's legendary progenitor, Andrew Jackson, in 1832.[21]

Amidst all the resulting Republican Party fallout was the most obvious disparagement ever between the Republicans' foremost party allies, TR and Lodge. According to one Lodge biographer, "He was 'reduced to gloomy desperation'" when he stated: "To the best of my ability, I have fought the battles of the Republican Party for the past 30 years. To the Republican Party I owe all that I have had in public life. With its policies and principles, I am in full accord and I believe in the policies set forth at Chicago." And with that depressed admission, he had backed the party's nominee and not his best friend. Regardless, another Lodge biographer noted that by refusing to consider Lodge's opposition or even take it seriously, TR had placed a temporary strain on their relationship, but not one that couldn't be overcome. Biographically speaking, "No hot words" would ever be exchanged between them and even during the heat of the 1912 campaign they continued to correspond.[22]

To the contrary, rather than cast stones at each other over TR's decision to break with the party and Lodge's decision to back the Republican incumbent over his closest friend, what might have been arrows of distrust or hurtful disloyalty were tactfully sheathed and laid aside in wait for the new administration. And just as "hell hath no fury like a woman scorned," so too American history hath no fury like a Roosevelt wrongfully denied a return to the White House by his former party and the fellow progressive whose cunning entry by the Democrats had relegated him to only a share of the electorate's progressive vote. Is there any doubt the majority of Republicans and additional progressives would have favored one of the most popular presidents ever if Taft had only stepped aside? Besides, the newcomer, Wilson, had essentially stolen his thunder by putting the Democrats on the same, progressive path that he (TR) had been first to advocate.

"Despite TR's early doubts that he could win against an entrenched party system, defeat was bitter, above all because so many of his oldest political allies had turned their backs on him, but he was constitutionally incapable of lengthy depression." So confirmed Chace in his synopsis of the 1912 campaign and election. At the same time, Wilson's first term would witness a surge in domestic legislation in keeping with the new president's political science background and congressional expertise. Among his first term accomplishments would be the lowering of tariff rates; the creation of the Federal Reserve System to make the U.S. money supply more adaptable to changing economic conditions; the establishment of a National Parks Service; and creation of the Federal Trade Commission to allow small businesses to better compete with big ones. Along with such domestic accomplishments, an insurrection in neighboring Mexico brought reactionary Victoriano Huerta to power in 1913, prompting Wilson to refuse Mexican recognition, which threatened relations between the two countries to the point of possible armed conflict and forced Huerta, under pressure, to resign in 1914. In his place, Wilson chose to back Venustiano Carranza, but he, too, failed to maintain order south of the border, as revolutionaries led by the bandit Pancho Villa took over the northern half of the country. This time, Wilson dispatched U.S. troops across the border to try and capture Villa, but throughout this Mexican entanglement, the President became the subject of repeated Republican attacks. While accepting of his domestic agenda for the most part, TR and Lodge became his most constant critics over foreign policy.[23]

In late February 1815, TR threatened: "Lord, I am feeling warlike with this administration," while by that spring "Lodge had become convinced that with the possible exception of James Buchanan, Woodrow Wilson was the worst president in American history." That warning and verdict were recounted by Berg and Garraty, respectively, in their biographies from a time of reunited and growing consternation by both Roosevelt and Lodge over the policies Wilson was undertaking. The latter of the two biographers also quoted Lodge with the following, very personal condemnation:

> Woodrow Wilson is a self-seeking, unprincipled, egotistical, timid, and narrow-minded politician. He has a talent for felicitous expression and for mouthing high-sounding principles, but he has no policy other than his own aggrandizement. In domestic affairs, he is a demagogue, in foreign affairs a coward. He cannot get along with men who are his intellectual equals, consequently he surrounds himself with sycophants and second raters and drives them relentlessly to do his bidding. Essentially he is a man of words, not a man of action. He is stubborn, but when faced with a crisis of his own intransigence he collapses, disregarding the implications of his own acts.[24]

Those sentiments would precede Wilson's decision to finally take the United States into the First World War. After earning re-election in 1916 when "He Kept Us Out of War" was both reality and his campaign slogan, the conflict that had embroiled Europe ever since the over-reactive summer of 1914 finally reached America, as U.S. shipping interests came under attack by German U-boats (aka submarines) in international waters as they tried to short-circuit trade with our principal European allies (and Germany's principal enemies), Great Britain and France. Once American merchant ships came under attack on a regular basis, Wilson realized staying out was no longer an option. For Lodge and Roosevelt, it was about time. Both had been constant critics of the President's lack of aggression, especially in his response to the sinking of the *Lusitania* in 1915, a British luxury liner with 120 Americans on board, and again with the 1917 interception of the infamous "Zimmerman Telegram," an official German communiqué to the Mexican government proposing a military alliance between the two countries with the promised return of previously lost territory in the American Southwest should Mexico take the side of Germany in the ongoing international struggle. In both instances, TR failed to contain his martial spirit or harsh rhetoric, as he denounced Wilson's reluctant policies (aka lack of backbone) in the face of German atrocities and provocation.[25]

Needless to say, upon America's entry into the war and with all four of his sons headed to the front lines, TR would become the war effort's biggest cheerleader with Lodge and the rest of the congressional Republicans in lockstep. On April 2, 1917, when Wilson went before a joint session of Congress to ask for a declaration of war, the cheers and applause were "deafening," and Arthur Link in his book *Woodrow Wilson and the Progressive Era* wrote that even Lodge had to admit the President's speech "epitomized his own thoughts." It would be the beginning of America's involvement in foreign wars and just as with World War II two decades later, there's little doubt U.S. entry on the side of the Western Allies tipped the balance in bringing the so-called "War to End All Wars" to a final conclusion and armistice a year and a half later, November 11, 1918.[26]

To consummate a treaty and devise a lasting worldwide peace, Wilson felt no one could possibly be better suited to head the American delegation to Paris, France and the Palace of Versailles than himself. He would be one of the Big Four along with the victorious leaders of France, Great Britain, and Italy, and a world hero because of his proposed "Fourteen Points" for the treaty, including the formation of a League of Nations to arbitrate and deter any future conflicts between nations and as a means of avoiding another world war. As Berg emphasized, "The eyes of the world were on one man."[27]

Embraced by the other allied nations for his leadership in negotiating the Treaty of Versailles, including Germany's acceptance of blame for the war and its required compensation to the winning Western Allies as a result, Wilson would win the Nobel Peace Prize a year later (1919), but fail to win approval from his own country for the League he had so determinedly conceived and built into the treaty. While the rest of the world looked to Wilson and America as the new Western colossus in defining a new world order rather than the crumbling monarchies and damaged democracies of Europe, the U.S. Senate of Henry Cabot Lodge did not. Rather than just following the lead of the man who had been the toast of Europe and the lead arbiter in the new international makeup, Republican leadership in the Senate would prove a lot more subjective in its approach to the treaty than the supposed Democratic "savior," who had orchestrated its content and

10. Political Enemies on a Collision Course 131

Shown here riding in an open carriage through the streets of Paris in 1919 with French Prime Minister Raymond Poincare, Woodrow Wilson (left) was viewed as something of a savior when he arrived in Europe to assume leadership of the peace conference that would officially end World War I. Having brought America into the war, he was expected to again lead in the new world order (Library of Congress Prints and Photographs Division—Reproduction Number LC-DIG-ggbain-27985).

brought it home in glory to be rubber stamped. After all, they had really not been included among the U.S. commission that went "over there" with him to draw it up, with only one token Republican, a retired diplomat, among the official U.S. contingent, and they were wary of America committing to too much and what that might portend for its future. To Lodge and his Senate cabal, one foreign war was enough regardless of the President's stringent blessing and what had been approved on his watch in France. Once again, political battle lines were drawn on Pennsylvania Avenue with an unsuspecting general public still celebrating the war's end and the return of the American "Doughboys" of the American Expeditionary Force from Europe, while at the same time the U.S. government embarked on a very contested state of affairs.[28]

11

The Ammunition of Lasting Animosity

Among the many major American happenings of 1918, one that did not garner headlines or political debate was one that transpired in the U.S. Senate, when New Hampshire's Jacob Gallinger died. Gallinger had been the leader of the Republican caucus for almost six years or ever since the retirement of Illinois' Shelby Cullom, who had inherited that same status from Rhode Island's legendary Nelson Aldrich, truly the leader of the Republican Old Guard at the end of the 1900s and start of the 20th century. Based on seniority, the new chairman of the Republican Caucus in 1918 was to be Henry Cabot Lodge and "he gloried in his new title," according to Richard Baker and Neil MacNeil in their combined history, *The American Senate*. Writing to his good friend TR at the time, Lodge would proclaim: "I am to be at the center to which everyone must come."[1]

Lodge was 68 years old when the First World War ended, and the Senate Republicans regained a majority in the midterm elections that same November. Not that being the Senate majority leader before that became an officially used title in 1925 came without sometimes mutinous caucus members, as Lodge would learn from a group within his party that came to be known as the "Irreconcilables." Led by outspoken William Borah of Idaho, they verged on being a separate party within the party, but they were still part of the bare bones Republican majority the midterms had fashioned and Lodge was anxious to make that majority work for the American people, who had made their feelings about President Woodrow Wilson's peace-making agenda obvious in the recent elections.[2]

It was made obvious by the fact the President had actually pressed for the election of Democrats in 1918 to help ensure his own peace prerogatives would be adopted in the coming year. In stressing his need for a Democratic support system while at the same time urging national unity in the war's final weeks, Wilson made what many considered a tactical error when he made the following appeal directly to the American people:

11. The Ammunition of Lasting Animosity

If you approve of my leadership and wish me to continue to be your unembarrassed spokesman in affairs at home and abroad, I earnestly beg that you express yourself immediately to that effect by returning a Democratic majority to both the Senate and the House of Representatives. I am your servant and will accept your judgment without cavil, but my power to administer the great trust assigned to me by the Constitution would be seriously impaired should your judgment be adverse, and I must frankly tell you so because so many critical issues depend upon your verdict. The return of a Republican majority to either House of Congress would, moreover, certainly be interpreted on the other side of the water as a repudiation of my leadership. In ordinary times I would not feel at liberty to make such a public appeal, but these are not ordinary times.[3]

Given what had been, for the most part, Republican adherence to the interests of national unity in a time of war, this statement injected politics into the coming peace process and provided a new source of ammunition to further fuel the animosity of the administration's chief Republican critics—critics like Roosevelt and Lodge. As biographers would note, "criticism and ridicule" were immediately hurled at Wilson for "lowering himself" to politicize the ongoing war effort, while also providing the opportunity for Lodge to sarcastically respond: "The President has thrown off the mask. [His] only test of loyalty is loyalty to one man no matter what he does."[4]

That was, however, but the first round of ammunition Wilson would load into Republican guns aimed at his leadership as the war played out and peace came into focus. Another would be the previously mentioned illogical makeup of the U.S. peace commission he selected. Behind the scenes, the Senate Republican leader was seething over the President ignoring consideration of any Senate Republican and particularly any Republican member of his Senate Foreign Relations Committee for the American team. After all, that would be the committee that any peace treaty would need to pass muster with. Nothing against Henry White, who was a Republican in good standing in addition to having been an ambassador to both Italy and France, but Lodge would have preferred a member of his own Senate committee and the fact no committee members were even consulted about the President's choice, much less considered, was for the senator from Massachusetts, "unforgivably insulting" in the words of one of his biographers. "The President has anointed himself with the appointment of Henry White," Lodge reportedly "snorted" upon seeing a list of the so-named "American Peace Commission." That same biographer, Kurt Schriftgiesser, also speculated as to how Wilson might have changed the fate of his League if only, he had made the effort to include one of Lodge's Republican Caucus colleagues in the peace process. Would that approach and inclusion on the front end have assuaged any of the majority leader's animosity on the back end of Senate consideration for the Treaty of

Versailles? Possibly but highly unlikely, it would seem, given the disdain Lodge and Wilson already felt for each other. At the same time, a little diplomatic honey in the midst of political vinegar wouldn't have hurt, as the succeeding months would clearly indicate.[5]

No, such was the passionate dislike of the President by both Lodge and his best friend, Theodore Roosevelt, that no outreach or olive branch by Wilson would have probably made a difference. Frank Cobb, an administration-friendly columnist of the time for the *New York World*, once stated that Lodge hated Wilson "as only a small-minded man can hate a great man," while Schriftgiesser even applied "Ovid's description of envy" to the Senator's demeanor at the mere mention of the President's name: "His face is livid; gaunt his whole body; his breast is green with gall; his tongue drips poison...."[6]

As overly dramatic as that example might seem, there was no denying that Lodge was plotting, scheming, and anxious for the moment he might deal America's suddenly idolized chief executive a decisive blow once he returned from his European sojourn. Just as anxious for the Presbyterian minister son's comeuppance, Roosevelt was a bed-ridden man by the time the World War I armistice was signed that fall, but even in the final months of his life (TR would die in early January 1919 at only 60 years of age), the former president still hated Woodrow Wilson. Despite the recent blow of his youngest son being killed in the war, TR along with Lodge determined to use their combined influence with Ambassador White to infiltrate and possibly even subvert the President's commission before it embarked. "Peace," they jointly emphasized to White, "must be determined by the United States and its allies. And it must be imposed upon Germany, who must be forced to accept terms, however harsh." That's the way Schriftgiesser explained their message to the only Republican on the commission. In much the same way, John Garraty made mention of the fact White's position would be difficult, especially as Republican pressure was brought to bear, including a memorandum about acceptable peace terms that should leave Germany "impotent" and include the postponement of any League of Nations discussion. At the same time, Lodge avoided the idea of America adopting an "isolationist attitude toward the rest of the world" even though much of the Republican rank and file would have supported such a concept. Their joint intervention with Ambassador White would prove to be their last shared political purpose, as TR died shortly thereafter, "of course, a hard blow for Lodge," who eulogized his great friend of 35 years with a formal tribute in the Senate.[7]

Regardless of their intercession with White, however, the majority of the peace process went about the way Wilson would have wanted it—or at least the way he and his co-lead negotiators from France and Britain would

11. The Ammunition of Lasting Animosity

have it. For Wilson, it was mostly about his dream of a new world order or League, while for France's Georges Clemenceau and Britain's David Lloyd George it was always about German acceptance of responsibility and payment of reparations to their battered nations given their immense wartime losses in money and men. Leaving Germany prostrate was the Allied European goal, but Wilson did not wish to condone or oversee a devastated German economy because of what he perceived as its financial importance to the whole continent.[8]

All toll, Wilson was in France four separate times to work on the treaty, December 13–25, 1918; January 7–February 14, 1919; March 14–18, 1919; and the last time, June 20–28, 1919. The Treaty of Versailles was officially signed (amidst great solemnity rather than pomp) on June 28, 1919, and on July 8, Wilson arrived back in the United States for the final time to what Berg termed "the largest crowd that had ever greeted him on the sidewalks of Manhattan."[9]

Despite torrential rain in Washington two days later, July 10, 1919, the President travelled the short distance down Pennsylvania Avenue to

An armistice on November 11, 1918, brought a stop to the First World War, but a peace treaty still had to be drawn up and signed to officially end hostilities and recognize the surrender of Germany. This was done during a conference involving hundreds of diplomats from all over the world at the Palace of Versailles outside Paris, France (Library of Congress Prints and Photographs Division—Reproduction Number LC-DIG-ppmsca-50568).

present the final draft of the treaty in person to the Senate. A welcoming committee that included Lodge, the nation's most senior senator, met him on the second floor of the Capitol and escorted him to the Senate Chamber. Upon seeing the 20 by 14 by six-inch document under his arm, Lodge is reputed to have asked, "Mr. President, can I carry the treaty for you?" to which Wilson supposedly responded, "Not on your life." He was about to become the first American president to hand deliver a treaty to the Senate and his entrance onto the Senate Floor received a standing ovation from many of those in attendance. The Republicans, however, "withheld their applause," according to Berg, foreshadowing events to come. Later, one GOP senator would also dismiss the President's speech that day as "soap bubbles of oratory and soufflé of praises," but through it all and despite the lukewarm Republican reception, Wilson was by then counting on American popular sentiment to ensure his League.[10]

Unfortunately, having been away from the U.S. so much with his concentration constantly on the treaty negotiations, the President did not fully comprehend the changes that had been taking place in the country since the war's end. For instance, prices in America had doubled between 1913 and 1919, and in just months had spiked by four percent. The U.S. media for the first time began to use the acronym HCL for "high cost of living." Strikes were threatened nationwide as the wartime economy changed over to peacetime, requiring adaptation by the labor force. Race riots erupted over bi-racial competition for jobs for the first time, especially with all the returning American Doughboys, Black and White. A post-war recession was all but inevitable.[11]

Wilson biographer John Milton Cooper, Jr., confirmed "public opinion had hardened" since the President's next to last trip to France and an organization named the League for the Preservation of American Independence (or simply "Independence League") was already trying to mobilize anti–League sentiment using a variety of oratorical stars to make its points heard in an era before television or even radio (which did not proliferate in the U.S. until the 1920s), including senators like the previously mentioned "Bill" Borah and the equally high profile Hiram Johnson of California, both staunch isolationists and more opposed to any kind of international governing body than Lodge. At the same time, Lodge and Elihu Root, another close colleague and confidant of the deceased TR, had also adopted a strategy of attacking individual parts of the treaty, hoping to limit American commitment and participation in the League as a prerequisite for ratification.[12]

The President faced the choice of either staying in Washington, trying to deal with the recalcitrant Republican senators, or taking his arguments for the League directly to the American people, an outside-the-box strategy that would require him to make a speaking tour of the whole country to better educate the public on the need for U.S. leadership and treaty buy-in, including commitment to his League of Nations. Initially he tried the former, remaining in Washington during the hot summer months and somewhat still removed from the domestic violence underway over race, unemployment, strikes, and the conflict-causing inflation that was occurring all over the country. Concerns over his health began to creep into the public psyche, but that did not deter him from staging numerous one-on-one meetings with senators of both parties (but the vast majority Republicans), as he sought to change enough minds about the League concept to ensure its passage along with the rest of the treaty. That, however, would prove totally unsuccessful as time after time Republican senators expressed appreciation in the press for the President's "cordial" invitations, but also how their minds had not been changed and why reservations on the league had to be addressed (or incorporated) before ratification could (or would) take place.[13]

By August Wilson had all but given up on his man-to-man approach, partly because other domestic issues were demanding his time, but also because no bi-partisan headway had been made. The HCL that needed addressing on the domestic front was a lot less difficult than the H.C.L. (as in Henry Cabot Lodge) he was confronted with over the League. There were other parts of the treaty that a few, individual Republicans objected to, but nothing like their nearly unanimous objection to Article X—the proposition that called for each League member to "undertake to respect and preserve against external aggression the territorial integrity and existing political independence of all members of the League." As a result, Lodge had the votes needed to stop passage without the proposed reservations and Wilson knew it. Nonetheless, the President remained in a stern, uncompromising mood, which Lodge obviously heard about from all the previous White House meetings. In early August, Lodge also began to hold Senate hearings, calling on other members of the President's delegation to the peace conference to testify, including Secretary of State Robert Lansing, who underwent five hours of what Cooper termed "mostly hostile interrogation." Lodge, Johnson, and other members of the Foreign Affairs Committee were all disappointed with Lansing's testimony (with Lodge going so far as to call it "pathetic") as he sought to negotiate around or avoid entirely any personal disagreements he may have had with Wilson on the treaty's final form, obviously doing his best not to arouse potential conflict with his boss, the President.[14]

There were fleeting moments when bipartisan cooperation seemed possible, but by August, Wilson effectively killed any compromise hopes when Lansing reported the President "would have none of it" in response to

Once the Treaty of Versailles with its League of Nations was signed by the Allied Powers and Germany, officially ending World War I and attempting to police the world's nation states in the future, the treaty went to the United States Senate for ratification. There it received rough treatment from Republican leader Henry Cabot Lodge and his Foreign Relations Committee, as depicted in this cartoon (Library of Congress Prints and Photographs Division—Reproduction Number LC-USZ62-8828).

just one accommodation with a few of the "milder reservationists." In that moment, someone recalled, "His face took on that stubborn, pugnacious expression which comes whenever anyone tells him a fact which interferes with his plans," and shortly thereafter, according to Cooper, Wilson authorized the ranking Democrat on Chairman Lodge's Foreign Relations Committee to share with the press that "the President did not believe any compromise should be discussed or negotiated at that time."[15]

Eventually, Lodge felt he had waited long enough on potential compromise by the administration and, still seething over Wilson's arrogance in excluding anyone from his U.S. Senate Foreign Relations Committee on the peace commission, he elected to initiate discussion himself. On August 12 he rose in the Senate to specifically address the treaty's well-publicized

Article X. His speech that day, which would last two hours, included the following:

> I object in the strongest possible way to have the United States agree, directly or indirectly, to be controlled by a league, which may at any time and perfectly lawfully with the terms of [this] covenant, be drawn in to deal with internal conflicts in other countries no matter what those conflicts may be. In Article X, the United States is bound on the appeal of any member of the [proposed] league not only to respect but to preserve its independence and its boundaries, and that pledge we give must be fulfilled. I, for one, hope the day will never come when the United States [cannot] keep its promises [and as a result] without reservations, this treaty should not be acted upon in its current form.[16]

Again according to Wilson biographer A. Scott Berg, in a posthumously published account of the League dispute, Lodge would later go to "great lengths to insist he never harbored any 'personal hostility to Mr. Wilson,' but after years of disagreement with the President on practically every major issue, the majority leader's hostility towards him had steadily increased"— and everyone in attendance in the Senate that day knew it. And with that and "each remaining step in the process," Lodge would introduce a myriad of "stalling tactics" when it came to Senate consideration of the Treaty of Versailles. Over the next several days in mid–September, 50 amendments to the treaty were considered by the Senate Foreign Relations Committee. Different reports were presented, with the majority report not surprisingly in support of the reservations to Article X while "caustically" answering charges of delay by then emanating from the White House. On the other hand, the Democratic report opposed reservations and urged immediate ratification. Traditional backers of the President like the *New York Times* also began to print criticism of the Senate procrastination like the following:

> If the President's interpretation of the treaty and his straight forward replies to the Senators' questions have not removed from their minds all reasonable doubts and misgivings, then evidently nothing can and the country will be forced to the conclusion that their objections do not lie in the treaty or in the League covenant, but somewhere outside of both. If that be true, then the people must deal with this senatorial obstruction, for the President has exhausted the resources of reasoning and exposition.[17]

Another reason Lodge was stalling was because it had become obvious Republican objections to the League covenant did not necessarily mean opposition to the peace treaty, but everything had been written so that there was no way to separate the two for separate votes. Only with their reservations on Article X would the Republican majority condone ratification. In 45 days, Lodge's committee had considered what the Versailles peace commissioners had taken six months to accomplish. It challenged what it labeled Wilson's "autocratic methods" before ending up with multiple amendments and the four critical reservations for the administration to review, but it was already becoming obvious the President would never accept any of those or any other compromise.[18]

The President, in fact, had already begun a long and laborious cross-country tour, taking his treaty and his League directly to the people. Believing that the vast majority of Americans favored an immediate and lasting international peace—one without the threat of another world war—Wilson hoped to force the people's representatives in the Senate to back down in their opposition and vote to ratify the Treaty of Versailles in its entirety. To his stubborn way of thinking, changes were unnecessary and dangerous, with the rest of the world waiting on America to assume leadership of what it had already put in place. Oh, he had offered a few concessions before leaving on his whirlwind national tour in early September, including one asserting that action by the League was "to be regarded only as advice and leaves each Member State free to exercise its own judgment as to whether it is wise or practicable to act upon that advice or not," but still without mention of Congress. On the surface, this appeared a significant concession, but it was merely Wilson "trying to retain presidential flexibility" as well as his notion of "a moral obligation" to the other nations the U.S. had led in Paris, according to Cooper. Clearly, it was not going to move the bipartisan needle or else a visibly fatigued and, some would say, ill-looking president would not have boarded his presidential railcar, the *Mayflower*, for the planned month-long journey that would resemble the most ambitious presidential election campaigns of the era. Under gray skies the next day, Wilson's tour opened in Columbus, Ohio, to a capacity crowd of 4,000 at that city's Memorial Hall (an additional 2,000 people had to be turned away). That became common at each stop, as big crowds gathered in city auditoriums and smaller but equally interested turnouts occurred at small town railroad stations, where he would speak and shake hands from the train's rear platform. Typical of his message at each stop was the one reprinted by Berg that he delivered in Richmond, Indiana, where he said:

> The chief thing to notice about the treaty is that it is the first treaty ever made by great powers that was not made in their own favor. It is made for the protection of the weak peoples of the world and the aggrandizement of the strong. The extraordinary achievement of this treaty is that it gives a free choice to people who never could have won it for themselves. It is for the first time in the history of international transactions an act of systematic justice and not an act of grabbing and seizing.

Berg also asserted that at each stop along the way he would plaintively ask: "My fellow citizens, what difference does a political party label make when [all] mankind is involved?"[19]

11. The Ammunition of Lasting Animosity

The first week took him through Ohio, Indiana, Illinois, Iowa, Minnesota, South Dakota, and Nebraska. Cooper confirmed, "Never before had a president made so many personal appearances in so short an amount of time." He also made specific appeals and comparisons whenever he thought appropriate. To downtown St. Louis, Missouri, businessmen, he "extolled the benefits to be reaped by restoring international trade"; in Omaha, Nebraska, where his audience presumably included a lot of farmers, he said the international system minus Article X would be like a community where everyone had to defend their own land without law enforcement; in Sioux Falls, South Dakota, he "singled out mothers who had lost their sons" in what was already termed "The Great War"; and in Kansas City, Missouri, he maintained he was "fighting for something 'as great as the cause of mankind' itself." All the while, he was actually aiming his speeches to go beyond the people who came out to hear him. Through the press he aimed for a constant, daily barrage to the nation as a whole, as well as any senators back in Washington who might be influenced or at least swayed.[20]

Meanwhile, sharing the nation's front pages as Wilson's tour got underway were the four reservations to the League that Lodge's Foreign Relations Committee had decided upon, three of which asserted "the absolute right of any country to withdraw from the covenant and exempt domestic questions as well as America's longstanding Monroe Doctrine [opposing all European colonialism in the Western Hemisphere] from its jurisdiction." The fourth, according to Berg, "declined 'any obligation to preserve the territorial integrity or political independence of any other country,' including joining economic boycotts, employing American armed forces, or accepting any mandate except by act of Congress." An even bigger publicity coup for Lodge came in the middle of the President's tour, when his committee heard testimony from William Bullitt, a young U.S. diplomat who had resigned in protest during the Versailles Peace Conference and who produced a memorandum of conversation in which Secretary of State Lansing had condemned a sizeable portion of the treaty, including the League. In it, Lansing had apparently stated, "I consider that the League of Nations at present is entirely useless."[21]

Needless to say, as Cooper acknowledged, "Wilson was furious," and remained so even after Lansing telegraphed his own account, calling Bullitt's conduct and testimony "most despicable and outrageous." If not for being on the road, Wilson would have probably fired his secretary of state on the spot and after his return Lansing offered a letter of resignation. The damage, however, had already been done and events would soon make either of those outcomes irrelevant.[22]

In addition, to the League reservations sought by Lodge's committee, six amendments to the treaty overall were retained, most of which were intended to reflect flaws in the moralist posture of the President and his American negotiating team while in France. These amendments, however, were all voted down, with a number of Republicans joining most of the Democrats in the Senate to render any other considerations moot. Then it became time to debate the committee's recommended reservations. To the original four, more were added. Of the reservations, Garraty wrote: "Though some were unnecessary and others plainly motivated by political considerations, the chief purpose of most of them was to define the League obligations of the United States more specifically and to make it clear the right of Congress to control American performance of these duties." The final form of the one dealing with the by then controversial Article X read:

> The United States of America assumes no obligation to preserve the territorial integrity or political independence of any country or to interfere in controversies between nations under the provisions of Article X unless in any particular case the Congress, which under the United States Constitution has the sole power to declare war or authorize the employment of the military or naval forces of the United States of America, shall by act or joint resolution so provide.[23]

By mid–September, Wilson's tour had reached the West Coast, where the *Seattle Post-Intelligencer* reported on the President's speech as suggesting, "a man very much fatigued" in his delivery. In a humorous interlude at the Portland Auditorium in Oregon, he read an old newspaper quote from 1915 that "peace can only be maintained by putting behind it the force of united nations determined to uphold it and prevent wars" before revealing the speaker had been none other than the distinguished Massachusetts Senator Henry Cabot Lodge. Obviously enjoying this journalistic revelation from a few years before, the President quite naturally concurred before adding the punch line that he would look forward to the Senate leader's assistance in bringing about just such a result as soon as he got back to Washington—earning both laughter and applause from his amused audience. Afterwards, as he turned south to California, support for Wilson and the treaty was growing. Berg attested to as much by reporting a turnout of 12,000 to hear him at the Oakland Municipal Auditorium, 10,000 at Cal State Berkley's outdoor Greek Theater, and 30,000 at the San Diego Stadium, "where he experimented with a new electrical device called a 'voice phone.'" And then in Los Angeles—population 503,812 in those days—more than 200,000 people "greeted Wilson on the streets" for one of the city's most enthusiastic demonstrations up to that time. Even *Los Angeles Times* publisher Harry Chandler, a normally loyal Republican, was compelled to admit that Southern California was pro–League as much as six to one.[24]

11. The Ammunition of Lasting Animosity 143

Turning for home through the center of the country, stops included the Mormon Tabernacle in Salt Lake, Utah, where between 13,000 and 15,000 people packed the unventilated Temple Square hall, but where applause at news of the Senate's acceptance of the reservations led the President to react angrily and lash out at the largely conservative crowd with the comment: "Wait until you understand the meaning of it and if you have a knife in your hand with which you intend to cut out the heart of the covenant, then applaud," before arguing the reservations would undermine the moral obligation of the peace treaty. In Cheyenne, Wyoming, the next day, he maintained that Article X "cuts at the taproot of war" while urging all senators to realize that the reservations would "leave other nations to guess [at] what they felt obligated to do in each [future] instance. And in Denver, Colorado, early on September 25, 1919, the President of the United States 'painted'" what Cooper termed, "a picture of the next war [with] the last war's weapons being merely toys when compared to what would be unleashed the next time"—a war that "would be the destruction of mankind" and one for which he was for insurance against.[25]

Later that same day, 112 miles further south, the President's incredibly ambitious speaking tour would come to an abrupt end in Pueblo, Colorado, where he once again offered a picture of a thoroughly militarized America out of necessity should the United States not enter the League of Nations as specified in the Treaty of Versailles. His closing words were "We have accepted the truth and we are going to be led by it, and through us the world will come into pastures of quietness and peace such as the world has never dreamed of before."[26]

Defiant in his resolve for a treaty and a League of Nations that would usher in a new era of worldwide peace and international tranquility, those would be the last words he would ever offer in a presidential speech. As Cooper and Berg had both revealed earlier in their biographies, Wilson had become increasingly subject to mood swings for over a decade and had long been dealing with dormant arteriosclerosis—hardening of the arteries—first diagnosed when he was president at Princeton in 1906. As a result, under the prolonged pressure of the war, the peace conference to end all wars, and finally his defense of the League of Nations he had worked so hard to sell on the world stage, only to see it attacked by his own government, it was not all that surprising that he was not a healthy man by the time he rose to speak at the Colorado State Fairgrounds in Pueblo. So, it was also not surprising when the pace of world events, painstaking negotiations, and finally political rejection caught up with the stubborn idealist, whose second term international goals, unlike his first term domestic agenda, would not come true and effectively crash down upon him that day with the beginnings of what would ultimately be a stroke. Later that evening, back on the train with an "unbearable" headache that prevented sleep, the rest of his tour was canceled, and it was decided the President should be returned to Washington ASAP.[27]

Once back at the White House, Wilson went into seclusion. "Unquestionably," according to Berg, the speaking tour to save his League had wrought a tremendous personal toll and was probably never worth the effort he had put into it. Lodge and the Republicans were waiting when he returned. By this time, Lodge wanted the treaty and League destroyed. But although at least one of his biographers framed this objective in just such a no-nonsense manner, he also pointed out that Lodge was coy enough to proceed with caution. But as October 1919 dawned and then expired with still no signs of compromise, it became increasingly apparent to the Democratic minority, who without any new signals or guidance from a suddenly silent White House were hunkered down to vote for the treaty and League as originally planned, that their equally determined Republican counterparts considered the time for talking past.[28]

Finally, on November 19, the Democrats received a hand delivered letter from the President advising them to refuse support for the Foreign Relations Committee (or Lodge) reservations. That same day, the Senate voted on the treaty with the Lodge reservations included and the Dems joining with the Borah-led Republican Irreconcilables, who opposed ratification in any form, to easily defeat that option 53 to 38. Upon that vote being taken, Lodge turned to a nearby colleague and reputedly said,

THEY WON'T DOVETAIL
—Bronstrup in San Francisco Chron.

President Woodrow Wilson's hope for a League of Nations to end the prospect of future wars and ensure world peace was met with contention in the United States Senate, as depicted in this political cartoon from that era. In it, the President is pictured realizing he cannot make his League work within the parameters and oversight of the U.S. Constitution, as a disapproving Uncle Sam looks on (Library of Congress Prints and Photographs Division—Reproduction Number LC-USZ62-30948).

11. The Ammunition of Lasting Animosity 145

"The door is closed." Nationwide reaction to that news was, according to Schriftgiesser, "consternation and regret." There followed a demand for compromise in the Senate Chamber, as Democrats believed public opinion demanded further consideration and even Lodge agreed to the effort.[29]

At the start of a new congressional session after Thanksgiving, Lodge contended that the President should withdraw entirely from the process, putting reconsideration back in committee, but the scheme was blocked, causing the majority leader to stand pat on the reservations, a clear sign he was in no compromising mood. A bipartisan committee of 10 senators was then proposed with Lodge clearly in opposition to the idea until the Republican "middle-grounders," as Schriftgiesser described them, reputedly warned him they would ignore his leadership unless he at least attempted a compromise. That's how things stood until after the holidays and when the Democrats re-gathered for their caucus on January 8, 1920, another letter from the President was waiting on them. Schriftgiesser also provided the following excerpts from that Wilson message: "'Personally, I do not accept the action of the Senate as the decision of the nation. We cannot rewrite this treaty. We must take it without changes, which would alter its meaning, or leave it and face the unthinkable task of making another, separate kind of treaty with Germany.' Otherwise, 'the clear and single way out' would be to 'submit the question to the voters of the nation in the next election [1920], making it a great and solemn referendum.'" For the Democrats, Wilson's political solution seemed less than ideal as they continued to press for compromise, but Lodge accepted the President's electoral challenge and made the case that it was the nation's chief executive, who was unyielding, "not himself."[30]

Threatened by the 16 Irreconcilables in his own party, however, Lodge was in no position to compromise either and rumors of him surrendering to pressure from across the aisle, the administration, or even the general public were greatly exaggerated. Ultimately, neither side, Democrats or Republicans, were willing, in Schriftgiesser's words, "to run the risk of giving the other side any chance to claim victory." On January 30, 1920, Lodge announced, "There can be no compromise on principle." Another month of oratory followed, with Wilson labeling the reservationists with a dirty word from the past—"nullifiers"—and another hopeless Senate vote ended with the treaty failing again—this time forever.[31]

"The fact the treaty could not command a simple majority" either way, "with or without the Lodge reservations [was] a tribute only to the stubbornness of both sides," Garraty concluded in his biography of the Senate leader. Blame was placed on both sides by both sides, while "less partisan observers were inclined to spread the blame." But in the more intimate circles of Republican politics, the Lodge family, and even among the

Roosevelts, the victory, as Schriftgiesser implied, would always be to the senator he chronicled as the *Gentleman from Massachusetts*. With Corinne Roosevelt Robinson, TR's younger sister, present at the Lodge home the day of the final vote, in fact, the mood was somber, without the trappings of victory or celebration, but Lodge's daughter probably summed up her father's feelings best, when she said:

> My father hated and feared the Wilson League, and his heart was really with the Irreconcilables of his party. At the same time, it was uncertain whether this League could be beaten straight out, his way, so the object of his reservations was to emasculate the Wilson League and ensure that [even] if it did pass, it would be valueless and United States [sovereignty] would be honorably safeguarded. My father never wanted the Wilson League and when it was finally defeated, he was like a man from whom a great burden was lifted.[32]

The fact was as recently as 1915 Lodge had endorsed the entreaty of his good friend TR ... the call Roosevelt had issued in his Nobel Prize-winning speech of 1910 for a "League of Peace," a convergence and agreement of the major international powers to police and enforce global conflicts among the nations of the world, including themselves. Funny how when the similarly visionary aspirations of a political rival were within mankind's reach, the gentleman from Massachusetts was suddenly opposed, or at least constrained by reservations. The difference, after all, was no coincidence. "When it [finally] came, it was the gift of a Democratic president, the gift of a man whom his closest friend [had] deeply hated and for whom he, himself, had built up a hatred equally intense. For that reason and because he wanted to bring back his party into power, he fought to the bitter end."[33] That was one biographer's final reasoning of one senator's victory in what would prove a less than beneficial Washington war. Ironically, the visionary goal that one Democratic president sought to achieve would have to wait for another Democratic president with the last name Roosevelt to be re-conceived and enacted in similar form a quarter century later, but not before another cataclysmic world war. Rather than the League of Nations, it would then be called the United Nations.[34]

12

One-and-Done and Back to Normal

As the calendar flipped from 1919 to 1920 in the America of Woodrow Wilson and Henry Cabot Lodge, the residue of their Washington war over the Treaty of Versailles and more specifically the League of Nations would linger for a while in the national psyche. The President himself became a post–World War I casualty; the peace earned on the battlefields of Europe would require a separate U.S. treaty with Germany in 1921, even as the Allied nations carried on with their League; and the country as a whole went looking for "normalcy" and a renewed sense of isolationism behind its two great ocean barriers, as it had always done before. Alongside the belief that participation in a one-time overseas war had been necessary and justified to ensure freedom of the seas, democracy, and the victory of our closest European partners, there was still a prevailing sense of one-and-done and back to normal as most Americans hoped to avoid foreign involvement from then on, concentrating instead on the home front and making America alone again.[1]

A League of Nations would still exist for 26 years without U.S. membership and enjoy several diplomatic successes, especially in its first decade, including the Locarno Pact of 1925, which guaranteed Germany's western border with France and Belgium, and the creation of the European Federal Union in 1929 to coordinate economic and political policies. Germany, the main Allied enemy during the war, the recipient of blame, and the nation responsible for reparation payments to its neighboring victors, even joined the League in 1926. Located in traditionally neutral Switzerland (Geneva), smack dab in the middle of Europe, the League would last until 1946 and, as already noted, be succeeded by President Franklin D. Roosevelt's United Nations at the end of World War II, another, even greater conflict that it had been unable to curb and probably intensified by ensuring German enmity left over from the Treaty of Versailles with the rise of divisive, racist elements such as Nazism and Adolf Hitler.[2]

In the words of a current online encyclopedia:

> With the United States refusal to join, the League of Nations fell short of its goal of universality and was subsequently doomed to failure. It remained a largely Eurocentric organization. Frequent fluctuation in membership exacerbated its effectiveness, but the League failed primarily in the end because its member states continued to pursue [their own] national interests and act independently without regard for the organization. [At the same time], the League was a key agent in the transition from a world of formal empires to a world of formerly sovereign states. [But] despite its effectiveness for [some] international cooperation, the League failed to safeguard peace.

Like the League, the presidency of Wilson would mark a transitional time in U.S. history, as his progressive domestic agenda would become a regular feature of Democratic Party politics throughout the 20th century and into the 21st, while his Republican counterparts, by forsaking the legacy of Theodore Roosevelt in favor of William Howard Taft and the Old Guard in 1912, would become the more conservative of the two parties ever since. At the same time, by taking the U.S. into foreign conflict, the first American chief executive to do so, and by advocating international cooperation on a global scale (small nations as well as large), Wilson also broke the mold of America-first presidents—just about all the men to hold that office since George Washington, who famously warned against foreign entanglements even as the world was becoming more and more interconnected. Only in the matter of race relations, the clear result of a Southern upbringing and the Solid South voting reality of all Democratic politics before the 1960s, did Wilson come up just short of the few presidents generally given A+ ratings.[3]

As transitional as the first six-plus years of his administration were, however, Wilson's presidency would end under the shadow of misfortune and not merely because of the defeat of his League. Instead, it was the end of his tour to save the League that would define his last months in office, as the symptoms described in the last chapter would manifest themselves in a massive stroke just days after his tour finale in Pueblo from which he never fully recovered. And "because neither the Constitution nor precedent provided guidance in coping with the disability of a sitting president, the nation faced a real crisis of leadership." Continuing to quote presidential historian William DeGregorio, "During his convalescence Wilson chose not to relinquish, even temporarily, the office and duties of the president"—not even to the vice president, little utilized or remembered Thomas Marshall of Indiana. Actually Vice President Marshall "spurned" the idea that he should assume presidential duties while Wilson was incapacitated—duties that were apparently handled by America's First Lady at that time, Edith Galt Wilson, the second Mrs. Wilson, having married the

12. One-and-Done and Back to Normal 149

President before his second term began after the death of his first wife from Bright's disease five years earlier.[4]

She, in fact, would screen all matters of state and decide which ones were important enough to bring to the attention of her bedridden husband

The victim of a major stroke while still president in October 1919, Woodrow Wilson would lean on his second wife, Edith Galt Wilson, for things no other First Lady was ever asked to do, as she served as America's unofficial chief executive for much of the remainder of his second term (ending in March 1921). With the left side of his body paralyzed, Wilson depended on her while his condition was kept secret (Library of Congress Prints and Photographs Division—Reproduction Number LC-USZ62-62850).

as he recovered behind mostly closed doors at the White House. This unique circumstance in American history was captured in detail by Wilson biographers Berg and Cooper. According to Berg, as the President's train sped back towards Washington in late September 1919 after cancellation of the rest of his tour, including planned stops in Wichita (Kansas), Oklahoma City (Oklahoma), Little Rock (Arkansas), Memphis (Tennessee), and Louisville (Kentucky), Wilson "remained indisposed in his stateroom and in pain." A few opposition newspapers suggested the cancellation of the remainder of his tour was merely "a ruse" to induce sympathy in the Senate, where at least two previously expected "nay" voters on the League were known to be wavering. Cooper concurred by offering that while his doctor never used the word "stroke" aboard the train, he did suspect something was amiss with Wilson's fragile circulatory system and thus the need to get him home as soon as possible.[5]

While attempting what Cooper also termed "the most extensive effort any president had ever made to try to educate the public about foreign policy," he had obviously gone too far physically, and his body had not held up under the strain. "Back at the White House, Wilson went into seclusion." Rest would be his only treatment, but "the awful pain in his head" was relentless. After seemingly minor improvement by October 1, his third day home, there was renewed hope that the worst was past, but then October 2 brought those hopes crashing down, when, as Berg described, the First Lady telephoned his doctor around 8:30 a.m. to let him know the President was very sick and even before she had finished her call, he had collapsed, unconscious on the bathroom floor.[6]

"The stroke and illness Woodrow Wilson suffered in October 1919 brought on the worst crisis of presidential disability in American history." So wrote Cooper as he began to unravel the period following Wilson's second and more severe stroke. From the outset, those around him contemplated the question of whether or not he should resign. The stroke paralyzed his left side, including his arm and leg, as well as the lower left side of his face, which drooped noticeably. At the same time, the right side of his body was apparently unaffected, leaving him with the ability to write and conduct his normal, right-handed tasks, and his mind was not affected, as he retained the ability to speak and answer questions slowly but clearly. He alone among White House insiders never considered resignation.[7]

His wife did at least bring up allowing Vice President Marshall to take over, but his doctors felt that might remove his greatest incentive for recovery. As a result, she took on the role of gate-keeper, filtering and analyzing everything before it reached the President, deciding what needed presidential scrutiny and what did not behind closed doors, tasks that many pundits have since asserted made her, in essence, the nation's first female president for a period of weeks while Wilson continued his recovery. In the biggest of his biggest political fight and with the chances of his League dwindling, there was no way he was going to allow his congressional adversaries to call him "a quitter," Cooper emphasized, so even the mention of resignation in his presence was not condoned. At the same time, his visitors were few and far between, and those that did get in to see him were thoroughly screened, with the President only available in ways that concealed the invalid nature of his condition. The First Lady would later come under severe criticism for her concealment and "stewardship," as she called it, which included the reading of all classified, state papers.[8]

Whether or not a surrogate president was needed became open to debate within the confines of the White House, as the country as a whole heard only rumors and hearsay evidence. Secretary of State Lansing was one of those who raised the question of "presidential disability" and even brought it up at a Cabinet meeting on October 6 by posing the question of vice-presidential intervention based on the constitutional provision—"in case of the inability of the President." The Secretary's exact motives in raising that question have also been the subject of debate. Bullitt's controversial testimony in the Senate had left a festering sore spot between Wilson and Lansing, who was advocating that all Cabinet members should "go about their business 'without attempting to consult the President,'" again according to Cooper. In that same vein, Berg acknowledged that Lansing believed Wilson's physical state was "dangerous" for the country and within days of that Cabinet meeting, newspapers were appearing with rumors of a "cerebral lesion or hemorrhage," forcing the President's medical team to issue "non denial denials," as they became total accomplices to the ongoing administration subterfuge.[9]

Eventually, the First Lady did agree to a briefing "through a third party" with the vice president, entrusting what Berg termed "the nation's darkest secret to a middleman"—a Washington correspondent of the *Baltimore Sun* named Fred Essary. In the shock of having the presidential rumors confirmed in such a way, Vice President Marshall was reputedly left "speechless" and had no response other than silence for his undercover messenger, who left the VP's office without another word being spoken. For years afterward, Theodore Roosevelt's oldest daughter, Alice Roosevelt Longworth, the wife of Republican Congressman and future Speaker of the House Nicholas Longworth, who, like her father, was an established critic of the Wilson administration, enjoyed embellishing this tale of supposed Democratic cowardice by telling willing listeners that the fear-stricken Marshall had actually fainted at the news—thus his silence.[10]

Always something of an outsider in the administration, Marshall seemed to remain "invisible" in the days after Wilson's return and his

Close associates of former President Theodore Roosevelt as his best friend and son-in-law (respectively), Massachusetts' Henry Cabot Lodge (left) and Ohio's Nicholas Longworth were Republican leaders during the early 1900s, with Lodge the ranking GOP member in the Senate and Longworth, who married Roosevelt's oldest daughter, an eventual Speaker of the House. Both opposed the League of Nations (Library of Congress Prints and Photographs Division—Reproduction Number LC-USZ62-64298).

obvious seclusion at the White House. Cooper indicated the Vice President actually avoided 1600 Pennsylvania Avenue and refused to speak with reporters. Finally, reports of the President's incapacity began to circulate on Capitol Hill and the vague physician denials of the gravity of Wilson's health influenced senators of both parties to begin making their own attempts to persuade the reluctant VP to intervene and take over. By late November, in fact, rumors about the President were so constant that as Congress reconvened following the Thanksgiving holiday, a group of senators were determined to learn the truth. As an excuse to do so, they utilized renewed tensions with Mexico over a seized and detained American citizen in that neighboring country. When Lansing confirmed he had not spoken with Wilson about the potential controversy, the Senate panel had the issue it needed to justify its own conference with the President. Prepared for just

12. One-and-Done and Back to Normal 153

such an approach and potential inquisition, however, the White House doctors, "put on a show designed to [again] hide the nature and extent of Wilson's disability," and on December 5, when Senators Albert Fall of New Mexico and Gilbert Hitchcock of Nebraska came calling, Cooper also recounted how they found him "propped up in his bed" with "all the lights in the room on" and his paralyzed left side well concealed under the bedcovers with papers on a table to the right of his bed, "where he could easily reach them with his good arm and hand." When Fall stated, "I hope you will consider me sincere that I have been praying for you, Sir," Wilson famously quipped, "Which way, senator?" ... exhibiting the dry wit that had always been a staple of his personality with the kind of clear-headed comeback that got their visit off to an amiable and less suspicious start. Cooper concluded: "The President performed beautifully" and in their ensuing discussion "counseled against haste in dealing with Mexico," putting to rest their fears of the administration not being able to deal with the problem.[11]

Afterwards, Hitchcock even shared with reporters: "The President looks much better than when I last saw him. His color was good, he was mentally alert, and physically seemed to me to have improved greatly." Fall agreed, telling the gathered press corps that Wilson should be perfectly capable of handling the Mexican situation. In other words, the ruse had worked, and the President had passed the necessary test to move Congress and the nation past growing concerns over his ability to remain in office. Just over a week later, in fact, he was able to stand up and take his first unaided steps since the stroke two months earlier. He was certainly not out of the woods health-wise, but he had overcome the greatest threat to the completion of his second term. Unfortunately for him, as already revealed, he would never be able to overcome Republican opposition to his League of Nations. As John Garraty concurred in his bio of Lodge and wrap-up of the League fight: "The decision of the Republican Party [in regard to the League] was unfortunate, but it was not unpopular in [the distracted] America [of 1920]"—an America still recovering from 600,000 deaths during the Spanish flu epidemic of 1918 and about to embark on the controversial "Era of Prohibition," with ratification of the Eighteenth Amendment on January 16, 1920.[12]

Lodge, meanwhile, issued a statement about how just "because the American people were [ultimately] opposed to the League of Nations formulated and brought home by Mr. Wilson [did] not in the least mean that they proposed to isolate themselves and have nothing to do with the affairs of the rest of the world." On the surface that sounded good in a rational, justifying, fence-mending sort of way, but in reality the country had moved past the international focus that had been so apparent when its ships were being attacked by German U-boats and later when its young men were being sent across the Atlantic to fight in a foreign war for democracy's sake. The presidential campaign of 1920 would result in the infamous, "smoke-filled-room" selection of a nondescript, compromise candidate on the Republican side, Ohio Senator Warren G. Harding, a self-made, former small town newspaper publisher, who would defeat another former newspaper publisher from the same state, Ohio's Democratic governor, James M. Cox. The all–Ohio race would result in a Harding landslide and obvious referendum against Democratic support for Wilson's League. Ironically, Harding would attempt to straddle the League issue during the campaign, while Cox openly "challenged war-weary Americans to remain active in world affairs." But as presidential historian Kenneth Davis noted: "Worn by war and Woodrow Wilson's aggressive reform agenda, America wanted to catch its breath" and with Harding running on the slogan "A Return to Normalcy," the outcome was never really in doubt.[13]

Harding truly was *The Available Man* of Andrew Sinclair's 1965 book and of the mainstream conservative doctrine Republicans would come to embrace.[14] Despite a major international naval conference in December 1920 shortly after Harding's election victory that belied Republican leanings away from foreign involvement, the "Era of Normalcy" for the American electorate was at hand. In addition, the relatively new Seventeenth Amendment to the Constitution changed the way U.S. senators had always been selected by state legislatures to being elected through statewide elections, just as governors always had been, and Harding was the first of that new type of senator to also be elevated to the White House. Up until 1913 Sinclair mentioned how senators were not viewed as "good presidential timber" because they had rarely proved their vote-getting potential among the general public. Harding's selection, however, marked a change in that belief, which actually had only been true since the Civil War, with Andrew Johnson (1865–1868) and Benjamin Harrison (1888–1892) the only presidents to have previously been senators during that span. Nonetheless, several multi-termed, business-backed senators from that period undoubtedly had more influence than the sitting presidents. Before the Civil War, senators becoming president had been much more common, as seven chief executives were elevated after being legislatively conferred senators. Also true is the fact senators have again become presidents with increasing frequency in modern times, as the elections of Harry Truman, John Kennedy, Lyndon Johnson, Richard Nixon, Barack Obama, and Joe Biden all attest.[15]

At the same time, Harding's ascension as a compromise candidate was not only a renewed political trend, but what Samuel Hopkins Adams, another of his biographers, viewed as his membership in the Republican Old Guard that conspired to produce him. Being "reliably compliant," as in making decisions and establishing policy the Old Guard would prefer, had

12. One-and-Done and Back to Normal

to be a primary consideration when the 1920 Republican National Convention devolved into a backroom selection process following nine inconclusive ballots and put him over the top ahead of a general (Leonard Wood), a governor (Illinois' Frank Lowden), and a much less controllable, progressive senator (the previously mentioned Hiram Johnson of California), all of whom had been ahead of him in balloting before the decisive, smoke-filled induced, 10th delegate count.[16]

Harding's victory was also an apparent mandate for a return to the less government, conservative style of politics so evident at the turn of the century during the administration of the twice-elected William McKinley of Ohio, Harding's personal hero, who had been felled by the assassin's bullet that ushered in the more progressive era of TR and Wilson. And Harding, who unexpectedly died of a heart attack himself only two and a half years into office, was the precursor to the Republican decade of the 1920s (ironically the "Roaring 20s" of live and let live trends and lifestyle changes), the forerunner of Calvin Coolidge, America's foremost tax cutter, and Herbert Hoover, the business and engineering whiz who would have the misfortune of being the president amid the greatest financial collapse in U.S. history. Although Harding's shortened administration would be marred by scandal brought on primarily by his Cabinet and other appointees, it nonetheless signaled the inward looking mood of the country that would turn to trickle-down economics, wild speculation, and ultimately too little, too late oversight (or foresight) by both Coolidge and Hoover.[17]

"The Great Depression," as we have come to know it, began with the stock market crash of October 1929 and resulted in another, nearly as lopsided presidential landslide in 1932, the turning away from conservative economics to the renewed TR/Wilsonian progressivism of FDR, who unleashed a decidedly more liberal "New Deal" in his administration's first 100 days, providing hope to a nation in desperate need of some (so much so, in fact, that he would be re-elected three times). In addition to the Great Depression, the second Roosevelt would lead the United States through a Second World War in just over two decades. Indeed, the Western democracies would have to unite once again with what was by then a strange ally, Communist Russia, to defeat a totalitarian Nazi Germany, an empire-crazed Japan, and a misguidedly fascist Italy, as the world had evolved in unimaginably dictatorial ways since America's failure to join the League of Nations. In her book on the peace conference that officially ended the First World War and produced the Treaty of Versailles and ill-fated League, Margaret MacMillan indicated near the end that "the picture of Germany crushed by a vindictive peace [could] not be sustained" so long as the frustrated German people, who had never been defeated, were made to accept all the blame and a majority of the cost. Instead, all it took was the rise of der Fuhrer, Adolf

Hitler, who aroused German frustrations in such a way that he was able to create a new Germany bent on revenge for what had happened at Versailles. Quoted by MacMillan, German Foreign Minister Joachim von Ribbentrop said in 1939, as World War II was beginning with Germany's invasion of its eastern neighbor Poland: "The Fuhrer had done nothing but remedy the most serious consequences which this most unreasonable of all dictates in history imposed upon a nation and, in fact, upon the whole of Europe—in other words, repair [for] the worst mistakes committed by none other than the statesmen of the Western democracies."[18]

One of those statesmen was Woodrow Wilson and a good thing for him he did not live long enough to hear that verdict of Versailles issued on the world stage at the outset of another world war, with his dreams of avoiding that obviously recurring nightmare not only shattered but mocked. That would have surely killed him, just as assuredly as his stressful wounds 15 years earlier had done in the League fight. After still being president when the Nineteenth Amendment was finally ratified, giving U.S women the right to vote for the first time on August 26, 1920, he would oversee a mostly uneventful final few months of his second term except for being named the 1920 Nobel Peace Prize recipient for his leadership at Versailles (small consolation) before exiting the White House for the last time on March 4, 1921. The 28th president would not stick around for the inaugural of the 29th and although he would surprisingly outlive his successor by five months, Wilson would never fully recover from his last stroke before dying on February 3, 1924, at age 68.[19]

Meanwhile, Wilson's great nemesis continued in the Senate during the Era of Normalcy, which Garraty titled the final chapter of his biography. Lodge actually won re-election in March of 1919 in the closest vote of his six-term Senate career before also dying from a severe stroke accompanied by the complications of prostate cancer in late 1924. At 74, he outlived Wilson by just nine months.[20]

Section Five

Surviving the Red Menace
Harry Truman vs. Joseph McCarthy

13

The Cold War Launch of a Red Hot Demagogue

On November 2, 1948, one of the biggest upsets in American political history took place. Missouri's Harry Truman, the "stand-in" president who had followed the four-time elected and hugely popular Franklin Delano Roosevelt into the White House only because he had been vice president at the time of FDR's death (April 12, 1945), was re-elected in a presidential campaign for the ages—one in which he was given no chance. Truman's come-from-behind victory over New York's Republican Governor Thomas Dewey was unlikely for a number of reasons. In the first place, the plain-spoken Truman was an improbable successor to the polished, Harvard-educated FDR, whose hopeful, progressive agenda during the Great Depression and World War II had rallied the country in ways not duplicated before or sense. But the need to balance the Democratic ticket of 1944 with a moderate from Middle America like Truman rather than the liberal Henry Wallace, FDR's incumbent vice president and preferred running mate, elevated the "Show-Me State" senator at the last minute to the VP position—a job he really did not want and repeatedly tried to decline. Only FDR's direct appeal in the face of party dissension over retaining Wallace finally convinced Truman to get on board, even as rumors of the President's increasingly fragile health began to surface.[1]

So, when Roosevelt, generally considered one of the top three presidents of all-time, did indeed suffer a fatal cerebral hemorrhage only a month into his fourth term, his new and little-known vice president became the last of our presidents to ascend to the White House without benefit of a college education. As summed up in the book The American Senate: "Truman seemed a sorry substitute for Franklin Roosevelt. He had none of FDR's debonair nonchalance, his persuasive eloquence, or grand manner. He had none of Roosevelt's arrogance either or his political guile." What Truman did have, however, was a great deal of common sense and plain-spoken honesty. The late, great journalist and author David

13. The Cold War Launch of a Red Hot Demagogue

Halberstam once described him as a "decisive man" and "easy to underestimate."[2]

Such qualities allowed him to pick up the gauntlet left by FDR without overcompensating in an attempt to measure up by bringing World War II to a successful close. In so doing, he made a world-changing decision to drop the first atomic bombs on Japan as a means of ending the war sooner with less American lives lost; he completed FDR's vision of a United Nations organization to try and limit future international conflict, avoiding the American tendency towards isolationism following overseas involvement that had been obvious in the Senate denial of Wilson's League of Nations; and he was proactive in his approach to the Cold War with the Soviet Union (formerly Russia) by rebuilding European democracies and seeking to contain the spread of communism in devastated or developing countries through establishment of his Truman Doctrine and the European Recovery Act that became known as the "Marshall Plan."[3]

Taking over for the hugely successful Franklin Delano Roosevelt as president in 1945, Harry Truman seemed an unlikely replacement. Already a more moderate vice-presidential replacement when he was made FDR's fourth term running mate in place of the liberal incumbent, Truman had to learn on the job as World War II wound to a close and the Cold War against the Soviet Union heated up (Library of Congress Prints and Photographs Division—Reproduction Number LC-USZ62-98170).

All of these early, first term achievements are made even more impressive by considering what his primary biographer, David McCullough, claimed in his 1992 Pulitzer-winning masterwork, *Truman*, when he wrote: "In just [his first] three months [in office], Harry Truman had been faced with a greater degree of history, with larger, more far-reaching decisions than any president before him"—a bold claim to be sure made even bolder as McCullough included both Abraham Lincoln, with the impending Civil War starring him in the face, and FDR in the midst of the nation's worst economic disaster. "Forthright to the point of bluntness," was how

Walter Isaacson and Evan Thomas characterized Truman in their book *The Wise Men* about the six U.S. diplomats primarily responsible for America's Cold War diplomacy. According to them, following the "haughty air" and self-assuredness of Roosevelt, it took Americans some time to get used to the "righteous indignation of President Truman." Far more reliant on his advisers when it came to foreign policy than FDR, Truman was a surprisingly steady, resolute leader early on, including his participation as Roosevelt's replacement at the Potsdam Conference, which was held in a suburb of the defeated German capital (Berlin), where he had every intention of continuing to negotiate in good faith with the Soviet Union, treating it as the ally it had been during the war. In addition, his decisive use of the atomic warheads at Hiroshima and Nagasaki to end the war in the Pacific and spare American lives that otherwise would have been lost in an invasion of the Japanese homeland, set the U.S. apart as the world's lone superpower (at least for the time being). At Potsdam, British Prime Minister Winston Churchill, FDR's famous partner in Allied leadership during World War II, judged Truman "a man of immense determination." In addition, after the new president made known his Truman Doctrine and the Marshall Plan in response to attempted communist intrusion in Greece and Turkey, and as war debts forced Britain to abandon more than four decades of leadership in the Eastern Mediterranean, Churchill would write to him to say how much he appreciated what had been done "for peace and freedom," and how his presidency had become "the one cause of hope in the [post-war] world."[4]

Relying on the grasp of world affairs of General George C. Marshall, one of FDR's most trusted confidants as Army chief of staff during World War II, Truman would first bring the general out of retirement as a special envoy to the nationalist government in China during its battle to avert communist takeover and later make him secretary of state, ultimately confirming his Cold War importance by virtue of his namesake Marshall Plan. Also central to Truman's expanding strategy of challenging the spread of communism with economic aid to European countries decimated or in jeopardy of succumbing to socialism was Dean Acheson, one of the six "architects of the American Century" featured in the previously mentioned book by Isaacson and Thomas. A product and prodigy of the Eastern elite, including Yale University and Harvard Law School, he may have been more responsible for the Truman Doctrine than the President himself and as responsible for the Marshall Plan as the secretary of state he previously served under before Truman elevated him to head of the State Department. Marshall, *Time* magazine's two-time Man of the Year (1943 and 1947), had actually retired a second time and been called back again by the President to be secretary of defense, when a controversial predecessor in that role

13. The Cold War Launch of a Red Hot Demagogue   161

had to be replaced over an unprecedented "Revolt of the Admirals." That so-named uprising among naval leadership was prompted by the National Security Act of 1947, which reorganized the U.S. military in lieu of the tremendous debt incurred during World War II, leading the Navy's leadership to assert its funding should not be cut in order to offset development of the Air Force as a separate service instead of its wartime status as the Army Air Corps.[5]

Although regarded by the President as irreplaceable members of his administration as the Cold War heated up and other foreign developments took place (for instance U.S. recognition of the new Jewish nation of Israel in the Muslim dominated and formerly British mandated area of Palestine), both Marshall and Acheson would become targets of criticism in Truman's second term. In Republican circles, Marshall was already being blamed for China becoming the world's second major communist country due to his perceived lack of oversight as World War II drew to a close, and Acheson was among the most disliked officials in post-war Washington, where his often aloof demeanor and what Isaacson and Thomas described as his equal "contempt for ignorance and congressmen" made him a logical GOP target.[6]

At the same time, Truman's own stock had begun to drop since being the common, every-man successor the country had rallied around when he manfully assumed the great responsibility that FDR's death had cast upon

A mainstay of the Allied effort during World War II, General George Marshall would become just as important as a statesman after the war, serving Truman as both secretary of state and later secretary of defense. Despite his five-star military service and post-war achievements, including the European Recovery Act also known as the Marshall Plan, he would become a target for Republican criticism (Library of Congress Prints and Photographs Division—Reproduction Number LC-USZ62-119186).

him. Since bringing another world war to a close with his decisive decision to decimate America's reviled attacker, Japan, and positioning the U.S. as the world's democratic leader, the soldiers were coming home and the country was ready to enjoy the fruits it felt were warranted by having been the "Arsenal of Democracy" for four years. With the Great Depression and war finally over, the desire to live in the "Land of Opportunity" was again on American minds and no one was under more pressure from those expectations than the President. By 1946, less than a year after Japan's surrender, work stoppages consumed the country as U.S. workers decried their sacrifices of the previous four years and anticipated a bigger slice of the American pie. Labor support remained key to the Democratic Party, but as coal miners and railway workers instigated simultaneous strikes, Truman threatened to use the Army to seize the railroads and the mines, and to draft strikers back into the armed services in peacetime. This time, however, such decisive action was deemed a bit too far in the land of the free, as the *Christian Science Monitor* plaintively asked the question, "is this Russia or Germany?" with both Democrats and Republicans combining to crush the President's dramatic proposal in the Senate by a vote of 70–13.[7]

"Unlike FDR and so many FDR mourners," according to David Pietrusza in what would be his book on the presidential election of 1948, "Truman did not wear his liberalism on his sleeve." Already he had replaced the liberals' "sainted" Wallace in 1944 and with FDR gone and the war completely over, many of those FDR loyalists now began to turn on the President so much, in fact, that talk of replacing him with Wallace in '48 became prevalent following his failed attempt to control labor.[8]

Also, as the grandson of slaveholders and son of Southern sympathizers living in rural Western Missouri from whence the pro-slavery Border Ruffians of Bleeding Kansas days had come, "the White South felt confidant," Truman, as president, "would be sympathetic to its racial code," when he replaced the obviously more liberal Roosevelt. William Leuchtenburg authored a book about such White Southern concerns and the three mid-20th century Democratic presidents who tried to move past them in *The White House Looks South*. Southern Blacks were just the opposite. Although Truman's voting record during his Senate days had been surprisingly pro-civil rights, African Americans found his sudden ascension "unsettling" and most believed him "a Negro hater," based on where he came from, according to Leuchtenburg. Both Southern groups had to be equally surprised when Truman asked Congress to again fund the Fair Employment Protection Committee (FEPC) and when he announced he would be creating a President's Committee on Civil Rights (PCCR). Their collective surprise was then turned to shock when he desegregated the U.S. military and all federal employment by executive order.[9]

13. The Cold War Launch of a Red Hot Demagogue 163

Once again according to Pietrusza, the political "timing" in both circumstances "revealed remarkable calculation" on his part when the Democratic Party became a party in revolt. As the 1948 Democratic National Convention neared, left-leaning party regulars, including FDR's sons, had sought to enlist popular General Dwight Eisenhower, World War II's overall Allied commander in Europe, as a replacement candidate for Truman, while Southern Dems, angry over the President's recent actions in support of civil rights jumped on the conservative candidacy of powerful Georgia Senator Richard Russell. Both efforts failed, however, with Eisenhower declining (only to run as a Republican four years later) and Russell failing to gain any traction outside the South and losing on the first ballot to Truman, who rallied delegates with what one historian termed "a two-fisted attack" on the Republicans now holding a majority in Congress (what he termed the "Do-Nothing Congress"), while also threatening to call a special congressional session to address a series of progressive bills, including slum clearance, low-cost housing, and the extension of FDR's popular Social Security Act. From lackluster, care-taker candidate, "Give 'em Hell Harry" was suddenly born and the convention hall in Philadelphia, by all reports, was "electrified."[10]

Truman would go on to stage a determined 30,000-mile "whistle-stop" campaign by train in which he delivered more than 300 outspoken speeches to an estimated six million people, but he remained a decided underdog. Not only was he going against a young, polished Republican opponent in Governor Dewey, who was running for a second time after losing to the FDR-Truman ticket four years earlier, but Wallace also filled a void for the most liberal Democrats by getting his own name on the ballot in 45 of the then 48 states, while Southern Democrats or "Dixiecrats," as they were called, coalesced around Strom Thurmond, the segregationist governor of South Carolina. Indeed, with three Democrats in the running, potentially splitting the party three ways, it was very reminiscent of the 1860 election of Abraham Lincoln. Truman's fate seemed all but sealed. Dewey was supremely confident and campaigned on a vague theme of national unity and an end to what he called the "waste and inefficiency" of Democratic rule the previous 16 years.[11]

Amazingly it was not to be. Truman's aggressive fighting style in the face of extremely long odds convinced enough of the country that he should be re-elected. He garnered 49 percent of the vote to Dewey's 45 percent, while the insurgent campaigns of Wallace and Thurmond managed just two percent each. As mentioned before, it was a stunning upset. Despite the pre-election polls and pundits giving him no chance, Truman continued to believe he could and would win, and in the end not only won himself, but also carried the Senate and House races with him, flipping both from

Republican majorities to Democratic control. Even most of the governors' mansions were left in decidedly Democratic hands.[12]

As a result, to say Harry Truman entered his second term on a high note would be an understatement. McCullough, his chief biographer, would write:

> The country was flabbergasted. It was called a "startling victory," "astonishing," "a major miracle." He had won it against the greatest odds in the annals of presidential politics. Not one polling organization had been correct in its forecast. Not a single radio commentator or newspaper columnist, or any of the hundreds of reporters who covered the campaign had called it right. Every expert had been proven wrong and, as was said, "a great roar of laughter arose from the land." The people had made fools of those supposedly in the know. Of all amazing things Harry Truman had turned out to be (he was) the only one who knew what he was talking about.[13]

His victory had come against the backdrop of the aptly named "Berlin Airlift," which he began along with the British as a means of not allowing Soviet held East Germany to cut off supplies from the Allied western sector of Germany's capital city once the fighting stopped—what McCullough described as "one of the most brilliant American achievements of the post-war era and one of Truman's proudest decisions, strongly affecting the morale of Western, non-communist Europe, the whole course of the Cold War, and his drive for re-election." In keeping with the Truman Doctrine and Marshall Plan, his decision to fly supplies into West Berlin, rendering the surrounding Soviet blockade irrelevant, was yet another example of his desire to contain communism without confronting it militarily, giving the world and particularly Europe a chance to recover from the carnage and devastation of World War II. And with FDR's visionary United Nations still in its diplomatic infancy, he would continue to utilize deterrence in the hope of avoiding future conflict in April 1949. That's when 12 nations under the leadership of his administration created the North Atlantic Treaty Organization (NATO) as a bulwark against further expansionist aims of the Soviet Union on the European continent (as most of Eastern Europe was already under Soviet control by war's end). With Marshall, by then between stints as secretary of state and secretary of defense, Acheson deserved most of the credit for negotiating the NATO defense pact, whereby an attack, Soviet or otherwise, on any of the 12 member nations would be treated as an attack on all—a deterrent that at this writing had lasted over 70 years.[14]

The Truman Doctrine; the Marshall Plan; the Berlin Airlift; the North American Treaty Organization; a history-making come-from-behind re-election victory that included majorities in both Houses of Congress; and sole possession of the world's most powerful weapon. Obviously,

13. The Cold War Launch of a Red Hot Demagogue   165

President Truman and his administration had enjoyed a glorious run of achievements by the summer of 1949, but their string of accomplishment was on the verge of an abrupt end.[15]

Along with the previously mentioned communist takeover of China, that fall would bring proof of the Soviet Union's detonation of their own atomic weapon, stunning America's sense of security with the realization that suddenly there was another superpower. And as the calendar changed to a new decade, 1950 dawned with new accusations—charges of communist infiltration in the Truman administration by congressional Republicans, an attention-getting mechanism that provided front page headlines for weeks and one that continued even when overshadowed by other news four months later. That's when a surprise attack—equally surprising to the Japanese attack on Pearl Harbor nine years earlier that ushered America into the Second World War—occurred on the Korean Peninsula. North Korea, the communist controlled half of that East Asian appendage invaded its southern neighbor, South Korea, on June 25, 1950, initiating the kind of ideological military confrontation Truman had hoped to avoid. Some 90,000 soldiers—more than seven infantry divisions and one armored brigade of the North Korean People's Army—crossed the 38th parallel and drove south in "an extremely well-planned, multi-pronged attack." That's the very simple way Halberstam described the start of the Korean War in his 2007 book *The Coldest Winter*. Following a United Nations mandate to expel the North Koreans engineered by Truman the "Korean Conflict," as it became known, would last three years (1950–1953) and eventually involve China, which also surprised U.S. military leadership by entering the war when American troops got too close to its border with North Korea, yet another massive headache for Truman as he sought to minimize the chances of a third world war and especially the threat of an atomic war between superpowers. As a result, Korea would be termed a "police action," not a war at all in the official administration lexicon of the day, but until the North Koreans and later the Chinese were pushed back within their original borders, it would cost the lives of over 33,000 Americans before ending in stalemate—thankfully without the use of any more atomic bombs.[16]

In the meantime, despite all its efforts to avoid military conflict at any Cold War flashpoints left over from World War II, the Truman administration was finally forced to deal with an armed invasion of localized origin that threatened global consequences, while back on the home front another equally insidious attack was underway on the President and his government. To address this other, domestic threat as early as 1946, Truman had established a Temporary Commission on Employee Loyalty to facilitate the removal of security risks from sensitive federal jobs. With communism making inroads around the world, however, Republicans in Congress had "criticized him [even then] for not going far enough." That implication, acknowledged by presidential historian William DeGregorio, presaged the coming storm that would be called the "Red Menace" or, more appropriately, the "Red Scare."[17]

The fear of communism had indeed come home to roost and not just on the battlefields of a little known or previously considered peninsula on the other side of the world, where localized ideological warfare had evolved into American soldiers suddenly being confronted by Communist Chinese. In 1949, in fact, a year before North Korea attacked its more democratic southern neighbor, a former member of the Communist Party in America and a former editor at *Time* magazine, Whitaker Chambers, alleged that one of the original Justice Department attorneys from FDR's first term, Alger Hiss, who had gone on to work at the State Department as director of the Office of Special Political Affairs and as secretary-general of the United Nations Conference on International Organization, was, in all probability, a Soviet spy. Into the vortex created by this very public allegation by an admitted former communist stepped the first of several political opportunists, relatively new California Congressman Richard Nixon, who, as a member of the House Un-American Activities Committee, knew an attention-grabbing issue when he saw one and pounced, understanding the lofty political aspirations that could be realized by pursuing (and perhaps proving) such a case. Later, as Nixon biographer Rick Perlstein would poignantly write in regard to hidden evidence that Chambers produced and Nixon revealed, leading to Hiss's conviction for perjury despite unwavering support and testimony from his superior at State, Secretary Acheson:

> The very next day, in the most stem-winding speech of his congressional career, Richard Nixon said that Dean Acheson's words [had been] sacrilege. Nixon called his oration "The Hiss Case—A Lesson for the American People." The lesson was that Alger Hiss's conviction [was an indictment] of Harry Truman himself. The Secretary of State had thrown the power and prestige of his office [and the Truman administration] behind Hiss after he had been convicted. In Nixon's words, that was just how liberals were. They coddled traitors. They [wrongly] invoked the Holy Name to do so. They traduced Americans' moral values.[18]

It would be the opening salvo in a concerted Republican effort to uncover more communists in the Truman administration and it set the stage for the launch of a senatorial witch hunt like no other in American history. Unwittingly, in making a name for himself within the Republican ranks (which he obviously did by becoming Dwight Eisenhower's vice-presidential running mate in 1952), Nixon illuminated a potential pathway to prominence that appealed to one Joseph R. McCarthy, the

13. The Cold War Launch of a Red Hot Demagogue   167

The successor to George Marshall as secretary of state, Dean Acheson emerged during the Truman years from a coalition of young American diplomats who had played roles during the Cold War aftermath of World War II. Considered arrogant by the political right, his testimony in the Alger Hiss perjury trial would be held against him as claims of communist infiltration in his State Department intensified (Library of Congress Prints and Photographs Division—Reproduction Number LC-DIG-hec-25820).

junior senator from Wisconsin. On February 9, 1950, just two weeks after Hiss was sentenced to five years in prison, the third year U.S. senator borrowed large tracts of Nixon's congressional address in a speech he would give in Wheeling, West Virginia. With midterm elections already on the minds of the Republican minority and Nixon's use of what noted historian Jon Meacham termed "domestic fears of communist influence" in his *Soul of America*, McCarthy delivered what the *Wheeling Intelligencer* called a "homey" address to 275 people at the McClure Hotel as part of a Lincoln Day celebration. Seemingly out of nowhere at this intimate small town gathering, McCarthy suddenly injected, "While I cannot take time to name all the men in the State Department who have been named as active members of the Communist Party and members of a spy ring, I have in my hand a list of 205 that were made known to the secretary of state as being members of the Communist Party and who, nevertheless, are still working and shaping policy in the State Department."[19] Suddenly, that same *Wheeling Intelligencer* had gone from covering a feel-good, local story to a block-busting national exclusive.

Of that same moment in another of his exceptional books before he was killed in a tragic 2007 automobile accident, Halberstam would write:

> The McCarthy era was about to begin. Joseph R. McCarthy, Republican senator from Wisconsin, stepped forward to lend his name to a phenomenon that, in fact, already existed. He was the accidental demagogue. Almost casually, he claimed that there were communists in the State Department and that they controlled American foreign policy. As one of the reporters who knew him well noted later, McCarthy himself had no idea his speech would prove so explosive. Otherwise, he would have taken along at least one of the handful of right-wing reporters who tutored him. Also, he would have picked a bigger town than Wheeling and a more prominent group than the Ohio County Women's Republican Club. His line about communists in the State Department was [actually] a throw away, but that began it. Later that night, Noman Yost, who worked as a stringer for Associated Press, phoned in a few paragraphs to the AP office in [West Virginia's capital] Charleston. The story moved over the AP wire on a Thursday night and made the Friday papers. The circus had begun.[20]

For President Truman, new Secretary of State Acheson, and former Secretary of State Marshall, a new and bitter nemesis was created with that AP story, a nemesis who would rise to so much prominence on the notion of communist infiltration of our federal government and what he called "20 years of treason" in the last two Democratic presidential regimes that a derivative of his name "McCarthyism," would become synonymous with the Red Scare. Not the first Republican to profit politically from such propositions (as future President Nixon's meteoric rise attested), Senator McCarthy would nonetheless make a name for himself without ever producing a shred of evidence and become one of the earliest right-wing heroes. Anthony Summers, a biographer of controversial FBI Director J. Edgar Hoover attested to as much despite the "bogus" nature of the accusations McCarthy would make over the next four years in a disgustingly profound

13. The Cold War Launch of a Red Hot Demagogue   169

way, when he quoted a reputedly inebriated McCarthy boasting to a gathered group of reporters shortly after his West Virginia speech: "Listen you bastards, I just want you to know I've got a pail full of this shit and I'm gonna use it where it does me the most good." And after he had flushed it "on an America [already] awash with [the] fear of communism," U.S. politics would never be the same.[21]

14

Turning the Other Cheek in a No-Win War

"National bonfire" was the way Lyndon Johnson's award-winning biographer Robert Caro described what Joe McCarthy ignited in early 1950. In his book, *Master of the Senate,* Caro described "a bonfire that was to consume or sear the reputations of thousands of innocent Americans, blazing for four years and 10 months, a period longer than America's participation in the Second World War." But who was the rogue senator that started this blaze? And how did he maintain membership in the nation's loftiest legislative body while making destructive accusations that would sully the nation's leadership without proof? Robert Sherrill, one of the leading investigative journalists of that era, called him "the most influential demagogue the United States has ever produced," and although that is no longer true, it certainly was in 1950.[1]

"Shrewd, insecure, and defensive," as David Halberstam described him in his book *The Fifties,* McCarthy was of "poor, Irish stock from the wrong side of the tracks" in Appleton, Wisconsin. He put himself through college in-state, attending Catholic, Marquette University in Milwaukee and finishing with a Law degree in five years. After working for a year at a small law firm in Shawano, Wisconsin, he ran for district attorney as a Democrat in 1936 and lost. In 1939, he ran again for an elected judgeship in his home state's 10th Circuit and defeated the incumbent, who had held the position for 24 years, by reputedly exaggerating his opponent's age. As controversial on the bench as he would later be in the Senate, he was censured in 1941 for misplacing evidence. Less than a year later he entered the Marine Corps as a first lieutenant, thanks to his college work qualifying him for a direct commission, and he would serve in World War II as an intelligence briefing officer for a dive bomber squadron based in the South Pacific for 30 months, exiting with the rank of captain in April 1945. A volunteer for 12 combat missions during the war as a gunner-observer, he would acquire what many believed the self-conferred nickname "Tail-Gunner Joe" by the

14. Turning the Other Cheek in a No-Win War 171

A relative unknown his first few years in Washington, Wisconsin Senator Joseph McCarthy would become a household name in American politics when he began making claims of communist infiltration of the U.S. State Department. Along with President Truman, George Marshall and Dean Acheson would become primary targets of the McCarthy accusations (Library of Congress Prints and Photographs Division—Reproduction Number LC-DIG-ds-07186).

time he left the service, and somehow receive a Distinguished Service Cross by falsely claiming 32 aerial missions on his wartime resume.[2]

Putting such personal propaganda to use even before the war was over, he campaigned unsuccessfully for a Republican nomination to the U.S. Senate while still on active duty in 1944 but was simultaneously re-elected unopposed to his old seat on the circuit court. Almost immediately after those results were in, he set his sights on Wisconsin's other Senate seat in 1946 and through the support of the state's Republican boss, Thomas Coleman, he achieved that primary victory by unseating Robert M. La Follette, Jr., the three-term Republican incumbent and son of Robert M. LaFollette, Sr., one of the most renowned politicians in state history.[3] With Coleman's backing, McCarthy attacked the younger La Follette for not enlisting in the wartime military, even though he was 46 years old at the time, and for war profiteering through the stock market. McCarthy's campaign funds, most of which came from out-of-state, were also 10 times those of La Follette and contributed to his upset victory by just over 5,000 votes. Then, in the general election, McCarthy hammered his Democratic opponent with a convincing 62 percent of the vote to 37.3 percent.[4]

Rapid recovery, stunning rise, or just plain lucky … actually all three applied to Joe McCarthy as he entered the Senate in January 1947. Most pundits would say his credentials did not warrant the position, but regardless, once in the Senate, he, like all politicians, needed to be productive to stay there and as McCullough pointed out in *Truman*:

> Until January [of 1950], Wisconsin's 41-year-old junior senator had been casting about for an issue that might lift him from obscurity [including his stunning concern for Nazi war prisoners convicted of the infamous massacre of unarmed American soldiers at Malmedy, Belgium in WWII due to the profusion of voters of Germanic ancestry in the "Badger State"]. All but friendless in the Senate and recently voted the worst member of the Senate in a poll of Washington correspondents, McCarthy appeared a hopeless failure [by his third year on the job]. [Then] over dinner one evening, Father Edmund A. Walsh of Georgetown, a Catholic priest from one Washington's most historic neighborhoods, suggested he might sound the alarm over communist infiltration of the government, and McCarthy, who had already made some loud, if unnotable, charges about communist subversion, seemed to have realized all at once he had found what he needed.

Suddenly he was making headlines throughout the country, claiming to have revealed "Truman's iron curtain of secrecy."[5]

Wild and unsupported though his claims were, he was making the kind of noise in the Senate that had not been seen since the days of Louisiana's Huey Long, another so-called demagogue, but without Long's flamboyance and charisma. Although initially a supporter of then President-elect Roosevelt when he first arrived in the Senate in 1932, the flamboyant former governor of the "Bayou State," who was known there as the "Kingfish," quickly unfurled his true colors in the Democratic ranks as he sought to at first influence and later usurp the New Deal policies of FDR, who once labeled Long one of the two most dangerous men in America. According to Long's biographer, T. Harry Williams, after one showdown meeting with FDR over administration policy moving forward, Long supposedly remarked, "What the hell is the use of coming down to see this fellow? I can't win any decision over him." And along those same lines, he would later state: "The trouble is Roosevelt hasn't taken all of my ideas; just part of them. I'm about one hundred yards ahead of him."[6]

While totally different, they were of the same party and Long's initial intent was to push the President and the Democratic Party to become even more progressive in the Depression. But his true intention of stepping into presidential power himself should Roosevelt falter was clear to FDR from the get-go. As a result, FDR managed to control him politically behind the scenes and keep him in his place, rendering Long impotent on the national stage.[7] On the other hand, Harry Truman would have no such power to control the Senate demagogue he and his administration would be confronted with. Instead, because they were of opposing parties, he had to hope the Republican leadership would rein in the irrational and unsubstantiated claims McCarthy was making and while at first that might have been the wishes of some GOP leaders, others, including Styles Bridges of New Hampshire, Owen Brewster of Maine, Homer

Before Joe McCarthy, the closest thing to a political demagogue in the U.S. Senate had to be Huey Long, the flamboyant former governor of Louisiana who attracted attention from the moment he arrived in Washington in 1932. An early supporter of FDR, he quickly became a potential rival for the new Democratic president, who once termed him one of the most dangerous men in America (Library of Congress Prints and Photographs Division—Reproduction Number LC-DIG-hec-38950).

Capehart of Indiana, Karl Mundt of South Dakota, and Kenneth Wherry of Nebraska began actively "egging him on." Eventually, even Ohio's Robert Taft, the ultra-conservative senator known as "Mr. Republican," offered McCarthy encouragement to "keep talking." Taft, in fact, coined the phrase "soft on communism" that became the mantra for an opposition party still angry over Truman's surprising second term. At the same time, Democrats in Congress would press for a "complete investigation of McCarthy's charges," resulting in a special subcommittee under the leadership of Maryland's Millard Tydings. The Tydings committee began hearings in March.[8]

The bright light of public exposure, however, only made McCarthy more magnified. When asked what evidence he had to substantiate his claims of rampant communist infiltration in the State Department, he would simply say that Acheson's staff at State had all the evidence under wraps, basing his accusations on the existence of FBI information, even though J. Edgar Hoover, whose biographer termed McCarthy "Edgar's protégé," would never own up to it. Hoover, in fact, would scold the senator—not over what he had said, but the specific way he said it. Subsequently, when President Truman ordered the State Department files opened, Hoover declared them intact, prompting McCarthy to assert they had been tampered with before the FBI gained access.[9]

In other words, it did not matter that the Tydings subcommittee findings found that McCarthy had perpetrated a "fraud and hoax" on the Senate, the senator from Wisconsin remained unrepentant in his ongoing claims. "Basking in his new visibility," according to Baker and MacNeil in *The American Senate*, he "learned the rhythms of the press, not only the daily deadlines, but the restraints of the 'objectivity' [the reporters] imposed on themselves." George Reedy of United Press International observed at the time, "We had to take what McCarthy said at face value. Joe couldn't find a communist in Red Square—he didn't know Karl Marx from Groucho [Marx]—but he was a United States senator." In *The Fifties*, Halberstam also mentioned how he became adept at making his communist claims in small towns, knowing full well the nearest Associated Press office would pick up the local story and run it without further scrutiny. And even though they knew better, as Halberstam also indicated, they were guilty of "chronicling each charge" in "his travelling road show, instead of bothering to follow up. It was news and he was news" and apparently "that was all that mattered."[10]

Amid McCarthy's litany of accusations and the Tydings hearings, Truman found time to hold a press conference on March 30 while enjoying a spring getaway at his Florida Little White House in Key West, during which he addressed the McCarthy saga. "I think the greatest asset the Kremlin has is Senator McCarthy," he asserted. It was an accusation of aiding

14. Turning the Other Cheek in a No-Win War

communism in reverse and a pre-planned strategy that the gathered scribes jumped on to report, with one exclaiming, "Brother will that hit page one tomorrow." According to Jon Meacham in *The Soul of America*, the President also reminded them of the 1946 loyalty commission he had instituted as the Cold War gathered steam to identify potential subversives—a proactive policy that obviously looked good in light of McCarthy's radioactive rhetoric.[11] Making it seem nothing but politics, Truman continued:

> For political purposes, the Republicans have been trying vainly to find an issue on which to make a bid for control of the Congress next year. They tried "statism." They tried "welfare state." They tried "socialism." And there are a certain number of the Republican Party who are trying to dig up that old malodorous dead horse called "isolationism." And in order to do that, they are perfectly willing to sabotage the bipartisan foreign policy of the United States. Now if anybody really felt that there were disloyal people in the employ of the government, the proper and the honorable way to handle the situation would be to come to the President and say, "This man is a disloyal person. He is in such and such department." We would investigate him immediately and if he were a disloyal person, he would be immediately fired. [But] that is not what they want. They are trying to create an issue.[12]

Just over two months later, North Korea's communist regime unleashed its surprise attack and the Korean conflict would take precedence in Truman's presidency for the remainder of his two plus years in office. In that vein, he would repeatedly downplay the constant irritation that was McCarthy. According to McCullough, the President considered him a temporary aberration—"a ballyhoo artist who has to cover up his [own] shortcomings by wild charges." Even before the Tydings subcommittee findings were announced, with no evidence of further communist subversion (other than the earlier Hiss case), Truman remained calm amid his staff's worry and repeatedly voiced the expectation that McCarthy was a "liar" who would ultimately "destroy himself." Writing to the sister of Owen Lattimore, a former State Department employee whom McCarthy had implicated as the potential "top Russian espionage agent" in the U.S. and Hiss's one-time boss, the President wrote:

> I think our friend McCarthy will eventually get all that is coming to him. He has no decency or honor. You can understand, I imagine, what [a] president has to stand [when] every day in the week he's under a constant barrage of people who have no respect for the truth and whose objective is to belittle and discredit him. While they are not successful in these attacks, they are never pleasant, so I know just how you feel about the attack on your brother. The best thing to do is to face it and the truth will come out.[13]

At the same time, nothing Truman or anyone else said seemed to quell the incessant abuse and drumbeat of McCarthy's accusations, and the resulting fear it spread through the federal government. The closest anyone in his own party came to admonishing the Wisconsin senator was a female colleague—Senator Margaret Chase Smith of Maine. Publicly acknowledging her as one of his personal heroes, historian Jon Meacham recounted an exchange between McCarthy and Chase on June 1, 1950, just 24 days before the Korean War began. At that time, Chase issued what she termed a "Declaration of Conscience," attacking McCarthy's methods. Confiding to another author, she stated that "Joe began to get publicity crazy and the other senators were now afraid to speak their minds [and] take issue with him, obviously for fear his communist claims might even include them—the next time. It had gotten to the point where senators were afraid to even be seen with certain people in Washington previously implicated or suspected. Smith had been on good terms with McCarthy before his communist accusations began, having even lauded her as a possible vice presidential candidate in 1952, so it was with no trepidation that he approached her before knowing what her Declaration was about and said, 'Margaret you look very serious; are you going to make a speech today?'"—to which she replied, "Yes and you will not like it." "Is it about me?" he inquired. "Yes," she continued, "but I am not going to mention your name." Frowning at this point, according to Meacham, McCarthy then reminded the first woman to serve in both Houses of Congress that he controlled 27 convention votes from the Wisconsin delegation—a warning that obviously did not faze Smith, who pushed by McCarthy and onto the Senate floor, where she famously rose and offered the following:

> I would like to speak briefly and simply about a serious national condition. It is a national feeling of fear and frustration that could result in national suicide and the end of everything that we Americans hold dear. I speak as a Republican. I speak as a woman. I speak as a United States senator. I speak as an American. I think it is high time we remembered that we have sworn to uphold and defend the Constitution. I think it is high time that we remembered the Constitution speaks not only of freedom of speech, but also trial by jury instead of trial by accusation. Those of us who shout the loudest about Americanism in making character assassinations are all too frequently those who, by their own words or acts, ignore some of the basic principles of Americanism—the right to criticize; the right to hold unpopular beliefs; the right to protest; the right of independent thought.[14]

Everyone in the Senate that day knew the intended target of Smith's rebuke, what Meacham termed being "four years ahead of most of her colleagues." But alas, only six other senators joined her in their condemnation of the tactics being utilized by Congress' badgering antagonist from the Badger State, and McCarthy was quick to defiantly label them "Snow White and the Six Dwarfs." Unfortunately, other Republicans were only too

14. Turning the Other Cheek in a No-Win War

willing to see where "McCarthy's act" might take them. One, John Bricker of Ohio, supposedly even said, "Joe, you're a real SOB, but sometimes it's useful to have SOBs around to do the dirty work." As for McCarthy's in-state approval among his Wisconsin constituents at that time, Milwaukee Mayor Frank Zeidler attested, "He's unbeatable right now. He's a Northern Huey Long."[15]

Most of McCarthy's attacks continued to be aimed at Truman's State Department and in particular Acheson, whose friends rallied to the Secretary's defense. After vowing not to turn his back on the convicted Hiss, he at first felt good about his statement that day and his support for his discredited former staffer. He labeled McCarthy and his Republican backers "primitives" and "beneath contempt." But along with Truman, he underestimated their staying power. Later he would acknowledge that his initial loyalty to Hiss had hurt the State Department and much later his wife would confide that the "attack of the primitives" had taken 10 years off his life. Meanwhile, "McCarthy's witch-hunt," as Walter Isaacson and Evan Thomas would term it in *The Wise Men*, resulted in the immediate firing of 91 employees and over the next three years the Loyalty Boards established by Truman to pre-empt right-wing attacks would end up dismissing hundreds more as security risks. Most, however, were "innocents." Acheson manfully tried to defend his subordinates whenever possible, but as the co-authors added, "He could not afford to take a high profile and make a crusade out of protecting his underlings," as "he was damaged goods" in the eyes of a Cold War wary public convinced that communists were lurking everywhere. By being "true to himself" and coming to Hiss' defense, "he had exhausted his

The only GOP senator to rebuke the dirty tactics of fellow Republican Joe McCarthy was also the first woman who would serve in both Houses of Congress, Maine's Margaret Chase Smith. In June 1950, Smith famously admonished the Wisconsin senator on the Senate floor for his rejection of basic American principles (Library of Congress Prints and Photographs Division—Reproduction Number LC-USZ62-42661).

moral capital," especially as Korea heated up and U.S. containment policy shifted from diplomacy back to the military.[16]

Among the more surprising supporters of Joe McCarthy was Joseph Kennedy, the wealthy former wartime ambassador to Great Britain and the father of a future Democratic president. Having himself experienced rebuke and recall for criticizing the British decision to stand alone against Germany at the start of World War II while representing the Roosevelt administration at the Court of St. James, the elder Kennedy "enjoyed McCarthy's company" and "admired his big mouth, his outspoken confrontation with the government establishment (especially the State Department), his take no prisoners attacks on the Truman administration, and his contempt for diplomacy and decorum." That's according to Kennedy biographer David Nasaw, who authored *The Patriarch: The Remarkable Life and Turbulent Times of Joseph P. Kennedy*. Like Kennedy an Irish Catholic, McCarthy would also benefit from Kennedy money in his re-election campaign, briefly date two of Kennedy's daughters, and even employ Robert Kennedy, the future president's younger brother (and recent University of Virginia Law graduate) as legal counsel for his Subcommittee on Investigations. As an assistant attorney under Roy Cohn, the subcommittee's soon-to-be infamous chief counsel, "Bobby" Kennedy would eventually have a falling out over the aggressive tactics witnesses were being subjected to in the Senate hearings and resign. He was convinced Cohn "was going to get McCarthy and everyone who worked for him in trouble." Ironically, four years later, when the Senate finally voted to censure McCarthy by a 67–22 vote, the only Democrat absent that day who did not cast a vote against the Wisconsin senator would be Senator John F. Kennedy of Massachusetts, conveniently absent due to illness.[17]

Long before that vote, however, the war in Korea was front and center on a daily basis for the Truman administration. After initially doing nothing but retreat in the face of the surprise North Korean onslaught pushing south, the United Nations forces, anchored primarily by American soldiers, rallied at the southeasternmost part of the peninsula, establishing what became known as the "Pusan Perimeter." By August 5, 1950, the retreating Americans had stopped their retreating and solidified their defenses on two sides, facing north and east with the Sea of Japan at their backs to the west and the Straight of Korea and seacoast city of Pusan behind them to the south. From there, the U.N. forces steadied themselves, repulsing repeated North Korean charges at different points along the perimeter as the enemy probed for a weak spot in the defensive line. Based in Tokyo as supreme commander of the Pacific Theater ever since accepting the surrender of Japan at the end of World War II, and overseeing that former enemy's occupied return to unmilitarized global acceptance, General Douglas MacArthur, one of five

14. Turning the Other Cheek in a No-Win War

legendary U.S. Army generals to attain five-star ranking from their leadership in World War II (the others being Marshall, Eisenhower, Omar Bradley, and Hap Arnold), had been slow to react to the North Korean assault. By then 70 years of age, MacArthur had ignored warning signs emanating from the ideologically divided peninsula ever since 1945, focusing instead on Japan's conversion from ancient monarchy that somehow achieved what Halberstam termed "economic and military modernity" despite "social and political feudalism" to a more "egalitarian, democratic society," and by 1950 the job he was doing there was being lauded both in Japan and Stateside. He rather obviously cared little for Korea, South or North, an attitude developed more from the primacy given Japanese and Chinese cultures in Western historical thought. Again, as Halberstam stated in *The Coldest Winter*:

One of five five-star American generals in World War II, Douglas MacArthur was the commanding officer in the Pacific when North Korea initiated the Korean War by invading the South in 1950. Initially taken by surprise, MacArthur would reverse the course of the conflict with some daring strategy before controversy marred his command (Library of Congress Prints and Photographs Division—Reproduction Number LC-USZ62-21027).

"Korea was a small, proud country that had the misfortune to lie in the historical path of three infinitely larger, stronger, more ambitious powers—China, Japan, and Russia." Speaking for MacArthur, Halberstam clearly felt Korea meant little to the U.S. without the threat of global communism.[18]

But as of summertime 1950 that was the threat and America's top general in that part of the world was suddenly on the clock to deal with it. Although fighting under a United Nations flag rather than American, thanks to the Truman administration's "police-action" approach, the commanding general in the Pacific was not one of the most decorated U.S. soldiers ever without good reason and after his forces retreated in the best order possible, he went to work devising an ingenious plan to get them relief and turn the tide of a conflict that was even entertaining talk of evacuation (a la the British at Dunkirk in World War II) if something dramatic wasn't forthcoming. That drama would take place at another Korean seacoast town, the Port of Inchon on the opposite, west coast and well behind the frontlines. Halberstam said, "It reflected the supreme self-confidence [of MacArthur] and the Tokyo command about what American troops could accomplish," but it would involve an amphibious landing, which was always "fraught with danger" and in a place the Navy felt must have been "created by some evil genius" without "beaches, only seawalls and piers," and with a heavily guarded island "smack in the middle of the harbor."[19]

Out of necessity, the landing and offensive would come at high tide and with the threat of mines throughout the harbor on September 15, 1950. A total of 13,000 U.S. Marines reached the seawalls and piers, and breached the North Korean defenses, including the heavily fortified island, immediately turning the American led U.N. war effort from defense to offense, as it recaptured Seoul, the South Korean capital, and erased North Korea's supply lines. After originally underestimating North Korea's fighting capacity, MacArthur had pulled off the totally unexpected against a now overconfident opponent. Inchon would forever be memorialized as the war's turning point. Unfortunately, it should have also been the reason for its conclusion. Soon enough the North Korean forces were in full retreat, back above the 38th parallel they had surged across less than three months earlier to begin the conflict. It's the boundary that still divides North and South Korea. Suing for peace in that moment and renewing the peninsula stalemate left over from World War II to avoid further aggression and bloodshed would have been a wise choice without the threat of another global confrontation. MacArthur, however, had other ideas.[20]

As far back as 1948, the General had made known through American media outlets his belief that the loss of China to communism would "imperil the United States" and along with the pro–China, right wing press, which included *Time*, *Life*, and *Fortune* magazines' magnate Henry Luce, the son of missionaries to China and leader of the China-first Republican lobby in Congress, MacArthur had stateside support. At about the same time, McCarthy and a sidekick, William Knowland of California, began to question whether the administration was doing enough in support of the besieged Nationalist Chinese government of General Chiang Kai-Shek, which would ultimately be forced to abandon the huge Chinese mainland to the Mao Zedong–led communists, setting up shop on the island of Formosa (now Taiwan). With China in communist hands, in fact, Acheson's State Department would be compelled to produce a China White Paper once General Marshall's previously mentioned mission to the "Middle Kingdom" proved "fruitless," as the Nationalist Chinese were unable to

14. Turning the Other Cheek in a No-Win War

shore up allegiances and their resources insufficient to forestall the Communist Chinese takeover or, at the very least, work out a compromise regime. The report covered the years 1944–1949 and was designed to head off Republican criticism of China policy during the Truman years, including acknowledgment of the suddenly wasted $2 billion expenditure in support of China's exiled government. In *Truman*, McCullough recounted Acheson's lament that this huge investment "had not been enough" and "the fault was in the internal decay of Chiang Kai-Shek's regime, its rampant corruption, lack of leadership, [and its] indifference to the aspirations of the Chinese people." The Secretary of State added: "The unfortunate but inescapable fact is that the ominous result of the civil war in China was beyond the control of the United States. It was the product of internal Chinese forces; forces which this country tried to influence but could not." Nevertheless, it remained a prime Republican talking point and it still was when MacArthur, a Republican presidential wannabe himself, reversed the Korean conflict and had, in his estimation, the communists on the run.[21]

"The specific issue being used against Truman was China," Halberstam emphasized. "Both Truman and Acheson were aware of the political game being played and they were contemptuous of the men who were leading the gathering force." The Republicans had their issue and were plotting a "political barbecue" in the lead-up to the 1950 midterms. To combat this anticipated attack over China and Korea, Truman reverted to what had worked so well for him during his 1948 presidential campaign—a cross country train tour during which he would make more than 50 speeches in 15 states. It was arranged in conjunction with the President's previous commitment to dedicate the massive Grand Coulee Dam in Washington State. According to McCullough, never once in all those speeches, however, did he mention McCarthy or "sound a call to arms" as he had so often done in his come-from-behind, whistle-stop crusade two years earlier. "Instead," his biographer wrote that "he seemed to glow with patience and optimism," while maintaining that although the Cold War figured to be around a while, it would produce no problems that could not be effectively resolved.[22]

Meanwhile, the Republicans were calling for Acheson's resignation, prompting Truman's assurance that his secretary of state wasn't going anywhere—"period." And when *Time* magazine speculated there was "suspicion" within Congress that the State Department had indeed "played footsie" with the communists "over China," McCarthy labeled the ongoing Asian conflict "the Korean death trap" and charged the whole thing could be laid "at the doors of the Kremlin [Russia's seat of power] and those who sabotaged rearming China [at the end of World War II], including Acheson and the President." McCarthy even attempted to frame Millard Tydings, the Democrat whose Senate subcommittee had found no evidence to support his claims of State Department malfeasance, by forging a fake photo of the Maryland senator in the company of Earl Browder, head of the American Communist Party. Obviously, such wanton accusations severely tested Truman's resolve to ignore the Wisconsin sensationalist. Even the First Lady, fed up with McCarthy's dirty politics, chastised the President for not using his "presidential bully-pulpit" to pressure his over-reaching Senate rival. Through it all, however, Truman remained, in McCullough's words, "calm and steady."[23]

About that time, speaking of over-reaching, MacArthur on his own would make a military and ultimately political evaluation that would change everything. Never one to interpret civilian authority and leadership as superior to his own (symptomatic of an old, family grudge left over from his father's bitter experience as a celebrated but stymied military lieutenant general), MacArthur believed North Korea, as the perpetrator of the conflict, could and should be made to collapse once its defeated army retreated back across the 38th parallel, so he sent his own forces across that boundary as well, seizing the initiative and taking advantage of what Halberstam called some "surprisingly ambiguous" orders coming out of Washington. Regardless of the North Korean response or ability to repulse the U.N. force, which had effectively turned the tables as far as potential reunification of the peninsula was concerned, the American commander was to "avoid any act that would engage the United States and the United Nations in a larger war with either the Russians or Chinese." But to that possibility, MacArthur was convinced the still fledgling Chinese Army would never come into the war—even as American troops drew closer and closer to North Korea's border with China at the Yalu River. With the wind of victory at his back after Inchon and the communists in full retreat, the old General's blood was up and his goal of a reunited, non-communist Korea was suddenly of paramount importance to him, without regard to signals emanating from across the Yalu. MacArthur was obviously fixated on putting an end to the first communist country history had sent against him and not particularly worried about the potential (and much more dangerous) enemy on the other side of the river.[24]

More than any other American military miscalculation of the 20th century, Halberstam believed MacArthur's decision to advance all the way to the Chinese border ranks as the worst, because by October 15, 1950, with the acknowledgment and approval of both the Soviet Union and the now desperate North Koreans, troops of the Red Chinese Army had begun crossing the Yalu relatively undetected at first, but soon in overwhelming numbers. But combined with the fact the Chinese had virtually no air force yet, giving the U.N. forces total air superiority, "the China that existed in MacArthur's mind was one that had actually not been touched

14. Turning the Other Cheek in a No-Win War 183

by revolution [the way Russia had in 1917]," Halberstam revealed. As would become painfully obvious, however, had been and Mao's mastery of that country through his "Long March" and the massive manpower at his disposal should have never been underestimated, as it was by MacArthur.[25]

Ironically, the Chinese offensive would secretly be planned the same day as the first ever, face-to-face meeting between Truman and his commanding general in the Pacific at Wake Island. MacArthur thought it a waste of time and a violation of his sense of hierarchy and deference due him at that time. According to a young officer on MacArthur's staff, Vernon Walters, the General did not believe anyone from Washington outranked him and that was especially true of the titular leader of the rival party. Needless to say, the meeting began in what Halberstam described as "an atmosphere of mutual suspicion" and did not go well. MacArthur remained dismissive of the signals coming out of the Chinese capital (Beijing) and, according to H.W. Brands in his 2016 book *The General vs. The President*, assured the President that "victory in Korea was [already] won." Upon departing at the Wake Airfield, MacArthur impetuously asked the President if he would run for re-election in 1952, to which Truman responded noncommittally with the same question of the General. "No," MacArthur reportedly answered before adding, "If you have any general running against you, his name will be Eisenhower, not MacArthur," a statement obviously predicting Republican intentions two years later. And by the time MacArthur had returned to Tokyo to oversee his highly anticipated wrap-up and reunification of Korea remotely, his "misread of Red China," as another historian labeled it, had come home to roost—regardless of air superiority or any other advantage.[26]

DeGregorio very concisely summarized what happened next, when he wrote:

> Hundreds of thousands of Chinese poured across the border in January 1951 and drove the Americans back south. MacArthur then called for all-out war against China. When Truman refused to extend the conflict for fear of touching off World War III and a possible nuclear exchange with the Soviet Union, MacArthur publicly criticized U.S. policy. Unwilling to tolerate such insubordination, Truman relieved the popular general of his command four months later—a decision that drew a firestorm of criticism from the political opposition.

And fellow presidential historian Kenneth Davis would take that description further, when he wrote:

> At home, "hawks" supported total commitment to the war effort and were led by MacArthur and the powerful China Lobby of Republican senators and media moguls [like the before mentioned Henry Luce], who all wanted all-out war against communism, including an assault on China. In one of the most dramatic moments of the Korean War, Truman fired General MacArthur, a World War II

hero, a presidential aspirant, and one of the most popular men in America, for insubordination. MacArthur wanted Truman to drop 30 to 50 atomic bombs on mainland China. A great general and icon in most Americans' eyes, MacArthur publicly rebuked Truman's decision not to commit U.S. air power to attacking China and the President's war strategy in general. He came home to a hero's welcome and Truman's approval ratings plummeted.[27]

Basically, everyone in the administration agreed with Truman's decision to relieve MacArthur, including his military peers and superiors on the Joint Chiefs; the Department of Defense with former General Marshall at the helm; as well as Acheson's State Department. Marshall biographer Forest Pogue pointed out that McCarthy had by now re-directed his attacks by focusing on the former general and secretary of state. "Defeats in Korea and the removal of MacArthur had aroused ancient hostilities against Marshall and particularly his ongoing defense of Acheson," his successor at State. McCarthy called Marshall "completely unfit," "completely incompetent," and demanded his dismissal from Truman's Cabinet, especially after he supported the decision to remove his fellow five-star general from command in Korea. On June 4, 1951, McCarthy rose in the Senate to castigate one American military icon, Marshall, in support of another, MacArthur. Given advance notice via the Washington press corps of what was coming, the galleries were packed to overflowing for his speech, which he had even titled "America's Retreat from Victory: The Story of George Catlett Marshall." *The Congressional Record* reported his speech lasted nearly three hours, "twisted quotes, drew unwarranted conclusions from the facts he did get right, and accused the revered Marshall of having made common cause with Stalin [the Soviet despot] in 1943." Although he later denied he had actually accused Marshall of treason, it "was not unreasonable to conclude that McCarthy was accusing Marshall of nothing less than being pro-communism." Again, in *Truman*, McCullough concluded: "The scourge of Joe McCarthy that Truman had thought would go away was by then still poisoning the entire political atmosphere." He accused both Marshall and Acheson of being part of a "mysterious" communist conspiracy "so immense" that it surpassed any "such venture" in history. He chided Marshall for the "disastrous" China policy after World War II and for a military strategy that was making the war in Korea "a pointless slaughter," and he insinuated Truman was "no longer master of his house" and of being guided by a world-wide conspiracy that had been hatched "in Moscow," the Soviet capital. Needless to say, the President was furious and finally sought advice on what he should do about McCarthy.[28]

An unofficial committee of four Democratic senators, the attorney general, solicitor general, Democratic Party chairman, veteran Kentucky

14. Turning the Other Cheek in a No-War War   185

Congressman Brent Spencer, and White House Council Clark Clifford was convened to consider what McCullough termed McCarthy's "hectoring and innuendo, his horrors and dirty tricks, his delight in the ruin of innocents," as well as the most effective "antidote" for such "poison." Mentioned was a "devastating dossier" that was being compiled on the Wisconsin senator, including "details on his bedmates" through the years—enough to blow up the whole "McCarthy show." There were suggestions that this material could be leaked to the press, but speaking in the third person, Truman emphatically put an end to "such talk" by emphasizing: "You must not ask the President of the United States to get down in the gutter with a guttersnipe. Nobody, not even the President, can approach too close to a skunk in skunk territory and expect to get anything out of it but a bad smell. If you think somebody is telling lies about you, the only way to answer is with the whole truth."[29]

From that point on at press conferences whenever asked for his views on McCarthy, Truman, "though plainly seething," according to his biographer, would simply answer "no comment." And taking the President's lead, Marshall also refused to respond, stating privately that if at this point in his long and distinguished service "he had to explain that he was not a traitor, then it was hardly worth the effort."[30] The furor over Truman's firing of MacArthur would eventually subside and the President would actually be exonerated by testimony given by the Joint Chiefs and others McCarthy had treated with contempt during additional Senate hearings in May 1951, with influential Georgia Democrat Richard Russell presiding. Throughout the inquiry, both Truman and MacArthur were treated fairly, for which Russell received acclaim for "defusing" what a biographer of his would term "a highly inflammatory situation." Once General Omar Bradley, Marshall, and Acheson all laid out the series of insubordinate actions MacArthur had committed while prosecuting the Korean Conflict, it became clear the President had no choice but to remove him in favor of a much younger and more efficient General Matthew Ridgway, who would lead the way until the war concluded in stalemate under President Eisenhower in 1953. Nonetheless, with the Senate still failing to rein in McCarthy's charges, Truman would have to continue his "no comment" posture for the remainder of his White House days.[31]

McCarthy, in fact, would carry over his anti-communist agenda into the early Eisenhower years, even though the presidency had finally been flipped to the Republicans after 20 years of Democratic rule. By then, his was a tired act and his own party really didn't need him mounting attacks or raising suspicions of Democrats anymore. Halberstam touches on that sudden non-partisan transformation by the Republicans in *The Fifties*, when he wrote:

For McCarthy, Eisenhower's election was the beginning of the end. Now that the Republicans had the White House, they wouldn't need McCarthy any longer. What would take place, of course, was the denouement. McCarthy did not understand, of course, that his real value was not in uncovering spy rings, which he almost certainly had not been doing, but as a partisan ploy, allowing worthier men to keep their hands clean.[32]

15

From Fearmongering to Covert Action

Harry Truman's successor in the White House wasn't so much elected president as preordained. For General Dwight D. Eisenhower—much like Generals George Washington and Ulysses Grant before him—the job was his whenever he wanted it. As with the American Revolution and Civil War, a grateful nation was more than happy to inaugurate its pre-eminent general of World War II, despite no prior political experience, in 1952. Chances are it would have done the same thing in 1948 if he had wanted the job then, but at that time, no one even knew which political party he would call his own. As a result, playing the partisan waiting game made sense (although several leading Democrats, including a couple of FDR's sons, did try to recruit him as a replacement for Truman in '48).

Once he made up his mind, World War II's victorious supreme Allied commander in Europe, "Ike," as Eisenhower was affectionately known, would win the 1952 GOP presidential nomination on the Republican Convention's first ballot after not entering the race until early June—just five months before the election. Senator Robert Taft, the favorite of the conservative wing of the Republican Party and the pre-convention favorite, was overwhelmed by a draft Eisenhower movement that began with the chant "Taft can't win" and ended in a rout, 845 delegate votes to only 280 for Taft, including a midnight switch of votes by the Minnesota delegation that ultimately put Ike over the top.[1]

In 2007, Mark Perry, a critically acclaimed author and journalist, wrote a book about the unique partnership that existed during World War II between Eisenhower and his immediate superior, General Marshall. As the story goes, Marshall had actually been in line to command the Allied armies in Europe, but because President Roosevelt wanted to keep Marshall close at hand in Washington, modern history's choicest military assignment, the liberation of Western Europe from Nazi Germany, including the now famous D-Day invasion (June 6, 1944), fell to Eisenhower, Marshall's hand-picked choice.

As a result, with that sort of mutual trust and admiration in their past, the most eye-opening episode of the 1952 Eisenhower presidential campaign and landslide victory over his Democratic opponent, urbane and intellectual Adlai Stevenson, the governor of Illinois, involved none other than the already infamous Joe McCarthy. Perry recounted the episode thusly:

> In the midst of his campaign ... Eisenhower was asked whether he would endorse the bid of Senator Joseph McCarthy for another term [in the Senate]. Eisenhower maintained his silence on the subject, but in private he hated McCarthy, resented his mindless criticisms of [Marshall], and refused to forgive him. When the time came, he vowed, he would denounce him. Eisenhower had even written a speech defending Marshall, to be delivered in Milwaukee, when McCarthy [would be] seated on the platform behind him. But the Republican gang, as well as leaders of the Republican Party and Wisconsin's governor, flew to Peoria, Illinois (where Eisenhower was campaigning), to urge Eisenhower to appear with McCarthy and say nothing. His criticism of McCarthy would do nothing to help Marshall now, they said, and it could hurt his majority in the state. Eisenhower reluctantly deleted the offending paragraphs, and one week later, in Milwaukee, he stood on the same stage as the senator. He remained silent. The next morning, the nation's papers commented on Eisenhower's apparent endorsement of McCarthy's views. That is what his silence meant, they said. Serving out his last months in the White House, Harry Truman was enraged. He denounced Eisenhower then and throughout the [remainder of] the campaign. Eisenhower was surprised by Truman's vitriol; he had made his views on Marshall clear in public. "There is nothing of disloyalty in General Marshall's soul," he told one audience. While never mentioning McCarthy's name, he told another audience that he had "no patience with anyone who can find in [Marshall's] record of service for this country anything to criticize." ... Even so, there it is: Eisenhower's silence remains a stain on the Eisenhower legacy.[2]

On that same affair, Jon Meacham would write of the Milwaukee omission:

> Eisenhower was slated to defend Marshall in no uncertain terms. "I know that charges of his disloyalty have in the past been leveled against General George C. Marshall," Eisenhower was to have said. "I have been privileged for 35 years to know General Marshall personally. I know him as a man and as a soldier to be dedicated with singular selflessness and the profoundest patriotism to the service of America. And this episode is a sobering lesson in the way freedom must not defend itself." Ike never uttered the words. Talked out of it by political advisers who thought it unwise to antagonize McCarthy and his supporters. Eisenhower always regretted his failure to say what he thought, and he hated that the world knew what had happened [after] word of the dropped paragraph leaked to the *New York Times*. "It turned my stomach," General Omar Bradley would later [say] of the Eisenhower-Marshall-McCarthy episode.[3]

Thus, for the sake of political expediency and party loyalty did the professed non-political Eisenhower side with the mudslinging

15. From Fearmongering to Covert Action

McCarthy at the expense of his longtime friend and colleague in arms, Marshall. Distasteful as that was for Truman, Bradley, and others in the administration and military establishment, it also gave notice that the Wisconsin senator was not going away just because a fellow Republican was about to enter the White House. "To Truman, with his devotion to George Marshall, Eisenhower had committed an act of unpardonable betrayal," McCullough would acknowledge. McCarthy would retain his Senate seat and resume his ceaseless diatribes and warnings. By then it was the only political game he knew, and Eisenhower would just have to put up with it—much like Truman. "Although documents reveal Eisenhower working behind the scenes to blunt McCarthy, Ike never publicly challenged the Wisconsin senator as he continued his vitriolic and dangerous campaign against communist subversion in America," Kenneth Davis stated in 2014.[4] At the same time, the eight-year Eisenhower administration would become more impactful behind the scenes than out in front of them.

After being re-elected in 1952, Senator McCarthy not only continued his anti-communist crusade, but expanded it even with a Republican at 1600 Pennsylvania Avenue. One historian of the era worded it this way: "For several years he captivated the nation by charging that communists had launched 'a conspiracy so immense and an infamy so black as to dwarf any previous venture in the history of man.'" Among the

President Dwight Eisenhower. With his ascension in 1952 as the first Republican president in 20 years, most political pundits felt Joseph McCarthy's scurrilous accusations of communist infiltration into the previously Democratic federal government would finally end. But they were sadly mistaken, as the junior senator from Wisconsin continued his fearmongering and guilt by association (Library of Congress Prints and Photographs Division—Reproduction Number LC-DIG-ppmsca-38556).

agencies he (again) singled out as having been infiltrated by communists were the State Department and the (increasingly influential Central Intelligence Agency or) CIA, which had come into existence just five years earlier under Truman as a clearinghouse for foreign intelligence and was becoming a huge contributor in the containment of communist expansion. In addition to its primary purpose to collect, analyze, evaluate, and disseminate foreign intelligence, it also became the only agency under the National Security Council authorized to conduct covert overseas operations. Exactly what that had entailed up to that time other than the gathering of foreign surveillance is hard to equate (although MacArthur would blame the CIA rather than his own military intelligence sources for his lack of advance knowledge of Communist China's entry into the Korean Conflict), but McCullough makes clear Truman "never intended the CIA to become what it did." On the other hand, what it became was evident almost immediately under his successor.[5]

Perhaps Eisenhower, given all his years in Europe as head of the Supreme Headquarters Expeditionary Force (SHAEF), with all the intricate, international give-and-take and behind the scenes maneuverings he must have experienced in that role, was more amenable to under-the-table overseas operations than his presidential predecessor had been. Or perhaps as a political novice he wasn't wary of using American power and influence to cut some diplomatic corners as long as he could maintain plausible deniability, but whatever the excuse, there's no denying the CIA became a much more aggressive foreign undercover operation during the Eisenhower years. Of that development, Davis would write: "Under Eisenhower, the CIA was allowed to run roughshod with covert operations." Eisenhower's new secretary of state, John Foster Dulles, was U.S. legal counsel at the First World War's Versailles Peace Conference more than three decades before and more recently a U.S. senator from New York. And his younger brother Allen Dulles, a veteran State Department diplomat, had become the first civilian head of the CIA. According to Stephen Kinzer, an award-winning foreign correspondent, in a 2013 book he authored on the Dulles brothers, Foster had made a convert of Eisenhower while he was still overseeing post-war Europe but already the presumptive Republican presidential nominee. As a private attorney at the prestigious New York law firm of Sullivan & Cromwell, the elder Dulles had "arranged to be invited to give a speech in Paris, where Eisenhower was serving. They had two long conversations, and Foster left the General with the manuscript of an article called, 'A Policy of Boldness' that he had just written for *Life* magazine. It charged the Democrats with following a cowardly policy, seeking only containment of communism, while Republicans would take the offensive. They would secure

15. *From Fearmongering to Covert Action* 191

As President Eisenhower's secretary of state, John Foster Dulles would oversee the United States' turn to covert action against foreign governments and individual leaders during the remainder of the Cold War. Assisting in this change of approach from the Truman years would be Dulles's brother, Allen, as the first civilian head of the still new Central Intelligence Agency (CIA) (Library of Congress Prints and Photographs Division—Reproduction Number LC-DIG-ds-01102).

the 'liberation' of 'captive nations' and crush 'communist stooges' around the world."[6]

This openly defiant and aggressive approach was John Foster Dulles' introduction to the next president of the United States, and it must have made an impression because gradually some of the sentiments in that article began to find their way into Ike's campaign speeches. Although exaggerated because of established knowledge that Truman had come to the aid of the Greek government in 1947; that he had met the Soviet challenge at Berlin and instituted the Marshall Plan in 1948; that he had entered NATO in 1949; and that he had stopped the communist takeover of Korea in 1950, all of which were evidence of the Truman Doctrine, Dulles' influence nonetheless must have resonated with the new president and his get-even-tougher message on communism obviously appealed to the voters, who gave Eisenhower a resounding victory in 1952.[7]

The Dulles worldview resonated with Eisenhower so much, in fact, that he named Foster secretary of state over the objections of several prominent foreign statesmen, including British Foreign Secretary Anthony Eden as well as, somewhat surprisingly, previously noted conservative mainstay Henry Luce, who recommended Dewey while privately hoping for the job himself. At his Senate confirmation, Dulles would assert that not only was the influence and spread of Soviet communism the "gravest threat ever faced by the United States, but the gravest threat ever faced by what we call Western civilization or indeed any civilization which was dominated by a spiritual faith," according to Kinzer.[8]

At the same time Allen Dulles was ascending from deputy director of the CIA to the intelligence agency's top spot, Eisenhower nominated his trusted World War II chief of staff, Walter "Beetle" Smith, to be undersecretary of state, even though Smith, again according to Kinzer's *The Brothers: John Foster Dulles, Allen Dulles and Their Secret World War*, "made no secret of his concern over Allen's enthusiasm for extravagant covert actions." Others also warned the President of the younger Dulles's unorthodox mind, which, they said, would make it problematic for him to run such a large, worldwide operation. But just as with Foster, Ike fell under the Dulles spell and Allen would be confirmed by the Senate on February 26, 1953, setting up a team of brothers in the nation's two most influential foreign policy posts, a unique collaboration that would facilitate an American transition to covert conspiracy on the international stage.[9]

As Walter Isaacson and Evan Thomas would concisely document in *The Wise Men*, with Foster orchestrating foreign policy in the State Department, the agency managed by his brother was "in its freebooting heyday." It organized the overthrow of a government deemed to be pro-communist in Iran in 1953 and Guatemala in 1954; helped install pro–Western

15. From Fearmongering to Covert Action 193

governments in Egypt in 1954 and Laos in 1959; tried and failed to overthrow the government of Indonesia in 1958; infiltrated refugees to disrupt Soviet-bloc governments in Eastern Europe; ran sabotage operations against Communist China from nearby Laos and Burma; and plotted assassination attempts against China's Chou Enlai, Prince Lumumba of the Congo, Cuba's Fidel Castro, and Rafael Trujillo of the Dominican Republic.[10] Needless to say, while McCarthy continued to warn of communist subversives in the U.S. government, his Red Menace rumors had nothing on the Dulles brothers when it came to America's actual foreign subversion.

Meanwhile, "isolationism was [also] back on Capitol Hill and it was back strong." That was the judgment of Robert Caro as he authored *Master of the Senate*, covering the life and times of Democratic Minority and later Majority Leader Lyndon Baines Johnson during the Eisenhower years. With a Republican administration in charge, in fact, LBJ proved much more amenable to working with the new moderate in the White House than did many of his more conservative Republican colleagues. As previously referenced, Eisenhower would have been an immensely popular choice for president regardless of which party banner he ran under in 1952 and working with the World War II hero became a prerequisite of Johnson's ability to stay in office and get things done. As Caro worded it: "Since Eisenhower was popular, Johnson explained, whoever was supporting him would be on the popular side. The Democrats, he said, could be on the popular side—particularly if they were supporting Eisenhower and the Republicans weren't." And as a product himself of the more conservative Southern faction of the Democratic Party, LBJ was prepared to make that happen, especially in the foreign policy realm, where the prospective return of Republican isolationism had the potential to drive a wedge between the former Allied commander, a globalist, and his party. Of course, Johnson had to convince his Democratic caucus that such bipartisan agreement made sense. Once he did, it paid huge dividends for both his and Eisenhower's legacy.[11]

For instance, the most conservative Republicans in Congress sought to impugn the legacy of Democratic icon FDR, especially in regard to Roosevelt's final "Big Three" conference with British Prime Minister Winston Churchill and Stalin, the Russian premier, at Yalta, a resort city on the Black Sea, shortly before FDR's death in 1945. Once Stalin also died in March of 1953, the resurgent GOP conservatives felt empowered to question what the Roosevelt administration had actually acquiesced to by signing a war-ending pact. "Yalta gave these throwbacks a focus for their rage, for it symbolized so much of what they detested and feared: the usurpation of the sacred constitutional powers of Congress by the hated Roosevelt; the 'softness' on communism that had left Eastern European nations under Stalin's heel; not to mention the treachery implicit in those 'secret' agreements that they were certain existed." Such was Caro's spin on that time of Republican majorities in both the House and Senate.[12]

There was one problem with that, however: Eisenhower, as supreme Allied commander in Europe, had been the "implementer" of Roosevelt's agreements, and as president he was not disposed to seeing the agreements he had overseen suddenly scrutinized for purely political purposes, especially if their repudiation could open the door to similar scrutiny and repudiation by Russia (aka the Soviet Union). Instead, again according to Caro, Ike rejected "interpretation of the accords that 'have been perverted to bring subjugation of free peoples'" with the knowledge that Dulles as secretary of state had already investigated and found nothing to substantiate any "secret" agreements. The same Republican congressional contingent, upon realizing that President Eisenhower would not repudiate the Yalta accords and only accuse the Soviets of subverting them, began plotting harsher amendments of their own until a new voice was heard in the person of the Senate minority leader, LBJ, who conveniently sided with the President— the Republican President.[13]

It was the start of America's most cooperative and peaceful bipartisan relationships even after LBJ went from minority to majority leader in 1955 and one that would resist the same kind of isolationist tendencies that had cloistered American interests after World War I (and even in the earlier era before Theodore Roosevelt at the turn of the 20th century). Johnson, in fact, would draw criticism from some Democrats "for failing to square off more often against the popular Republican president," as presidential historian DeGregorio recounted LBJ's mastery on Capitol Hill, but their unusual symbiotic political relationship would contribute to a 1950s decade that seemed, according to Halberstam, "slower, almost languid," an "orderly era, one with a minimum of social dissent" and one of "general goodwill and expanding affluence." Unfortunately, this political era of truces and understanding at the highest levels of the federal government would not silence the cacophony of discordant accusations that continued, at least early on, from the mouth of Senator McCarthy. Davis, as a presidential historian, would confirm that "Ike never publicly challenged McCarthy" and the "great fear" that he continued to cultivate "would ruin lives and careers with 'guilt by association.'" For example, at least 300 people were "blacklisted" in Hollywood (as communists), as the Senator's accusations continued to fly "with little regard for due process or constitutional rights." With Truman comfortably enjoying retirement in Independence, Missouri, as of 1953, Johnson, as the highest-ranking Democrat, continued the waiting game—waiting on the Wisconsin senator's own, personal demise—waiting for him to take a step too far that would effectively silence him forever.[14]

15. From Fearmongering to Covert Action

That moment finally came in 1954, the fifth and final year of the McCarthy era, when he made the mistake of picking on the worst possible, most unassailable target—the United States Army. For a nation steeped in political wars and name-calling political campaigns, that would prove a bridge too far and the breaking point of public patience. Ultimately embarrassed by a documentary on national television by the famous broadcaster Edward R. Murrow, McCarthy followed that up with a fatal mistake by agreeing to his Senate subcommittee hearings being shown on live TV—investigative hearings pitting McCarthy vs. the U.S. Army—a dual development that exposed the shamefully fabricated nature of his accusations. Exposed as never before, his popularity plummeted right along with his credibility, allowing Johnson to bring charges that Republicans had to accept, which led to his censure by the Senate and showcased LBJ's legislative skill. Three years later, still in the midst of his second term in the Senate, Joe McCarthy would die of complications brought on by alcoholism at Bethesda Naval Hospital. Humbled and again an inconsequential (and by then unelectable) senator, he was just 49 years old.[15]

Meanwhile, Truman, who was already 69 when he left the White House, would live two more decades, dying in December 1972. Although at lower than low approval rankings when he left office, his legacy and presidential ranking would enjoy an amazing recovery in the years ahead. And with the collapse of Russia's Soviet government in 1991, in fact, his visionary policy during the Cold War, which always included avoiding all-out confrontation with the major communist nations if possible, was "vindicated." Speaking of that, historian Robert Dallek assessed Truman this way: "His contribution to victory in the Cold War without a devastating nuclear conflict elevated him to the stature of a great or near-great president."[16]

SECTION SIX

Civil Rights or Segregation
*Lyndon Johnson
vs. Richard Russell*

16

Anatomy of an Impending Political Breakup

No one was more instrumental in the political rise and acumen of future president Lyndon Baines Johnson of Texas than Richard Brevard Russell of Georgia. Both Southerners, they were nearly inseparable Senate colleagues as members of the powerful "Southern Bloc" during the early to mid–1950s, when racial segregation was finally having an impact on the national consciousness after World War II as a result of President Truman's post-war integration of the U.S. military, and the intensified demands of young African Americans for a better stake in the American way of life. For almost 100 years, or ever since the end of slavery and the Civil War, segregation—the social separation of the races—had been practiced in the South through the unceasing dedication and efforts of devout Southern leaders like Russell, a good man in every other respect and a loyal New Deal Democrat since rapidly ascending from speaker of the Georgia House of Representatives at just 30 years of age; to the youngest governor in the country by 33; and ultimately to the Senate by a twist of fate just 18 months later, when he decided to exit his gubernatorial term early in favor of a successful bid for Congress' Upper Chamber, following the death in office of Georgia Senator William Harris.[1]

With what his recent biographer and niece, Sally Russell, termed his "well-honed sense of timing in the political arena," this product of a large Georgia political family (15 children and his father as the elected chief justice of the Georgia Supreme Court when he died), who never married, captured the first of seven straight elections to the U.S. Senate in 1932, a run that would last through 1971 and make him one of the most powerful politicians of the 20th century. Eventually, such prestige would elevate his status to the point of having not one, but two federal office buildings named in his honor in Washington and Atlanta. "Quiet, self-effacing" and "a workhorse in the Senate, not a show horse," Russell was described by his niece as "a liberal in bad times and a conservative in good times," who refused minority

16. Anatomy of an Impending Political Breakup

and majority leadership posts in order to remain "archly conservative on race relations" at a time of growing pressure within the Democratic Party to support the civil rights so long denied Southern Blacks. For him, defending the traditional White Southern view of segregated society became "a heavier and heavier burden," as he led defense of it on the Senate floor in the decade of the 1950s.[2]

Nonetheless, it was a burden Richard Russell had accepted as early as 1948. As emphasized by his biographer, he had emerged as the undisputed leader of a group of Southern senators determined to derail all civil rights legislation. Although there is no evidence that he sought this role, Georgia's junior senator (Walter George was an even longer serving "Peach State" senator at the time) had earned this status with his clear understanding of the way the Senate worked and his ability to react quickly with well-organized defensive measures whenever Truman and others put forth civil rights legislation. Johnson biographer Robert Caro would illustrate Russell's influence this way: "Among Democratic senators, it was not the liberals who held the power in the Senate; it was the Southerners. Of the eight most powerful Senate committees, Southerners held the chairmanships of five

With federal office buildings named in his honor in both Washington and Atlanta, Georgia's Richard Russell was a mainstay of the Senate for 38 years. He actually died while still in office in 1971, having been elected to six consecutive terms after initially leaving the governor's mansion to run for the Senate in a special election (Library of Congress Prints and Photographs Division—Reproduction Number LC-DIG-ggbain-12826).

and another was held by a dependable Southern ally." As chairman of the Armed Services Committee, Russell usually spoke for this Southern caucus and hosted its regular meetings in his office. During a quarter century of his leadership up to that time, Southerners had never lost a civil rights battle and as a legislative strategist he was considered so masterful that political pundits even labeled him "the South's greatest general since Robert E. Lee."[3]

Into this Southern Senate dominance, confidently strode the ambitious presence of the newly elected junior senator from Texas, where he had staged a controversial, 87-vote upset of one of the most popular politicians in Lone Star State history, former Governor Coke Stevenson, in 1948. But 44-year-old Lyndon Johnson was not like most freshman senators. He was a politician in a hurry, and it did not take him long to assess who and what offered the best chance for rapid ascendance up the Senate pecking order. Explaining it in simple terms, esteemed historian Doris Kearns Goodwin described Johnson's entry into the Senate in her book *Leadership in Turbulent Times* this way:

> The Senate's "folkways" and "unwritten rules of the game" called upon freshman senators to serve a period of apprenticeship, show deference to their elders, refrain from speaking too often on the floor, concentrate on learning the expected "norms of behavior"—[all] habits of mind Johnson had long cultivated. Had he become a senator in a different era, he might not have been able to exercise his unique leadership talents to full effect, but the Senate Johnson entered was perfectly suited to his leadership style. No sooner had he arrived than he set about figuring out the structural machinery of the institution and it quickly became apparent to the freshman senator that power resided in an informal coalition, an inner club of Southern Democrats and conservative Republicans. A bargain had been struck whereby the conservative Republicans would vote with the South against civil rights legislation and, in return, the Southern Democrats would oppose liberal social and economic measures. The undisputed leader of this inner club, commanding the respect of almost every member of the Senate, was Richard Russell.[4]

Like Texan Sam Rayburn before him, the Speaker of the House of Representatives and another old bachelor whom Johnson had cultivated since first arriving in Washington as a congressional aide in 1931 (and later as a four-term congressman), Russell would become the next willing target of the LBJ admiration blitz. Recognizing that Russell, like Rayburn, was "lonely," the Texas freshman began "courting" the Georgian, Sally Russell confirmed, carving out a plan whereby he might ascend the Senate ranks as quickly as possible. Obviously married to his job and public service (again, much like Rayburn), Russell normally spent his evenings and weekends in the District of Columbia alone in his small apartment reading, without

16. Anatomy of an Impending Political Breakup 201

much social interaction away from work. "The Senate is my life and work," Caro reported Russell once told a reporter. "I don't have any family or home life." With the advent of Senator Johnson, however, that would gradually change.[5]

Originally striving for one of the coveted seats on the Senate Appropriations Committee regardless of his freshman status, Johnson would soon drop that request, focusing instead on the committee whose chairman was Richard Russell and his Armed Services Committee. Caro would note that Johnson believed there was only one way to get close to a man whose life was his work. "I knew there was only one way to see Russell every day, and that was to get a seat on his committee," he often said. "Without that, we'd most likely be passing acquaintances and nothing more. So, I put in my request for the Armed Services Committee." And once he landed one of the four vacant seats on the lesser-in-demand committee, he "threw himself" into the work and made a point of dropping by Russell's office every afternoon to seek advice on whatever committee assignment he had been given, making sure to keep his approach deferential as he began to fashion a mentor-protégé relationship with the man he would nickname "The Old Master." LBJ had always cultivated older, well-connected men who could aid his political rise and with Russell, as he had with Rayburn and so many others, he would take that practice and talent to another level. So much so, in fact, that the old bachelor—so used to big family gatherings and interactions whenever he was back home in Georgia—would become a regular guest at the Johnsons' Washington abode and a favorite of LBJ's wife ("Lady Bird"), and two young daughters (Lynda and Luci). Russell's niece turned biographer even admitted "it became a great pleasure for him to be included in the Johnson family circle, usually on short notice," and amidst Lady Bird favoring him with Southern cooking and the Johnson girls calling him "Uncle Dick," it's easy to understand just how close these old and new Southern senators would become. In the second of his volumes on the Johnson years, Caro even spelled out the bewitching ability LBJ had in this regard, when he wrote:

> Cultivating and manipulating older men possessed of power that could advance his ambitions, the young Lyndon Johnson employed obsequiousness and flattery so striking that contemporaries mocked him as a "professional son"—but that was no more striking than the openness with which he explained to them in detail his techniques of cultivation and manipulation, and boasted and gloated over his success in bending older men to his will. Each stage of his political climb was marked by perhaps the ultimate manifestation of [such] pragmatism in politics in a democracy.[6]

Johnson, who had entered New Deal politics by successfully cultivating the notice of then President Franklin Roosevelt as an up-and-coming young congressman in 1937, enhanced his Texas reputation and resources through his intimacy with Rayburn, "Mr. Sam," and ultimately he would subscribe to what he believed all "schoolchildren of mid-century America learned" through their so-called "three Rs—readin', riten', and 'rithmetic" … only for LBJ, the three R's would prove to be Roosevelt, Rayburn, and Russell.[7]

Throughout the 1950s, Johnson would not only entrench his relationship with Russell, but also his good standing with all of the Southern Bloc, strict segregationist senators like South Carolina's previously mentioned Thurmond, Virginia's Harry Byrd, Mississippi's John Stennis, and 17 other Southern Democrats under Russell's leadership. The benefits of this relationship would be manifested in 1955, just six years after LBJ's election to the Senate, when he was named Senate minority and later majority leader, primarily because of Russell's unflinching support. In the midst of the McCarthy years and Eisenhower's ascendance to the White House, the Democrats (as revealed in the last section) were cast as being soft on communism. As a result, when the Republicans became the majority party in Congress in 1952, the shakeup in seniority and leadership on the Democratic side of the aisle provided opportunity for anyone willing to take hold of their minority reality and bipartisan necessity. Such

After achieving a seat in the Senate in 1948 in a legendary Texas election decided by a mere 87 votes, Lyndon Johnson would rise to leadership of the Democratic Caucus five years later and become the most powerful Senate majority leader ever between 1955 and 1960. A master parliamentarian and arm-twisting vote-counter, he often kept the Senate in session over extended hours to get things done (Library of Congress Prints and Photographs Division—Reproduction Number LC-DIG-ppmsca-03141).

16. Anatomy of an Impending Political Breakup

a man (and opportunist) was LBJ, even though his first senatorial term was due to expire in two years. With the Democrats divided between progressive and conservative camps, but the liberals feeling more the brunt of Eisenhower's victory over Adlai Stevenson, the path was open for the caucus' most conservative voice, Russell, to either become the minority leader himself or decide who would be. In *Master of the Senate*, Caro described what initially transpired as Johnson, indeed, pushed Russell to become the Leader, promising, "I'll do the work and you'll be the boss." But Russell declined as he had been doing for years, realizing that as the Southern spokesman, he could not hope to maintain overall command of a divided party when any compromise of his states' rights leadership would no longer be possible. What he could do, however, was offer command to his Southern protégé, Johnson, which was probably what LBJ suspected he would do all along. So, when Russell's name was "put forth to become the minority leader" in January 1953, his biographer confirmed he "instead backed Johnson," who obviously wanted it and would have "the ability to affect compromise." LBJ's only condition, according to Caro ... that Russell move his desk directly behind his own desk in the Senate Chamber, since he "would be constantly needing the Old Master's advice."[8]

"With Dick Russell's endorsement, Johnson was unanimously elected." Thus was unleashed the most impactful Senate leader in modern American history and arguably all time. As mentioned previously and acknowledged in Russell's biography, "the goal" for Johnson and Russell "was not to oppose" the proposals of the new Eisenhower administration, but to see how they might be modified to "Democratic specifications." And for two years, this minority approach and relationship with Ike would produce unusual bipartisanship. With Democrats split between Russell's conservative South and the more liberal North and West, "Johnson, indeed, proved the man for the job and under his leadership, Democrats as opposite as Russell and the ultra-progressive Hubert Humphrey of Minnesota were soon working together within the caucus confines."[9]

As a result, when the Senate and House reverted to Democratic majorities in 1955 (with LBJ having been easily re-elected in 1954), the Johnson-Russell strategy of bipartisanship had been vindicated and as Caro asserted, the position of majority leader was about to become "powerful." Presidential historian William DeGregorio also acknowledged the youngest majority leader up to that time (46) "would emerge a dynamic, skilled parliamentarian with a keen instinct for workable compromise. Characteristically" DeGregorio continued, "he discouraged protracted debate [and] preferred instead to hammer out differences on the [Senate] floor. Unlike his predecessors, he routinely kept the Senate in night session to conclude pressing business." In other words, he set the agenda; set the legislative schedules; and despite "criticism from some Democrats for failing to square off more often against the popular Republican president," he got things done/passed[10]—what, unfortunately, has too often not been the case in American congressional history.

Over the next four years, Johnson would further inculcate his standing not only as a protégé of Richard Russell, but indeed, as the promising adherent of the entire Southern Bloc. As alluded to earlier, Lyndon Johnson was not just a Southern senator. Whenever it suited him, he could also be a Western senator, a rancher from the Texas Hill Country who shared Western as well as Southern ideals and roots. At the same time, he was a presidential aspirant despite being from the South and the existing belief in both major parties that no Southerner could be a legitimate presidential contender given the prevailing national bias against a section consumed with

The leader of the Southern Bloc of senators who controlled the Upper Chamber of Congress during the 1940s and '50s, Richard Russell of Georgia, shown here (third from left) with fellow Southerners (from left) Tom Connally of Texas, Walter George of Georgia, and Claude Pepper of Florida, was only 36 years old when he stepped down as Georgia's governor to successfully run for the Senate in 1933 (Library of Congress Prints and Photographs Division—Reproduction Number LC-DIG-hec-23959).

maintaining racial segregation. In *The White House Looks South*, William Leuchtenburg wrote:

> A national identity Johnson may have had, but for two decades no one could differentiate his behavior from that of any other Southern congressman, who dutifully followed the lead of ardent White supremacists such Tom Connally, the senior senator from Texas. Not long after Johnson first came to the House [in 1937], Connally is said to have told him, "Lyndon, you're a Texan. And don't forget that as a Texan you're a Southerner. If you throw down on the South and forget your origins, you're going to foreclose your progress, because the only people that will stand with you are the people from the South. The people from the North are never going to have any respect for you."

Meanwhile, Virginia Senator Willis Robertson voiced similar sentiments of the young LBJ when he said, "He was a Southern man ... and some people called him Western, but we called him Southern and Texas [had been] in the Confederacy."[11]

In keeping with such regionalized politics and in order to maintain electability as he first sought re-election in the House and eventually higher office in the Senate, LBJ would consistently oppose civil rights measures that came before Congress for two decades. Beginning with his initial election to the U.S. House of Representatives and continuing once he squeezed into the Senate in 1948, Leuchtenburg contended, "Lyndon Johnson gave the country good reason to think he was just another member of the Dixie [or Southern] Bloc." Although younger than the majority of his vested Southern colleagues in the Senate, LBJ gave every impression that he was in lockstep with the older Harry Byrds, Strom Thurmonds, and Richard Russells of Capitol Hill, a next generation defender, so to speak, of the Southern faith, but someone who might also serve the South as a more youthful and thus more useful intermediary between the sections. As a narrative about the "strange friendship" of "Richard B. Russell and Lyndon B. Johnson" in a 1989 issue of the *Missouri Historical Review* quoted by Leuchtenburg assessed: "Johnson had been raised in a segregated society and had voted with Southerners on civil rights bills, but was not identified so clearly with White supremacy and segregation that he could not work with Northern liberal and moderate Democrats."[12]

But "if conciliator, his inclinations retained a decidedly southward bend" as Leuchtenburg worded it, and he usually never strayed far from his power base—both his fellow Southerners in the Senate and the predominantly White, segregated voters of the Lone Star State. Perhaps the first time he did so as Senate majority leader followed the landmark *Brown vs. Board of Education* Supreme Court ruling in May 1954, which supposedly struck down racial segregation in public schools as unconstitutional, even if segregated schools were deemed equal in quality. That "separate but equal" mantra had become a mainstay of the South's defense of its divided public education system and whether true or not (with most people believing the latter), the unanimous Court decision was deemed "a catastrophe" by the vast majority of White Southerners and something that must be overcome in the days ahead by their elected representatives. Reacting to the ruling as one of those elected representatives caught in the middle of a regionally divided party and nation, LBJ is reputed to have said, "I'm damned if I do and damned if I don't. The Southern caucus and a lot of my people at home will be on me like stink on shit if I don't stand up and bray against the Supreme Court's decision. [And] if I do bray like a jackass, the red hots and senators with big minority [voting] blocs in the East and North will gut shoot me."[13]

One thing he did not do, however, was sign what became known as the "Southern Manifesto," a document issued by the South's congressional contingent less than two years after the *Brown* decision that, according to Leuchtenburg, "exalted Jim Crow" segregation as "'a part of the life of the people of many of the states,'" while also praising "'the motives of those states, which have declared the intention to resist forced integration by any lawful means.'" It also accused the U.S. Supreme Court of substituting "'naked judicial power for the established law of the land'" and denounced "'outside meddlers'" for trying to destroy "'the amicable relations between the White and Negro races'" that had been built over 90 years, inflicting "'chaos'" in its place. Sources agree, it was intended as a call on the Southern states to resist the *Brown* decision.[14]

Resisting what was described as "a calculated declaration of defiance by 100 men in the Houses of national political power" by John Egerton, a Southern journalist of the time, Johnson, as the Democratic Senate majority leader, would not sign the Manifesto (suffering a burned cross by night riders on his ranch property in Texas as a result). Instead, Caro confirmed that LBJ stayed as clear of the controversial document as possible and as far as Russell allowed him to stay. Admittedly, a few other Southern senators stayed clear as well, including Tennessee's more progressive duo of Albert Gore and Estes Kefauver, both of whom retained national aspirations, but none was more conspicuous in their absence from the Manifesto than the Majority Leader. Indeed, Johnson would first claim he had never seen it before it was released, a somewhat "disingenuous assertion," according to Caro, and later contend the Southerners had purposely not shown it to him in order to not put his Senate leadership in the compromised position of regional bias. He would also proffer the more heroic impression that they had not asked him to sign because they knew he would not bend to regional pressure. More likely was the idea that Russell and the other Southern Bloc leaders did not want to subject their suddenly ascendant political acolyte and potential national candidate to excessive media scrutiny or criticism.[15]

16. Anatomy of an Impending Political Breakup

As already touched on, this latter rationale for the absence of his signature on the Southern Manifesto resided in the concept that in the Jim Crow era, a Southern politician, no matter how powerful or high ranking in the congressional pecking order, would have an impossible path to the presidency. Russell had already experienced the liability that was Southern roots on the national stage, as his presidential nomination at the Democratic Convention of 1952, although flatteringly promising early on and based on his burgeoning influence in the Senate, was doomed to a third place finish once national electability became a second ballot issue and a Northern liberal, Stevenson, emerged as the majority choice. Though his biographer called him "a gracious loser" for stepping aside in that moment of regional, intra-party tension, the loss nevertheless had to hurt, especially for a consummate Democratic mainstay like Russell, who realized his path to the nomination would be forever blocked by his segregationist history. Leuchtenburg also addressed the revered Georgian's political limits when he quoted then North Carolina Governor Terry Sanford as saying, "I would have liked to have voted for Richard Russell, but [he] never had a chance because of the stance he had to take on the race issue. You know every real leader in the South was held back."[16]

With Russell's blessing, however, Johnson was determined to find a way around that roadblock. Always excessively ambitious, to the point of doing whatever it took to ensure electoral success and political progression, this was brought out repeatedly by Caro throughout his multi-volume masterpiece. In his *Means of Ascent* Introduction, Caro wrote: "Without the lure of new, greater power, the power he [already] possessed was meaningless to him." Later, in the third chapter of that same book, he wrote: "If one characteristic of Lyndon Johnson was a boundless ambition, another was a willingness on behalf of that ambition to make efforts that were also without bounds." And by the time he wrote *Master of the Senate*, LBJ's principal biographer would address the Senate majority leader's elephant-in-the-room ambition when he penned: "No Democrat could become president without the North's support—support not available to an advocate of segregation. It was therefore an article of faith in Washington that no Southerner could ever become president of the United States.... Lyndon Johnson was from Texas, one of the eleven states of the Confederacy. The taint of the South was upon him. For him to realize his greatest ambition, the taint would have to be removed."[17]

Immediately after the Southern Manifesto and with Russell's compliance, he set about removing the taint. Leuchtenburg also wrote about this new LBJ, who in 1957 would guide a watered-down civil rights bill through Congress—the first federal civil rights legislation passed in America since Charles Sumner's landmark Reconstruction bill in 1875. Although the bill was drastically limited from the original voting rights legislation proposed by Minnesota's Hubert Humphrey and other Northern Democratic progressives, the Majority Leader was labeled "a traitor to his own people," "a renegade," and "a double-crosser" by newspapers throughout the South for even allowing such a thing to come to a Senate vote. Meanwhile, there's every indication Russell was privately hoping LBJ might enjoy the presidential possibilities he had been denied and in so doing limit the civil rights bills he had to know were coming. As a result, Leuchtenburg recounted how Johnson was allowed to pursue this initial civil rights passage as a "safeguard" for "his party, the nation, and his career." Although threatening filibuster, the constitutional mechanism by which the Southern Bloc had always blocked past civil rights attempts, LBJ would secure enough amendments to the bill "to get it down to just a 'right to vote' bill that won't be too hard to live with," meaning just enough that his Southern colleagues in the Senate could stomach, keeping their filibuster under wraps ... at least for the time being.[18]

As determined as Johnson was to have the historic passage of a civil rights bill on his resume, Russell and the other Southerners "knew that he would give them some 'face savers' and that he had sufficient understanding of their plight [with their Southern constituents] to do things in such a way that they would not be isolated from the legislative process." And "what was much more important," according to Leuchtenburg, was that "the most important Southerners, led by Russell, thought of LBJ as the only Southerner who could become president and were [very] aware that he could not become president if he shared their unyielding opposition to civil rights." In other words, there was an ulterior motive involved in how the Southern Bloc inexplicably stood down on Johnson's 1957 bill, calculating they might gain more in the long run by not agitating their fellow Democrats from the North and West. After all, there was another presidential nomination already on the horizon for 1960 and when LBJ framed the impending Senate vote as "national rather than sectional legislation," it might as well have been code for a modest step that merely enhanced Democratic chances (and his own) three years hence. "In truth," as Leuchtenburg confirmed, "the [1957] law did not amount to much."[19]

What it most certainly did not do was address the school desegregation that had been mandated by the *Brown* decision or the ongoing racial separation taking place in all other public places throughout the South, something intrinsic to its original intent from both the progressive and African American perspectives, but also something Johnson had assured Russell would be removed before any serious voting began. Was it in essence all for show (?)—probably. Ever the "master" politician as Caro labeled him, LBJ held a meeting at his ranch in 1958 among veterans of

16. Anatomy of an Impending Political Breakup 209

his political campaigns. "He was convinced that he was the best man to be president," Caro acknowledged in the fourth volume of his Johnson biography, *The Passage of Power*. "He was very aggressive," one of those in attendance confirmed. "Anyone who didn't agree was wrong. He knew in his own mind that he was destined to be president of the United States."[20]

Equally focused on the big picture nationally at this time was Richard Russell, "who had," in Caro's words, "made his Southern caucus understand that the only way to make the South part of the United States again, 'to really put an end to the Civil War,' would be to elect a Southerner president, and they understood that their beloved 'Dick,' [having given] up his own dream, had anointed Lyndon as that Southerner." He had also made them understand "that in order for Johnson to attain the nomination he would first have to be perceived as a strong, successful Senate Leader, and therefore he would have to have a united party behind him and they must bend their views to support him."[21]

Thus, did Lyndon Johnson enter the last two years of his second Senate term at the peak of his legislative power. Newspapers throughout the country had considered passage of the 1957 Civil Rights Act the pinnacle of his congressional career and he would add more of those laurels in 1960, when he "engineered passage," according to William DeGregorio, of another civil rights bill establishing federal inspection of voter registration polls, effectively eliminating discriminatory practices that had been utilized throughout the South for decades. Rated "the most powerful majority leader in the history of the Senate," by award-winning historian Doris Kearns Goodwin, Johnson had also been judged "the best qualified candidate" by 1956 nominee Adlai Stevenson, and at one time (rather surprisingly) fellow senator and eventual 1960 Democratic nominee John F. Kennedy opined that he was "owed the nomination." But for Stevenson, Kennedy, and the prevailing party leadership, there would always be that one negative to the chances of a Johnson presidential run—his Southern roots.[22] That had to be why JFK felt comfortable in making his "owed" comment.

Regardless, LBJ sought to become the 1960 Democratic nominee despite his Southern heritage. To do so would have required just the right mix of a less than exciting field of candidates; the Democrats' most formidable campaign apparatus; and the kind of never-say-die, in-it-to-win-it attitude from the get-go that had always characterized Johnson's past political efforts. Unfortunately for him, none of those would be true. Although believing the nomination should be his by 1958, he delayed truly going for it until it was too late because of his belief that all of the other potential candidates had at least one fatal flaw, while he would be able to command the largest bloc of delegates—the South—going into the convention. At the same time, the field became more cluttered than he had assumed, as Kefauver, Humphrey, Missouri's Stuart Symington, and Stevenson (for a third time) all appeared likely to throw their influential hats in the ring along with the young and suddenly formidable Kennedy of Massachusetts, who would mount one of the best campaigns of the modern political era, relying on his large and politically motivated family, and his father's financial fortune. Taken by surprise as to the level of appeal for Kennedy, who would become the first Catholic president in U.S. history (finally overcoming the church-state bias that had doomed Democrat Al Smith's candidacy three decades earlier), Johnson completely underestimated the Kennedy charisma that along with his campaign organization overcame every primary obstacle and earned JFK the nomination with almost twice as many delegate votes—806 to 409.[23]

Ironically, Johnson would ultimately become Kennedy's vice-presidential running mate for the same reason most thought he could never be the top-of-ticket nominee—his Southern roots. Needing to ensure support from the traditionally Democratic South with what figured to be a very close election against Eisenhower's two-term vice president, Richard Nixon, Kennedy opted for LBJ as his VP over the objections of his family and party liberals because of the aid Johnson's presence on the ticket might provide the Northeastern-bred, Harvard-educated JFK among Southern voters (and indeed with Johnson on the ticket, the Dems would hold off the GOP in six Southern states, just enough to win one of the closest presidential elections ever). Johnson, meanwhile, also faced criticism from his backers for accepting the No. 2 slot, but after the requisite soul-searching and recovery from his earlier convention disappointment, his rationale for taking the VP job was simple—the fact that a return to the Senate would get him no closer to his presidential ambitions, while the vice presidency just might, as it had seven times before in American history when vice presidents ascended to the White House due to a presidential death in office. With Kennedy set to be the second youngest chief executive ever at 43, such developments did not seem likely in 1960, but given his lifelong ambitions and party loyalty, LBJ chose the course that made the most sense in that moment and following the narrow Kennedy-Johnson victory later that fall, he would faithfully serve the next three years in whatever assignment the President came up with despite never being in his inner circle.[24]

Through all kinds of foreign policy ups and downs, including the Bay of Pigs invasion disaster in Cuba in April of 1961, another Cold War Berlin Crisis later that same year, and the Cuban Missile Crisis in October 1962, probably the closest the United States would ever come to nuclear war with the Soviet Union, the Kennedy administration rolled with the punches and generally came off the better for it in the eyes of history. But in the domestic arena, where much had been expected, JFK's legislative initiatives had

16. Anatomy of an Impending Political Breakup

been stalled in Congress until the fate-filled day of November 22, 1963, forever changed the legacies of Kennedy, who was famously assassinated while riding in an open convertible motorcade through the downtown streets of Dallas, Texas, and his successor, Lyndon Johnson. Sworn in as president before ever leaving Dallas once Kennedy was pronounced dead, LBJ became president, not as he wanted, but just as he had always planned to be. And with his ascension to the White House, the Kennedy domestic agenda would be revisited in ways no one could have expected, least of all the senators of the Southern Bloc. All, that is, except Richard Russell.[25]

17

The End of Debate; the Start of Equality

Long the domain of long-winded speakers and speeches, the U.S. Senate's most time-honored function has always been policy discourse and debate. Since its inception as supposedly the more rational (or sensible) and thus more consistent (or reliable) Upper House in America's bicameral system of legislative democracy, the Senate idea probably came from the British House of Lords in Great Britain's Parliament, which had always been based on heredity or appointment. Usually composed of more established (or secure) representatives as a result, it theoretically provided an alternative to the more idealistic type of mass-driven representation to be found in the House of Commons—the British equivalent of the House of Representatives. From the get-go, America's Founding Fathers, while understanding the democratic need for a legislative branch with local representation based on the general populations of the individual states, also perceived possible danger if this large and potentially undisciplined House of the common man wasn't offset by older, wiser, more established decision-makers—men like themselves—to avoid the pitfalls of rash decisions that could result from more emotional, less experienced leadership.[1]

As a result, their elected House of Representatives would choose two senators from each state for what was expected to be a much steadier, more level-headed Senate. And in keeping with this concept of a wiser Senate being able to mitigate a more impulsive House was born the necessity of debate—of being able to hash out the various issues from all sides and constituencies in order to make the best, majority-based decisions on any legislation before becoming law. And ably fulfilling this crucial function after the original founders would be a progression of outstanding debaters, some of whom have been covered in these pages, senators like Henry Clay, Stephen Douglas, Charles Sumner, and yes, Richard Russell and Lyndon Johnson, two Southern Democrats whose careers intersected at a moment of great national debate. Upon the death in office of President John F. Kennedy and the ascension of Johnson to the White House in late 1963, their successful Senate partnership would come to an end, but their revised relationship would still command center stage as the country finally faced its inevitable question of civil rights.²

Perhaps the first great Senate debater, as credited in *The American Senate* by Richard Baker and Neil MacNeil, and the first to hold court on the Senate floor for hours at a time was John Randolph of Roanoke, Virginia. He apparently loved to lecture his fellow senators, holding them captive in the mid–1820s until they asked for something called a "corrective" or began the practice of walking out on his most excessive harangues. His fellow Virginian, the Revolutionary orator Patrick Henry, once even drew up "articles" against Randolph's "most flagrant indecencies of vilification," calling on the sitting vice president to restrain Randolph's abuse of debate from his presiding chair—a request the VP steadfastly refused, citing his intended role as impartial overseer. While fellow senators could call another senator to order for excessive speech-making—this established the vice president should not.³

Although not considered a filibuster at that time, ultimately debate would become a regional or partisan tactic designed to delay, obstruct, and hopefully stop legislation through a succession of long, drawn-out speeches—an early American hint of what was to come by 1837, when it became accepted minority strategy. That's when the previously referenced Thomas Hart Benton moved to "expunge" the Senate's earlier censure of President Andrew Jackson over the extended, all-night speeches of Clay and other Whigs seeking to preserve the previous reprimand. Fast forward from there to the post–Civil War period, when partisanship achieved new identity levels by 1879; when reinstated Southerners suddenly created a Democratic majority in the Senate; and when Republicans resorted to filibuster to slow the prohibiting of Army regulars from guarding Southern polling places in light of the South's emerging segregationist tendencies. Then again in 1891, a new kind of one-man filibuster emerged when West Virginia's Charles Faulkner held court on the Senate floor for eleven and a half straight hours, a situation that unnerved congressional observers and portended the threat of other individuals purposely tying up Senate business until their colleagues conceded to their wishes. Some filibusters would last for weeks, as one did in 1908 when progressives from the Midwest spoke out against emergency currency legislation they considered nothing more than a scheme to benefit the wealthy. For Senate historians like Baker and MacNeil, the bottom line was: "When Republicans were in the minority, they filibustered Democratic bills. When the Democrats were in the minority, they filibustered Republican bills." And at other times, "the filibusters came from regional blocs like farmers or ideological blocs like isolationists."⁴

Needless to say, it became a practice that brought criticism to the Senate to the point of some senators proposing a stronger majority cloture rule, which is the only procedure the Senate has to place a time limit on the debate of a bill and thereby overcome protracted filibuster—Senate Rule XXII. With 60 votes this time limit could be applied to any issue under debate, effectively containing a filibuster if a three-fifths majority could be cobbled together.[5] George Norris, the great senator from Nebraska spotlighted in this book's Prologue, offered another, at least partial filibuster solution in 1923, which was ultimately approved by both Houses of Congress and ratified in 1934. In order to preserve the sanctity of debate and yet end the practice of a filibuster and its primary intended obstruction in the final days of a congressional session, Norris proposed leaving each session's final day of adjournment "open-ended." To his nuanced way of thinking, "No limitation of a session would exist and no filibuster would [then] be attempted." Unfortunately, Norris' claim that such an open-ended congressional schedule would prevent blatant filibusters was not the easy fix he prophesied and senators' use (and abuse) of the filibuster continued.[6]

Perhaps the worst abuser of the filibuster was the previously mentioned Huey Long of Louisiana, whose flamboyant, self-promoting use of the tactic captured national attention during his short Senate career in the mid–1930s. One day in 1935, Long held the Senate floor for 15 hours and 35 minutes, an extraordinary feat that was both irrelevant and offensive to Senate norms, but also instructive to other Southerners, who were soon using well-timed filibusters to waylay votes on basic civil rights in fear that giving an inch to federal intervention might lead to having to accept a mile on other, integration measures. In 1922, the House of Representatives passed just such a measure, a bill that would have made lynching (aka, mob murder of African Americans), which had been happening in the racially unrepentant Deep South ever since Reconstruction, a federal crime. Amazingly, when that most virtuous of bills reached the Senate, it was immediately filibustered to death by Southern senators, the first of many such victories of delay and disruption that would lead to Alabama's Oscar Underwood, the minority leader at the time, snidely remarking, "Under the rules of the Senate, when 15 or 20 or 25 say you cannot pass a bill, it cannot be passed." In the words of *The American Senate*:

> That was the beginning of the calculated obstruction by filibustering Southern senators of all civil rights measures, a systematic campaign that would torment the Senate's deliberations for the next half-century and more. And in that vein, Southern senators flaunted what they were doing, sure of enthusiastic support from voters back home. They argued that these bills were unconstitutional and by opposing them they were defending "the Southern way of life" by which they meant the subjugation of Blacks to legally enforced racial segregation.

17. The End of Debate; the Start of Equality 215

In this struggle, the Senate's filibuster became for them a positive good, the means of protecting their cherished principles, such as they were, from outside intrusion.[7]

This then was the backdrop in which Senate Majority Leader Lyndon Johnson got Richard Russell and the Southern Bloc to go along with, or at least acquiesce to, his ice-breaking civil rights bills in 1957 and 1960, the latter of which authorized federal inspection of local voter registration polls and was only passed via some of Johnson's parliamentary sleight-of-hand. That was still the backdrop three years later when John Kennedy was assassinated with his own expanded civil rights legislation languishing in Congress. It was also the legislative backdrop when the modern Civil Rights Movement came into determined, full-throated prominence like never before.[8]

That's not to say it had not been building in the late 1950s and early '60s through protests and the resulting media exposure of such things as a Southern city bus boycott by African Americans over racially segregated seating; through National Guard enforced integration in a Southern state

During the 1950s and early '60s, the nonviolent Civil Rights Movement would reach its zenith in America, as demonstrations and marches took place throughout the South, prompting President John F. Kennedy to seek a landmark civil rights bill and his successor, President Lyndon Johnson, to utilize the JFK legacy and his own mastery of the Senate to finally get it passed (Library of Congress Prints and Photographs Division—Reproduction Number LC-DIG-ppmsca-04297).

capital in the wake of the *Brown versus Board of Education* Supreme Court decision; through multi-city sit-ins by young Blacks at several White-only lunch counters in the South; through the premeditated travel of Negroes called "Freedom Riders" on interstate buses throughout the Deep South and the numerous physical attacks they encountered along the way; through the heinous murders of civil rights workers seeking to register Black voters in the Deep South; through the police use of water hoses and snarling dogs to disperse urban protest marches in the South; and through a Sunday morning church bombing by the notoriously racist Ku Klux Klan that left four African American girls dead in a major Southern city. Indeed, by the time JFK was gunned down in the streets of Dallas and LBJ was sworn in as president, the rest of the nation had been made painfully aware of the ongoing racial discrimination and violence occurring in the American South. So, with momentum building for a more determined response, including action on Kennedy's pending civil rights bill, the threat of filibuster became the accepted legislative tactic of choice for the Senate's Southern Bloc.[9]

In the 12 months preceding his assassination, according to presidential historian William DeGregorio, Kennedy had "ordered an end to racial discrimination in housing owned, operated, or financed by the federal government; had established [a] Presidents Committee on Equal Employment Opportunity; had appointed numerous African Americans to prominent federal positions; and had exerted moral leadership on the race issue in a televised address. Nonetheless, his domestic civil rights agenda as a whole remained under wraps along with a new, recession-proof tax bill [overseen by previously mentioned Southern stalwart Harry Byrd] in the Senate despite what Johnson biographer Robert Caro labeled 'demonstrations throughout the South rising in intensity' and despite the fact 200,000 demonstrators had descended on the national capital in a so-called 'Freedom March' that August. In other words, the country was already inundated with civil rights talk and tension when its young president was killed. That's when a clear majority came to the realization there had to be change."[10]

So too had Lyndon Johnson. Because he had been excluded from much of the Kennedy administration's day-to-day deliberations, as Caro confirmed repeatedly in his fourth volume of the Johnson life story, *The Passage of Power*, "he did not know what he needed to know" about the exact status of the deceased president's domestic agenda—the tax stalemate and civil rights paralysis. So, once the solemnity of three days of Kennedy remembrance, homage, and burial in the nation's capital had taken place, he set about learning the updated lay of the congressional landscape he had mastered the previous decade. For instance, he learned that Senator Byrd's Senate Finance Committee was holding up the tax bill until the overall Kennedy budget became apparent in January. If it amounted to more

17. The End of Debate; the Start of Equality 217

than $100 billion as he expected it would, Byrd was determined to stop the tax cuts. LBJ was advised to give up the idea of lowering the tax rate because so much ill will against the Kennedy measures had been built up in Congress before his tragic demise. "No, no," Johnson is reputed to have replied. "I can't do that [without] destroying the Democratic Party. We can't abandon that fella's program because he's a national hero now and his people [the Kennedy Cabinet] want his program passed. We've got to keep the Kennedy aura around through the election [1964]," which was less than a year away.[11]

Those comments, made to Senate "Whip" George Smathers, a Floridian whom LBJ had relied on as a vote counter during his majority leader days, were apparently the first admission by the new president of the legacy of the previous one that he would endorse and rely on to get things done in time for his own 1964 presidential re-election campaign. In recent months, the Civil Rights Movement had been encouraged by the Kennedy administration's apparent commitment to their cause after so many decades of false hope and incremental accommodation designed to placate rather than truly solve the inequality of ongoing segregation in a third of the country. And a Southerner suddenly in the White House in Kennedy's place had to send the fear of another aborted Reconstruction through the Movement's leadership, just as the first President Johnson had done nearly a century before following the assassination of Abraham Lincoln. Jon Meacham addressed what had to be the mindset of Martin Luther King and other Movement leaders in *The Soul of America* when he speculated: "Now we may never get our freedom," as the logical reaction of MLK and other Civil Rights officials all too familiar with the disappointments of previous administrations, especially those of the more liberal Democrats, hamstrung politically as they were by their Southern brethren/senators of the previously Solid South. To turn its back on Dixie always threatened electoral division and doom for the Democratic Party, a national tightrope that Franklin Roosevelt, Harry Truman, and JFK had all had to master. But the Dems' high stakes balancing act would be different this time. Ever the master politician, LBJ sensed it had to be.[12]

In her 2018 book, *Leadership in Turbulent Times*, Doris Kearns Goodwin established Johnson's vision at the time, when she wrote:

> Everyone agreed that Lyndon Johnson was a master mechanic of the legislative process. What became apparent from the first hours of his presidency, however, was that he meant to use those unparalleled skills in the service of a full-blown vision of the role government should play in the lives of the people. From the outset, he knew exactly where he wanted to take the country in domestic affairs [including civil rights] and he had a working idea of how to get there. In his mind's eye, he could already envision a future in which all of Kennedy's progressive legislation, then deadlocked in Congress, had become law. "I'm going to get

Kennedy's tax cut out of the Senate Finance Committee and we're going to get [the] economy humming. Then I'm going to pass Kennedy's civil rights bill. And I'm going to pass it without changing a single comma or word."[13]

In that same vein, Meacham's 2018 *The Soul of America* summarized LBJ's transformation this way:

> Johnson had hardly been a progressive in his pre–White House years. As a Texan with an acute sense of politics and a consuming ambition, he [had previously] erred on the side of appeasing his segregationist constituents. [As a result], his commitment to the cause after Dallas would form one of the great chapters of personal transformation and political courage in the history of the presidency—one akin to Lincoln's move from tolerance of slavery in 1861 to emancipation in 1862–63. In the story of Johnson and civil rights, we [were to] see the difference a singular president can make when the circumstances are right.[14]

Caro acknowledged that "in confrontations with the former president during the [previous] three years, Congress, and in particular the Senate, had won so often [and] blocked so many Kennedy legislative proposals, that Congress felt power rested on Capitol Hill, not in the White House." In other words, Congress, and more specifically the Senate, was emboldened and confident in such a fight. But that was with the former chief executive, as Senator Byrd and his Senate Finance Committee would soon find out, as well as the previously impervious Southern Bloc.[15]

On November 27, 1963, just four dramatic days after becoming the fourth accidental U.S. president to assume office via an assassination and the first since Theodore Roosevelt in 1904, LBJ spoke to the combined Houses of Congress and the nation. "All I have I would have gladly given not to be standing here today," he began. "Eloquent and sorrowful," is how Caro described his tone, as he continued: "The greatest leader of our time has been struck down by the foulest deed of our time. Today, John Fitzgerald Kennedy lives on in the immortal words and works he left behind." A few sentences later, he would add: "No words are strong enough to express our determination to continue the forward thrust of America he began." Never considered a great speaker, Johnson, nevertheless, hit a responsive chord from that point on in the way Caro said he spoke. So slowly, with a deep, grave dignity that seemed to reverberate across the rows of listeners. It was the determined LBJ his former Senate colleagues had known so well and with each carefully crafted phrase, he added to the Kennedy legacy of progressive ideals and charismatic leadership.[16]

For members of the Kennedy administration in attendance that day, Johnson's effusive eulogizing of their boss had to be gratifying and somewhat surprising, especially given the way the vice president had been shunned from most policy decisions the previous three years, but it proved

17. The End of Debate; the Start of Equality

another example of LBJ's well-timed political instincts when it came to getting things done. In death, Johnson knew President Kennedy's hopes and wishes had a better chance than they enjoyed while he was alive—and as his successor, he was determined to take advantage.

In the run-up to his speech, Johnson received advice from a number of people, including his party's foremost progressive voice, Senator Humphrey; respected economist and diplomat John Kenneth Galbraith; Associate Supreme Court Justice Abe Fortas; National Urban League Executive Director Whitney Young; and several administration insiders such as Ted Sorenson, a longtime JFK adviser and speech consultant. However, he already knew what he wanted to say. At some point, in fact, someone advised him "not to press for civil rights," to which Johnson supposedly replied, "Well what the hell's the presidency for [then]?" Meacham even headlined one of his *Soul of America* chapters with that query—an obvious, spur-of-the-moment retort by LBJ and a clear indication of his intent and determination to be the president who finally got meaningful civil rights done. As Meacham concluded: "Fate had given him ultimate power and he intended to use it."[17]

And as his speech that day reached its climax, LBJ famously stated: "No memorial oration or eulogy could more eloquently honor President Kennedy's memory than the earliest possible passage of the civil rights bill for which he fought so long. We have talked long enough in this country about equal rights. We have talked 100 years or more. It is now time to write the next chapter and to write it in the book of law."[18]

Caro's recounting of that historic moment, the moment the whole country, North and South, East and West, knew there was a new sheriff in town, so to speak, a new Southern president who was going to go to greater lengths than his Democratic predecessors, FDR, Truman, and JFK, had ever felt able to go. In that moment, with the moral outrage of a nation still in mourning over an assassin's bullet, Lyndon Johnson was truly going for it, shaking down the echoes of Lincoln and Sumner from so long ago. There was no turning back, the gauntlet had been cast, and as applause rained down from almost every corner of the House Chamber, LBJ spoke directly to the gathered legislators when he said: "I urge you, as I did in 1957 and 1960, to enact a civil rights law [that will] eliminate from this nation every trace of discrimination and oppression that is based upon race or color."[19]

But not everyone in the House Chamber was applauding, as Caro took time to emphasize. Seated directly behind the Cabinet were "two rows of Southern senators," mostly veterans of the Southern Bloc—Byrd, Eastland, Talmadge, Thurmond, Russell, and others—men who had lifted LBJ to power in the Senate, who had swallowed hard on his limited 1957 and 1960 civil rights bills in order that he might become a national candidate. They were not applauding. According to Caro, they were "islands of silence in a sea of cheers."[20]

Johnson's commitment to civil rights that day constituted a decisive departure from his past, as Leuchtenburg confirmed in *The White House Looks South*, but Russell may have already known, or at lease sensed, what was coming. Immediately after his speech, the new president called on his old mentor from Georgia, asking him to serve on a commission he was putting together to be led by Supreme Court Chief Justice Earl Warren for the purpose of investigating the Kennedy assassination, with the hope of putting to rest countless conspiracy theories running rampant throughout the country. Russell, however, was adamant that he could not serve. He knew that defeating the impending civil rights legislation would require his guidance, so he declined LBJ's assignment, claiming no time in the midst of the current legislative schedule. Besides, he had "no affection for Earl Warren," according to his niece, "feeling as he did that the Warren Court had brought about too much judicial law"—the rightful realm of Congress. Not taking no for an answer, however (as was often the case), Johnson purposely included Russell's name among the committee members when the Warren Commission was announced in the press. Upon being informed by LBJ that his name was still on the list and that he "would just have to deal with it," Russell angrily compared it to being "conscripted" into the military.[21]

Although there was no suggestion that Johnson wanted Russell on the Warren Commission to potentially weaken his impact in the upcoming civil rights fight, the President was undoubtedly cognizant of the fact his old ally might serve as a useful confidant, if need be, or as a counterweight to the chief justice, whom LBJ knew he did not get along with. Plus, knowing that Russell had become a trusted congressional committeeman, as evidenced by his heralded chairmanship of the previously mentioned Truman-MacArthur hearings, his name added to what would ultimately become the "Warren Report," was intended to lend credibility to the findings. Nonetheless, the timing of his commission assignment simultaneous to the pending civil rights bill was too suspicious to ignore, especially given Johnson's penchant for political advantage.[22]

And it's not like Russell didn't know what (or whom) he was up against. His biographer pointed out how "early in the fight," during one of his frequent visits to the White House, Johnson had told him outright: "Dick, I love you. I owe you. But I am going to run over you if you challenge me or get in my way. I aim to pass the civil rights bill, only this time Dick, there will be no caviling, no compromise, no falling back. This bill is going to pass." For Russell it was the realization of a long-anticipated inevitability, the fact that sooner or later a civil rights champion was going to emerge

17. The End of Debate; the Start of Equality 221

with the political skills to overcome Southern obstruction tactics in the Senate. That inevitability, however, did not mean he would go down without a fight. According to Caro, he knew "the new odds against the South were long, but that did not stop him from famously rallying the Southern Bloc with the classical retort: 'It's clear that the only thing we can do now is gird our loins and shout the cry of centuries—The enemy comes to our tents, O Israel.'"[23]

By early 1963, it had become clear that the entire Kennedy domestic agenda was being intentionally bottled up in the Senate. Along with tax cuts and civil rights, this legislation included Medicare (the eventual federal health insurance program for America's senior citizens) and federal aid for education. The media termed it just another congressional "logjam," but LBJ recognized it as more than that. With the "public outcry for civil rights" and "an end to Jim Crow" growing stronger by the day, Johnson realized it was more than that—that, in fact, it was a strategy and probably the only one available to his former associates in the Southern Bloc. The President knew a Southern strategy when he saw one and how, behind the scenes,

Known for his confrontational style of politics, Lyndon Johnson could even resort to the same tactics with allies, as was the case after becoming president when he met with old friend and mentor, Georgia Senator Richard Russell, to let him know in no uncertain terms that he intended to pass meaningful civil rights legislation over the objections and obstruction of Russell's Southern Bloc in the Senate (courtesy LBJ Presidential Library, W98-30).

his old friend and new rival, Russell, was indeed laying it all out; drawing up a list of all federal laws set to expire and explaining to his Southern co-conspirators how they would build a blockade around the civil rights bill in the committees chaired by senators from the South. And if and when that logjam was broken, the Southerners would need to be prepared to filibuster, Caro advised—"not on the civil rights bill itself, but on the motion to bring the civil rights bill to the floor." Only should cloture be imposed to end the filibuster on that motion would the South have to fall back on its last line of defense, another filibuster of the bill itself, which by that point in the proceedings would probably signal the doom of debate and overwhelming civil rights momentum.[24]

Cloture, a seldom heard word even in the world of legislative assembly, was the procedure for ending debate in the Senate and forcing a vote. Caro pointed out early on in *The Passage of Power* that there were, after all, only two ways to end a Senate filibuster—by a vote of cloture or by abandoning the bill being filibustered altogether, effectively withdrawing it from Senate consideration. The latter way had actually played out in the South's favor 11 times before between 1929 and 1962. Whenever the South decided to fight civil rights with the filibuster for as long as necessary by not allowing the Senate to move on to other bills—in effect rendering those other bills hostages of civil rights—that was the very effective Southern strategy LBJ knew only too well. To defeat the strategy first required getting any other important bills off the table, so to speak. Only by eliminating the pressure of other key legislation did the 1964 Civil Rights Act, which outlawed discrimination based on race, color, religion, sex, or national origin in the workplace, schools, or public accommodations, get passed into much needed law.[25]

The day Johnson issued his challenge to Russell, nose-to-nose, in the White House, saying he fully intended to pass the civil rights bill, the very careful, deliberate senator from Georgia supposedly replied: "Well Suh, you may very well do that, but if you do ... you will lose the South forever." That would remain the prevailing political fallout Johnson had to come to terms with, not only for himself in what would be his re-election campaign later that year, but also for the future of the Democratic Party. Leuchtenburg, in *The White House Looks South*, even indicated LBJ went so far as to lecture the Southern Bloc in advance of the upcoming showdown, remarking: "Boys, you've got a Southern president and if you want to blow him out of the water go right ahead, but [if you do] you will never see another one."[26]

As had happened before, including his first year in the Senate (when as one of the youngest members of the Southern Bloc he had witnessed the Southern strategy work to stop the hoped for civil rights legislation of newly re-elected Harry Truman), LBJ knew it could happen again if he didn't do something to counteract it. And as Caro acknowledged, Russell

17. The End of Debate; the Start of Equality 223

would first try to make time the ally of the South. If the Southerners could keep debate in the Senate going long enough, proponents of the civil rights legislation were expected to again tire and seek to move on to other bills with a better chance of consensus passage. Almost as imperative, if not as contentious as the civil rights bill was sure to be, was the tax bill, then in its 11th month before Congress and, as previously noted, under the control of Senate Finance Committee Chairman Harry Byrd, an unflinching, 31-year member of the Southern Bloc and someone with personal strings attached to both bills.[27]

Debate on the civil rights bill began in early March and led by Russell, the well drilled Southerners filibustered from the start. Seeking to derail such tactics, Johnson pressured his successor as Senate majority leader, Mike Mansfield of Montana, to hold around-the-clock sessions, which would have forced Russell and his Southern colleagues to keep debate going into the wee hours. Mansfield, however, refused, citing the fact that tactic had failed to crack Southern resolve before and with the rebuke: "This is not going to be a circus or a sideshow. We are not operating in a pit with spectators late at night to see senators of the republic come out in (their) bedroom slippers. There will be no pajama sessions of the Senate." According to Baker and MacNeil's history of the Senate, Mansfield did relent some by starting sessions "early each morning" and letting them run "well into each night," but his refusal to use harsher methods made it easy for Russell and company as they filibustered the motion for three full weeks. Only then, fearing to stall any longer might prompt a successful motion for cloture did the Southerners back off, allowing debate on the bill itself to begin.[28]

Taking the lead in arguments for the civil rights bill was Humphrey, the Democratic majority whip, who coordinated cogent arguments among his more liberal colleagues in a procession of speakers on both sides. Mansfield and Humphrey were relying on the prospect of an eventual settlement through cloture, but as so often before, with the Southern Bloc of Democrats as their opposition, they knew they could never muster enough party-line votes to achieve the two-thirds needed to end debate. What they needed were Republicans, who as conservatives themselves had often sided with the Southern Dems, especially whenever they could safely trade their votes on civil rights for similar favors on their own minority legislation.[29]

At the same time, LBJ was behind the scenes maneuvering what became the Tax Reduction Act of 1964, which cut federal income taxes by approximately 20 percent across the board, out of the tight-fisted clutches of Harry Byrd by getting the federal budget below the $100 billion mark, the Virginia senator's deal or no-deal cutoff as far as negotiations were concerned. Once Johnson had managed the necessary reductions, a feat of fiscal responsibility rarely equaled in such a short amount of time by a sitting U.S. chief executive, and proven his handiwork to "Old Harry," who was growing tired of hearing how he was the hold-up on reducing taxes, the bill was finally moved out of committee and onto the floor, where it became law on February 26, 1964. It would be a precursor of the administration's final push on civil rights legislation just over four months later.[30]

Meanwhile, Johnson's floor generals in the Senate, Mansfield and Humphrey, had gone out of their way to make an unlikely ally on civil rights in the person of the Republican minority leader, Everett Dirksen of Illinois. Mansfield, a modest man to the point of "self-abnegation" (again according to *The American Senate's* co-authors), had no trouble deferring to the droll, spotlight-seeking Dirksen. LBJ had urged them both to flatter Dirksen by offering him the role of statesman in a history-making undertaking. As a result, Humphrey reported: "[We] began a public massage of [Dirksen's] ego and appealed to his vanity."[31]

Nearly identical versions of this courtship appear in the previously referenced historic narratives of Doris Kearns Goodwin and Jon Meacham, while the biography of Russell provided the opposition take. In Goodwin's text she wrote:

> A legendary nose-counter, Lyndon Johnson was certain that without Republican support [given the sectional split in the Democratic Party] "we'd have absolutely no chance of securing the two-thirds vote to defeat the filibuster. And I knew there was but one man who could secure us that support—the senator from Illinois, Everett Dirksen." Just as he had identified Senate Finance Chair Harry Byrd as the key to success in the tax struggle, so now he saw that the Republican minority leader was the one man able to corral the 25 or so Republicans needed to invoke cloture. "The bill can't pass unless you get Dirksen," Johnson [told] Humphrey. "You and I are going to get him. You make up your mind now that you've got to spend time with [him]. You've got to let him have a piece of the action. He's got to look good [in this] all the time."

Both versions would conclude with the following exhortations: "You get in there to see Dirksen! You drink with Dirksen! You talk to Dirksen! You listen to Dirksen!"[32] On the other hand, Russell's biographer would simply note:

> As the civil rights fight of 1964 heated up, the President sent Hubert Humphrey to court and win over Republican giant Everett Dirksen. Although the Southern Bloc mounted a formidable filibuster campaign, Humphrey took pages from Russell's book and kept his people on hand with [speaking] schedules that allowed everyone rest time. Including the debate on the motion, this became the longest filibuster in the history of the U.S. Senate, lasting 74 working days.[33]

Dirksen had issues to deal with if he was to support the civil rights bill. During his last re-election campaign in 1962, Illinois' African American

17. The End of Debate; the Start of Equality

Photographed at the White House with Senate Republican Leader Everett Dirksen (left) and Democratic Majority Leader Mike Mansfield (center), Lyndon Johnson as president took advantage of his vast parliamentary experience, honed during his own years of Senate leadership, to break through the Southern strategy of filibuster that had previously limited meaningful civil rights legislation. Dirksen's influence was key to bipartisan passage of the 1964 Civil Rights Act (courtesy LBJ Presidential Library, A2550-3a).

leadership had come out against him and that still annoyed him. At first, he pronounced the bill unsatisfactory, but as the filibuster continued week after week, he eventually put aside personal issues while entering into what Baker and MacNeil described as:

> A complex series of backroom negotiations with senators sponsoring the legislation, staff experts, and officials of the Justice Department led by Attorney General Robert Kennedy. A gifted legislator able to compose law, unlike many of his colleagues, Dirksen began to propose changes in the pending bill, which had already been passed in the House [of Representatives]. Resentful [of] Dirksen's sudden prominence in the [process], Robert Kennedy tried to block [the changes], but Dirksen had his way. He had a telling argument, [as] without the changes he could not hope to deliver the votes of his Republicans for cloture. Dirksen offered 70 amendments in all and he insisted on them as his price for supporting the bill. He so altered the bill that it became known as "the Dirksen package."[34]

In the middle of these negotiations, Russell made one last effort to woo Dirksen away from the bill's sponsors, but the Johnson-inspired and

Humphrey-implemented recruitment of the Republican leader had been too deferential and empowering for him to ignore. In addition, Dirksen had taken his party's prospects for the coming presidential election into account and with his good friend, fellow Senator Barry Goldwater of Arizona, as the presumptive Republican nominee, he wanted to position the GOP and its candidate in as favorable a light as possible. But even with his own amendments added, he still faced a daunting task getting at least 25 of 33 Republican senators to vote for cloture.[35]

Nonetheless, with Republicans numbering less than one third of the Senate's membership, he had achieved remarkable influence for the party, far in excess of its numerical strength, and through his remarkable talents of persuasion he was going to decide not only whether the bill passed, but also its substance. During the debate, making the most of his theatrical style of oratory, he urged his fellow senators to endorse a cause long overdue, when he uttered the phrase: "Stronger than all the armies whose time had come, this is an idea whose time has come. It will not be stayed. It will not be denied."[36]

And it was not. As Russell's niece, Sally Russell, recorded: "On 10 June, the Senate voted 71 to 29 [with four more 'ayes' than actually needed], to close off debate" on what would become the landmark Civil Rights Act of 1964. Clearly the Senate had changed since Russell repeatedly blocked civil rights legislation via the filibuster, as well as two attempts to amend the filibuster rule. Realizing he could no longer stop what he termed "the resulting stampede of amendments," the Georgian ironically complained that "a lynch mob" had been loosed on the Senate floor. In a last-ditch try to preserve Southern segregation, he proposed that certain provisions of the bill be submitted to a national referendum, but that proposal was easily turned back by a 73–27 vote two days later, the same tally by which the legislation itself would ultimately pass on June 19. And on July 2, LBJ, a Southerner, triumphantly signed a bill officially putting an end to 90 years of segregation in the South.[37]

Having maneuvered his former Southern colleagues turned foes into submission, Johnson had proven he was still "master of the Senate." Former Atlanta mayor and U.S. ambassador to the United Nations under President Jimmy Carter, Andrew Young, who along with Martin Luther King, Jr., John Lewis, and others became icons of the Civil Rights Movement, would later write: "It was a powerful symbol ... that a president born and raised in a [former] Confederate state was the one to [finally] sign the [1964] Civil Rights Act into law." However, as Johnson would later reflect, "The decision to press for the civil rights bill in 1964 was not without penalties for me. It was destined to set me apart forever from the South."[38]

Richard Russell would serve one more term in the Senate, dying while

17. The End of Debate; the Start of Equality

Upon assuming the presidency in the wake of the Kennedy assassination, Lyndon Johnson would invoke the memory of JFK and the honor that would be afforded him by passage of the 1964 Civil Rights Act, which he would doggedly pursue to this historic signing on July 2, 1964 (Library of Congress Prints and Photographs Division—Reproduction Number LC-DIG-ppmsca-03196).

still in office on January 21, 1971. Always admired by former constituents and colleagues, though viewed disparagingly by the rest of the country for his decades-long defense of segregation, he would remain cordial with LBJ even in defeat of what he had termed the "Southern way of life." Although he never again addressed Johnson as "Lyndon"—only "Mr. President"—he would mostly support the remainder of his presidency and take pride in the fact their friendship had played a big part in elevating him to the Oval Office. Later their relationship did "cool," according to Sally Russell, near the end of her uncle's life as the result of a disagreement over the appointment of a federal judge from Georgia. Russell again felt betrayed and this time would go to his grave having lost all trust in Johnson, his former Southern protégé.[39]

18

Personal Legacy Waylaid by Foreign Escalation

In the first volume of his voluminous, multi-volume biography of Lyndon Baines Johnson, *The Path to Power*, Robert Caro laid out the political strategy of a very young, 28-year-old LBJ, seeking to become the representative of Texas' 10th Congressional District in just three words—Franklin Delano Roosevelt. Indeed, the most popular and generally recognized most successful president of the 20th century, the always engaging and politically astute FDR was Johnson's hero and role model even before he became a freshman congressman in 1937. While virtually all down-ballot Democrats would profess allegiance to the undisputed titular head of their party in the mid–1930s, Johnson, in Caro's words, had to be "more pro–Roosevelt" than the rest. And in his own words, especially as a largely unknown first-time candidate, Johnson was a "Roosevelt man" all the way when it came to addressing Texas voters in the all-important 1936 Democratic primary and general election that followed.[1]

LBJ had actually jumped on the Roosevelt bandwagon in 1931 as a young congressional aide for then–Texas Congressman Richard Kleberg, "one of the wealthiest men in Texas" and the grandson of Richard King, founder of the world-famous King Ranch. With his new boss a typical, conservative Southern Democrat, in fact, it was Johnson who first impressed on Kleberg the absolute necessity of casting his lot with FDR's New Deal as a means of political survival, since most of the Great Depression masses had embraced their new president's progressive, government-induced strategy for economic recovery upon his arrival in the White House in 1933. As a young congressman himself four years later, Johnson would take full advantage of a Roosevelt fishing excursion along the Texas coast that ended at the Port of Galveston. He arranged to meet FDR at the conclusion of the President's 11-day cruise with Texas Governor James Allred there to facilitate introductions. It would be the first of many well-timed ploys by Johnson and a valuable photo op as he ascended the political ladder. So well

18. Personal Legacy Waylaid by Foreign Escalation

timed, in fact, that he was invited to ride in the President's open touring car (along with Allred and Galveston's mayor) amidst a tremendous turnout for FDR by the citizens of Galveston all along the way from the port to the city train depot, where Johnson also got to accompany Roosevelt aboard his private railroad car, first to review 3,000 ROTC cadets at Texas A&M University and then on to Fort Worth before de-training and bidding the President adieu, having spent an entire day in his company, a rare opportunity indeed for any young Democratic congressman.[2]

Later in *Means of Ascent*, his second volume in the Johnson series, Caro reported on the instant rapport of Johnson and Roosevelt from that first meeting, which would enable LBJ to gain access to a small circle of FDR associates in the nation's capital that assisted his political rise. At the same time, no one could have predicted how the fates aligned that day in Galveston—the coming together of two U.S. presidents, both of whom ascended to the White House nearly three decades apart. Johnson, however, was always of the mindset to seek to control fate, especially his own, and his desire to emulate Roosevelt as his career moved forward would often resurface, especially after he became an accidental president through a totally unexpected historic twist—the death in office of the second youngest U.S. president ever. And in that tragic moment, when LBJ sought to use the passing of John Fitzgerald Kennedy to inspire Congress to finally adopt meaningful civil rights, it should have come as no surprise that Johnson would also adopt the legacy of FDR—tackling the depths of the Great Depression with his New Deal—by announcing a "War on Poverty" in 1964. Doris Kearns Goodwin illuminated this connection to FDR when she acknowledged Johnson's hope to "surpass" the New Deal with his own, so-called "Great Society," a series of programs by which Johnson could model himself after the president he admired most, carrying "the people though a dark hour in their national life," and "exhorting them to action."[3]

In *The Soul of America*, Jon Meacham echoed this connection, when he wrote: "Both [FDR and LBJ] believed in the transformative power of the presidency and sought to marshal federal power in the service of government." But an even more personal illustration of FDR's influence on his fellow, future president was confirmed in a 2012 online article that deciphered the simultaneous use of three initials, à la FDR, by aspiring young Democrats of the next generation like LBJ and JFK. Its conclusion: "The most enthusiastic and calculating adopter of the [three initial] convention was LBJ. As a congressman, long before he was vice president, he had instructed his assistants to always refer to him by his initials in the FDR mode." Johnson would even name his two daughters using the same three initials (Luci Baines and Lynda Byrd), a political ploy and subliminal connection with the preeminent Democrat of the 20th century.[4]

And perhaps nothing illustrated how much Johnson measured himself and greatness by the legacy of Roosevelt than his immediate reaction to FDR's death in 1945, explicitly described in Caro's *The Path to Power* as the depiction of a reporter friend who spied LBJ by himself in "a gloomy capitol corridor" after news of the President's passing had just been announced. That eye-witness account follows:

> "With tears in his eyes" and "a white cigarette holder"—similar to Roosevelt's—clamped in "a shaking jaw," he told the reporter that when the news came, "I was just looking up at a cartoon on the wall—a cartoon showing the President with that cigarette holder and his jaw stuck out like it always was. He had his head cocked back; you know. And then I thought of all the little folks and what they had lost. He was just like a Daddy to me; he talked to me that way.... God! God! How he could take it for all of us!"[5]

All of that to say ... even with the nation in mourning as he ascended to the presidency due to an assassin's bullet; and even with his embrace of

There's no doubt Franklin Delano Roosevelt, shown here addressing the nation via radio in the 1930s, was Lyndon Baines Johnson's political hero and role model as president. Following his re-election in 1964, in fact, LBJ's series of legislative programs aimed at lifting people out of poverty were intended to emulate FDR's New Deal in the midst of the Great Depression (Library of Congress Prints and Photographs Division—Reproduction Number LC-DIG-hec-47601).

18. Personal Legacy Waylaid by Foreign Escalation 233

After the national disgrace that was Bloody Sunday in March of 1965, the Civil Rights Movement's planned march from Selma, Alabama, to the state capitol in Montgomery to demonstrate for African American voting rights was allowed to proceed as the result of intervention by the Johnson administration two weeks later with over three thousand taking part under National Guard protection (Library of Congress Prints and Photographs Division—Reproduction Number LC-USZ62-133090).

embraced would provide one more milestone on the Johnson presidential resume, thanks to another seminal event in the Deep South. That one would occur in Selma, Alabama, on March 7, 1965, and forever become ingrained in American history as "Bloody Sunday"—the day approximately 600 marchers set out on foot from that sleepy Southern town for the state capital, Montgomery, a 54-mile trek designed to bring attention to the one thing the 1964 Civil Rights Act had not fulfilled for African American equality—voting rights—for without voting rights there could be no Black equality regardless of what other desegregation (or integration) occurred.[11]

On the now famous Edmund Pettus Bridge, which sits where the highway exits Selma's downtown over the Alabama River, the marchers were met by state troopers, some mounted, and brutally beaten when they did not disperse and call off their march. Under the direction of Alabama's segregationist governor, George Wallace, the troopers' actions that day were captured by network television, to the horror and revulsion of the entire nation. And when the march triumphantly resumed a few days and federal-state-Movement negotiations later, this time under National Guard protection, it would lead directly to President Johnson finishing what he had started the previous year with his 1965 Voting Rights Act, which once-and-for-all prohibited any kind of racial discrimination in voting when it was passed by both Houses of Congress six months later.[12]

How Selma and Bloody Sunday led to that historic follow-up legislation on August 6, 1965, has been retold in numerous narratives of the Civil Rights Movement. A young newspaper reporter at the time, David Halberstam was there representing the *Nashville Tennessean* during the Southern sit-ins and went on to cover that period in detail, including Vietnam while working for the *New York Times*, where he earned a Pulitzer Prize in 1964. His 1998 book, *The Children*, made the young Black adults who were the Movement's leaders better known and understood. Twelve years earlier, David Garrow, a professor at Emory University in Atlanta, Georgia, conceptualized the whole era in greater detail with his Pulitzer Prize-winning book, *Bearing the Cross*, about Martin Luther King (MLK) and the Southern Christian Leadership Conference (SCLC), which evolved into the Movement's most influential leadership organization. And in 1998, John Lewis, one of the young titans Halberstam had prominently profiled in his book, authored his own bestselling memoir of the Movement, *Walking with the Wind*, including his first person participation and near death experience on Bloody Sunday. All three books, in fact, would lend credence to the far-reaching impact of the Selma confrontation and the transformative, concluding legislation it directly produced.

Taking Lewis' recounting first, his thoughts on the aftermath of Bloody Sunday, during which the future and longtime Georgia congressman (33 years) sustained a fractured skull were as follows:

> The American public had already seen so much of this sort of thing, countless images of beatings and dogs and cursing and hoses. But something about that day in Selma touched a nerve deeper than anything that had come before. Maybe it was the concentrated focus of the scene, the mass movement of those troopers on foot and on horseback, rolling into and over two long lines of stoic, unarmed people. This was a faceoff in the most vivid terms between a dignified, completely nonviolent multitude of silent protesters and the truly malevolent force of a heavily armed, hateful battalion of troopers. The sight of them rolling over us like human tanks was something that had never been seen before. People just couldn't believe this was happening, not in America.[13]

Halberstam, meanwhile, described the aftermath from the role of the perpetrators when he wrote:

> It had been nothing less than state-sponsored mayhem that day, the State of Alabama using its full force to beat and intimidate its poorest citizens and thereby keep them from being able to participate in the political process. Yet, it was the

most short-lived of segregationist victories, for yes, they had succeeded momentarily in stopping the march … but they called national attention to Black grievances in Alabama. It had been America at its ugliest.[14]

Meanwhile, the following excerpt from *Bearing the Cross* touched on how media reports began to permeate and influence the country, as Garrow documented:

> It was early evening by the time that news reports of the bloody attack began to spread across the country. Many television viewers were astounded by the graphic film of the troopers' assault on peaceful marchers. ABC interrupted a movie, *Judgement at Nuremberg*, to present footage that depicted how racial hatred could generate awful violence in America, not just Nazi Germany.[15]

As a result of the optics of Selma, which had been set up by ongoing African American demonstrations over Southern voting rights, it was relatively easy for Johnson to go back to Congress the following year for what the 1964 Civil Rights Act had obviously lacked—federal voting guarantees for minorities. In describing the 1965 legislative process that dealt with voting rights, co–Senate historians Richard Baker and Neil MacNeil kept it simple as they explained: "The debate began in mid–April and the Southerners filibustered. Once again, Dirksen conceded that they were having the usual difficulty persuading senators to vote for cloture despite some promised conversions. The day before the scheduled vote, Senator Russell said in resignation, 'If there is anything I could do, I'd do it, but I assume the die is cast.' The vote for cloture was 70 to 30 and the next day the Senate approved the [1965 Voting Rights Act], 77 to 19. Larry O'Brien, Johnson's chief liaison to Congress, gave the credit to Dirksen. 'You can't get cloture in the Senate,' O'Brien said, 'without Dirksen working like hell for it!'" But even with Johnson's and Dirksen's passage of the 1964 and 1965 bills, their passage still did not remove one more racially charged problem, prompting Johnson and Dirksen to join together yet again to pass a Fair Housing Act in 1968. When completed, it signaled the enactment of all the "long-pending civil rights measures," according to Baker and MacNeil. "Only dimly understood at the time, the three bills of 1964, 1965, and 1968 would dramatically change the nation politically," not only ending the Democrats hold on the South, but in their estimation "radically altering the way voters chose presidents and members of Congress. In this new form, the filibuster would fundamentally change the Senate. Within the Senate, the filibuster became an entirely different mechanism, freed at last from the onus of racial discrimination, but caught up in its revised use as an instrument of even more frequent legislative gridlock."[16]

SECTION SEVEN

The Canal Giveaway
Jimmy Carter vs. Paul Laxalt

19

From "Perpetuity" to "Inviting Disaster"

As secretary of state under both Presidents Richard Nixon and Gerald Ford, Henry Kissinger, a naturalized, German-born U.S. citizen and former Harvard University professor, became perhaps the best-known diplomat on the world stage during the 1970s and later authored a book with the rather simple title, *Diplomacy*. More specifically, it's a book about the history of Western diplomacy, basically from the time of Cardinal Richelieu in France through the likes of French Emperor Napoleon and the unifier of Germany, Otto von Bismarck, with the gist prefacing leadership of the United States in the 20th century and what he termed "The Hinge"— the "watershed," internationalist presidencies of Theodore Roosevelt (1901–1909) and Woodrow Wilson (1913–1921) that European history helped initiate. Included in Kissinger's text would be many of his own contributions on the back side of the century, but, ironically, nothing of his most direct link to the legacy of the irrepressible TR—the transformative Panama Canal, the 51-mile long lifeline of maritime trade that crosses the Central American Isthmus at its narrowest point, connecting the Atlantic and Pacific Oceans and significantly lessening the distance and costs of global commerce.[1]

Or to be more specific, the role Kissinger played in the ultimate transfer of the Panama Canal, Roosevelt's vision, acquisition, and creation, and truly one of America's greatest contributions to the world. Instead, the Canal is mentioned only once in the 912-page Kissinger text published in 1994, 17 years after the Ford administration gave way to the presidential election of Georgia Governor Jimmy Carter in 1976. On page 39, Kissinger merely stated: "With American help, the local population wrested independence from Colombia, but not before the Roosevelt administration had established the Canal Zone under United States sovereignty on both sides of what was to become the Panama Canal."[2]

It was mentioned in the context of TR's more assertive, "muscular

19. From "Perpetuity" to "Inviting Disaster" 239

diplomacy" in the Western Hemisphere and America's "new global role," but it failed to assert the diplomatic liberties and foreign policy short cuts our first President Roosevelt would take in 1903 to make it happen and keep it American for "perpetuity." For more on the whole dramatic story of America's incredible Canal achievements, read David McCullough's *The Path Between the Seas: The Creation of the Panama Canal—1870-1914*, but for the purposes of this book, suffice it to say that TR tried to deal with Colombia before Panama seceded from that South American nation, but when the asking price got too unrealistically high he was more than happy to support and deal with the suddenly independent nation of Panama instead. That's another story of diplomatic intrigue for another day that obviously did not make Kissinger's book. Flash forward seven decades and what's equally surprising is how Kissinger's diplomatic efforts with Panama in early 1974 also didn't make it—what became known as the "Kissinger-Tack Principles," the agreement the then U.S. secretary of state would reach with Juan Antonio Tack, Panama's foreign minister, promising to replace the 1903 Hay-Bunau-Varilla Treaty "with one providing a prompt end to U.S. control of the [Panama] Canal Zone, a greater share of Canal profits for Panama, and a promise that Panama would join in the administration and defense of the Canal." This according to another book that does deal specifically with the Canal issue, a 2018 narrative by Adam Clymer titled *Drawing the Line at the Big Ditch: The Panama Canal Treaties and the Rise of the Right*.[3]

Perhaps Kissinger's omission of his Panama negotiations under Nixon and Ford was just a sign of the times, as Clymer made note of the fact only one major newspaper, the *Los Angeles Times*, considered the Kissinger-Tack announcement front page news. Coming out of the Johnson and Nixon presidencies, which were ultimately consumed by the specter of Vietnam and Watergate, respectively, the move towards relinquishing seven decades of control of the Panama Canal did not seem so important and as Clymer noted, "they spent no political capital trying to prepare the American people to accept their belief that this national treasure would be best preserved not by a continuation of colonial rule, but by cooperation on terms modern Panama could accept." The limited media coverage was enough, however, to stir reaction that blurred party lines. Strom Thurmond, by then a converted Southern Republican, having abandoned the Democratic Party in 1964 after Democratic President Johnson's assumption of civil rights leadership, said the Panama agreement would "invite disaster," while Democrats like John Murphy of New York stated: "Kissinger was undertaking 'a course of action which borders on insanity.'" Yet another Democratic congressman, Daniel Flood of Pennsylvania, who had been inspired as a child by the building of the Panama Canal after actually meeting then ex–President Theodore Roosevelt, even warned of his fear of communist takeover and

Taking advantage of a planned Panamanian revolution and separation from the nation of Colombia, President Theodore Roosevelt first rejected the extortionist demands of the Colombian government, as this 1903 *Harper's Weekly* cartoon illustrated, supporting Panama's independence instead in order to secure for America the best deal and chance to begin construction of the Panama Canal in 1904 (Library of Congress Prints and Photographs—Reproduction Number LC-DIG-ppmsca-50509).

19. From "Perpetuity" to "Inviting Disaster"   241

the problem of the U.S. "yielding 'to politically and communistically motivated demands of Panama [that] at times featured mob violence.'"[4]

With all of Latin America looking to the United States for good faith in its mentorship of the Western Hemisphere, including the relinquishing of what increasingly seemed seven decades of imperialistic control of the Canal Zone, the United Nations Security Council convened a meeting in Panama in the spring of 1973. Its purpose was to consider a resolution demanding, "without delay" a new "just and fair" treaty that would fulfill Panama's legitimate aspirations and guarantee full respect for Panama's sovereignty over all its territory, with the authoring and signing of a new treaty to replace the old, 1903 version. The U.S. had promptly vetoed that resolution and no other Security Council nation had voted with the Americans, not even the British, who abstained.[5]

That was the moment, however, that prompted Kissinger to act and to convince Nixon that serious problems could result from turning away from the Panamanian, and indeed, the entire Latin American aspirations of

Still one of mankind's greatest engineering achievements over 100 years after its completion, the Panama Canal made the global transport of goods much easier by connecting the Atlantic and Pacific Oceans with a manmade, 51-mile waterway that eliminated the necessity of sailing around South America (Library of Congress Prints and Photographs Division—Reproduction Number LC-DIG-npcc-19345).

the late 20th century. As a result, that winter Kissinger and Tack developed their agreement, which promised a replacement for the 1903 treaty that would end U.S. control of the Canal Zone; provide a greater share of Canal profits to Panama; and affirm partnership between the two countries in the administration and defense of the Canal. The United States would still retain the use of land, water, and airspace necessary to defend the Canal and priority access to Canal passage for its shipping over every other nation in the future. "Most important," according to Clymer, "the document (also) promised to abrogate the 1903 treaty and replace it with one having a fixed termination date" and elimination of the concept of "perpetuity."[6]

At the time, Kissinger stated, "The world we live in today is not the world of Teddy Roosevelt," but it was the world Gerald Ford inherited when he became an accidental president as surely as any, following Nixon's historic resignation from office over the Watergate scandal (or maybe more so than any other considering he was also an accidental vice president after his appointment a year earlier under the new Twenty-Fifth Amendment following VP Spiro Agnew's disgraced resignation over tax evasion). Despite their acknowledgment of the congressional opposition to be faced from the likes of Senator Thurmond and Congressman Flood, Ford instructed Kissinger to move ahead on the agreement for a new treaty. The threat of Panamanian unrest or insurrection, already evident in past instances of violence in 1958 and 1964, or even possible sabotage of the Canal locks, presented the new president with a Latin American situation that he would just as soon negotiate away as he dealt with the last vestiges of the Vietnam War, which did not come until 1975, and Watergate, which would include his controversial pardon of Nixon issued later that year, September 8, 1974.[7]

Many conservatives, including Alabama's segregationist governor, George Wallace, felt that because of America's abdication from Vietnam and the resulting communist takeover of that entire country, many Americans believed it was more than strategic, diplomatic, or geopolitical issues that were tied into giving away the Canal. Indeed, it was, as Floyd Haskell, a Republican turned Democratic senator from Colorado, uttered regarding the agreement and planned giveaway, when he said, "We were giving away a piece of American folklore." That was the essence of the Panama Canal controversy that became front and center fodder for the 1976 presidential campaign. While most Americans were focused on the breakdown of trust in the American government brought on by Vietnam and Watergate, and the choice between a Washington outsider in Democrat Jimmy Carter and the replacement Republican incumbent Gerald Ford, another name surfaced bringing conservative values into the national discussion, Ronald Reagan, a former movie star and the governor of California. Normally, an incumbent president has the complete support of his party when seeking re-election. But exceptions to that rule had occurred: for instance, President Franklin Pierce, who was replaced on the 1856 Democratic ticket by James Buchanan, and three other accidental presidents, Millard Fillmore, Andrew Johnson, and Chester Arthur, none of whom ever enjoyed the overall support of the parties that put them in position as vice presidents to ascend to the White House in place of deceased predecessors. Likewise, Ford, as the most accidental of accidental presidents, felt he had earned another term, but unlike fellow 20th century accidentals Theodore Roosevelt (1904), Harry Truman (1948), and Lyndon Johnson (1964), he would not get one in '76—not because of Reagan's candidacy, but because of the tainted Nixon legacy and his pardon, which set him far behind what Carter biographer Stuart Eizenstat described as "an outsider's nonideological appeal to restore trust and confidence in the presidency." That outsider appeal produced an insurmountable 30-plus point deficit in the polls early on and eventual defeat despite a ferocious comeback that made the final 1976 presidential election results much closer than expected—297 electoral votes for Carter to 240 for Ford.[8]

The 1970s congressional battle over the Panama Canal was actually a proxy war brought about by the leading conservative of that era, Ronald Reagan, California's governor and a first-time presidential candidate in 1976. Reagan identified American intentions to turn the Canal over to Panama as a major campaign issue and the battle was continued for him during the administration of President Jimmy Carter (Library of Congress Prints and Photographs Division—Reproduction Number LC-DIG-ppmsca-50509).

But Reagan's conservative infusion into the Republican primary had not helped Ford's chances either and the esteemed, longtime Michigan congressman and Speaker of the House wanna-be (before he was literally drafted by the GOP for his brief VP role), would go to his grave believing he deserved better after coming to the rescue of the Nixon administration. As a result, he would always harbor a grudge against Reagan, who entered the race on November 20, 1975, and generally made life miserable for the incumbent through the primaries. "Decades later," according to Ford biographer David Brinkley, "[he] still bristled about Reagan's decision to challenge him in 1976. To Ford, that rendered an earlier Reagan pronouncement: 'A Republican should never criticize another Republican'" totally hypocritical.[9]

Nonetheless, challenge him Reagan did and one of the best ways he found to carry out that challenge was by casting Ford's decision to continue negotiating away the Panama Canal as un–American. At speaking engagements, Reagan discovered that one of the best avenues for rallying the crowd to his candidacy was the phrase "we built it, we paid for it, it's ours and we are going to keep it," forcing President Ford to address what Brinkley referred to as "The dull nuances behind the official U.S. position in the complex negotiations over the inevitable eventual transfer of control of the Canal to Panama." Clymer, again in *Drawing the Line at the Big Ditch*, would make Reagan's stance on the issue the subject of two early chapters leading up to the 1976 general election. He confirmed that in mid–July the year before, Regan had asked his good friend and Nevada Senator Paul Laxalt to establish an exploratory Reagan for President Committee. That allowed their conservative backers to raise money and begin a drumbeat over the impending Canal transfer, including the demand that Congress stand up to the State Department's intention to surrender the Canal, and comments by Reagan like: "I think we'd be damn fools to turn over the Panama Canal. The Panamanians seceded from Colombia in 1903 because they wanted to participate in the benefits the Canal would bring to their part of the world and they identified their future success with the United States, having watched the French fail in their attempts." As well as: "Panama has the highest standard of living in Central America"—as if to say (according to Clymer), why would Panamanians want to "kill the goose that laid the golden egg?"[10]

The Reagan campaign continued to draw applause whenever the issue came up. Meanwhile, the Carter campaign, according to Eizenstat, "declared [it] was ready to negotiate with Panama on physical improvements, tolls, and practical matters," but "would not relinquish practical control of the Panama Canal Zone anytime in the foreseeable future." It was a convenient abdication by the Democratic nominee of an issue that was roiling the Republican Party, but it was an issue that would not be going away and one that President Ford would soon turn over to his successor. That would set up a rare proxy war in the Halls of Congress and particularly the Senate, a proxy war that would ensure, once and for all, the rise of Reagan and the right wing of the Republican Party.[11]

20

Reversing Course into a Proxy War

A Southern-born and bred conservative, Jimmy Carter was an anomaly when he earned the Democratic presidential nomination in 1976. A devout, "Born-again Christian" in his Southern Baptist beliefs, he was the epitome of the Washington outsider that he campaigned to be. Ultimately, that's what got him elected in the aftermath of Vietnam and Watergate, when mistrust of the federal government was rampant. "Enlightened when it came to race," while at the same time offering a "commonsense approach to economics," according to presidential historian Kenneth Davis, Carter was an acceptable crossover candidate at the perfect time, when honesty seemed to be valued more than anything else by American voters.[1]

During the campaign, Carter had artfully framed the Panama Canal as "a hot political issue, particularly with his Southern political base," according to his political adviser turned biographer Stuart Eizenstat. Strategically, he turned Gerald Ford's "good-faith negotiations" with Panama against him, "accusing his opponent of being prepared to cave on sovereignty," and thus "outflanking him from the right." At the same time, Adam Clymer, in his book on the Canal saga, emphasized Carter "never raised" the issue "on his own in the campaign," giving credence to the idea it was merely fodder he could use against the incumbent until the race was over and he had actually replaced Ford in the White House. At that point, as Eizenstat testified, it came as a surprise that Carter "vaulted one of the most contentious, emotional foreign-policy issues of the era to the top of his priority list." Clymer tried to make sense of this policy shift by the new chief executive, when he wrote:

> For Carter's [immediate] predecessors, Canal negotiations were driven by the sense they could enhance the security of the waterway. For Carter they were also, and more significantly, an opportunity to show a new face of American foreign policy, one that conveyed respect for human rights, small nations, and moral principle. [He] certainly had not planned to make Panama the first

foreign issue he tackled. Launching [his] Mideast peace process had been his first foreign policy priority, but he said in a 2006 interview that Panama had been very important to him, too [by admitting] "I wanted to treat Panama fairly. I had studied the issue thoroughly and I was convinced that it was an unfair original agreement that was foisted upon the Panamanian people against their will. I was determined to go through with the Panama Canal [treaty] because I thought I could succeed, and I did not anticipate the antipathy and the concerted effort that was aroused against it. I underestimated the opposition."[2]

Long before Carter's determination to move forward on the Canal in 1977, in fact, battle lines on the issue had been forming in Washington. In his autobiography, Laxalt, the Nevada senator and confidant that future President Reagan would rely on to keep his Republican primary manifesto versus Ford simmering after Carter was elected, remembered his earliest recollection of the Canal controversy when he was asked during his own Senate campaign in 1974 if he agreed with the plan "to give away the Canal." Laxalt, who was running for the Senate after previously serving as Nevada's governor, was caught totally unaware of the

Jimmy Carter, the little-known governor of Georgia, was a surprise presidential winner in 1976 over incumbent Gerald Ford when he skillfully used Ford's negotiations with Panama against him before reversing course on the issue once he was in the White House. Carter also gained a huge campaign edge from Ford's controversial pardon of his disgraced predecessor, Richard Nixon (Library of Congress Prints and Photographs Division—Reproduction Number LC-DIG-ppmsca-09782).

possibility and "filibustered vaguely," to use his words, that it was not a very good idea. It was an admittedly unprepared answer to a question that was about to become a conservative, "hot-button issue"—truly Laxalt's "wakeup call."[3]

Once elected, he further learned (and wrote) that, indeed, Kissinger's State Department was full of diplomats who believed the Panamanians had been treated unfairly "and that it was time to expiate our guilt and return the Canal to its rightful owners." But with Republican Gerald Ford as president, he assured himself that no such "giveaway" could possibly be imminent, an assumption obviously proven false when Regan's right-wing backers convinced him of the issue's relevance during their '76 campaign versus Ford. No such assumptions would be necessary with Carter, however, as "immediately after the election [as previously noted and confirmed by Laxalt], the Carter people entered into negotiations with the government of Panama's Omar Torrijos to settle on treaty terms."[4]

Ah yes, Omar Torrijos, who is commonly referred to as a Panamanian dictator by almost any source—a former commander of the Panamanian National Guard, who took over individual leadership of the country during a military coup d'état and served in that role from 1968 to 1981 and enacted a variety of social reforms without ever adopting the title of president. Admittedly inspired by the likes of Marshal Josip Tito, Yugoslavia's independent leader during Soviet domination of the rest of Eastern Europe, and Egypt's Abdel Nasser, the most popular Arab leader at a time of shrinking European influence in the Middle East (including nationalization of the Suez Canal), Torrijos was also notoriously linked to Cuba's Fidel Castro and branded a pro-communist friend and ally of the Cuban strongman. As a result, Reagan accused him of censoring the Panamanian press, extinguishing civil liberties, and threatening sabotage or guerrilla attacks on the Canal Zone in order to leverage treaty talks.[5]

Regardless, Carter's sudden reversal and follow-up on the Kissinger-Tack Agreement thrust Torrijos into the Latin American catbird seat, and by December of 1976, Eizenstat confirmed that "half a dozen presidents of other Latin American countries had signed a letter to the President-elect," urging "the need for a new Panama Canal Treaty" to improve "inter-American relations." And Carter, who had "always been devoted to Latin America," and had "a strong sense of kinship with them would never do anything that was not conducive to improved relations [between] the United States" and its hemispheric neighbors. As a result, multiple sources acknowledge there is little doubt that immediately after the '76 election, the Carter administration entered into renewed treaty negotiations with the Torrijos government.[6]

Accordingly, as yet another source, Laura Kalman, who authored a book titled *Right Star Rising* on the "new politics" between 1974 and 1980, reported: "By the summer of 1977, the President's negotiators had actually prepared two treaties, which, [when] combined, embodied the principles of Kissinger-Tack." The first was simply named the Panama Canal Treaty and established provisions for immediately increasing Panamanian participation in the operation of the Canal Zone through the end of the century, with the assertion that Panama would gain ultimate control in 2000. The second was labeled the Treaty Concerning Permanent Neutrality and Operation of the Panama Canal, and "spelled out" what Kalman called, "the obligation of [both] the United States and Panama to defend the Canal and any threat to its status as a neutral waterway," as well as assuring U.S. ships priority in times of excess traffic.[7]

Likewise, Laxalt's memoir confirmed that in September: "The announcement was made, the Panama Canal treaties had been signed, and the fat was in the fire," so to speak. "Conservatives were shocked. They just did not believe that when push came to shove Carter would actually go along" ... that "regardless of what had been said, if the Democrats did win, they would give away the Canal."[8]

With Panamanian leader Omar Torrijos seated next to him and anxiously looking on, President Jimmy Carter hosted the 1977 treaty signing ceremony in Washington, during which the Panama Canal, America's creation and prize possession since the days of "Teddy" Roosevelt, was officially turned over to the host country, Panama (Library of Congress Prints and Photographs Division—Reproduction Number LC-DIG-ppmsca-09785).

20. Reversing Course into a Proxy War

Torrijos had come to Washington along with 17 other Latin American heads of state for what would be an extravagant signing ceremony at the Pan American Union Building. Also present were former President Ford, Lady Bird Johnson, Lyndon Johnson's widow (LBJ having died in 1973), and Kissinger, U.S. architect of the original agreement. Speaking in the broadest of foreign policy terms at the time, President Carter said: "Fairness, not force, should be at the heart of our dealings with the nations of the world. In a world very different from ours today, an original treaty was signed which has become an obstacle to better relations with Latin America. The new treaties can open a new era of understanding and comprehension, friendship and mutual respect throughout not only this hemisphere, but the world."[9] In his book, Senator Laxalt would again concur, when he wrote: "Under the terms of the treaties, the U.S. would gradually relinquish control over the waterway until the year 2000, when Panama would complete the take-over. Until that time, the U.S. would operate the Canal as well as the 14 military bases located in the Canal Zone. If, after the year 2000, the Canal's safety was [ever] endangered, the U.S. would be free to intervene with military force"—an important concession, but not one that came close to appeasing the most conservative Republicans.[10]

And it didn't take long for representatives of conservative groups to begin contacting Reagan's surrogate in the Senate. Laxalt acknowledged these groups viewed Carter, like Ford, as "soft" on the issue and formally asked him to lead Senate opposition to ratification. At the same time, those groups were prepared to begin a grass roots campaign to raise funds with which to initiate combative, direct mail opposition. Laxalt also set about organizing a Senate team to confront the issue, with Jim Allen of Alabama as its floor leader, strategist, and "superb parliamentarian," to go along with Bob Dole of Kansas, Jake Garn of Utah, John Tower of Texas, Pete Domenici of New Mexico, Bill Scott of Virginia, California's S. I. Hayakawa, and the previously mentioned Thurmond plus Jesse Helms of North Carolina and Utah's Orin Hatch. It was literally a who's who of Senate conservatives and a group made even more formidable by the fact it included five members of the powerful Armed Services Committee, lending, in Laxalt's words, "important weight" to their opposition.[11]

The first order of business for this opposition force was what Laxalt termed a "reliable headcount" to determine where each of their Senate colleagues stood on the Canal issue. "Within days," Laxalt had his somewhat reliable count, including 23 "hard votes" and five "possibles," with the rest of their fellow senators "leaning heavily" in the other direction. To defeat ratification of the Carter-Torrijos treaties, at least 34 of the 100 senators would be needed to vote against them, so with only 23 "assureds," much work loomed for the Laxalt-led team.[12]

Immediately, Laxalt and the others took to the airwaves, aggressively challenging the treaties on television and radio. Laxalt was paired against Carter's chief negotiator, Ambassador Sol Linowitz, at the prestigious Commonwealth Club of San Francisco, where they debated their opposing positions. Going second, Laxalt confronted each of Linowitz's pro-treaty arguments, while the Carter team indicated rejection of the treaties would serve as a direct slap to the newly elected president and could seriously diminish his administration before it had a chance to get started. Laxalt reminded the nation that while the president had the power to negotiate treaties, only the Senate had the power to approve them and should never be treated as merely a "rubber stamp" for the chief executive. And although accepted by the U.S. military in the persons of the Joint Chiefs, Laxalt and his conservative cohorts polled 245 Navy officers, establishing some opposition among 241 of them.[13]

Linowitz also contended that America had basically short-changed the Panamanians, a "poor Panama syndrome" that Laxalt attacked as utter nonsense based on the economic advantages American presence had brought to the Panamanian people; the infrastructure gained by American dollars and know-how; and by medical advances achieved during the Canal's construction, including the eradication of yellow fever and control of malaria and other mosquito-borne diseases. In conclusion, Laxalt said "it was high time the U.S. stopped apologizing to poorer countries we had befriended or helped save." And to further their arguments against the treaties, Laxalt and Dole were soon on their way to Panama for an inspection tour of the Canal Zone and their own personal visit with Torrijos. It was during that visit, in fact, that Torrijos candidly admitted his friendship with Castro, while also demonstrating his devotion to his people when he took the two senators for a stroll through the streets of Panama City. Nevertheless, just four years later Torrijos would be mysteriously killed in a helicopter accident that paved the way for a far more unsavory successor, Manuel Noriega, to eventually emerge as president (Noriega would later be forced out of power in a U.S. invasion in 1989).[14]

Upon his return stateside, Laxalt and his fellow conservatives also embarked on another initiative as the Canal issue intensified. They called it a "Truth Squad" and they prepared to take their campaign on an extensive aerial road trip to counter the Carter administration's assertions about transferring the Canal and despite the rejection of any funding assistance by the Republican National Committee and its moderate chairman Bill Brock of Tennessee, a rejection that drew immediate condemnation from Reagan. Nevertheless, the Truth Squad raised the funds necessary to take to the air on a highly publicized five-day, seven-city tour designed to alert the American people to the supposed fatal flaws in the Panama Canal treaties.

20. Reversing Course into a Proxy War

Travelling with the Laxalt team were several ex-military officials to help spread the word in Nashville, Atlanta, Miami, Cincinnati, St. Louis, Denver, and Portland. Included in their case was the fear the U.S. would eventually be turning over the Canal to a government friendly with both Cuba and Russia, and by March 1978, "the debate over the Panama Canal treaties was," in Laxalt's estimation, "the Number One political topic in the United States." Undecided senators were, again in his words, "subjected to unbelievable pressure from both sides," and White House invitations to review the treaties "were commonplace."[15]

Eizenstat, who was in the middle of it all from the administration's standpoint, pointed out that Joint Chief of Staff General David Jones was warning that Senate rejection "was likely" to touch off violence and guerrilla warfare in Panama, probably "threatening the Canal even more than a change to local control." At the same time, conservative activist and talk show host Pat Buchanan was sarcastically pointing out the U.S. had always grown through questionable land grabs like the Canal Zone— so, he said, "what was next ... giving back New Mexico, Arizona, and California?" After all, they too had been extracted from another country. Should they be returned to Mexico, too, just to satisfy what Kalman re-quoted as the "Chablis-and-cheese set?" But it was the battle on Capitol Hill that was attracting the most interest. Meeting regularly in Laxalt's office, the treaty opponents got their marching orders from conservative insurgents like Paul Weyrich, founder of the Heritage Foundation and reportedly originator of the term "Moral Majority." Meanwhile,

Senator Paul Laxalt of Nevada was the Senate leader in the battle to stop two decades of negotiations over the Panama Canal during the mid 1970s. After waging this proxy war for his good friend Ronald Reagan, who instigated the Canal fight as a presidential candidate in 1976, he would remain a key congressional supporter of the future president (permission granted by the Paul Laxalt Group via Wikimedia Commons, U.S. Senate Photo).

the White House established a war room under the leadership of Carter Chief of Staff Hamilton Jordan to coordinate the campaign for ratification, beginning with lobbying efforts to keep senators neutral and open-minded until the administration had a chance to explain how the treaties would protect U.S. interests, as well as defend that idea in the court of public opinion.[16]

Polls were showing the American public was with Laxalt and the treaty opponents, as the battle cry of "don't give up our Canal" echoed among Americans by as much as 78 percent. A feeling of "vanished mastery" was how one historian categorized the U.S. psyche after Vietnam and the possibility of a Canal giveaway being more of the same. And then there was the specter of Reagan, with his initial warnings about the Ford administration's negotiations with Panama still looming as an ever-more pervasive voice of Republican aspiration. Already in February of 1977, Reagan had addressed the Conservative Political Action Conference in Washington and denounced negotiating with a dictator, and others, including Democrat Bob Sikes of Florida, had cautioned about Russian ambitions in Latin America. Meanwhile, Laxalt and company were bringing enormous pressure on avowed undecideds like Henry Bellmon of Oklahoma, Louisiana's Russell Long, Arizona's Dennis DeConcini, Sam Hayakawa of California, Kentucky's Wendell Ford, and Ed Zorinsky of Nebraska. In writing about the Senate machinations of the Laxalt (and Reagan) team, Kalman called it a "milestone in the development of conservatism."[17]

Meanwhile, the Carter administration was busy developing a campaign to increase public support for the Canal treaties. While key senators were being inundated with anti-treaty mail by the Laxalt-Reagan team, the bipartisan Committee of Americans for the Canal treaties was unveiled in Washington composed of military and diplomatic luminaries from past administrations, as well as corporate leaders anxious to avoid the threat of Latin American supply chain instability. At the same time, Carter took on a huge role, according to Adam Clymer. While personally telephoning, wiring, and/or meeting with all 100 senators, he took copious notes on their individual responses and/or reservations in order to better frame his message and combat the negative polling numbers his administration was facing with public opinion. In the days before the final, amended version of the treaties came up for a vote in the Senate, the President treated the issue like a political campaign while seeking momentum and a feeling of inevitability. There was the spectacle of Latin American leaders journeying to Washington in a show of hemispheric support; the achievement of clarity over the fact no limitations would be placed on American intervention in defense of the Canal; and the way Carter was able to prod Torrijos toward expanding democracy and human rights. At the time Carter said:

We made a tremendous effort to woo Congress. Many nights when I was tired and would like to have relaxed, we had a supper for maybe a hundred [congressmen] and I would spend two more hours in the East Room describing either domestic or foreign policy. We had them in groups ad nauseam, night after night, going through the same basic questions and why they ought to support the Panama Canal legislation.[18]

Like Laxalt and Dole, Republican Minority Leader Howard Baker was one of numerous senators Carter encouraged to make fact-finding trips to Panama. Baker finally made his in January 1978. Torrijos assured him he would be flexible and amenable to an amended treaty within reason. But the most difficult of the uncommitted senators to sway for different reasons, according to the Carter camp, were Hayakawa and Domenici, one a Republican and the other a Democrat (respectively). Hayakawa, a best-selling author, was willing to commit his vote in exchange for future foreign policy access and input, while Domenici wanted to specify in the treaties what would constitute the need for American force and not just in the Canal Zone, but Panama proper as well—a potential deal breaker since Carter and Torrijos had kept that part of the negotiations ambiguous, intentionally avoiding specifics. The President and his team had to remedy both, with Carter reading Hayakawa's book, *Language in Action*, and praising its content as a means of stroking his ego to secure his vote, while Jordan would save the day by rushing to Panama to assure Torrijos that the inclusion of a Domenici amendment could (and would) be watered down by the later actions of Senate Leaders Baker and Robert Byrd, who were both committed to the administration.[19]

On March 16, 1978, all the behind the scenes cajoling by both sides finally came down to the actual Senate vote, which Laxalt spoke directly about in his autobiography, when he wrote:

> The day of the vote could only be described as wild. The galleries filled to the ceiling early. Leader Robert Byrd insisted upon "order" in the galleries. He even ordered the well of the Senate cleared during the vote. Shortly before the vote was called, there was bad news for our side—my colleague from Nevada, Howard Cannon. All along we had assumed Cannon was with us because of overwhelming sentiment in Nevada against the treaties. Just before the vote, Senator Cannon, who was chairing the Senate at the time, signaled me to come to the chair. He asked, "How are you doing?" That should have been a tip-off. I told him it could go either way and that we were at a hard 32 count and looking for two more votes in a pool of six, [still] undecideds. "How are you counting me?" he asked [and I responded] "I'm counting you with us, of course!" To this he gravely remarked, "I wouldn't if I were you." My heart sank. Without Cannon, that left us looking for three votes instead of two, which was a huge difference. The time for debate was divided equally between the two sides [and] as floor

leader it became my questionable honor to parcel out time to my colleagues and leave myself enough time to close with a summary of our position. I had figured I would need at least 30 minutes to close properly, but as time progressed, it was clear that I would be lucky to speak at all.

Sure enough, debate time ended and Laxalt's chance for a stirring close was lost to history—certain though it was, nothing he could have said at that point would have probably changed a single vote.[20]

The vote itself was unusual as the senators cast their votes seated at their desks, which was rare. Usually, Senate votes were recorded with senators milling about in the well and many after the first call, but not this one—not the one on relinquishing America's Panama Canal. As the roll call proceeded, the pool of remaining undecideds, including Belmon, Domenici, Hayakawa, and the others, one by one voted in favor of the treaties. "The final vote was 68–32," two votes shy of what was needed to deny ratification. Laxalt's conclusion: "The White House pressure on the undecideds [had been] too great. We had made it to the one-yard line but couldn't push the ball over the goal line."[21]

But, as everyone knows, close only counts in horseshoes and the political fallout at home for those who voted in favor of the treaties was intense to say the least. Both Baker and Bellmon, fellow Republicans, asked Laxalt to join them at appearances in their states for damage control, which he did. As for Cannon, four years later he would be defeated while Hayakawa soon decided against running for re-election with his vote in favor of the treaties the main reason. To the end of his political days, Laxalt felt opposition to relinquishing control of the Canal was vindicated by his belief Panama, Latin America, and the U.S. would have been better served if Senate ratification had failed.[22]

On the other hand, Carter would always label the win one of his proudest moments. It had come at the end of the longest Senate debate over foreign policy since then President Wilson and Senator Lodge had squared off over the League of Nations. Vice President Walter Mondale observed at the time that the administration had indeed achieved "a Pyrrhic victory," but at a cost of good will and trust. And sure enough, in late 1989 then President George H.W. Bush was compelled to authorize "Operation Just Cause," a month-long U.S. military invasion of Panama, ensuring protection of some 35,000 Americans still living and working in the Canal Zone and as a means of capturing and deposing Noriega.[23]

Nonetheless, following 13 years of negotiations, beginning under the administration of Lyndon Johnson, the United States and Panama concluded a treaty in September 1977 that provided for the transfer of the Panama Canal and return of the Canal Zone to Panama on December 31, 1999. As noted earlier, Torrijos would not live to see it (as the result of the mysterious accident in 1981), but Carter would be there at age 75, heading a 29-member U.S. delegation commissioned by then President Bill Clinton, who, along with Secretary of State Madeline Albright, was notably absent. According to a *Baltimore Sun* story at the time, Clinton rebuffed a personal appeal for him to attend from Panamanian President Mireya Morosco, fearing his presence or anyone else from his administration could be used against Vice President Albert Gore, Jr., who would be running for president in 2000. Obviously, even by the turn of the century, giving up the Panama Canal remained a very controversial political issue.[24]

21

The Diminishing Returns of Global Leadership

Despite public opinion to the contrary, Jimmy Carter was well satisfied with his achievement of the two Panama Canal treaties early in his presidency. An avowed proponent of U.S. support for small developing nations, human rights, and better hemispheric relations, his decision to finish what Lyndon Johnson had initiated and his presidential opponent, Gerald Ford, had negotiated in the face of opposition from conservatives in both parties was a bold foreign policy and legislative triumph that seemed to embolden the new, "outsider" administration to tackle even greater international initiatives. Speaking on that in the foreword to Eizenstat's biography of the 39th president, then Secretary of State Albright wrote: "Those who dismiss Jimmy Carter's considerable accomplishments as president are doing a disservice to the historical record. This is particularly true in the realm of foreign policy. President Carter was idealistic; he wanted America to present a morally untainted image to the world."[1]

By taking on the Laxalt-Reagan team and taking over efforts to deliver the Panama Canal to its host country as a gesture designed to promote democratic principles and hemispheric unity in the later, more advanced stages of America's Cold War with the Soviet Union, Carter surprised the U.S. establishment. It was a signal of things to come. Equally surprising would be his next diplomatic move towards Middle East peace, a challenge other presidents had been hesitant to confront, especially early in their administrations, as Eizenstat established. Through his more pro-active approach, Carter would achieve an historic "first peace treaty between [the Jewish state of] Israel and any Arab [or Muslim] state," when he consummated his hard-won "Camp David Accords" between the Israelis and their most powerful Middle Eastern rival, Egypt, in September 1978—a truly global diplomatic milestone that neither country would have achieved on its own. In so doing, he became the first American president to successfully negotiate an international

21. The Diminishing Returns of Global Leadership

peace treaty between warring nations since Theodore Roosevelt's Nobel Prize–winning settlement of the Russo-Japanese War in 1905 (an irony of sorts given Carter's previous giveaway of TR's most iconic achievement, the Panama Canal).[2]

Ever since President Harry Truman went out on a limb in 1947 by officially recognizing the new nation of Israel over the objections of many within his administration, including Secretary of State George Marshall, "the United States had a moral commitment to Israel's survival," again according to Carter's biographer. It was an unwritten rule of American foreign policy and public support that viewed Israel as the biblically ordained "Holy Land" and an "island of democracy in a sea of autocratic, Muslim regimes." And by the time President Carter came along, in fact, Israel had established military supremacy over its surrounding Arab neighbors, as well as an overall reliance on the U.S. At the same time, Carter had been preparing to take on the major foreign policy issues of the era ever since deciding to run for president, knowing full well his lack of international experience could he used against him. As Georgia's outgoing governor, he prepped for his next job by connecting with the likes of the Trilateral Commission in 1975, an organization of political, economic, and academic leaders from Japan, Europe, and the U.S., establishing contacts that could be pressed into service should he reach the White House. Special emphasis was also given during the '76 campaign to the Middle East and Israel, which he had made a point to visit while a governor three years earlier.[3]

Initially, Carter's lack of experience with the inner workings of Washington politics and his own, egotistical self-reliance were held against him. Democratic Speaker of the House Tip O'Neill once called him "The smartest public official [he had] ever known, but when it came to the politics of Washington, he never understood how the system worked." As a result, his initial approach to the Middle East was somewhat disjointed, but he eventually settled on a more balanced view of the Israeli-Arab conflict that was fraught with pro–Israel, anti–Arab public opinion concerns, but necessary for meaningful diplomacy. The Six-Day War of 1967 had left Israel in control of far more territory than ever before, both the Sinai Peninsula and Gaza Strip from Egypt, the West Bank along the Jordan River from neighboring Jordan, and the Golan Heights of Syria, all of which contained remnants of the Palestinian population, many of whom had been displaced in the Jewish nation's founding. In the aftermath of war, United Nations Resolution 242 attempted to restore (and return) the conquered territories to their previous boundaries (and governments), but Israel did not see it that way, instead allowing its own settlers to gradually move into the subjugated areas. And despite another, 19-day Arab-Israeli war in 1973, that was still the situation when Anwar el Sadat, the new president of Egypt, determined to seek a more progressive Arab future instead of the conservative Arab past, a development that would ultimately make Jimmy Carter's Middle East peace initiatives possible.[4]

In November of 1977, Sadat engaged in the boldest possible step by deciding to visit Israel to begin peace negotiations, a previously unthinkable gesture by an Arab head of state who would be subjecting himself to condemnation from the other rulers of the six-nation Arab League and the rest of the Muslim world. By deigning to visit and negotiate with the Jews, Sadat would become the first Muslim leader to recognize Israel, an act of extreme political and personal courage that would eventually lead to his assassination four years later. That tragedy, however, was not until he had become part of an agreement that would surprise the rest of the world and elevate Carter to the pinnacle of his presidency.[5]

But, "how was the administration to proceed" to make it happen? That's the question Eizenstat posed in writing about the Carter formula—what he hoped would be a lasting Mideast peace, a world-changing moment, and a major landmark for his own legacy. Just as with the Canal, gone would be the campaign's more electable emphasis on Israel's preferred position and security needs; on opposition to Arab arms sales; and on the dangers of Arab/Muslim states. Already Sadat had realized he needed American help. He needed American intervention to reclaim the Sinai Peninsula, which was still in Israeli hands since the Six-Day War. At the same time, because of that "other," Arab-Israeli War in 1973 and the resulting Arab oil embargo, Carter needed Sadat to avoid another economic shakedown of the world's economy that might cost him re-election. Eizenstat stressed that the President "was not" interested in an Israel-Egypt agreement alone, but instead hoped "to forge a comprehensive peace with all parties in the [regional] conflict," including the other neighboring Arab nations, Syria and Jordan, and most "critically," the Palestinians.... Arabs who had co-existed alongside Jews in Palestine for centuries, but who had become refugees in their own land when the suddenly insolvent British Empire ended its between world wars Palestinian Mandate. Thousands of European Jews had since returned to reclaim their "Promised Land." Their lives and lively hoods had been devastated by World War II and more specifically by expansionist Nazi Germany's immoral ethnic cleansing, and by whatever means necessary, these Jews intended to have a nation of their own.[6]

Cyrus Vance, a former New York City lawyer and veteran diplomat whom Carter had retained from his campaign team to be secretary of state, would be sent to the Middle East within weeks of the inauguration to begin the process. While there he would visit Israel, Egypt, Syria, and Saudi Arabia, with the latter already a behind-the-scenes regional force due to its oil

21. The Diminishing Returns of Global Leadership 259

dominance, even though not a bordering nation in the conflict. At the same time, "the Israeli elections of 1977 had changed the calculus," according to Eizenstat, with the new prime minister, Menachem Begin, much more committed to the traditional Jewish view of Gaza and the West Bank as "liberated—not occupied—territories" and more symbolically, the restored biblical lands once called Judea and Samaria. Meanwhile, Sadat went from hoping the new American president would negotiate for Egypt with the Israelis to shocking the world on November 9, 1977, when he announced during a speech to the Egyptian Parliament that he would actually do the previously unthinkable for an Arab leader by going to Israel to meet with Begin, his new Israeli counterpart and someone who had previously called Sadat, "an enemy of Israel."[7]

The 1999 PBS documentary, *The 50 Years War: Israel and the Arabs*, portrayed Sadat's dramatic announcement as "writing his name indelibly in the history books." Faced, in fact, with this courageous act, Begin had no choice but to issue an official invitation to the Egyptian president to address the Israeli Knesset. And so, with the eyes of the world watching, Sadat flew to Israel just over a week later on November 19, 1977, and was greeted, according to the documentary, like a modern day "Moses" while making his way to the Israeli capital, Tel Aviv, the next day. On the other hand, one member of the Egyptian entourage would confess it felt like he was visiting "outer space," so unprecedented was that moment in the history of Israeli-Arab relations and the Middle East.[8]

Admittedly, Sadat's address to the Knesset that day was not nearly as conciliatory as his visit had rather hopefully implied, and after seven more months of talks between the foreign ministers of the two countries amounted to nothing, a frustrated Sadat proclaimed the peace process "terminated" and his gesture in going to Israel "fruitless." That's when Carter, against the advice of his advisers, who repeatedly thought it a very bad idea, decided to enter the impasse by inviting both Sadat and Begin, and all of their respective advisers, to join him and his diplomatic team at the U.S. presidential retreat in the Catoctin Mountains near Washington, Camp David, for two weeks of intense negotiation that he hoped would broker a lasting peace agreement between the warring rivals and prove a starting point for lasting Middle East peace. That, after all, was the long sought dream ever since the modern state of Israel had come into being as an ongoing Cold War threat to world peace.[9]

Twice Carter had to literally issue personal appeals to keep the negotiations going, once each to both sides, but eventually he was able to achieve an historic agreement between the two that became the Camp David Accords. Actually, the compromise agreed upon included Israel's return of the Sinai and the dismantling of its new settlements there by 1982 in exchange for Egypt becoming the first Arab nation to officially recognize the Jewish State. Not addressed (and a problem ever since) was the Arab call for a separate Palestinian state in the Israeli controlled West Bank. Nevertheless, on March 26, 1979, at the White House, two documents—a "Framework for Peace in the Middle East" and a "Framework for the Conclusion of a Peace Treaty between Egypt and Israel"—were signed by Sadat and Begin amid much fanfare, including their official handshake photo op with Carter that would be seen around the world. Both Begin and Sadat would win Nobel Peace Prizes (Carter would as well following his presidency for his work on peaceful solutions to international conflicts; his advancement of democracy; and his advocacy for worldwide economic and social development) and the peace between Israel and Egypt has lasted ever since despite many other Middle Eastern conflicts.[10]

From the Canal and the Egypt-Israel peace agreement, Carter would move on to other tricky foreign policy issues. Unlike his six immediate predecessors, in 1979 Carter became the first president to establish diplomatic

In perhaps the high point of his presidency, Jimmy Carter (center) joyfully congratulates Egyptian President Anwar Sadat (left) and Israeli Prime Minister Menachem Begin in the White House Rose Garden after the signing of the landmark Egyptian-Israeli peace treaty he negotiated at Camp David. Sadat, who was under intense pressure from the rest of the Arab/Muslim world for negotiating with the Jewish state, would be assassinated two years later. (Library of Congress Prints and Photographs Division Reproduction—Number LC-DIG-ppmsca-0324).

21. The Diminishing Returns of Global Leadership

relations with Communist China, officially recognizing the government in Peking as the legitimate Chinese government instead of the exiled Nationalist Chinese regime on the island of Taiwan; he negotiated a second Strategic Arms Limitation Treaty with the Soviet Union, only to see its ratification denied by conservatives in the Senate; and he cut off humanitarian aid to the nation of Afghanistan in response to the slaying of the U.S. ambassador there, an unrelated prelude to the Soviet Union's invasion of that country later the same year—an invasion that would spark a U.S. embargo on high tech equipment and grain, U.N. resolutions calling for the withdrawal of all foreign troops, and a 63-nation boycott of the 1980 Moscow Summer Olympics. All of those paled in comparison, however, to the last foreign policy dilemma of the Carter administration—the takeover the U.S. embassy in Tehran, Iran and the taking of 60 American hostages by government backed Islamist militants in response to the deposed Iranian Shah's presence and medical treatment in the U.S. The militants demanded that the Shah (King) be returned to Iran to stand trial for human rights atrocities. Only eight of the hostages, all either African Americans or women, would be released and returned home immediately, while the 52 others were held captive for more than a year. Still, Carter would not negotiate and send back the Shah, a former U.S. ally, to what would have surely been his execution. Instead, he embarked on a major diplomatic, economic, and even secret military operation to try and gain the hostages freedom, all of which failed and as much as anything cost him re-election in 1980.[11]

On the domestic front, things got almost as bad for Carter, ensuring he was a one-term president. Inflation peaked amidst an energy crisis that featured long lines at gas pumps and the President didn't help himself when he referred to "the malaise" of the American people. One presidential historian's way of putting it: "His much-admired idealism ran up against the harsh reality of geopolitics in the 1970s," which he was unprepared to deal with. As a result, he has long been revered for making his greatest contributions in the area of human rights after leaving office. At this writing, he was the longest living U.S. president ever at age 96 (and still counting with his next birthday just months away).[12]

As for Laxalt, who would be referred to as "The First Friend" once Ronald Reagan entered the White House in 1981, he would serve one more term in the U.S. Senate while also being general chair of the Republican National Committee from January 1983 until January 1987. Before leaving the Senate, he would become a special envoy for Reagan to the beleaguered Philippines government of U.S. ally Ferdinand Marcos, whom he advised to step down as president to avoid civil war and possible communist takeover, which Marcos famously did on February 25, 1986, after 21 years in power, leaving his homeland (along with his family) for asylum in the United States.[13]

Along with an entire chapter on the Marcos affair in his memoir, Laxalt also devoted a significant amount of another chapter to the Iran-Contra controversy, which tarnished the Regan legacy, and yet another to his own controversial legal battle with the *Sacramento Bee* newspaper, which accused him and his family in November 1983 of an "illegal diversion" of up to $2 million in cash from their ownership of the Ormsby House, a former restaurant and casino in Carson City, Nevada. Purchased by Laxalt's father in the early 1900s, it was rebuilt by then Governor Laxalt in 1972. The

Dubbed the First Friend of President Ronald Reagan, Senator Paul Laxalt led Ronald Reagan's efforts to stop transfer of the Panama Canal to Panama during the Carter Administration without success, but also served his good friend as a special envoy to the Philippines during their Washington years together in the 1980s (permission to use granted by the Paul Laxalt Group via Wikimedia Commons).

21. The Diminishing Returns of Global Leadership 263

Bee indicated that his political connections at the time had "sidetracked any potential investigation and that there was evidence of organized crime involvement." Following a complete denial, Laxalt entered into an extensive libel suit that took three years to win, an exoneration that netted him and his family a $647,452.52 settlement in 1987.[14]

At about the same time, Reagan was having to admit his administration's trading in armaments to Iran in exchange for freeing seven American hostages held by the Iranian-backed terrorist organization Hezbollah in Lebanon. It would prove a dastardly reckoning considering how the Iranian regime had been vilified ever since the embassy takeover, but a reckoning nonetheless made worse by the fact proceeds from those arm sales were going to the "Contras," a rebel insurgency battling the communist "Sandinista" government in the Central American nation of Nicaragua. It was a twisted tale of covert operations that Reagan denied knowing about, but it threatened to destroy his credibility, "his greatest strength," according to Laxalt. After a special review board found fault with the process and the administration's handling of it, Reagan had to take responsibility for the subversive action less than a year before the end of his second term. In conclusion, his First Friend wrote: "Undoubtedly, Iran-Contra was by far the most severe crisis of the Reagan administration, but Ron still survived. A president with less credibility with his people [might] have been destroyed." Laxalt would outlive Reagan by 14 years, dying in 2018 at 96.[15]

Epilogue: If Keeping Score, Closer Than Anticipated

As alluded to in both the Introduction and Preface of this book, the scorecard for the seven legendary Washington wars examined herein was a lot closer than you probably anticipated for a nation where the presidency has attained such pre-eminence in national consciousness and political power. But nonetheless, four to three in favor of the Presidents was the final tally, with the chief executives having come out on top in the Bank war, the Red Menace accusations, in support of the Civil Rights Movement, and the Panama Canal giveaway, while senators ultimately held sway in the pre–Civil War Bleeding Kansas controversy, the all-too-brief Reconstruction period, and the League of Nations deliberations at the end of World War I. By any historic measure and despite the obvious advantage of the presidential Bully Pulpit, those would be the accepted results handed down by American historians in their judgment of each—the whys, what happened, and immediate outcomes.

The presidential winners, Andrew Jackson, Harry Truman, Lyndon Johnson, and Jimmy Carter, were ironically all Democrats, while the senators who came out on top, Stephen Douglas, Charles Sumner, and Henry Cabot Lodge, did so by claiming the political high ground versus stubborn, overreaching presidents unwilling to compromise regardless of the political or personal consequences. While each individual winner would not necessarily benefit politically from the Washington war they waged, most of the losers, Henry Clay, James Buchanan, Andrew Johnson, Woodrow Wilson, Joseph McCarthy, and Richard Russell, would all pay a price politically at the time or to their legacies. Only Paul Laxalt, the proxy for Ronald Reagan, could be judged a winner even in defeat by virtue of the next election cycle (1980).

Chapter Notes

Chapter 1

1. William DeGregorio, *The Complete Book of U.S. Presidents*, 98, 107, 111–112; Jon Meacham, *American Lion: Andrew Jackson in the White House*, 44; Glyndon G. VanDeusen, *The Jacksonian Era: 1828-1848*, 61–67.
2. H.W. Brands, *Heirs of the Founders: Henry Clay, John Calhoun, and Daniel Webster—The Second Generation of American Giants*, 117–118.
3. Robert V. Remini, *Henry Clay: Statesman for the Union*, 212–213, 218–219; Jon Meacham, *American Lion*, 37; Glyndon G. VanDeusen, *The Jacksonian Era*, 31.
4. Robert Remini, *Henry Clay*, 373; Richard A. Baker and Neil MacNeil, *The American Senate: An Insider's History*, 62.
5. Robert Remini, *Henry Clay*, 1; William DeGregorio, *The Complete Book of U.S. Presidents*, 112; Kenneth C. Davis, *Don't Know Much About the American Presidents*, 165.
6. William DeGregorio, *The Complete Book of U.S. Presidents*, 109–110; Michael F. Holt, *The Rise and Fall of the American Whig Party: Jacksonian Politics and the Onset of the Civil War*, 8.
7. Kenneth C. Davis, *Don't Know Much About the American Presidents*, 156; Jon Meacham, *American Lion*, 20–21.
8. Robert Remini, *Andrew Jackson: The Course of American Freedom—1822-1832*, 59–60.
9. Robert Remini, *Henry Clay*, 2–5, 34–35.
10. Richard A. Baker and Neil MacNeil, *The American Senate*, 280.
11. Robert Remini, *Henry Clay*, 77.
12. Robert Remini, *Henry Clay*, 77; "Henry Clay," en.wikipedia.com; Glyndon G. VanDeusen, *The Jacksonian Era*, 47.
13. Glyndon VanDeusen, *The Jacksonian Era*, 47; Robert Remini, *Henry Clay*, 225.
14. Glyndon G. VanDeusen, *The Jacksonian Era*, 51; Michael F. Holt, *The Rise and Fall of the American Whig Party*, 10–20, 841–842.
15. Glyndon G. VanDeusen, *The Jacksonian Era*, 1; Michael F. Holt, *The Rise and Fall of the American Whig Party*, 6; Kenneth C. Davis, *Don't Know Much About the American Presidents*, 164–166.
16. Kenneth C. Davis, *Don't Know Much About the American Presidents*, 164-166; H.W. Brands, *American Lion*, 120–122.
17. H.W. Brands, *Heirs of the Founders*, 186–190; Glyndon G. VanDeusen, *The Jacksonian Era*, 48–52; Robert Remini, *Henry Clay*, 376; H.W. Brands, *American Lion*, 273–274.
18. Glyndon G. VanDeusen, *The Jacksonian Era*, 48–50; William DeGregorio, *The Complete Book of U.S. Presidents*, 116; H.W. Brands, *Heirs of the Founders*, 186.
19. H.W. Brands, *Heirs of the Founders*, 185.
20. H.W. Brands, *American Lion*, 139–140, 201, 203–205.
21. Andrew T. Hill, "The First Bank of the United States," federalreservehistory.org, December 4, 2015.
22. Robert Remini, *Andrew Jackson*, 36; H.W. Brands, *American Lion*, 48; Kenneth C. Davis, *Don't Know Much About the American Presidents*, 48–51.
23. Kenneth C. Davis, *Don't Know Much About the American Presidents*, 117, 119, 121; William DeGregorio, *The Complete Book of U.S. Presidents*, 63, 66; William Safire, "Essay; 'Little Jemmy,'" *New York*

Times, March 19, 2001; Andrew Burstein and Nancy Isenberg, *Madison and Jefferson*, 544–545.

24. Kenneth C. Davis, *Don't Know Much About the American Presidents*, 164; Glyndon G. VanDeusen, *The Jacksonian Era*, 62.

25. Glyndon G. VanDeusen, *The Jacksonian Era*, 63–64; Robert Remini, *Daniel Webster: The Man and His Time*, 261–262; Robert Remini, *Henry Clay*, 195, 198–199, 569; H.W. Brands, *Heirs of the Founders*, 190.

26. H.W. Brands, *Heirs of the Founders*, 189–190; Robert Remini, *Henry Clay*, 379–380.

27. Michael F. Holt, *The Rise and Fall of the American Whig Party*, 15–17; H.W. Brands, *American Lion*, 208–212; Kenneth C. Davis, *Don't Know Much About the American Presidents*, 165–166.

28. Richard A. Baker and Neil MacNeil, *The American Senate*, 61, 169, 281.

Chapter 2

1. Robert Remini, *Henry Clay*, 379–380; H.W. Brands, *Heirs of the Founders*, 189–191; Glyndon G. VanDeusen, *The Jacksonian Era*, 65–66; William DeGregorio, *The Complete Book of U.S. Presidents*, 112; Michael F. Holt, *The Rise and Fall of the American Whig Party*, 15–16.

2. H.W. Brands, *American Lion*, 53, 75, 76, 103–104, 121; Glyndon G. VanDeusen, *The Jacksonian Era*, 62–64; Robert Remini, *Henry Clay*, 139–140, 379; Andrew T. Hill, "The Second Bank of the United States," federalreservehistory.org, December 5, 2015; H.W. Brands, *Heirs of the Founders*, 186–190.

3. H.W. Brands, *Heirs of the Founders*, 190, 195.

4. Robert Remini, *Henry Clay*, 379; Richard A. Baker and Neil MacNeil, *The American Senate*, 281.

5. Michael F. Holt, *The Rise and Fall of the American Whig Party*, 14–15; Robert Remini, *Henry Clay*, 379–380.

6. Robert Remini, *Henry Clay*, 380–381.

7. *Ibid.*, 381.

8. *Ibid.*, 382.

9. Glyndon G. VanDeusen, *The Jacksonian Era*, 65.

10. Robert Remini, *Daniel Webster*, 29, 360–361; "The Devil and Daniel Webster," en.wikipedia.org.

11. Robert Remini, *Andrew Jackson*, 303–304; Robert Remini, *Daniel Webster*, 361; H.W. Brands, *Heirs of the Founders*, 191; Glyndon G. VanDeusen, *The Jacksonian Era*, 65.

12. Glyndon G. VanDeusen, *The Jacksonian Era*, 65; H.W. Brands, *Heirs of the Founders*, 192.

13. Robert Remini, *Henry Clay*, 398.

14. Robert Remini, *Henry Clay*, 1; H.W. Brands, *Heirs of the Founders*, 186–194, 195.

15. H.W. Brands, *American Lion*, 275.

16. Glyndon G. VanDeusen, *The Jacksonian Era*, 66.

17. *Ibid.*

18. Robert Remini, *Andrew Jackson*, 323.

19. Robert Remini, *Henry Clay*, 398.

20. Robert Remini, *Henry Clay*, 398–399; Glyndon G. VanDeusen, *The Jacksonian Era*, 66.

21. Glyndon G. VanDeusen, *The Jacksonian Era*, 66; Robert Remini, *Daniel Webster*, 367; Robert Remini, *Henry Clay*, 399.

22. Robert Remini, *Henry Clay*, 400.

23. Robert Remini, *Daniel Webster*, 368.

24. Robert Remini, *Andrew Jackson*, 346–349.

25. *Ibid.*, 347.

26. *Ibid.*, 348–349.

27. Jon Meacham, *American Lion*, 275.

28. *Ibid.*, 276.

29. Kenneth C. Davis, *Don't Know Much About the American Presidents*, 164; Glyndon G. VanDeusen, *The Jacksonian Era*, 66.

30. Michael F. Holt, *The Rise and Fall of the American Whig Party*, 16.

31. Glyndon G. VanDeusen, *The Jacksonian Era*, 66.

32. Michael F. Holt, *The Rise and Fall of the American Whig Party*, 16.

33. Glyndon G. VanDeusen, *The Jacksonian Era*, 67.

34. *Ibid.*; Robert Remini, *Daniel Webster*, 370–371; Michael F. Holt, *The Rise and Fall of the American Whig Party*, 16.

35. Robert Remini, *Henry Clay*, 399–402.

36. Robert Remini, *Henry Clay*, 403.

37. *Ibid.*

38. *Ibid.*

39. Robert Remini, *Henry Clay*, 373–374, 403; Glyndon G. VanDeusen, *The Jacksonian Era*, 56; H.W. Brands, *Heirs of the Founders*, 185.

40. Robert Remini, *Andrew Jackson*, 382.
41. Robert Remini, *Andrew Jackson*, 382–384; H.W. Brands, *American Lion*, 219.
42. William DeGregorio, *The Complete Book of U.S. Presidents*, 112; Kenneth C. Davis, *Don't Know Much About the American Presidents*, 164.
43. Robert Remini, *Henry Clay*, 662; H.W. Brands, *Heirs of the Founders*, 300–301.

Chapter 3

1. Robert Remini, *Henry Clay*, 394–410; Glyndon G. VanDeusen, The *Jacksonian Era*, 67; H.W. Brands, *Heirs of the Founders*, 195–196; Kenneth C. Davis, *Don't Know Much About the American Presidents*, 164; William DeGregorio, *The Complete Book of U.S. Presidents*, 112; Michael F. Holt, *The Rise and Fall of the American Whig Party*, 17.
2. Robert Remini, *Henry Clay*, 403–404.
3. Ibid., 1–2.
4. Robert Remini, *Henry Clay*, 239, 249, 658, 662–663.
5. H.W. Brands, *American Lion*, 218–219; Robert Remini, *Henry Clay*, 404; Michael F. Holt, *The Rise and Fall of the American Whig Party*, 17.
6. William DeGregorio, *The Complete Book of U.S. Presidents*, 112.
7. Michael F. Holt, *The Rise and Fall of the American Whig Party*, 17, 18, 957, 983; F. Martin Harmon, *Presidents by Fate: Nine Who Ascended through Death or Resignation*, 72.
8. Kenneth C. Davis, *Don't Known Much About the American Presidents*, 164–165.
9. H.W. Brands, *Heirs of the Founders*, 229–230, 234–236.
10. Ibid., 230–231.
11. H.W. Brands, *American Lion*, 278–279, 335.
12. H.W. Brands, *Heirs of the Founders*, 235.
13. Kenneth C. Davis, *Don't Know Much About the American Presidents*, 165; Glyndon G. VanDeusen, *The Jacksonian Era*, 104–106, 113, 116.
14. Robert Remini, *Daniel Webster*, 445, 452, 464–465.
15. Glyndon G. VanDeusen, *The Jacksonian Era*, 119–120, 128.
16. Glyndon G. VanDeusen, *The Jacksonian Era*, 52, 69; H.W. Brands, *Heirs of the Founders*, 185; William DeGregorio, *The Complete Book of U.S. Presidents*, 82–83; Glyndon G. VanDeusen, *The Jacksonian Era*, 113–114, 167, 206–207.
17. William DeGregorio, *The Complete Book of U.S. Presidents*, 115.
18. Glyndon G. VanDeusen, *The Jacksonian Era*, 39.
19. Glyndon G. VanDeusen, *The Jacksonian Era*, 71–80; H.W. Brands, *Heirs of the Founders*, 197–201; Kenneth C. Davis, *Don't Know Much About the American Presidents*, 168.
20. H.W. Brands, *Heirs of the Founders*, 202–205; William DeGregorio, *The Complete Book of U.S. Presidents*, 82, 115; Margaret Coit, *John C. Calhoun: American Portrait*, 255.
21. Fergus M. Bordewich, *America's Great Debate: Henry Clay, Stephen A. Douglas, and the Compromise That Preserved the Union*, 1; Scott Farris, *Almost President: The Men Who Lost the Race But Changed the Nation*, 20–21, 45, 55; Richard A. Baker and Neil MacNeil, *The American Senate*, 171, Martin H. Quitt, *Stephen A. Douglas and Antebellum Democracy*, 117; Robert Remini, *Henry Clay*, 786.
22. Michael Kazin, *A Godly Hero: The Life of William Jennings Bryan*, xiii–xiv, 10, 40, 47–49, 122–123; Phillip Bump, "What's The Optimal Number of Times to Run For President?" *Washington Post*, September 12, 2014.
23. Glyndon G. VanDeusen, *The Jacksonian Era*, 86.
24. Kenneth C. Davis, *Don't Know Much About the American Presidents*, 568–569; Scott Farris, *Almost President*, 32–33.
25. Brian McClanahan, *Nine Presidents Who Screwed Up America*, 15–16, 22–23.
26. Kenneth C. Davis, *Don't Know Much About the American Presidents*, 166.
27. Glyndon G. VanDeusen, *The Jacksonian Era*, 49; "Indian Removal Act," en.wikipedia.org.
28. Kenneth C. Davis, *Don't Know Much About the American Presidents*, 124; H.W. Brands, *Heirs of the Founders*, 140–141.
29. Glyndon G. VanDeusen, *The Jacksonian Era*, 28–30; Kenneth C. Davis, *Don't Know Much About the American Presidents*, 157, 159–160, 166; William DeGregorio, *The Complete Book of U.S. Presidents*, 114.
30. William DeGregorio, *The Complete Book of U.S. Presidents*, 114, 384–387; 498–501.

Chapter 4

1. Richard A. Baker and Neil McNeil, *The American Senate*, 285.
2. Debra McArthur, *The Kansas-Nebraska Act and "Bleeding Kansas,"* 39–40.
3. Martin H. Quitt, *Stephen A. Douglas and Antebellum Democracy*, 66–86; William Gardner, *The Life of Stephen A. Douglas*, 25–30; Jean H. Baker, *James Buchanan*, 23–29, 32–34, 38–43, 57–67; Garry Boulard, *The Worst President*, 16–23.
4. Garry Boulard, *The Worst President*, 36; William Gardner, *The Life of Stephen A. Douglas*, 43–47; Martin H. Quitt, *Stephen A. Douglas and Antebellum Democracy*, 107–114; Jean H. Baker, *James Buchanan*, 77–78, 79, 81.
5. William DeGregorio, *The Complete Book of U.S. Presidents*, 82; Debra McArthur, *The Kansas-Nebraska Act and "Bleeding Kansas,"* 17–18; Kenneth C. Davis, *Don't Know Much About the American Presidents*, 133.
6. Kenneth C. Davis, *Don't Know Much About the American Presidents*, 133; Walter Stahr, *Seward: Lincoln's Indispensable Man*, 51.
7. Fergus M. Bordewich, *America's Great Debate*, 9, 11; William DeGregorio, *The Complete Book of U.S. Presidents*, 157, 170–171.
8. William DeGregorio, *The Complete Book of U.S. Presidents*, 171; Walter Stahr, *Seward*, 486.
9. Fergus M. Bordewich, *America's Great Debate*, 8; Walter R. Borneman, *Polk*, 224; Kenneth C. Davis, *Don't Know Much About the American Presidents*, 202, 204; Robert Utley, *The Indian Frontier of the American West: 1846-1890*, 340.
10. Debra McArthur, *The Kansas-Nebraska Act and "Bleeding Kansas,"* 18–19; Fergus M. Bordewich, *America's Great Debate*, 11–12.
11. Fergus M. Bordewich, *America's Great Debate*, 11-12; Kenneth C. Davis, *Don't Know Much About the U.S. Presidents*, 217, 218; "Mason-Dixon Line," en.wikipedia.org.; William DeGregorio, *The Complete Book of U.S. Presidents*, 192.
12. Williiam DeGregorio, *The Complete Book of U.S. Presidents*, 192; Richard A. Baker and Neil MacNeil, *The American Senate*, 64–65; Fergus M. Bordewich, *America's Great Debate*, 358; William Gardner, *The Life of Stephen A. Douglas*, 33.
13. "Arkansas," "Iowa," "Missouri," "Oklahoma," "Texas," "Wisconsin," The States, History Channel Video, 2007; Glyndon G. VanDeusen, *The Jacksonian Era*, 48–50.
14. Debra McArthur, *The Kansas-Nebraska Act and "Bleeding Kansas,"* 21; William DeGregorio, *The Complete Book of U.S. Presidents*, 180–181; Scott Farris, *Almost President*, 57.
15. William Gardner, *The Life of Stephen A. Douglas*, 35; Martin H. Quitt, *Stephen A. Douglas and Antebellum Democracy*, 6, 89, 184.
16. Nicole Etcheson, *Bleeding Kansas*, 9–11; David Dury, *The Oregon Trail: An American Saga*, 59, 81.
17. Nicole Etcheson, *Bleeding Kansas*, 11, 14.
18. *Ibid.*
19. Nicole Etcheson, *Bleeding Kansas*, 14–15; Scott Farris, *Almost President*, 57.
20. Debra McArthur, *The Kansas-Nebraska Act and "Bleeding Kansas,"* 27–40.
21. Nicole Etcheson, *Bleeding Kansas*, 15.
22. *Ibid.*, 20.
23. *Ibid.*
24. Scott Farris, *Almost President*, 56; Kenneth C. Davis, *Don't Know Much About the American Presidents*, 226; Debra McArthur, *The Kansas-Nebraska Act and "Bleeding Kansas,"* 27–28.
25. Debra McArthur, *The Kansas-Nebraska Act and "Bleeding Kansas,"* 28–29.
26. *Ibid.*, 40.
27. Mark Stein, *How the States Got Their Shapes*, 102, 169; William DeGregorio, *The Complete Book of U.S. Presidents*, 205; Scott Farris, *Almost President*, 59.
28. Scott Farris, *Almost President*, 58, 59; Debra McArthur, *The Kansas-Nebraska Act and "Bleeding Kansas,"* 41–43.
29. Debra McArthur, *The Kansas-Nebraska Act and "Bleeding Kansas,"* 41–45; Kenneth C. Davis, *Don't Know Much About the American Presidents*, 228; Nicole Etcheson, Bleeding Kansas, 69–78.
30. Nicole Etcheson, *Bleeding Kansas*, 59, 77–82.
31. Kenneth C. Davis, *Don't Know Much About the American Presidents*, 227–228, 229; William DeGregorio, *The Complete Book of U.S. Presidents*, 215.

32. Jean H. Barker, *James Buchanan*, 62, 67–68, 70.
33. William DeGregorio, *The Complete Book of U.S. Presidents*, 231–232.
34. Walter Stahr, *Seward*, 177.

Chapter 5

1. Jonathan Alter, *The Defining Moment: FDR's Hundred Days and the Triumph of Hope*, 139, 178–181.
2. Jean H. Baker, *James Buchanan*, 75–78.
3. Jean H. Baker, *James Buchanan*, 76; Kenneth C. Davis, *Don't Know Much About the American Presidents*, 152, 196.
4. Garry Boulard, *The Worst President*, 33–34; Jean H. Baker, *James Buchanan*, 83–85; Richard Carwardine, *Lincoln: A Life of Purpose and Power*, 71.
5. Kenneth C. Davis, *Don't Know Much About the American Presidents*, 238, 240; Garry Boulard, *The Worst President*, 33–34.
6. Garry Boulard, *The Worst President*, 34.
7. Jean H. Baker, *James Buchanan*, 84–85; William DeGregorio, *The Complete Book of U.S. Presidents*, 219.
8. William DeGregorio, *The Complete Book of U.S. Presidents*, 217; Jean H. Baker, *James Buchanan*, 74.
9. Jean H. Baker, *James Buchanan*, 80, 81.
10. Jean H. Baker, *James Buchanan*, 90–93; Garry Boulard, *The Worst President*, 40.
11. Richard A. Baker and Neil MacNeil, *The American Senate*, 285.
12. Scott Farris, *Almost President*, 59.
13. William Gardner, *The Life of Stephen A. Douglas*, 135.
14. *Ibid.*, 41–42; Tony O'Bryan, "Topeka Constitution," civilwaronthewesternborder.org., January 30, 2020; Zack Garrison, "Lecompton Constitution," civilwaronthewesternborder.org., January 30, 2020.
15. Jean H. Baker, *James Buchanan*, 93, 97; Debra McArthur, *The Kansas-Nebraska Act and "Bleeding Kansas,"* 73; William DeGregorio, *The Complete Book of U.S. Presidents*, 219–220.
16. Garry Boulard, *The Worst President*, 41.
17. William Gardner, *The Life of Stephen A. Douglas*, 135; William DeGregorio, *The Complete Book of U.S. Presidents*, 219.
18. Garry Boulard, *The Worst President*, 41.
19. Garry Boulard, *The Worst President*, 42; Jean H. Baker, *James Buchanan*, 101–102.
20. William Gardner, *The Life of Stephen A. Douglas*, 135.
21. *Ibid.*, 136–137.
22. Jean H. Baker, *James Buchanan*, 102, 103–104; Garry Boulard, *The Worst President*, 43.
23. Garry Boulard, *The Worst President*, 43.
24. Jean H. Baker, *James Buchanan*, 104–105, Nicole Etcheson, *Bleeding Kansas*, 174–176.
25. F. Martin Harmon, *Presidents by Fate*, 77–95; William DeGregorio, *The Complete Book of U.S. Presidents*, 425; Margaret McMillan, *Paris: 1919*, 7; Garry Boulard, *The Worst President*, 42.
26. Nicole Etcheson, *Bleeding Kansas*, 175.
27. "Speech of Honorable S.A. Douglas of Illinois Against the Admission of Kansas Under the Lecompton Constitution. Delivered in the Senate of the United States, March 22, 1858," Library of Congress, Scholar Select Series.
28. Jean H. Baker, *James Buchanan*, 103, 105.
29. *Ibid.*, 105.
30. *Ibid.*, 6, 105-106.
31. Martin H. Quitt, *Stephen Douglas and Antebellum Democracy*, 128–131.
32. *Ibid.*, 134.
33. William DeGregorio, *The Complete Book of U.S. Presidents*, 233–234.

Chapter 6

1. William C. Davis, *Look Away: A History of the Confederate States of America*, 428; William E. Leuchtenburg, *The White House Looks South*, 22; Pedro Hernandez, "The United States' History of Third Party Candidates," fairvote.org, May 19, 2020; H.W. Brands, *American Colossus: The Triumph of Capitalism, 1865–1900*, 438.
2. William Gardner, *The Life of Stephen A. Douglas*, 141; Scott Farris, *Almost President*, 64.
3. Scott Farris, *Almost President*, 64–65.

4. *Ibid.*, 65.
5. *Ibid.*, 65–66.
6. William DeGregorio, *The Complete Book of U.S. Presidents*, 234.
7. *Ibid.*, 271, 285; Kenneth C. Davis, *Don't Know Much About the American Presidents*, 306, 308.
8. Kenneth C. Davis, *Don't Know Much About the American Presidents*, 253; H.W. Brands, *American Colossus*, 537; Walter Stahr, *Seward*, 186.
9. Jean H. Baker, *James Buchanan*, 107–110.
10. Garry Boulard, *The Worst President*, 68–70.
11. *Ibid.*, 87.
12. Richard Carwardine, *Lincoln: A Life of Purpose and Power*, 137, 141.
13. *Ibid.*, 135, 141.
14. David Herbert Donald, *Lincoln*, 257, 259–260.
15. *Ibid.*, 268–270.
16. *Ibid.*, 277–279, 282, 284–285, 291–292.
17. Robert P. Broadwater, *Did Lincoln and the Republican Party Create the Civil War? An Argument*, 7–8; Martin H. Quitt, *Stephen A. Douglas and Antebellum Democracy*, 170; William Gardner, *The Life of Stephen A. Douglas*, 150.
18. William Gardner, *The Life of Stephen A. Douglas*, 170–171; William DeGregorio, *The Complete Book of U.S. Presidents*, 221, 233.
19. Jean H. Baker, *James Buchanan*, 6, 159.
20. Brion McClanahan, *Nine Presidents Who Screwed Up America*, 25–26.
21. *Ibid.*, 26, 28–31; Kenneth C. Davis, *Don't Know Much About the American Presidents*, 257–258.

Chapter 7

1. David Herbert Donald, *Charles Sumner and The Coming of The Civil War*, 27–28, 33–35, 39–40, 189, 191, 199, 202–203, 267; Barry M. Goldenberg, *The Unknown Architects of Civil Rights*, 75.
2. Hans L. Trefousse, *Andrew Johnson: A Biography*, 51–83, 84–127; Eric Foner, *Reconstruction: America's Unfinished Revolution, 1863–1877*, 176.
3. Hans L. Trefousse, *Andrew Johnson*, 26–27, 28–34, 35–50.
4. *Ibid.*, 53, 88, 107, 150–152, 177–179.
5. F. Martin Harmon, *Presidents by Fate*, 84–85; Hans L. Trefousse, *Andrew Johnson*, 130–131, 144–145; Kenneth C. Davis, *Don't Know Much About the American Presidents*, 268, 271, 272; "The Impeachment of Andrew Johnson," *The Week*, October 25, 2019.
6. David Herbert Donald, *Charles Sumner and The Coming of The Civil War*, 281, 282–286, 289–296, 297–304, 336.
7. Hans L. Trefousse, *Andrew Johnson*, 132, 137, 139, 140, 142–143.
8. William DeGregorio, *The Complete Book of U.S. Presidents*, 250; Barry M. Goldenberg, *The Unknown Architects of Civil Rights*, 78; Robert Remini, *Daniel Webster: The Man and His Time*, 281; David Herbert Donald, *Charles Sumner and The Coming of The Civil War*, 181, 186–187, 194–195.
9. David Herbert Donald, *Charles Sumner and The Coming of The Civil War*, 213–219, 274–275; Hans L. Trefousse, *Andrew Johnson*, 42, 44, 50.
10. Kenneth C. Davis, *Don't Know Much About the American Presidents*, 273, 275; William DeGregorio, *The Complete Book of U.S. Presidents*, 253, 254; Hans L. Trefousse, *Andrew Johnson*, 197–198.
11. Hans L. Trefousse, *Andrew Johnson*, 197-198; William DeGregorio, *The Complete Book of U.S. Presidents*, 251.
12. Richard A. Baker and Neil MacNeil, *The American Senate*, 69; Hans Trefousse, *Andrew Johnson*, 197, 198, 207.
13. Kenneth C. Davis, *Don't Know Much About the American Presidents*, 273; William DeGregorio, *The Complete Book of U.S. Presidents*, 253.
14. Walter Stahr, *William Seward*, 417.
15. William DeGregorio, *The Complete Book of U.S. Presidents*, 253.
16. Hans L. Trefousse, *Andrew Johnson*, 216.
17. *Ibid.*, 379; David Herbert Donald, *Charles Sumner and The Rights of Man*, iv.

Chapter 8

1. Philip Dray, *Capitol Men: The Epic History of Reconstruction Through the Lives of the First Black Congressmen*, x; Eric Foner, *Reconstruction: America's Unfinished Revolution, 1863–1877*, xix, xx.

Notes—Chapter 8

2. Hans L. Trefousse, *Andrew Johnson*, 197, 207, 215, 216, 218–219, 220, 229, 230.
3. *Ibid.*, 223, 225; "The Impeachment of Andrew Johnson," *The Week*, October 25, 2019.
4. Eric Foner, *Reconstruction*, 177, 183.
5. Hans Trefousse, *Andrew Johnson*, 215.
6. Eric Foner, *Reconstruction*, 69, 199.
7. Hans L. Trefousse, *Andrew Johnson*, 241–242.
8. *Ibid.*, 165–166, 196, 219–223, 235, 238, 242–243; Eric Foner, *Reconstruction*, 179–180.
9. Eric Foner, *Reconstruction*, 180; Hans L. Trefousse, *Andrew Johnson*, 223–224.
10. Hans. L. Trefousse, *Andrew Johnson*, 299; Eric Foner, *Reconstruction*, 176–181, 217, 219–220, 223, 379.
11. Eric Foner, *Reconstruction*, 178; Hans L. Trefousse, *Andrew Johnson*, 237.
12. David Herbert Donald, *Charles Sumner and The Rights of Man*, 218–223.
13. *Ibid.*, 224.
14. *Ibid.*, 225–226.
15. F. Martin Harmon, *Presidents by Fate*, 88.
16. Hans L. Trefousse, *Andrew Johnson*, 234–237.
17. Eric Foner, *Reconstruction*, 178.
18. *Ibid.*, 190–192; "The Impeachment of Andrew Johnson," *The Week*, October 25, 2019.
19. David Herbert Donald, *Charles Sumner and The Rights of Man*, 226, 228–229.
20. *Ibid.*, 229–230.
21. *Ibid.*, 237–238.
22. *Ibid.*, 238.
23. *Ibid.*, 239.
24. *Ibid.*, 240–241.
25. *Ibid.*, 242, 243, 244–245.
26. Barry M. Goldberg, *The Unknown Architects of Civil Rights*, 83–84.
27. David Herbert Donald, *Charles Sumner and The Rights of Man*, 245; Walter Stahr, *Seward*, 468.
28. Walter Stahr, *Seward*, 468; F. Martin Harmon, *Presidents by Fate*, 89; Hans L. Trefousse, *Andrew Johnson*, 252–253.
29. Hans L. Trefousse, *Andrew Johnson*, 252; Walter Stahr, *Seward*, 468.
30. Hans L. Trefousse, *Andrew Johnson*, 252–253, 254.
31. *Ibid.*, 255; Walter Stahr, *Seward*, 468–469; William DeGregorio, *The Complete Book of U.S. Presidents*, 252–253.
32. David Herbert Donald, *Charles Sumner and The Rights of Man*, 247, 248.
33. Hans L. Trefousse, *Andrew Johnson*, 256, 257, 258, 259, 262.
34. *Ibid.*, 265, 266, 267; "The Impeachment of Andrew Johnson," *The Week*, October 25, 2019.
35. Walter Stahr, *Seward*, 477.
36. *Ibid.*; David Herbert Donald, Charles Sumner and The Rights of Man, 254–255.
37. Barry M. Goldenberg, *The Unknown Architects of Civil Rights*, 83, 84; "Civil War and Reconstruction, 1861–1877," loc.gov.
38. David Herbert Donald, *Charles Sumner and The Rights of Man*, 255.
39. *Ibid.*
40. *Ibid.*, 268; F. Martin Harmon, *Presidents by Fate*, 84, 177; "The Confederate States of America," infoplease.com; Doc Halliday, "Georgia's Readmission to The Union," *Marshall News Messenger*, July 15, 2015.
41. David Herbert Donald, *Charles Sumner and The Rights of Man*, 267–268; F. Martin Harmon, *Presidents by Fate*, 91; Eric Foner, *Reconstruction*, 276–277, 333.
42. Eric Foner, *Reconstruction*, 277.
43. *Ibid.*
44. Kenneth C. Davis, *Don't Know Much About the U.S. Presidents*, 274, 275; Jon Meacham, *The Soul of America: The Battle for Our Better Angels*, 3.
45. Jon Meacham, *The Soul of America*, 62–63.
46. Eric Foner, *Reconstruction*, 275.
47. David Herbert Donald, *Charles Sumner and The Rights of Man*, 277–278.
48. *Ibid.*, 280–281; Jason Silverstein, "Presidential Vetoes: How They Work, Who Issued the Most, and How Congress Stops Them," cbsnews.com, March 5, 2019.
49. David Herbert Donald, *Charles Sumner and The Rights of Man*, 284.
50. Robert A. Caro, *The Passage of Power: The Years of Lyndon Johnson*, 569–570; Barry M. Goldenberg, *The Unknown Architects of Civil Rights*, xv, xvii.
51. David Herbert Donald, *Charles Sumner and The Rights of Man*, 330–331; Hans L. Trefousse, *Andrew Johnson*, 150, 257–258, 291.
52. Hans L. Trefousse, *Andrew Johnson*, 291–292, 293–295.
53. *Ibid.*, 296–298.
54. *Ibid.*, 298–299.

55. Eric Foner, *Reconstruction*, 269–271.
56. Walter Stahr, *Seward*, 479–480.
57. Kenneth C. Davis, *Don't Know Much About the American Presidents*, 277; David Herbert Donald, *Charles Sumner and The Rights of Man*, 332.
58. David Herbert Donald, *Charles Sumner and The Rights of Man*, 333–334.
59. *Ibid.*, 334–335.
60. *Ibid.*, 336–337; John F. Kennedy, *Profiles in Courage*, 126, 138, 139; William DeGregorio, *The Complete Book of U.S. Presidents*, 254.
61. William DeGregorio, *The Complete Book of U.S. Presidents*, 254; David Herbert Donald, *Charles Sumner and The Rights of Man*, 337.
62. Hans L. Trefousse, *Andrew Johnson*, 327.
63. *Ibid.*; Barry M. Goldenberg, *The Unknown Architects of Civil Rights*, 51, 53; William DeGregorio, *The Complete Book of U.S. Presidents*, 266.
64. William DeGregorio, *The Complete Book of U.S. Presidents*, 255, 265; Hans L. Trefousse, *Andrew Johnson*, 345.
65. Barry M. Goldenberg, *The Unknown Architects of Civil Rights*, 85, 87, 89, 94.

Chapter 9

1. Eric Foner, *Reconstruction*, 532–533; Philip Dray, *Capitol Men*, xiii; F. Martin Harmon, *Presidents by Fate*, 183; David Herbert Donald, *Lincoln*, 314; Barry M. Goldenberg, *The Unknown Architects of Civil Rights*, 4, 91.
2. Barry M. Goldenberg, *The Unknown Architects of Civil Rights*, 89, 91; William DeGregorio, *The Complete Book of U.S. Presidents*, 97–98, 271–272, 284–286; Eric Foner, *Reconstruction*, 576; Martin Kelly, "Presidents Elected Without Winning the Popular Vote," thoughtco.com, August 5, 2019; Kenneth C. Davis, *Don't Know Much About the American Presidents*, 297–298.
3. Kenneth C. Davis, *Don't Know Much About the American Presidents*, 298; Eric Foner, *Reconstruction*, 582.
4. Barry M. Goldenberg, *The Unknown Architects of Civil Rights*, 89.
5. *Ibid.*, 89, 95.
6. *Ibid.*, 54, 56, 60.
7. *Ibid.*, 49, 51, 53.
8. *Ibid.*, 45, 49, 57–59.
9. *Ibid.*, 61–62.
10. Philip Dray, *Capitol Men*, 57, 64, 65, 188; Eric Foner, *Reconstruction*, 39, 40.
11. Eric Foner, *Reconstruction*, 145; Philip Dray, *Capitol Men*, xi, 36, 40, 64; Elwood Watson, "Richard H. Cain," blackpast.org, January 18, 2007.
12. Eric Foner, *Reconstruction*, 106–108, 137–138, 199–201, 342–343; "Reconstruction: The Second Civil War," PBS-American Experience video, 2004.
13. H.W. Brands, *American Colossus*, 390, 432, 436; Jon Meacham, *The Soul of America*, 68.

Chapter 10

1. Bill Cromartie, *Clean, Old-Fashioned Hate: The Game-By-Game Story of One of America's Most Heated and Colorful Football Feuds*, 1; John A. Garraty, *Henry Cabot Lodge: A Biography*, 297; A. Scott Berg, *Wilson*, 680, 695; Kurt Schriftgiesser, *The Gentleman from Massachusetts: Henry Cabot Lodge*, 265.
2. Kurt Schriftgiesser, *The Gentleman from Massachusetts*, 5, 22; Ella Nilsen, "Why Isn't Elizabeth Warren More Popular in Massachusetts?" vox.com, July 30, 2019; Douglas Martin, "Edward W. Brooke III, 95, Senate Pioneer Is Dead," *New York Times*, January 3, 2015.
3. Kurt Schriftgiesser, *The Gentleman from Massachusetts*, 12, 23, 30, 38, 42, 52.
4. *Ibid.*, 80; H.W. Brands, *T.R.: The Last Romantic*, 57; F. Martin Harmon, *Presidents by Fate*, 98–100; William DeGregorio, *The Complete Book of U.S. Presidents*, 217, 325–326; John A. Garraty, *Henry Cabot Lodge*, 68, 76–80, 86–87, 88.
5. John A. Garraty, *Henry Cabot Lodge*, 70, 88–90; Kurt Schriftgiesser, *The Gentleman from Massachusetts*, 93; F. Martin Harmon, *The Roosevelts and Their Descendants: Portrait of an American Family*, 7–8.
6. H.W. Brands, *T.R.*, 191–192; John A. Garraty, *Henry Cabot Lodge*, 90–91.
7. H.W. Brands, *T.R.*, 228, 546, 595; William DeGregorio, *The Complete Book of U.S. Presidents*, 379; Doris Kearns Goodwin, *The Bully Pulpit: Theodore Roosevelt, William Howard Taft, and the Golden Age of Journalism*, 7; John A. Garraty, *Henry Cabot Lodge*, 221.
8. John A. Garraty, *Henry Cabot Lodge*,

312, 348; Kurt Schriftgiesser, *The Gentleman from Massachusetts*, 296-298; 304-305; H.W. Brands, *T.R.*, 735-736, 805; Richard A. Baker and Neil MacNeil, *The American Senate*, 183; Kenneth C. Davis, *Don't Know Much About the American Presidents*, 391.

9. John Milton Cooper, Jr., *Woodrow Wilson: A Biography*, 8-10, 177-178; James Chace, *1912: Wilson, Roosevelt, Taft and Debs—The Election That Changed the Country*, 268-269.

10. Kurt Schriftgiesser, *The Gentleman from Massachusetts*, 5, 25-29; H.W. Brands, *T.R.*, 3, 55, 104; A. Scott Berg, *Wilson*, 29-41, 45-47, 51-73.

11. Kenneth C. Davis, *Don't Know Much About the American Presidents*, 387-388, 391; John Milton Cooper, Jr., *Woodrow Wilson*, 18, 23-25, 33-40; Edward L. Ayers, *The Promise of The New South*, 20-21; Peter Collier with David Horowitz, *The Roosevelts: An American Saga*, 31-33; Kurt Schriftgiesser, *The Gentleman from Massachusetts*, 23.

12. John A. Garraty, *Henry Cabot Lodge*, 86-87; James Chace, *1912*, 105, 112.

13. Karl Schriftgiesser, *The Gentleman from Massachusetts*, 118, 358-359, 361; "Henry Cabot Lodge," American Experience, pbs.org; Edmund Morris, *The Rise of Theodore Roosevelt*, 477-478, 560-561, 614-615, 686, 725, 726-729.

14. Kenneth C. Davis, *Don't Know Much About the American Presidents*, 388; William DeGregorio, *The Complete Book of U.S. Presidents*, 411-412, 414.

15. A. Scott Berg, *Wilson*, 181-186.

16. Ibid., 190-192; William DeGregorio, *The Complete Book of U.S. Presidents*, 414.

17. William DeGregorio, *The Complete Book of U.S. Presidents*, 415; John Milton Cooper, Jr., *Woodrow Wilson*, 142.

18. William DeGregorio, *The Complete Book of U.S. Presidents*, 416; Richard A. Baker and Neil MacNeil, *The American Senate*, 182; James Chace, *1912*, 107-113.

19. James Chace, *1912*, 113, 116.

20. Ibid., 7; Kenneth C. Davis, *Don't Know Much About the American Presidents*, 388; William DeGregorio, *The Complete Book of U.S. Presidents*, 416-417.

21. William DeGregorio, *The Complete Book of U.S. Presidents*, 417; James Chace, *1912*, 230-239.

22. Karl Schriftgiesser, *The Gentleman from Massachusetts*, 255-258; John A. Garraty, *Henry Cabot Lodge*, 292.

23. James Chace, *1912*, 246; William DeGregorio, *The Complete Book of U.S. Presidents*, 422; Kenneth C. Davis, *Don't Know Much About the American Presidents*, 392-393.

24. A. Scott Berg, *Wilson*, 410; John A. Garraty, *Henry Cabot Lodge*, 312.

25. Arthur S. Link, *Woodrow Wilson and the Progressive Era: 1910-1917*, 175-177, 178, 271-273, 274; William DeGregorio, *The Complete Book of U.S. Presidents*, 417; John Chace, *1912*, 249, 256; H.W. Brands, *T.R.*, 468, 750.

26. Arthur S. Link, *Woodrow Wilson and the Progressive Era*, 282.

27. William DeGregorio, *The Complete Book of U.S. Presidents*, 424; A Scott Berg, *Wilson*, 20.

28. William DeGregorio, *The Complete Book of U.S. Presidents*, 425; John Milton Cooper, Jr., *Woodrow Wilson*, 456-457, 462-463, 575-576; Margaret Macmillan, *Paris 1919: Six Months That Changed the World*, 15-16, 488; Barbara W. Tuchman, "The Case of Woodrow Wilson," *The Atlantic*, September 29, 2014.

Chapter 11

1. H.W. Brands, *American Colossus*, 544; Richard A. Baker and Neil MacNeil, *The American Senate*, 182-183.

2. Richard A. Baker and Neil MacNeil, *The American Senate*, 183.

3. A. Scott Berg, *Wilson*, 504.

4. John A. Garraty, *Henry Cabot Lodge*, 342.

5. Karl Schriftgiesser, *The Gentleman from Massachusetts*, 299-300.

6. Ibid.

7. John A. Garraty, *Henry Cabot Lodge*, 348-349.

8. Margaret MacMillan, *Paris 1919*, 93-97, 162, 175-176, 180-192, 202, 475.

9. Andrew Glass, "President Wilson Lands in France," *Politico*, December 13, 1918; A Scott Berg, *Wilson*, 599-601, 604.

10. A. Scott Berg, *Wilson*, 605-606, 608.

11. Ibid., 609-611; Chad Williams, "African American Veterans Hoped Their Service in WWI Would Secure Rights at Home. It Didn't," *Time*, February 25, 2019.

12. John Milton Cooper, Jr., *Woodrow

Wilson, 506; James Stewart, "Timeline: The Rise of Radio," vpr.org, December 30, 2019.
  13. John Milton Cooper, Jr., *Woodrow Wilson*, 507, 510.
  14. *Ibid.*, 511, 512, 513; David Pietrusza, *1920: The Year of the Six Presidents*, 39.
  15. John Milton Cooper, Jr., *Woodrow Wilson*, 514.
  16. Karl Schriftgiesser, *The Gentleman from Massachusetts*, 337–338; Henry Cabot Lodge, "Objection to Article X of the Treaty of Versailles," wwwphs.sharpschool.com, August 12, 1919.
  17. Karl Schriftgiesser, *The Gentleman from Massachusetts*, 340–342.
  18. *Ibid.*, 341, 342.
  19. A. Scott Berg, *Wilson*, 621; John Milton Cooper, Jr., *Woodrow Wilson*, 520–521.
  20. John Milton Cooper, Jr., *Woodrow Wilson*, 522–523.
  21. *Ibid.*, 524.
  22. *Ibid.*, 524–525.
  23. John A. Garraty, *Henry Cabot Lodge*, 373–374, 375, 376–377.
  24. A Scott Berg, *Wilson*, 628–630.
  25. John Milton Cooper, Jr., *Woodrow Wilson*, 528–529.
  26. *Ibid.*, 529.
  27. *Ibid.*, 530.
  28. *Ibid.*, 531, 532; Karl Schriftgiesser, *The Gentleman from Massachusetts*, 343–344.
  29. Karl Schriftgiesser, *The Gentleman from Massachusetts*, 345–346.
  30. *Ibid.*, 348.
  31. *Ibid.*
  32. *Ibid.*, 350–351; John A. Garraty, *Henry Cabot Lodge*, 378–379.
  33. Theodore Roosevelt, "International Peace," nobelprize.org, May 5, 1910; Karl Schriftgiesser, *The Gentleman from Massachusetts*, 351.
  34. James MacGregor Burns, *Roosevelt, The Soldier of Freedom: 1940–1945*, 427–429, 515, 533, 559, 582–583.

Chapter 12

  1. David Pietrusza, *1920*, 3, 5; A. Scott Berg, *Wilson*, 693; Kenneth C. Davis, *Don't Know Much About the American Presidents*, 390; William DeGregorio, *The Complete Book of U.S. Presidents*, 437–438, 440; John Milton Cooper, Jr., *Woodrow Wilson*, 572; Andrew Sinclair, *The Available Man: The Life Behind the Masks of Warren G. Harding*, 163, 198–199, 200, 205.
  2. C.N. Truman, "League of Nations," historylearningsite.co.uk, March 17, 2015; Richard Overy, *The Dictators: Hitler's Germany, Stalin's Russia*, 13–22.
  3. Kenneth C. Davis, *Don't Know Much About the American Presidents*, 385, 388–389, 391; David Pietrusza, *1920*, 326; John Milton Cooper, Jr., *Woodrow Wilson*, 599; James Chace, *1912*, 7, 8; David McCullough, *Truman*, 586, Robert Dallek, *An Unfinished Life: John F. Kennedy, 1917–1963*; Joseph J. Ellis, *His Excellency: George Washington*, 222–223; F. Martin Harmon, *Presidents by Fate*, 147, 152.
  4. William DeGregorio, *The Complete Book of U.S. Presidents*, 413, 419, 425.
  5. *Ibid.*, 413; A. Scott Berg, *Wilson*, 637; John Milton Cooper, Jr., *Woodrow Wilson*, 530.
  6. John Milton Cooper, Jr., *Woodrow Wilson*, 531–532; Berg, *Wilson*, 639–640.
  7. John Milton Cooper, Jr., *Woodrow Wilson*, 533, 535.
  8. *Ibid.*, 535–536.
  9. *Ibid.*, 538, A. Scott Berg, *Wilson*, 645.
  10. A Scott Berg, *Wilson.*, 646; Stacy A. Cordery, *Alice: Alice Roosevelt Longworth, from White House Princess to Washington Power Broker*, 251, 273, 285–286.
  11. John Milton Cooper, Jr., *Woodrow Wilson*, 539, 547–548.
  12. *Ibid.*, 548; Kenneth C. Davis, *Don't Know Much About the American Presidents*, 394; John A. Garraty, *Henry Cabot Lodge*, 401
  13. *Ibid.*, 402; William DeGregorio, *The Complete Book of U.S. Presidents*, 437–438; Kenneth C. Davis, *Don't Know Much About the American Presidents*, 397, 399.
  14. Andrew Sinclair, *The Available Man*, VIII, 299.
  15. *Ibid.*, 57–58; John A. Garraty, *Henry Cabot Lodge*, 402; Kenneth C. Davis, *Don't Know Much About the American Presidents*, 398; Andrew Sinclair, *The Available Man*, 57–58; William DeGregorio, *The Complete Book of U.S. Presidents*, 76, 110–111, 126–127, 142, 154, 200–201, 215, 251, 335, 512, 551, 568–569, 586, 800–801.
  16. Samuel Hopkins Adams, *Incredible Era; The Life and Times of Warren Gamaliel Harding*, 134; David Pietrusza, *1920*, 201–237; Amity Shlaes, *Coolidge*, 12; William DeGregorio, *The Complete Book of U.S. Presidents*, 437.

17. Andrew Sinclair, *The Available Man*, 59–60, 160; Kenneth C. Davis, *Don't Know Much About the American Presidents*, 400–402, 408, 418–419.
18. Margaret MacMillan, *Paris 1919*, 481, 482–483.
19. William DeGregorio, *The Complete Book of U.S. Presidents*, 425–426; Kenneth C. Davis, *Don't Know Much About the U.S. Presidents*, 387, 395.
20. John A. Garraty, *Henry Cabot Lodge*, 408–414, 422–424.

Chapter 13

1. David McCullough, *Truman*, 292, 298–299; Robert H. Ferrell, *The Dying President: Franklin D. Roosevelt, 1944-45*, 27, 76–78; William DeGregorio, *The Complete Book of U.S. Presidents*, 495, 512, 513, 514–515.
2. William DeGregorio, *The Complete Book of U.S. Presidents*, 503; Richard A. Baker and Neil MacNeil, *The American Senate*, 115–116; Kenneth C. Davis, *Don't Know Much About the American Presidents*, 458; Tom Murse, "Presidents Without College Degrees," thoughtco.com, June 26, 2019; David Halberstam, *The Coldest Winter: America and the Korean War*, 202–203.
3. William DeGregorio, *The Complete Book of U.S. Presidents*, 518–519.
4. David McCullough, *Truman*, 741–742; F. Martin Harmon, *Presidents by Fate*, 137; Walter Isaacson and Evan Thomas, *The Wise Men: Six Friends and the World They Made*, 256.
5. David McCullough, *Truman*, 741–742, 798; Jeffery Barlow, *Revolt of The Admirals: The Fight for Naval Aviation*, Kindle; John T. Correll, "The Revolt of The Admirals," *Air Force Magazine*, May 29, 2018.
6. Forest C. Pogue, *George C. Marshall, Statesman*, 422; Walter Isaacson and Evan Thomas, *The Wise Men*, 465–466.
7. David Pietrusza, *1948: Harry Truman's Improbable Victory and the Year that Transformed America*, 53, 55.
8. *Ibid.*, 55, 288.
9. David McCullough, *Truman*, 27–28, 53; William E. Leuchtenburg, *The White House Looks South: Franklin D. Roosevelt, Harry S. Truman, Lyndon B. Johnson*, 147–156, 161, 162, 163, 165, 178.
10. David Pietrusza, *1948*, 288; William DeGregorio, *The Complete Book of U.S. Presidents*, 513–514; Richard A. Baker and Neil MacNeil, *The American Senate*, 115.
11. Richard A. Baker and Neil MacNeil, *The American Senate*, 493, 513, 514.
12. *Ibid.*, 515; David Pietrusza, *1948*, 362–364, 393, 397, 399.
13. David McCullough, *Truman*, 710.
14. *Ibid.*, 630–631, 734–735; Kenneth C. Davis, *Don't Know Much About the American Presidents*, 460.
15. Kenneth C. Davis, *Don't Know Much About the American Presidents*, 461.
16. *Ibid.*, 456–457; David Halberstam, *The Coldest Winter: America and the Korean War*, 4, 47; William DeGregorio, *The Complete Book of U.S. Presidents*, 520.
17. William DeGregorio, *The Complete Book of U.S. Presidents*, 520.
18. Walter Isaacson and Evan Thomas, *The Wise Men*, 466–467; Rick Perlstein, *Nixonland: The Rise of a President and the Fracturing of America*, 33.
19. Rick Perlstein, *Nixonland*, 33; William DeGregorio, *The Complete Book of U.S. Presidents*, 537, 586–587; Robert Halberstam, *The Fifties*, 49; Jon Meacham, *The Soul of America*, 186.
20. Robert Halberstam, *The Fifties*, 49.
21. William DeGregorio, *The Complete Book of U.S. Presidents*, 520; Anthony Summers, *Official and Confidential: The Secret Life of J. Edgar Hoover*, 178.

Chapter 14

1. Robert A. Caro, *Master of the Senate: The Years of Lyndon Johnson*, 542.
2. David Halberstam, *The Fifties*, 53; David M. Oshinsky, *A Conspiracy So Immense: The World of Joe McCarthy*, 2, 11, 18–19, 22–23, 24, 26, 29–32.
3. David M. Oshinsky, *A Conspiracy So Immense*, 34–35, 36.
4. *Ibid.*, 39–49, 52.
5. Richard A. Baker and Neil MacNeil, *The American Senate*, 247–248; Larry Tye, "Senator McCarthy's Nazi Problem," *Smithsonian* magazine, July-August 2020; David M. Oshinsky, *A Conspiracy So Immense*, 74–80; David McCullough, *Truman*, 765.
6. David McCullough, *Truman*, 765; T. Harry Williams, *Huey Long*, 572–573, 619–620, 636–637, 640.

7. T. Harry Williams, *Huey Long*, 794–795.

8. *Ibid.*, 766; Richard A. Baker and Neil MacNeil, *The American Senate*, 248.

9. Richard A. Baker and Neil MacNeil, *The American Senate*, 248; David McCullough, *Truman*, 766; Robert A. Caro, *Master of the Senate*, 543–544.

10. Richard A Baker and Neil MacNeil, *The American Senate*, 248; David Halberstam, *The Fifties*, 55.

11. Jon Meacham, *The Soul of America*, 188.

12. *Ibid.*, 188–189.

13. David McCullough, *Truman*, 766, 768–769, 770.

14. Jon Meacham, "*The Soul of America* Conversation and Audience Q&A," Atlanta, Georgia (Carter Center), May 21, 2018; Jon Meacham, *The Soul of America*, 190.

15. Jon Meacham, *The Soul of America*, 191.

16. Walter Isaacson and Evan Thomas, *The Wise Men*, 493–495.

17. David Nasaw, *The Patriarch: The Remarkable Life and Turbulent Times of Joseph P. Kennedy*, 667–668, 671–672.

18. David Halberstam, *The Coldest Winter*, 60–63, 165.

19. *Ibid.*, 140, 295; William Manchester, *American Caesar*, 683–684.

20. William Manchester, *American Caesar*, 684, 688; David Halberstam, *The Coldest Winter*, 12, 295, 306–308, 335; Forest C. Pogue, *George C. Marshall*, 453–454; Tim Marshall, "Korea: A History of The North-South Split," news.sky.com, April 4, 2013.

21. David Halberstam, *The Coldest Winter*, 215, 238–239; Robert E. Herzstein, "Henry Luce: Political Portrait of the Man Who Created the American Century," foreignaffairs.com, May 1, 1994; Forest C. Pogue, *George C. Marshall*, 73–143; David McCullough, *Truman*, 743.

22. David Halberstam, *The Coldest Winter*, 247–248; David McCullough, *Truman*, 772–773.

23. David McCullough, *Truman*, 813–814.

24. H.W. Brands, *The General Vs. The President: MacArthur and Truman at the Brink of Nuclear War*, 193; William DeGregorio, *The Complete Book of U.S. Presidents*, 520; David Halberstam, *The Coldest Winter*, 331, 332, 334.

25. David Halberstam, *The Coldest Winter*, 355, 364, 369, 370; H.W. Brands, *The General Vs. The President*, 200.

26. H.W. Brands, *The General Vs. The President*, 179, 183; David Halberstam, *The Coldest Winter*, 365–368; William DeGregorio, *The Complete Book of U.S. Presidents*, 520.

27. William DeGregorio, *The Complete Book of U.S. Presidents*, 520; Kenneth C. Davis, *Don't Know Much About the American Presidents*, 457.

28. Forest C. Pogue, *George C. Marshall*, 488–489; David McCullough, *Truman*, 860–861.

29. David McCullough, *Truman*, 861.

30. *Ibid.*, 861–862.

31. *Ibid.*, 852; Sally Russell, *Richard Brevard Russell: A Life of Consequence*, 186–188; David Halberstam, *The Coldest Winter*, 605, 613; Kenneth C. Davis, *Don't Know Much About the American Presidents*, 456.

32. David Halberstam, *The Fifties*, 250.

Chapter 15

1. Mark Perry, *Partners in Command: George Marshall and Dwight Eisenhower in War and Peace*, 403; David McCullough, *Truman*, 612, 633; William DeGregorio, *The Complete Book of U.S. Presidents*, 532–533.

2. William DeGregorio, *The Complete Book of U.S. Presidents*, 533–534; Mark Perry, *Partners in Command*, 404.

3. Jon Meacham, *The Soul of America*, 197.

4. David McCullough, *Truman*, 911; Kenneth C. Davis, *Don't Know Much About the American Presidents*, 472; Stephen Kinzer, *The Brothers: John Foster Dulles, Allen Dulles, and The Secret World War*, 3.

5. Stephen Kinzer, *The Brothers*, 143; Rhodri Jeffreys-Jones, "Why Was the CIA Established in 1947?" tandfonline.com, January 2, 2008; David McCullough, *Truman*, 604, 990.

6. D. J. Hancock, *Eisenhower and The Art of War: A Critical Approach*, 69; Kenneth C. Davis, *Don't Know Much About the American Presidents*, 472; Stephen Kinzer, *The Brothers*, 103–105.

7. Stephen Kinzer, *The Brothers*, 104–105.

8. *Ibid.*, 106.

9. *Ibid.*, 107–108.

10. Walter Isaacson and Evan Thomas, *The Wise Men*, 574.
11. Robert A. Caro, *Master of the Senate*, 521, 523, 524.
12. Ibid., 524.
13. Ibid., 524–525.
14. William DeGregorio, *The Complete Book of U.S. Presidents*, 568; David Halberstam, *The Fifties*, ix, x, xi; Kenneth C. Davis, *Don't Know Much About the American Presidents*, 472; Robert A. Caro, *Master of the Senate*, 547–550.
15. Robert A. Caro, *Master of the Senate*, 551; Kenneth C. Davis, *Don't Know Much About the American Presidents*, 472.
16. Kenneth C. Davis, *Don't Know Much About the American Presidents*, 458–459.

Chapter 16

1. William E. Leuchtenburg, *The White House Looks South*, 250–252; Sally Russell, *Richard Brevard Russell*, xi, 80, 88, 105–106, 109, 141–143, 208–209.
2. Sally Russell, *Richard Brevard Russell*, 109–110, 114, 182, 190, back cover; Brian O'Shea, "Who Is the Russell Senate Building Named For?" ajc.com, August 27, 2018; Richard A. Baker and Neil MacNeil, *The American Senate*, 6–7.
3. Sally Russell, *Richard Brevard Russell*, 182; Robert A. Caro, *Master of the Senate*, xiv, final photo spread.
4. Robert A. Caro, *Means of Ascent: The Years of Lyndon Johnson*, 141, center photo spread, 317; Doris Kearns Goodwin, *Leadership in Turbulent Times*, 193–194; Robert A. Caro, *Master of the Senate*, 157–158.
5. Robert A. Caro, *Master of the Senate*, 157–159, 203–207.
6. Ibid., 207, 208, 209; William DeGregorio, *The Complete Book of U.S. Presidents*, 564–565, 566; Sally Russell, *Richard Brevard Russell*, 191; Robert A. Caro, *Means of Ascent*, 8, 16–17.
7. F. Martin Harmon, *Presidents by Fate*, 150; Robert A. Caro, *Master of the Senate*, 163.
8. Robert A. Caro, *Master of the Senate*, 96, 474–475; F. Martin Harmon, *Presidents by Fate*, 151; Sally Russell, *Richard Brevard Russell*, 197.
9. Sally Russell, *Richard Brevard Russell*, 197–198.
10. Robert A. Caro, *Master of the Senate*, 557–558; William DeGregorio, *The Complete Book of U.S. Presidents*, 568.
11. William E. Leuchtenburg, *The White House Looks South*, 229–239, 245–246, 248–249.
12. Ibid., 246, 250–251.
13. Ibid., 249, 251.
14. Ibid., 251; Robert A. Caro, *Master of the Senate*, 785–786.
15. Robert A. Caro, *Master of the Senate*, 786–787; William E. Leuchtenburg, *The White House Looks South*, 251.
16. William E. Leuchtenburg, *The White House Looks South*, 277; Sally Russell, *Richard Brevard Russell*, 193–195.
17. Robert A. Caro, *Means of Ascent*, xxvii, 36; Robert A. Caro, *Master of the Senate*, 125.
18. William E. Leuchtenburg, *The White House Looks South*, 255–257.
19. Ibid., 260–263; Sally Russell, *Richard Brevard Russell*, 211.
20. William E. Leuchtenburg, *The White House Looks South*, 260–261; Robert A. Caro, *Passage of Power: The Years of Lyndon Johnson*, 11–12.
21. Robert A. Caro, *Master of the Senate*, 599.
22. Doris Kearns Goodwin, *Leadership in Turbulent Times*, 198, 205; William DeGregorio, *The Complete Book of U.S. Presidents*, 568.
23. Robert A. Caro, *Passage of Power*, 10, 23–27, 33, 34–35, 47, 84–87, 107, 114, 155; Kenneth C. Davis, *Don't Know Much About the American Presidents*, 484.
24. Kenneth C. Davis, *Don't Know Much About the American Presidents*, 484; Robert A. Caro, *Passage of Power*, 109–115, 118–123, 132, 200–203, 224, 243; Doris Kearns Goodwin, *Leadership in Turbulent Times*, 205–206; William DeGregorio, *The Complete Book of U.S. Presidents*, 569.
25. William DeGregorio, *The Complete Book of U.S. Presidents*, 555, 557, 560; Kenneth C. Davis, *Don't Know Much About the American Presidents*, 484–487; Robert A. Caro, *Passage of Power*, 311–312, 323, 354–355; Sally Russell, *Richard Brevard Russell*, 228–229, 230.

Chapter 17

1. David McCullough, *John Adams*, 374–379; Andrew Burstein and Nancy Isenberg, *Madison and Jefferson*, 152–157.

2. Richard A. Baker and Neil MacNeil, *The American Senate*, 276, 278, 280, 284–286.
3. *Ibid.*, 305–306.
4. *Ibid.*, 306–307, 311, 313, 315–316; Molly F. Reynolds, "What Is the Senate Filibuster and What Would It Take to Eliminate It?" brookings.edu, October 15, 2009.
5. Richard A. Baker and Neil MacNeil, *The American Senate*, 317.
6. *Ibid.*, 318.
7. *Ibid.*, 319–320.
8. William E. Leuchtenburg, *The White House Looks South*, 263, 269–270; Sally Russell, *Richard Brevard Russell*, 219; Doris Kearns Goodwin, *Leadership in Turbulent Times*, 308; Jon Meacham, *The Soul of America*, 211–212; John Lewis with Michael D'Orso, *Walking with the Wind: A Memoir of the Movement*, 46–48.
9. John Lewis with Michael D'Orso, *Walking with the Wind*, 46–48, 128, 175–176, 199, 276; David Halberstam, *The Children*, 11, 92–94, 102–105; David J. Garrow, *Bearing the Cross: Martin Luther King and the Southern Christian Leadership Conference*, 11–82, 154–161, 239, 248–250, 291; Robert A. Caro, *The Passage of Power*, xiii–xv, 347, 444.
10. Robert A. Caro, *The Passage of Power*, 346; William DeGregorio, *The Complete Book of U.S. Presidents*, 557.
11. Robert A. Caro, *The Passage of Power*, 393–395.
12. Jon Meacham, *The Soul of America*, 212.
13. Doris Kearns Goodwin, *Leadership in Turbulent Times*, 308.
14. Jon Meacham, *The Soul of America*, 212–213.
15. Robert A. Caro, *The Passage of Power*, 398.
16. *Ibid.*, 429–430; F. Martin Harmon, *Presidents by Fate*, 36.
17. Jon Meacham, *The Soul of America*, 209, 212, 213; Robert A. Caro, *The Passage of Power*, 427–428.
18. Robert A. Caro, *The Passage of Power*, 430.
19. *Ibid.*, 431.
20. *Ibid.*, 431–432; F. Martin Harmon, *Presidents by Fate*, 152.
21. Sally Russell, *Richard Brevard Russell*, 231.
22. *Ibid.*, 232; Robert A. Caro, *The Passage of Power*, 443, 446–449.
23. Robert A. Caro, *The Passage of Power*, 457; Sally Russell, *Richard Brevard Russell*, 232.
24. Robert A. Caro, *The Passage of Power*, 455, 457–458.
25. *Ibid.*, 258–259; Sam Berger and Alex Tausanovitch, "The Impact of the Filibuster on Federal Policymaking," americanprogress.org, December 5, 2019; William DeGregorio, *The Complete Book of U.S. Presidents*, 574.
26. William E. Leuchtenburg, *The White House Looks South*, 303.
27. Robert A. Caro, *The Passage of Power*, 458–459, 462.
28. Richard A. Baker and Neil MacNeil, *The American Senate*, 330.
29. *Ibid.*, 330–331.
30. Martin Fridson, "Why the Kennedy Tax Cut Never Really Happened," forbes.com, December 11, 2017; Robert A. Caro, *The Passage of Power*, 471–475, 482–483.
31. Richard A. Baker and Neil MacNeil, *The American Senate*, 331.
32. Doris Kearns Goodwin, *Leadership in Turbulent Times*, 323; Jon Meacham, *The Soul of America*, 230.
33. Sally Russell, *Richard Brevard Russell*, 235.
34. Richard A. Baker and Neil MacNeil, *The American Senate*, 331.
35. *Ibid.*
36. *Ibid.*, 332.
37. Sally Russell, *Richard Brevard Russell*, 235.
38. William E. Leuchtenburg, *The White House Looks South*, 308–309; Robert A. Caro, *The Passage of Power*, 9.
39. Robert A. Caro, *The Passage of Power*, 431–432; Brian O'Shea, "Who Is the Russell Building Named For?" ajc.com, August 27, 2018; Sally Russell, *Richard Brevard Russell*, 257.

Chapter 18

1. Robert A. Caro, *The Path to Power*, 219, 271–272, 395; F. Martin Harmon, *Presidents by Fate*, 150.
2. Robert A. Caro, *The Path to Power*, 446–448; David M. Kennedy, "FDR and LBJ," *American Heritage*, December 1984.
3. Robert A. Caro, *Means of Ascent*, 10–11; Robert A. Caro, *The Passage of Power*, 550; Doris Kearns Goodwin,

Leadership in Turbulent Times, xv–xvi, 312, 328.
  4. Jon Meacham, *The Soul of America*, 46; Will Oremus, "RFK, DSK, OBL, WTF: When did we start referring to famous people by three initials," slate.com, June 11, 2012.
  5. Robert A. Caro, *The Path to Power*, 766.
  6. Robert A. Caro, *The Passage of Power*, 601; William DeGregorio, *The Complete Book of U.S. Presidents*, 574.
  7. Jonathan Alter, *The Defining Moment: FDR's Hundred Days and the Triumph of Hope*, 280–304; Michael Hiltzik, *The New Deal: A Modern History*, 66–69, 72–78, 106, 162, 164, 168; Kenneth C. Davis, *Don't Know Much About the American Presidents*, 431–433.
  8. Kenneth C. Davis, *Don't Know Much About the American Presidents*, 500–502.
  9. Jon Meacham, *The Soul of America*, 212; William DeGregorio, *The Complete Book of U.S. Presidents*, 575–576; Kenneth C. Davis, *Don't Know Much About the American Presidents*, 502–503.
  10. Kenneth C. Davis, *Don't Know Much About the American Presidents*, 508; F. Martin Harmon, *Presidents by Fate*, 153–154; Jon Meacham, *The Soul of America*, 235.
  11. Christopher Klein, "How Selma's Bloody Sunday Became a Turning Point in the Civil Rights Movement," history.com, March 6, 2015.
  12. *Ibid.*; Mary Schons, "The Selma-to-Montgomery Marches," nationalgeographic.org, January 21, 2011.
  13. John Lewis, *Walking with the Wind*, 344.
  14. David Halberstam, *The Children*, 513–514.
  15. David J. Garrow, *Bearing the Cross: Martin Luther King, Jr., and the Southern Christian Leadership Conference*, 399.
  16. Richard A. Baker and Neil MacNeil, *The American Senate*, 333–334.

Chapter 19

  1. Henry Kissinger, *Diplomacy*, 17, 29, 58, 65, 74, outside cover bio.
  2. *Ibid.*, 39.
  3. David McCullough, *The Path Between the Seas: The Creation of the Panama Canal, 1870–1914*; Adam Clymer, *Drawing the Line at the Big Ditch: The Panama Canal Treaties and the Rise of the Right*, 8–9.
  4. Adam Clymer, *Drawing the Line at the Big Ditch*, 9.
  5. *Ibid.*, 8.
  6. *Ibid.*, 8–9.
  7. *Ibid.*, 5, 13, 15; F. Martin Harmon, *Presidents by Fate*, 38, 159; David Brinkley, *Gerald R. Ford*, 67, 99–100.
  8. F. Martin Harmon, *Presidents by Fate*, 75–76, 89–90, 108; Jean H. Baker, *James Buchanan*, 69–70; Stuart E. Eizenstat, *President Carter: The White House Years*, 6–7, 54, 64.
  9. David Brinkley, *Gerald R. Ford*, 133–139; F. Martin Harmon, *Presidents by Fate*, 160; Adam Clymer, *Drawing the Line at the Big Ditch*, 23.
  10. Adam Clymer, *Drawing the Line at the Big Ditch*, 20, 22, 23; David Brinkley, *Gerald R. Ford*, 136.
  11. David Brinkley, *Gerald R. Ford*, 23; Stuart E. Eizenstat, *President Carter*, 556.

Chapter 20

  1. Kenneth C. Davis, *Don't Know Much About the American Presidents*, 537, 541; William DeGregorio, *The Complete Book of U.S. Presidents*, 623–624.
  2. Stuart Eizenstat, *President Carter*, 556–557; Adam Clymer, *Drawing the Line at the Big Ditch*, 44, 45.
  3. Paul Laxalt, *Nevada's Paul Laxalt: A Memoir*, 222.
  4. *Ibid.*, 222–223.
  5. Britney Schering, "A Brief History of Omar Torrijos," theculturetrip.com, November 23, 2017; Adam Clymer, *Drawing the Line at the Big Ditch*, 26, 34.
  6. Adam Clymer, *Drawing the Line at the Big Ditch*, 42; Stuart Eizenstat, *President Carter*, 557; Paul Laxalt, *Nevada's Paul Laxalt*, 223.
  7. Laura Kalman, *Right Star Rising: A New Politics, 1974–1980*, 266.
  8. Paul Laxalt, *Nevada's Paul Laxalt*, 223.
  9. Stuart Eizenstat, *President Carter*, 563; Adam Clymer, *Drawing the Line at the Big Ditch*, 50.
  10. Paul Laxalt, *Nevada's Paul Laxalt*, 223.
  11. *Ibid.*, 224–225.
  12. *Ibid.*, 225–227.

13. *Ibid.*, 228–231.
14. Ibid., 229–231; John Perkins, *The New Confessions of An Economic Hit-Man*, 65–82, 166–168.
15. Paul Laxalt, *Nevada's Paul Laxalt*, 232–234.
16. Stuart Eizenstat, *President Carter*, 565; Laura Kalman, *Right Star Rising*, 267.
17. Laura Kalman, *Right Star Rising*, 266, 268; Stuart Eizenstat, *President Carter*, 565; Paul Laxalt, *Nevada's Paul Laxalt*, 234. Adam Clymer, *Drawing the Line at the Big Ditch*, 45.
18. Adam Clymer, *Drawing the Line at the Big Ditch*, 48–49, 51; Stuart Eizenstat, *President Carter*, 565–567.
19. Stuart Eizenstat, *President Carter*, 567, 569, 570–571.
20. Paul Laxalt, *Nevada's Paul Laxalt*, 234–236.
21. *Ibid.*, 236.
22. *Ibid.*, 237, 238.
23. Laura Kalman, *Right Star Rising*, 270; Andrew Glass, "United States Invades Panama, December 20, 1989," politico.com, December 20, 2018; "Panama City: Documenting U.S. Invasion," *The Week*, July 3, 2020.
24. William DeGregorio, *The Complete Book of U.S. Presidents*, 627; Andrew Glass, "Panama Takes Control of The Canal, December 31, 1999," politico.com, December 30, 2016; Jonathan Weisman, "Clinton Decides Not to Attend Transfer of Panama Canal: White House Is Wary, Fearing Political Fallout Could Land on Gore," *Baltimore Sun*, November 30, 1999.

Chapter 21

1. William DeGregorio, *The Complete Book of U.S. Presidents*, 627–628; Stuart Eizenstat, *President Carter*, xv.
2. Stuart Eizenstat, *President Carter*, 409, 530; William DeGregorio, *The Complete Book of U.S. Presidents*, 628; F. Martin Harmon, *The Roosevelts and Their Descendants*, 181; F. Martin Harmon, *Presidents by Fate*, 25, 118.
3. F. Martin Harmon, *Presidents by Fate*, 190; Stuart Eizenstat, *President Carter*, 410, 411–412, 414.
4. Stuart Eizenstat, *President Carter*, 413–414, 415; Richard A. Baker and Neil MacNeil, *The American Senate*, 134; Norma Percy, "The 50 Years War: Israel and the Arabs," PBS video, 1999.
5. Norma Percy, "The 50 Years War," PBS video, 1999; William DeGregorio, *The Complete Book of U.S. Presidents*, 628.
6. Stuart Eizenstat, *President Carter*, 418–420; Norma Percy, "The 50 Years War," PBS video, 1999; F. Martin Harmon, *Presidents by Fate*, 190.
7. Stuart Eizenstat, *President Carter*, 49, 420, 438–439; Norma Percy, "The 50 Years War," PBS video, 1999.
8. Norma Percy, "The 50 Years War," PBS video, 1999.
9. *Ibid.*; F. Martin Harmon, *Presidents by Fate*, 190.
10. William DeGregorio, *The Complete Book of U.S. Presidents*, 628; Moni Basu, "Carter Wins Nobel Peace Prize," ajc.com, October 12, 2002.
11. William DeGregorio, *The Complete Book of U.S. Presidents*, 628.
12. Kenneth C. Davis, *Don't Know Much About the American Presidents*, 541–542; Ernie Suggs, "Jimmy Carter Gets New Title—Oldest Living Former President," ajc.com, March 21, 2019.
13. Norman Kempster, "By Leaving Quietly, Marcos Is Assured U.S. Asylum, *Los Angeles Times*, February 26, 1986; Paul Laxalt, *Nevada's Paul Laxalt*, 271–280.
14. Paul Laxalt, *Nevada's Paul Laxalt*, 359–367.
15. *Ibid.*, 349–351; Adam Clymer, "Paul Laxalt, Senator from Nevada, Reagan Confidant Dies at 96," *New York Times*, August 6, 2018.

Bibliography

Adams, Samuel Hopkins, *Incredible Era: The Life and Times of Warren Gamaliel Harding*. New York: Capricorn Books, 1964.

Alter, Jonathan, *The Defining Moment: FDR's Hundred Days and the Triumph of Hope*. New York: Simon & Schuster, 2006.

Baker, Jean H., *James Buchanan*. New York: Times Books, 2004.

Baker, Richard A., and Neil MacNeil, *The American Senate: An Insider's History*. New York: Oxford University Press, 2013.

Berg, A. Scott, *Wilson*. New York: G. P. Putnam's Sons, 2013. Book Group, 2012.

Bordewich, Fergus, *America's Great Debate: Henry Clay, Stephen A. Douglas, and the Compromise That Preserved the Union*. New York: Simon & Schuster, 2012.

Borneman, Walter, *Polk: The Man Who Transformed the Presidency and America*. New York: Random House, 2008.

Boulard, Garry, *The Worst President: The Story Of James Buchanan*. Bloomington, Indiana: iUniverse, 2015.

Brands, H.W., *American Colossus: The Triumph of Capitalism, 1865-1900*. New York: Anchor Books, 2010.

Brands, H. W., *The General vs. The President: MacArthur and Truman at the Brink of Nuclear War*. New York: Anchor Books, 2018.

Brands, H. W., *Heirs of the Founders: Henry Clay, John Calhoun, and Daniel Webster, The Second Generation of American Giants*. New York: Anchor Books, 2018.

Brands, H. W., *TR: The Last Romantic*. New York: BasicBooks, 1997.

Brinkley, Douglas, *Gerald R. Ford*. New York: Times Books, 2007.

Broadwater, Robert P., *Did Lincoln and Republican Party Create The Civil War? An Argument*. Jefferson, North Carolina: McFarland, 2008.

Burns, James MacGregor, *Roosevelt: The Soldier of Freedom: 1940-1945*. New York: History Book Club, 1970.

Burstein, Andrew, and Nancy Isenberg, *Madison and Jefferson*. New York: Random House, 2010.

Caro, Robert A., *Master of the Senate: The Years of Lyndon Johnson*. New York: Alfred A. Knopf, 2002.

Caro, Robert A., *Means of Ascent: The Years of Lyndon Johnson*. New York: Alfred A. Knopf, 1990.

Caro, Robert A., *The Passage of Power: The Years of Lyndon Johnson*. New York: Alfred A. Knopf, 2012.

Caro, Robert A., *The Path to Power: The Years of Lyndon Johnson*. New York: Vintage Books, 1983.

Carwardine, Richard, *Lincoln: A Life of Purpose and Power*. New York: Alfred A. Knopf, 2003.

Chace, James, *1912: Wilson, Roosevelt, Taft & Debs—The Election that Changed the Country*. New York: Simon & Schuster, 2004.

Clymer, Adam, *Drawing the Line at the Big Ditch: The Panama Canal Treaties and the Rise of the Right*. Lawrence, Kansas: University of Kansas Press, 2008.

Coit, Margaret L., *John C. Calhoun: American Portrait*. Boston: Houghton Mifflin Company, 1950.

Cooper, John Milton, *Woodrow Wilson: A Biography*. New York: Alfred A. Knopf, 2009.

Cordery, Stacy A., *Alice: Alice Roosevelt Longworth, from White House Princess* to *Washington Power Broker*. New York: Viking, 2007.

Dallek, Robert, *An Unfinished Life: John F. Kennedy—1917-1963*. Boston: Little, Brown and Company, 2003.

Dary, David, *The Oregon Trail: An American Saga*. New York: Alfred A. Knopf, 2004.

Davis, Kenneth C., *Don't Know Much About The American Presidents*. New York: Hyperion Hatchett, 2012.

DeGregorio, William, *The Complete Book of U.S. Presidents*. Fort Lee, New Jersey: Barricade Books, 1984.

Donald, David Herbert, *Charles Sumner*. New York: DaCapo Press, 1996.

Donald, David Herbert, *Lincoln*. London: Jonathan Cape, 1995.

Dray, Philip, *Capitol Men: The Epic Story of Reconstruction Through the Lives of the First Black Congressmen*. New York: Houghton Mifflin Company, 2008.

Eizenstat, Stuart E., *President Carter And The White House Years*. New York: Thomas Dunne Books, 2018.

Etcheson, Nicole, *Bleeding Kansas: Contested Liberty in the Civil War Era*. Lawrence, Kansas: University of Kansas Press, 2004.

Farris, Scott, *Almost President: The Men Who Lost the Race but Changed the Nation*. Guilford, Connecticut: Lyons Press, 2012.

Ferrell, Robert H., *The Dying President: Franklin Roosevelt, 1944-1945*. Columbus, Missouri: University of Missouri Press, 1998.

Foner, Eric, *Reconstruction: America's Unfinished Revolution, 1863-1877*. Baton Rouge, Louisiana: Louisiana State University Press, 1988.

Gardner, William, *The Life of Stephen A. Douglas*. Orlando, Florida: Black Oyster Publishing Company, 2012.

Garraty, John A., *Henry Cabot Lodge: A Biography*. New York: Alfred A. Knopf, 1953.

Garrow, David J., *Bearing The Cross: Martin Luther King, Jr., and the Southern Christian Leadership Conference*. New York: William Morrow, 1986.

Goldenberg, Barry M., *The Unknown Architects of Civil Rights*. Los Angeles: Critical Minds Press, 2011.

Goodwin, Doris Kearns, *The Bully Pulpit: Theodore Roosevelt, William Howard Taft, and the Golden Age of Journalism*. New York: Simon & Schuster, 2013.

Goodwin, Doris Kearns, *Leadership in Turbulent Times*. New York: Simon & Schuster, 2018.

Halberstam, David, *The Children*. New York: Fawcett Books, 1998.

Halberstam, David, *The Coldest Winter: America and the Korean War*. New York: Hyperion, 2007.

Halberstam, David, *The Fifties*. New York: Villard Books, 1993.

Hancock, D. J., *Eisenhower and the Art of War: A Critical Appraisal*. Jefferson, North Carolina: McFarland, 2004.

Harmon, F. Martin, *Presidents by Fate: Nine Who Ascended through Death or Resignation*. Jefferson, North Carolina: McFarland, 2019.

Harmon, F. Martin, *The Roosevelts and Their Descendants: Portrait of an American Family*. Jefferson, North Carolina: McFarland, 2017.

Hiltzik, Michael, *The New Deal: A Modern History*. New York: Free Press, 2011.

Holt, Michael F., *The Rise and Fall of the American Whig Party: Jacksonian Politics and the Onset of the Civil War*. New York: Oxford University Press, 1999.

Isaacson, Walter, and Evan Thomas, *The Wise Men: Six Friends and The World They Made*—New York: Touchstone Books, 1986.

Kalman, Laura, *Right Star Rising: A New Politics, 1974-1980*. New York: W. W. Norton & Company, 2010.

Kazin, Michael, *A Godly Hero: The Life of William Jennings Bryan*. New York: Alfred A. Knoff, 2006.

Kennedy, John F., *Profiles in Courage*. New York: Harper & Row Publishers, 1955.

Kissinger, Henry, *Diplomacy*. New York: Simon & Schuster, 1994.

Leuchtenburg, William E., *The White House Looks South: Franklin D. Roosevelt, Harry S. Truman, Lyndon B. Johnson*. Baton Rouge, Louisiana: Louisiana State University Press, 2005.

Lewis, John, with Michael D'Orso, *Walking with the Wind: A Memoir of the Movement*. New York: Harcourt Brace, 1998.

MacMillan, Margaret, *Paris 1919: Six Months That Changed the World*. New York: Random House, 2001.

Manchester, William, *American Caesar:*

Douglas MacArthur, 1880-1964. New York: Laurel Books, 1978.

McArthur, Debra, *The Kansas-Nebraska Act and "Bleeding Kansas" in American History*. Berkley Heights, New Jersey: Enslow Publishers, 2003.

McClendon, Brian, *Nine Presidents Who Screwed Up America and Four Who Tried to Save Her*. Washington: Regnery Publishing, 2016.

McCullough, David, *John Adams*. New York: Simon & Schuster, 2001.

McCullough, David, *The Path Between the Seas: The Creation of the Panama Canal, 1870-1914*. New York: Touchstone Books, 1977.

McCullough, David, *Truman*. New York: Simon & Schuster, 1992.

Meacham, Jon, *American Lion: Andrew Jackson in the White House*. New York: Random House, 2008.

Meacham, Jon, *The Soul of America: The Battle for Our Better Angels*. New York: Random House, 2018.

Morris, Edmund, *The Rise of Theodore Roosevelt*. New York: Ballantine Books, 1979.

Nasaw, David, *The Patriarch: The Remarkable Life and Turbulent Times of Joseph P. Kennedy*. New York: Penguin Books, 2012.

Oshinsky, David M., *A Conspiracy So Immense: The World of Joe McCarthy*. New York: Free Press, 1983.

Overy, Richard, *The Dictators: Hitler's Germany, Stalin's Russia*. New York: W. W. Norton & Company, 2004.

Perlstein, Rick, *Nixonland: The Rise of a President and the Fracturing of America*. New York: Scribner's, 2008.

Perry, Mark, *Partners in Command: George Marshall and Dwight Eisenhower in War and Peace*. New York: The Penguin Press, 2007.

Pietrusza, David, *1948: Harry Truman's Improbable Victory and the Year That Transformed America*. New York: Union Square Press, 2011.

Pietrusza, David, *1920: The Year of the Six Presidents*. New York: Carroll & Graf Publishers, 2007.

Pogue, Forest C., *George C. Marshall: Statesman*. New York: Penguin Books, 1987.

Quitt, Martin H., *Stephen A. Douglas and Antebellum Democracy*. New York: Cambridge University Press, 2012.

Remini, Robert V., *Andrew Jackson: The Course of American Democracy*. New York: Harper & Row Publishers, 1984.

Remini, Robert V., *Andrew Jackson: The Course of American Freedom*. New York: Harper & Row Publishers, 1981.

Remini, Robert V., *Daniel Webster: The Man and His Time*. New York: W. W. Norton & Company, 1997.

Remini, Robert V., *Henry Clay: Statesman for the Union*. New York: W. W. Norton & Company, 1991.

Russell, Sally, *Richard Brevard Russell: A Life of Consequence*. Macon, Georgia: Mercer University Press, 2011.

Schriftgiesser, Karl, *The Gentleman from Massachusetts: Henry Cabot Lodge*. Boston: Little Brown And Company, 1944.

Shlaes, Amity, *Coolidge*. New York: Harper Perennial, 2013.

Sinclair, Andrew, *The Available Man: The Life Behind the Masks of Warren G. Harding*. Chicago: Quadrangle Books, 1965.

Stahr, Walter, *Seward: Lincoln's Indispensable Man*. New York: Simon & Schuster, 2012.

Stein, Mark, *How the States Got Their Shapes*. New York: Smithsonian Books, 2008.

Summers, Anthony, *Official and Confidential: The Secret Life of J. Edgar Hoover*. New York: G. P. Putnam's Sons, 1993.

Trefousse, Hans L., *Andrew Johnson: A Biography*. New York: W. W. Norton & Company, 1989.

Utley, Robert M., *The Indian Frontier of the American West: 1846-1890*. Albuquerque, New Mexico: University of New Mexico Press, 1984.

Van Deusen, Glyndon G., *The Jacksonian Era: 1828-1848*. New York: Harper & Row Publishers, 1959.

Williams, T. Harry, *Huey Long*. New York: Vintage Books, 1981.

Index

Numbers in **_bold italics_** indicate pages with illustrations

Acheson, Dean 160, 166, 167, 171
Adams, John Quincy 10
Afghanistan 261
African Americans (or Blacks/Negroes) 84, 87, 89–91, 97, 99–101, 105, 107, 111, 113–118, 162, 198–199, 214, 216, 233–235, 261
Agnew, Spiro 242
Agricultural Adjustment Act (AAA) 232
Air Force (formerly Army Air Corps) 161
Alabama Crimson Tide 1
Alabama River 233
Albany, New York 98
Albright, Madeline 255–256
Aldrich, Nelson 132
Allen, Jim 249
Allied Powers **_138_**
Allred, James 228–229
American Century 160
American Communist Party 166, 168, 182
American Expeditionary Force (or Doughboys) 131, 136
American Party (or Know-Nothings) 53
American Peace Commission 131, 133
American President Series 55
American System 15, 31, 36–37
America's Resort 30
America's Retreat from Victory speech 184
Andersonville 9
Anti-Masonic Party 30–31
Appalachian Mountains (or Appalachia) 10, 79
Appleton, Wisconsin 170
Arab-Israeli War 257–258
Arab League 258
Arab/Muslim states (or world) 258, **_260_**
Arabs 258
Army 71, 93, 103, 106–107, 160, 162, 179, 195
Arnold, Hap 179
Arsenal of Democracy war slogan 162
Arthur, Chester 121, 243
Ashland 30
Asian continent 232
Associated Press (or AP) 168, 174
Atchison, David 46–47

Atlantic Ocean 238, 241
Atlanta, Georgia 123–124, 198, **_199_**, 226, 234
Auburn Tigers 1
Augusta, Georgia 123

Baker, Howard 253–254
Baltimore, Maryland 61, **_68_**, 69, 73, 98, 124
Baltimore Sun 255
Bank of England 16
Barkesdale, William 68
Bay of Pigs invasion 210
Beauregard, P.G.T. 73
Begin, Menachem 259–260, **_260_**
Beijing, China 183
Belgium 147, 172
Bell, John 69, **_70_**
Bellmon, Henry 252, 254
Benton, Thomas Hart 22, 26, **_26_**, 46, 47, 49, 213
Berlin, Germany (or West Berlin) 160, 164
Berlin Airlift 164
Berlin Crisis 210
Bethesda Naval Hospital 195
Biddle, Nicholas 17, 20–21, **_21_**, 34
Biden, Joe 155
Big Four countries 130
Big Three conferences 193
Bismarck, Otto von 238
Black Codes 87, 91, 97, 117
Black Sea 193
Blaine, James G. 121
Blair, Francis Preston 29
Blair, Montgomery 98
Blanche, Bruce 116
Bleeding Kansas 49, 162, 264
Bloody Sunday 233, **_233_**, 234
Bonaparte, Napoleon 238
Borah, William 132, 136, 144
Border Ruffians 50, 162
Border States 26, 99
Boston, Massachusetts 78, **_81_**, 111, 120, 122
Boston Celtics 1
Boston Daily Advertiser 122

285

Index

Boston Public Garden *81*
Boston Red Sox 1
Bradley, Joseph 113
Bradley, Omar 185, 188–189
Breckinridge, John 51, *68*, 69, *70*
Brewster, Owen 173
Bricker, John 177
Bridges, Styles 173
British Empire 258
British House of Commons 212
British House of Lords 212
British Parliament 212
Brock, Bill 250
Brooke, Edward 120
Brooks, Preston 80, 82
Browder, Earl 182
Brown, John 50
Brown vs. Board of Education (or *Brown* decision) 205–206, 208
Bryan, William Jennings 38, 126
Bryn Mawr College 124
Buchanan, James 42–43, 45, 51, *52*, 53–63, 65–67, *68*, 69–70, *70*, 71–76, 129, 243, 264
Buchanan, Pat 251
Buffalo, New York 98, 124
Bullitt, William 141
Bully Pulpit 7, 182, 264
Burma 193
Bush, George H.W. 38–39, 254
Butler, Andrew 80
Byrd, Harry 202, 205, 216–219, 223, 224
Byrd, Robert 253

Cabinet 24, 27, 29, 34, 55, 57, 61–62, 64, 83, 97, 103–104, 106, 108, 151, 155, 217, 220
Cabot, George 120–121
Cain, Richard 116
Cal State Berkley Greek Theater 142
Calhoun, John C. 5, 11, 27, 37, 38, 39, 48, 213
California Gold Rush 44
Calvin Coolidge 155
Camp David 259, *260*
Camp David Accords 256
Canada 44
Cannon, Howard 253–254
Capehart, Homer 173–174
Capitol Dome 3
Capitol Hill 93, 152, 193–194, 205, 218
Capitol Rotunda 111
Carpetbaggers 117
Carranza, Venustiano 129
Carson, Kit 44
Carson City, Nevada 262
Carter, Jimmy 2, 228, 238, 242–243, *243*, 244–246, *246*, 247–248, *248*, 249–250, 252–260, *260*, 261, *262*, 264
Cass, Lewis 46
Castro, Fidel 193, 247, 250
Catoctin Mountains 259
Catron, John 55–56

Central America (or Central American) 244, 246, 263
Central American Isthmus 238
Central Intelligence Agency (CIA) 190, *191*, 192
Chambers, Whitaker 166
Chandler, Harry 142
Charleston, South Carolina 68, 73
Charleston, West Virginia 168
Charleston Harbor 73
Chase, Salmon P. 108
Cherokees tribe 16
Cheyenne, Wyoming 143
Chicago, Illinois 49, 98, 121, 126, 128
Chicago Bears 1
Chicago Tribune 99
China (or Chinese, Middle Kingdom) 160–161, 165, 179–184
China Lobby 183
China White Paper 180
Choctaws tribe 16
Christian Science Monitor 162
Churchill, Winston 160, 193
Cincinnati, Ohio 98, 251
Civil Rights Act of 1864 222–224, *225*, 226, *227*, 232–233, 235
Civil Rights Act of 1875 100, 112, 114, 207
Civil Rights Movement 3, *111*, 120, *199*, 215, 217, 226, 232, *233*, 234, 264
Civil Service Commission 122–123
Civil War 1, 3, 37, 42, 45, 47, 53, 59, 65, 67, 69, 73, 75–76, 78–80, 86, *87*, *94*, *101*, 103, 107, *111*, 114, *115*, 120–121, 123, *125*, 126, 154, 159, 187, 198, 209, 213, 264
Civilian Conservation Corps (CCC) 231
Clay, Henry 2, 5, 7, 10–12, *14*, 15–16, 18–21, *21*, 22–23, *23*, 25–26, *26*, 27, *28*, 29–39, 42–43, 45, 67, 72, 111–112, 212–213, 264
Clean, Old Fashioned Hate rivalry 120
Clemenceau, Georges 135
Cleveland, Grover 69, 121, 125
Cleveland, Ohio 98
Clifford, Clark 185
Clinton, Bill 255
Clinton, George 16
Cobb, Frank 134
Cohn, Roy 178
Cold War 3, 159, *159*, 160, 161, 164, 165, *167*, 175, 177, 181, *191*, 195, 210, 256, 259
Coleman, Thomas 171–172
Colombia 238, 239, *240*, 244
Colorado State Fairgrounds 143
Columbia, South Carolina 123
Columbus, Ohio 98, 140
Committee of Americans for the Canal Treaties 252
Commonwealth Club of San Francisco 250
Communist China (or Red China) 183, 190, 193, 261
Communist Chinese Army 182

Communist Party (in America) 166, 182
Community Action Program 231
Compromise of 1850 38, 42, 44–45, 47, *47*, 73
Compromise Tariff 38
Conclusion of a Peace Treaty between Egypt and Israel 260
Confederate States (or Confederacy) 75, 86, 95, 99, 103, 117, 205
Congo 193
Congress 5, 12, 20–23, 26, 29, 35, 37, 39, 43, 45–46, *47*, 48, 51, 59, 62–65, 71, 80, *81*, 83–84, 86, 90, 92–100, 102–108, 110, 113, 116, 121, 133, 140–142, 152–153, 162–164, 166, 174–177, 180–181, 193, 198, 202, 204, 207, 211, 217–218, 220, 223, 229, 232, 234–235, 244, 253
Congressional Government 124
Connally, Tom *204*, 205
Conservative Political Action Conference 252
Constitution 25, 26, 35, 39, 55–56, 62–64, 75, 84, 96, 107–108, 113, 116, 133, 142, 148, 154, 176
Constitutional Union Party 69
Contras insurgency 263
Coolidge, Calvin 155
Corrupt Bargain 10, 112
Court of St. James 178
Covode, John 71
Cowan, Edgar 98
Cox, James M. 154
Credit Mobilier scandal 114
Creeks tribe 10, 16
Crime Against Kansas speech 80
Crittenden, John 72
Cromwell, Sullivan 190
Cuba (or Pearl of the Antillies) 71, 193, 210, 247, 251
Cuban Missile Crisis 210
Cullom, Shelby 132

D-Day invasion 187
Dallak, Robert 195
Dallas, George 22
Dallas, Texas 210, 216, 218
Dallas Cowboys 1
Davidson College 123
Davis, Jefferson 92, 100
Debs, Eugene 127
Declaration of Conscience 176
Declaration of Independence 98
Deep South 39, 56, 72–73, 116, 214, 216, 233
Democrat (or Democrats) 22–23, 30–34, 38, 42, 48–49, 51, 56–57, 59–60, 63–64, 66, 69, 74, 78, 82, 87, 90, 100, 102, 104, 107, 109, 113, 117, 125–126, 128, 132, 142, 144–145, 162–163, 185, 187, 190, 193–194, 199–200, 202–210, 212–213, 217, 219, 222–224, *225*, 235, 239, 248, 264
Democratic Caucus 145, 193, *202*, 203
Democratic National Convention of 1856 51

Democratic National Convention of 1860 68, *68*
Democratic National Convention of 1868 109
Democratic National Convention of 1948 163
Democratic National Convention of 1952 207
Democratic Party 25, 31, 38, 42–43, 47, *47*, 51, 56, 58–59, 61, 63–64, 67–68, *68*, 69, 74, 76, 91, 105, 109, 113, 121–122, 124–125, *125*, 127, 132, 146, 148, 151, 158, 162–163, 168, 173, *173*, 184–185, 188, 193, 99, 200, 202, *202*, 203–210, 213, 217, *219*, 223–225, 229, 235, 239, 242, 244, 248, 264
Democratic South (or Solid South) 107, 113, 148, 210, 277
Denver, Colorado 143
Department of Defense 184
Deserving Dozen (of Senate) 7
Detroit, Michigan 98
Dewey, Thomas 158, 163, 192
Dirksen, Everett 224–225, 225, 226, 235
Distinguished Service Cross 171
Dixie 67, 95, 206, 217
Dixiecrats 163
Do Nothing Congress 163
Dodge, Augustus 46–47, 58
Dole, Bob 249–250, 253
Domenici, Pete 249, 253–254
Dominican Republic 193
Doolittle, James 98
Douglas, Stephen A. 7, 38, 42–43, 45–47, *47*, 48–52, 57, *57*, 58–60, *60*, 61, 63–68, *68*, 69, *70*, 73–74, 76, 80, 212, 264
Dred Scott decision (or case) 56–59
Duke Blue Devils 1
Dulles, Allen 190, *191*, 192–193
Dulles, John Foster 190, *191*, 192–194
Dunkirk evacuation 180

The East (or Eastern) 44–45, 206, 219
East Asian 105
East Coast 114
East Germany 164
East Tennessee 79, 82
Eastern elite 160
Eastern Europe 164, 193, 247
Eastern Kansas 50
Eastern Mediterranean 160
Economic Opportunity Act 231
Eden, Anthony 192
Edmund Pettus Bridge 233
Egerton, John 207
Egypt (or Egyptians) 193, 247, 256–260, *260*
Egyptian Parliament 259
Eighteenth Amendment 153
Eisenhower, Dwight 163, 166, 179, 183, 185–189, *189*, 190, *191*, 192–194, 203, 210
Electoral College 5, 10, 31, 56, 112
Electoral Commission 112–113
Elementary and Secondary Education Act 231

Ellsworth, Roger 7
Emancipation Proclamation 76, 79
Emerson, Ralph Waldo 111
Emory University 234
Enforcement Acts of 1870 and 1871 116
Enlai, Chou 193
Era of Normalcy 154, 156
Era of Prohibition 153
Essary, Fred 151
Europe 37, 46, 78, 126, 129–131, *131*, 134, 141, 147, 156, 159–160, *161*, 163–164, 187, 190, 193–194, 238, 257
Euopean continent 164
European Jews 258
Evarts, William 108
Ewing, Thomas 22

Fair Employment Protection Committee (FEPC) 162
Fair Housing Act of 1968 235
Fall, Albert 153
Famous Five (of Senate) 5
Famous Nine (of Senate) 7
Federal Reserve 128
Federal Trade Commission 128
Ferguson, Champ 91
Fessenden, William 109
Fifteenth Amendment 100, 115
Fifth Amendment 56
Fillmore, Millard 45, 53, 56, 243
Fire-Eaters 68
The First Friend 261, *262*
The First Lady (Bess Truman) 182
First National Bank 16–17
Five Civilized Tribes 45
Flood, Daniel 239
Florida Little White House 174
Force Bill 37, 39
Ford, Gerald 238, 242, 245–246, *246*, 247, 256
Ford, Wendell 252
Foreign Relations Committee 133, 138, *138*, 139
Formosa (now Taiwan) 180, 261
Fort Sumter 73, 75
Fort Worth, Texas 229
Fortress Monroe 100
Fortune magazine 180
Foster Grandparents Program 231
Founding Fathers 16, 28, 212
Fourteen Points 130
Fourteenth Amendment (or Reconstruction Amendment) 96–97, 99–100, 103, 105, 109
Fowler, Josiah 109
Framework for Peace in the Middle East 260
France (or French) 44, 129–131, *131*, 133–134, *135*, 136, 142, 147, 238, 244
Fraser, Steve 18
Free Soil Party (or Free Soilers) 49, 78, 82
Freedmen's Bureau 84, 87, 116
Freedom March 216

Freedom Riders 216
Frémont, John C. 44, 53, 56
Fugitive Slave Act of 1850 45

Gallinger, Jacob 132
Galveston, Texas 229
Garfield, James 69, 121
Garn, Jake 249
Gaza Strip 257, 259
Geneva, Switzerland 147
George, David Lloyd 135, *205*
George, Walter 199, *204*
Georgetown neighborhood (Washington, D.C.) 172
Georgia House of Representatives 198
Georgia Supreme Court 198
Georgia Tech Yellow Jackets 120
German U-boats (submarines) 129, 153
Germany 130, 134–135, *135*, *138*, 145, 147, 153, 155–156, 160, 162, 164, 178, 187, 234, 238
Goddess Columbia (early American symbol) *60*
Golan Heights 257
Goldwater, Barry 226
Gore, Al, Jr. 255
Gore, Al, Sr. 206
Gould, Lewis 113
Grand Coulee Dam 181
Grant, Ulysses 69, 106–107, 109–110, 112, 114–115, *115*, 116–117, 187
Great Britain (or British) 10, 15, 27, 43–44, 129, 134–135, 160–161, 164, 178, 180, 192, 212, 241
Great Depression 155, 158, 162, 228–229, *230*
Great Smoky Mountains 79
Great Society slogan 229, 231–232
Great Triumvirate 5
Greece 160, 192
Green Bay Packers 1
Greeneville, Tennessee 79
Grier, Robert 56
Grimes, James W. 109
Guatemala 192
Gulf of Tonkin Resolution 232

Hamilton, Alexander 15, 16
Hamlin, Hannibal 79
Hancock, Winfield Scott 69, 107
Harding, Warren G. 154–155
Harris, William 198
Harrison, Benjamin 122, 154
Harrison, William Henry 37
Harvard Law School 160
Harvard University 78, 120, 123, 158, 210, 238
Harvey, George 125
Haskell, Floyd 242
Hatch, Orin 249
Hay-Bunau-Varilla Treaty 239
Hayakawa, S.I. (also Sam) 249, 252–254
Hayes, Rutherford B. 69, 112–113

Index

Haynie, Robert 22
He Kept Us Out Of War campaign slogan 129
Head Start program 231
Helms, Jessie 249
Henderson, John B. 109
Henry, Patrick 213
Heritage Foundation 251
Hermitage 31
Hezbollah 263
Hickory Clubs 31
Hill, Andrew 16
The Hinge presidencies 238
Hiroshima bombing 160
Hiss, Alger 166–167, *167*, 175, 177
"The Hiss Case—A Lesson for the American People" 166
History News Network 6
History of the American People 124
Hitchcock, Gilbert 153
Hitler, Adolf 147
Holden, William 90
Holmes, Oliver Wendell 111
Holy Land (also Promised Land) 257–258
Hoover, Herbert 54, 72, 155
Hoover, J. Edgar 168, 174
House Chamber 219
House Judiciary Committee 106
House of Representatives (or Lower House/Chamber) 10, 12, *13*, *14*, 22–23, 33, 48–49, 58, 62–64, 69, 71, 78–80, 82–84, 94, *94*, 95, 98–100, 102, 105–106, 108, 112, 120–123, 133, 151–152, *152*, 163, 166, 205–206, 212, 214, 225
House Un-American Activities Committee 166
Houston, Sam 48–49
Huerta, Victoriano 129
Humphrey, Hubert 203, 208, 210, 219, 223–224, 226

Inauguration Day (1860) 72
Inchon, South Korea 180, 182
Independence League (or League for the Preservation of American Independence) 136
Independence, Missouri 194
Indian Removal Act of 1830 39
Indian Territory 15, 45
Indianapolis, Indiana 98
Indonesia 193
Iran 192, 261, 263
Iran-Contra controversy 262–263
Irreconcilables 132, 145–146
Iscariot, Judas 99
Israel (or Israelis) 161, 222, 256–260, *260*
Israeli Knesset 259
Italy 130, 133, 155
Ivy League 123–124

Jackson, Andrew 2, 10–12, 13, 15–16, 18, 20–21, *21*, 22–24, *24*, 25–27, *28*, 29–31, 33–36, 36, 37–40, 42, 45, 55, 59, 61, 64, 69, 75, 79, 99, 108, *125*, 128, 213, 264
Jacksonian Era (or Jacksonians) 2, 11, 12, 15, *26*, 31, 37, 39, 42, 55, 59, 61
Japan (or Japanese) 159–160, 162, 165, 178–179, 257
Jefferson, Thomas 12, 16–17, 85
Jim Crow segregation 114, 206, 207, 222
Job Corps 231
Johns Hopkins University 124
Johnson, Andrew 2, 79–80, *80*, 82–87, *87*, 88–93, *94*, 95–100, 102–110, *110*, 112–113, 115–118, 154, 243, 264
Johnson, Hiram 136, 155
Johnson, Lady Bird 201, 248
Johnson, Luci 201, 229
Johnson, Lynda 201, 229
Johnson, Lyndon Baines (or LBJ) 2, 5, 105, 110, 114, 154, 170, 193–195, 198–202, *202*, 203–204, *204*, 205–211, 213, 215, *215*, 216–221, *221*, 222–225, *225*, 226–227, *227*, 228–230, *230*, 231–233, *233*, 234–235, 249, 254, 256, 264
Joint Chiefs 184–185, 250
Joint Committee (of Congress) 94–97
Jones, David 251
Jordan 257–258
Jordan River 257
Judea 261
Judgement at Nuremberg 235
Justice Department 34, 166, 226

Kai-Shek, Chiang 180–181
Kansas City, Missouri 141
Kansas-Nebraska Act 42, 47, *47*, 48–51, 57–58, *60*, 80
Kansas Territory 49, 50, 63
Kearney, Stephen W. 44
Kefauver, Estes 207, 210
Kendall, Amos 24
Kennedy, Joe 178
Kennedy, John F. (JFK) 5, 7, 108–109, 154, 178, 209–212, 215, *215*, 216–221, *227*, 229, 231
Kennedy, Robert (or Bobby) 178, 225
Kennedy, Ted 6, 120
Kennedy Cabinet 217
Kerry, John 120
Key West, Florida 174
King, Martin Luther (MLK) 217, 226, 234
King, Richard 228
King Ranch 228
Kissinger, Henry 238–239, 241, 242, 247–249
Kissinger-Tack Principles (or Agreement) 239, 242, 247–248
Kleberg, Richard 229
Knowland, William 180
Korean Peninsula 165, 178–180, 182
Korean War (or Conflict) 165, 175–176, *179*, 181, 183, 185, 190, 232, 275
Kremlin 174, 181

Index

Ku Klux Klan 117, 216
Ku Klux Klan Act of 1871 116

LaFollette, Robert, Jr. 171–172
LaFollette, Robert, Sr. 5, 172
Lancaster, Pennsylvania 75
Land of Opportunity 162
Language in Action 253
Lansing, Robert 137, 141, 151–152
Laos 193
Latin America 53, 241–242, 247, 249, 252, 254
Lattimore, Owen 175
Lawrence, Amos 50
Lawrence, Kansas 50
Laxalt, Paul 7, 244, 246–251, *251*, 252–254, 256, 261–262, *262*, 263–264
League of Nations 3, *121*, 130, 134–137, *138*, 139–144, *144*, 146–148, *152*, 153, 155, 159, 254, 264
Leavenworth, Kansas 50
Lecompton, Kansas 50
Lecompton constitution 50–51, 59–64, 71
Lee, Robert E. 200
Lewis, John 228, 234
Lexington, Kentucky 16, 35
Life magazine 180, 190
The Life and Letters of George Cabot 121
Lincoln, Abraham 2, 38, 51–52, *52*, 57, *57*, 58–59, 67, 69–70, *70*, 71–75, 79, *80*, 82–83, 84, 86, 88–89, 91, 102–108, 111–113, 120, 159, 163, 217–218, 220
Lincoln Day Celebration 168
Linowitz, Sol 250
Little Rock, Arkansas 150
Locarno Pact of 1925 147
Lodge, Henry Cabot 7, 120–121, *121*, 122–124, 128–134, 136–138, *138*, 139, 141–142, 144–147, *152*, 153, 156, 254, 264
Long, Huey 172–173, *173*, 177, 214
Long March 183
Longfellow, Henry Wadsworth 78, 111
Longworth, Alice Roosevelt 151
Longworth, Nicholas 151, *152*
Los Angeles, California 142
Los Angles Dodgers 1
Los Angeles Lakers 1
Los Angeles Times 142, 239
Lost Cause 91, 177
Louisiana Purchase 43–44, 46
Louisiana-Texas district 106
Louisville, Kentucky 98, 150
Louisville Courier Journal 125
Lowden, Frank 155
Loyalty Boards 177
Luce, Henry 180, 183, 192
Lusitania 129

MacArthur, Douglas 178–179, *179*, 180–185, 190, 221
Madison, James 15, 17

Malmedy massacre 172
Manifest Destiny 43, 46
Mansfield, Mike 223–224, *225*
Marcos, Ferdinand 261–262
Marine Corps 170
Marquette University 170
Marshall, George C. 160, 161, *161*, *167*, *171*, 179, *179*, 184, 188, 189, 257
Marshall, Thomas 148, 150–152
Marshall Plan (or European Recovery Act) 159–160, *161*, 192
Marx, Groucho 174
Marx, Karl 174
Mason, James 80
Mason-Dixon Line 45
Massachusetts Emigrant Aid Company 50
Massachusetts House of Representatives 78, 120
Massachusetts Republican State Central Committee 121
Massachusetts Republican State Convention 92
Massachusetts 6th Congressional District 122
Mayflower railroad car 140
Maysville Road 30, 35
McCain, John 6
McCarthy, Joseph 2, 7, 166, 168–170, *171*, 172–173, *173*, 174–177, *177*, 178–182, 184–186, 188–189, *189*, 193–195, 202, 264
McCarthyism 168
McClure Hotel 168
McCullough, Hugh 97
McCullough vs. Maryland 25
McKinley, William 124, 155
Medicaid 232
Medicare 222, 231
Memphis, Tennessee 98, 150
Mexican Cession 44, 48, 73
Mexican War 44, 76
Mexico (or Mexican) 33, 43–45, 48, 71, 104, 129–130, 152–153
Miami, Florida 251
Michigan Wolverines 1
Middle America 158
Middle Atlantic 39
Middle East 246, 256–260
Middle Kingdom 180
Midwest 213
Millionaires Club (also Most Exclusive Club) 7
Milwaukee, Wisconsin 170, 177, 188
Minh, Ho Chi 232
Mississippi River 47, 53, 71
Missouri Compromise (or Compromise of 1820) 38, 43, 45, 47–49, 56, 72
Missouri Historical Review 205
Missouri Supreme Court 55
Mr. Buchanan's Administration on the Eve of Rebellion 75
Mobile Bay 71

Index

Mondale, Walter 254
Monroe, James 17
Monroe Doctrine 141
Montgomery, Alabama **227**, 233
Moral Majority 251
Mormon (or Mormons) 57, 62, 65
Mormon Migration 44
Mormon Tabernacle 143
Moscoso, Mireya 255
Moscow, Russia 184
Moscow Summer Olympics (1980) 261
Mount Auburn Cemetery 111
Mundt, Karl 174
Murphy, John 239
Murrow, Edward R. 195

Nagasaki bombing 160
Nashville, Tennessee 31, 251
Nashville Tennessean 234
Nasser, Abdel 247
National Bank (or Second Bank of United States) 1, 3, 10, **14**, 15–16, **17**, 18, 20–21, **21**, 22–23 **23**, 24, **24**, 26, **26**, **28**, 29–31, 33–36, 39
National Democratic Party 69
National Guard 215, **233**, 234, 247
National Historic Preservation Act 232
National Hotel 90
National Park Service 128
National Recovery Act (NRA) 232
National Republican Party (or National Republicans) 15, 22, **23**, 31, 33, 34
National Security Act of 1947 161
National Security Council 190
National Union Convention 97, 100
Nationalist Chinese 180, 261
Native Americans 15, 39
Navy 161
Nazi Germany 155, 187, 235, 258
Nebraska Territory 46, 49
New Deal 155, 172, 198, 201, 228–229, **230**
New England 10, 12, 22, 30, 31, 39, 50, 51, 92, 111, 120
New Freedom 127
New Jersey Democratic Committee 125
New Jersey Democratic Party 124
New Nationalism 127
New Orleans, Louisiana 61, 98
New South 123
New York City, New York 98, 122–123, 258
New York City Board of Police Commissioners 123
New York Courier & Enquirer 18
New York Independent 99
New York Times (or *Daily Times*) 48–49, 71, 73, 97
New York Tribune 73, 99
New York World 134
New York Yankees 1
Nicaragua 263

Nineteenth Amendment 156
Nixon, Richard 154, 166–168, 210, 238–239, 241–243, **246**
Nobel Peace Prize 130, 146, 156, 257, 260
Noriega, Manuel 250, 254
Norris, George 5–6, **6**, 7, 214
The North (or Northern) 37–38, 43–44, 48–49, 51, 56, 58, 65, 67, 69–70, 72, 80, 82, **101**, 111, **111**, 116, 123, 203, 205–208, 219
North American Review 125
North Atlantic Treaty Organization (NATO) 164, 192
North Carolina Tar Heels 1
North Korea (or North Koreans) 165, 175, 178–179, **179**, 180, 182,
North Korean People's Army 165
North Vietnam 232
Northeastern elite 34, 122, 211
Northwest Ordinance of 1787 49–50
Nullification Crisis of 1832 39, 72

Oakland Municipal Auditorium 142
Obama, Barack 154
Office of Special Political Affairs 166
Ohio Repository 62
Ohio River 16, 36
Ohio State Buckeyes 1
Ohio County Women's Republican Club 168
Oklahoma City, Oklahoma 150
Omaha, Nebraska 141
O'Neill, Tip 257
Operation Just Cause 254
Ordinance of Nullification 37
Oregon Territory 44
Oregon Trail 44, 46
Ormsby House 262
Ostend Manifesto 53, 70
Oto language 46
Oval Office 3

Pacific Ocean 43, 160, **179**, 238, 241
Pacific Theater 178, 183
Palace of Versailles 130, **135**, 156
Palestine (or Palestinians) 258, 260
Palestinian Mandate 258
Pan American Union Building 249
Panama (or Panamanians) 3, 239, **240**, 241–242, **243**, 244–248, **248**, 249–251, **251**, 252–254
Panama Canal 2, 3, 238–239, **240**, **241**, 242, **243**, 244–251, **251**, 252–257, **262**
Panama Canal treaties (or Carter-Torrijos treaties) 248–254, 256
Panama Canal Treaty 246, 247, 248, 252
Panama Canal Zone 239, 239, 241–242, 244, 247–251, 253–254
Panama City, Panama 250
Panamanian National Guard 247
Panic of 1837 34, **37**
Panic of 1873 114, 117

292   Index

Paris, France 130, *131*, *135*, 140, 190
Pearl Harbor 165
Peking, China 261
Penn State University 114
Pennsylvania Avenue 3, 73, 131, 135, 152, 189
Peoria, Illinois 188
Pepper, Claude *204*
Pet Banks 34
Philadelphia, Pennsylvania 17, *17*, 98, 100, 163
Philadelphia North American 62
Philippines 261, *262*
Pierce, Franklin 47–48, 51, 54, 58, 80, 243
Pinkerton Detective Agency 73
Pittsburgh, Pennsylvania 98
Platte River 46
Poincare, Raymond *131*
Poland 156
A Policy of Boldness article 190
Polk, James K. 33, 37, 55, 99
popular sovereignty 42, 46–47, *47*, 48, 51, 57–59, 63, 80
Port of Galveston 228
Port of Inchon 180
Portland, Oregon 251
Portland Auditorium 142
Potsdam Conference 160
Pottawatomie Creek 50
President's Committee on Civil Rights (PCCR) 162
Prince Lumumba 193
Princeton University (or College of New Jersey) 123–125, *125*
Progressive Party (or Bull Moose Party) 127
Public Works Administration (PWA) 232
Pueblo, Colorado 143, 148
Pulitzer Prize 2, 5, 11, 104, 122, 159, 233–234
Pusan, South Korea 178
Pusan Perimeter battle line 178

Radical Republicans *81*, 82–84, 89–90, 92, 96–98, 100, 102, 106–107, 109, 113, 117
Raleigh, North Carolina 79
Randolph, John 213
Rayburn, Sam 200–202
Raymond, Henry 97
Reagan, Ronald 38–39, 242–243, *243*, 244, 246–247, 249–250, 252, 256, 261, *262*, 263–264
Reagan for President Committee 244
Reconstruction 2–3, 78, *81*, 83–84, 86, *87*, 88–98, 103–104, 106–110, *110*, 111–115, *115*, 116–117 208, 214, 217, 264
Reconstruction Act of 1867 103, 110
Red Scare (or Red Menace) 166, 168, 193, 264
Red Square 174
Redemption (racial backlash) 117
Reedy, George 174
Republic of Texas 33, 44–45
Republican (or Republicans) 15, 61, 63, 67, 69–72, 74, 79, 23–83, 90, 92, 95, 97–100, 102, 107–109, 113, 117, 127–128, 130, 132, 136–137, 142, 144–145, 154, 162, 166, 175, *176*, 181, 185–186, 193, 195, 200, 213, 224, 226, 249, 254
Republican Caucus 132–133
Republican Party (or GOP for Grand Old Party or Party of Lincoln) 5, 53, 56, 62, 67, 69–70, 74, 76, 113–116, 120–123, 126, *127*, 128, 132, 152, 153, 161, 173, 175, 177, 187–188, 193, 211, 226, 243–244
Republican National Committee 126–127, 250, 261
Republican National Convention of 1884 131
Republican National Convention of 1912 126
Republican Old Guard 126–127, 132, 148, 154
A Return to Normalcy campaign slogan 154
Revels, Hiram 116
Revolt of the Admirals 161
Revolutionary War 16, 213
Rhett, Robert 68
Richelieu, Cardinal 238
Richmond, Indiana 140
Ridgway, Matthew 185
Rio Grande River 104
Roanoke, Virginia 213
Roaring 20s 155
Robertson, Willis 205
Robinson, Corinne Roosevelt 146
Roosevelt, Alice 151
Roosevelt, Franklin D. (or FDR) 40, 54–55, 72, 147, 155, 158, *159*, 160–164, 166, 172–173, 187, 193, 201, 202, 217, 228–230, *230*, 231
Roosevelt, Theodore (or TR) 40 121, 121, 122–123, 130, 132, 136, 146, 148, 151, *152*, 194, 218, 238–239, *240*, 243
Roosevelt's Rough Riders 123
Root, Elihu 136
Ross, Edmund 108
Roswell, Georgia 123
Rural Electrification Act 5
Russell, Richard Brevard 2, 7, 163, 185, 198–199, *199*, 200–204, *204*, 205–209, 211–212, 215, 219–220, *221*, 220–221, *221*, 222–227, 235, 264
Russia/Soviet Union (or Russians/Soviets) 43–44, 55, 127, 155, 159, *159*, 160, 162, 164–165, 175, 179, 181–183, 194–195, 210, 251–252, 256, 261
Russo-Japanese War 257

Sacramento Bee 262
Sadat, Anwar 257–260, *260*
St. Louis, Missouri 98–99, 141, 251
Salt Lake City, Utah 143
San Diego Stadium 142
San Francisco, California 250
San Francisco Giants 1
Sandinista government 263
Sanford, Terry 207
Santa Fe Trail 44
Saturday Evening Post 22

Index

Scott, Bill 249
Scott, Dred 55–56
Scott, Winfield 71, 72
Sea of Japan 178
Seattle Post-Intelligencer 142
Selma, Alabama 233, *233*, 235
Seminoles tribe 10, 16, 27
Senate (or Upper House/Chamber) 3, 5–7, 11–12, *14*, 16, 18–19, 22–23, *23*, 25–26, *26*, 27, 29, 34–35, 43, 46–47, *47*, 48–49, 51–52, 57, *57*, 58, 61, 63–64, 73, 78–80, 82–84, 88–90, 92, 94–95, 100, *101*, 102, 104–105, 107–108, 110, 123, 130, 132–134, 136–138, *138*, 139–140, 142–145, 151–152, *152*, 156, 159, 162–163, 170–173, *173*, 176, *177*, 178, 181–182, 184–185, 188–189, 192, 194–195, 198–199, *199*, 200–202, *202*, 203, *204*, 205–210, 212–215, *215*, 216–219, 221, *221*, 222–224, *225*, 226, 235, 244, 246, 249–254, 261
Senate Armed Services Committee 200–201, 249
Senate Chamber 145, 203
Senate Committee on Territories 46, *47*, 63
Senate Finance Committee 216, 218, 223
Senate Foreign Relations Committee 133, 138, *138*, 139, 144
Senate Rule XXII 214
Senate Subcommittee on Investigations 178, 181, 195
Seoul, South Korea 180
Seventeenth Amendment 154
Seward, William 18, 49, 70, 84, 90
Seymour, Horatio 109
Shah (or King) of Iran 261
Shawano, Wisconsin 170
Sheridan, Phil 106–107
Sherman, Roger 7
Sherman, William Tecumseh 107
Sherrill, Robert 170
Sikes, Bob 252
Sinai Peninsula 257–259
Sioux Falls, South Dakota 141
Six-Day War 257–258
Smathers, George 213
Smith, Al 210
Smith, Joseph, Jr. 124
Smith, Margaret Chase 176, *177*
Smith, Walter 192
Snow White and the Six Dwarfs taunt 176
Social Security Act 163
The South (or Southern) 2, 23, 31, 33, 37, 43–45, 49, 56, 58–59, 6d1–62, 67, 73–74, 79–80, 82–84, 86, 87, *88*, 89, 91–95, 98, 100, *101*, 104, 106–108, 110–111, *111*, 112–115, *115*, 116–118, 123, *125*, 163, 198, 199–210, 212–215, *215*, 216–217, 219, 221, 222–223, 225, 226–228, 233–234, 235
South America (or South American) 239, 241
South Korea (or South Korean) 165, 180
South Pacific 170

South Vietnam 232
Southern Baptist beliefs 245
Southern Bloc (or Caucus) 198, 202, 204, *204*, 205–206, 208–209, 211, 215, 216, 218–219, 221, *221*, 222–224
Southern California 142
Southern Christian Leadership Conference (SCLC) 234
Southern Manifesto 206, 207
Southern Unionists 73, 107
The Southwest 46, 130
Southwest Georgia 91
Spain (or Spanish) 1, 53
Spanish American War 123
Spanish flu 153
Specie Circular executive order 35, *36*
Spencer, Brent 185
Springfield, Illinois 73, 98
Springfield Daily Republican 62, 90
Stalin, Joseph 184, 193
Stanton, Edwin 97, 103
State Department 160, 166, *167*, 168, *171*, 174–175, 178, 180–182, 184, 190, 244, 247
State of the Union address (1964) 231
Staunton, Virginia 123
Stennis, John 202
Stephens, Alexander 92
Stevens, Thaddeus 84, 92, 94, *94*, 96, 97, 99, 102, 105, 108, 113
Stevenson, Adlai 188, 203, 207, 209–210
Stevenson, Coke 200
Story, Joseph 78
Straight of Korea 178
Strategic Arms Limitation Treaty 261
Suez Canal 247
Sullivan & Cromwell 190
Sumner, Charles 2, 7, 78–81, *81*, 82, 84–85, 89–94, *94*, 95–100, *101*, 102–111, *111*, 112–114, 117, 120, 207, 212, 220, 264
Supreme Court 16, 25, 55–56, 58, 61, 75, 78, 111, 113, 126, 205–206, 216, 219–220
Supreme Headquarters American Expeditionary Force (SHAEF) 190
Sutter, John 44
Sutter's Mill 44
Swing Around the Circle campaign 98
Symington, Stuart 210
Syria 257–258

Tack, Juan Antonio 239
Taft, Robert 5, 7, 174, 187
Taft, William Howard 69, 126–128, 148
Taney, Roger B. 21, 24, 34, 55, 75
Taney Supreme Court 75
Tariff of Abominations 37
Tax Reduction Act of 1964 223
Taylor, Zachary 44–45
Tehran, Iran 261
Tel Aviv, Israel 259
Temple Square 143

Index

Temporary Commission on Employee Loyalty 165, 175
Tennessee 1st Congressional District 79
Tennessee Valley Authority (TVA) 5, 232
Tenure of Office Act 102, 104, 106–108
Texas A&M University 229
Texas Hill Country 204
Texas 10th Congressional District 228
Thurmond, Strom 163, 202, 205, 219, 239, 249
Tilden, Samuel 69, 113
Time magazine 160, 166, 180–181
Tito, Josip 247
Tokyo, Japan 178, 180, 183
Toledo, Ohio 98
Toombs, Robert 48
Topeka, Kansas 58
Topeka constitution 50–51, 58, 62
Torrijos, Omar 247, **248**, 249–250, 252–254
Tower, John 249
Trail of Tears 16
Treasury Department 34–35, 114
Treaty Concerning Permanent Neutrality and Operation of the Panama Canal 248
Treaty of Guadalupe Hidalgo 44
Treaty of Versailles 130, 134, 135, **138, 139**–140, 143, 147, 155
Treaty of Versailles Article X 137, 139, 141–143
Trilateral Commission 257
Trujillo, Rafael 193
Truman, Harry 2, 154, 158–159, **159**, 160–161, **161**, 162–166, **167**, 168, **171**, 172–175, 177–179, 181–185, 187–192, 194–195, 198–199, 217, 219–220, 222, 243, 257, 264
Truman Doctrine 159–160, 164, 192
Trumbell, Lyman 109
Truth Squad 250
Turkey 160
Tydings, Millard 174–175, 181

Uncle Sam (American symbol) **60, 70, 144**
Underwood, Oscar 214
Union League 116
Union Party 90, 98, 100, 109
United Nations (or U.N.) 146, 147, 159, 164–166, 178–179, 182, 228, 257, 261
United Nations Conference on International Organization 166
United Nations Resolution 242 257
United Nations Security Council 241
United Press International (or UPI) 174
University of Georgia Bulldogs 120
University of Michigan 231
University of Virginia Law School 124, 178
Upper South 30, 56
Upstate New York 30
Upward Bound program 231

Van Buren, Martin 24, 27, 35, **36**, 37–39
Vance, Cyrus 258
Vandenburg, Arthur 6
Van Winkle, Peter 109
Versailles (or Paris) Peace Conference 141, 190
Viet Cong 232
Vietnam War 232, 239, 242, 245, 252
Villa, Pancho 129
Virginia Dynasty 39
Volunteers in Service to America (VISTA) 231
Von Ribbentrop, Joachim 156
Voting Rights Act of 1965 234–235

Wade, Ben 83, 90, 92
Wagner, Robert 6
Wake Airfield 183
Wake Island 183
Wallace, George 233, 242
Wallace, Henry A. 158, 163
Walsh, Edmund A. 172
Walters, Vernon 183
War Department 106–107
War Democrat 79
War Hawks 12
War of 1812 (or America's Second Revolution) 1, 17, 20, 36, **60**
War on Poverty 229, 231–232
Warren, Earl 220
Warren, Elizabeth 120
Warren Report 220
Warren (Supreme) Court 220
Washington, George **13**, 16, 148, 187
Washington, D.C. 2, 3, 10, 12, 22, 24, 34, 42–43, 55, 61, 73, 76, 79, 82, 84–85, 93, 98, 104, 122–123, 135–137, 141–142, 144, 146–147, 150–151, **171**, 172, **173**, 176, 183–184, 187, 198, 200–201, **221**, 242, 245, 249, 252, 257, 259, **262**, 264
Washington Globe 29, 31
Washington National Intelligencer 11
Washington Redskins (former name) 1
Washington Union 62
Watergate scandal 239, 242, 245, **246**
Watterson, Henry 125
Waving the Bloody Shirt 67, 69
Webb, James Watson 18
Webster, Daniel 2, 11, 18, 22–23, **23**, 25–26, **26**, 27, 29, 35, 78, 82, 120
Weed, Thurlow 98
Welles, Gideon 97
Wesleyan University 124
The West (or Western) 10–12, 23, 31, 33, 37, 43–44, 46, 203–205, 208, 219
West Bank 257, 259–260
West Coast 44, 114, 142
Western Allies 130
Western civilization 192
Western diplomacy 238
Western Europe 164, 187
Western Hemisphere (or New World) **60** 141, 239, 241

Western Missouri 162
Western territories 3, 44
Weyrich, Paul 251
Wheatland 75
Wheeling, West Virginia 167
Wheeling Intelligencer 168
Wherry, Kenneth 174
Whig Party (or Whigs) 15, 22, 34, 48, 49, 69, 78, 82, 213
Whiskey Ring 114
White, Henry 133
White House 1, 3, 10, *13*, 17, 22–24, 32, *36*, 37–39, 42–43, 45, 51, *52*, 53–55, 57, 65, 69, *70*, 71–72, 74, 79–80, 82, 89, 93–94, *94*, 100, 102, 109, *110*, 112–113, *115*, 124, 126, 128, 137, 139, 144, 150–154, 156, 158, 185–189, 193, 195, 202, 210, 211, 213, 217–218, 220, 222, *225*, 228–229, 231, 243, 245, *248*, 251–252, 254, 257, 260, *260*, 261
White House East Room 253
White House Rose Garden 260, *260*
White Sulphur Springs, Virginia (now West Virginia) 30
White North 117
White South 103, 162
White supremacy 78–79, 90, 92–93, 112, 205
Whites (or Caucasians) 39, 89, 95, 97, 99–100, 109, 116–117
Whittier, John Greenleaf 111
Wigfall, Louis 68
Wilderness Act 232
Wilson, Edith Galt (or First Lady) 148, *149*, 151
Wilson, Kirt 114
Wilson, Woodrow 2, 85, 120, *121*, 122–125, *125*, 126–127, *127*, 128–130, 131, 132–144,
144, 145–149, *149*, 150–156, 159, 238, 254, 264
Wirt, William 30–31
Wirtz, Henry 91
Wisconsin Territory 55
Wisconsin's 10th Judicial Circuit 170–171
Wichita, Kansas 150
Wood, Leonard 155
Woodbury, Levi 24
Work Experience Program 231
Work Study Program 231
Works of Alexander Hamilton 122
Works Progress Administration (WPA) 231
World War I (or First World War /War to End All Wars) 1, 3, 120, *121*, 122, 129–130, *131*, 132, 134, *135*, *138*, 147, 155, 194, 264
World War II (or Second World War) 1, 130, 147, 156, 158–159, *159*, 160–161, *161*, 163–165, *167*, 170, 178–179, *179*, 180
World War III 183
Wyandotte, Kansas 65
Wyandotte constitution 65

Yale University 160
Yalta, Ukraine 193
Yalta accords 194
Yalu River 182
Yancey, William Lowndes 68
Yost, Norman 168
Young, Andrew 228
Young, Brigham 57

Zedong, Mao 180, 183
Zeidler, Frank 177
Zimmerman Telegram 130
Zorinsky, Ed 252

www.ingramcontent.com/pod-product-compliance
Lightning Source LLC
Chambersburg PA
CBHW021347300426
44114CB00012B/1116